# COTTON MATHER

Cotton Mather in his sixty-fifth year.
Mezzotint engraving by Peter Pelham, 1727.

# COTTON MATHER

❧

*The Young Life
of the
Lord's Remembrancer,
1663-1703*

DAVID LEVIN

*Harvard University Press
Cambridge, Massachusetts
and London, England
1978*

*Library of Congress Cataloging in Publication Data*

Levin, David, 1924-
    Cotton Mather: the young life of the Lord's
Remembrancer, 1663-1703.

    Includes bibliographical references and index.
    1. Mather, Cotton, 1663-1728.  2. Congregational
Churches—Clergy—Biography.  3. Clergy—Massachu-
setts—Biography.  4. Massachusetts—Biography.
F67.M43L48      973.2'092'4  [B]      78-2355
ISBN 0-674-17507-7

*For David and Rebecca*

Our authority should be so tempered with kindness, and meekness, and loving tenderness, that
our children may *fear* us with *delight*, and see that
we *love* them with as much *delight*.

Cotton Mather, *A Family Well-Ordered*

His Name is like to live a great while among us in his *printed Works;* but yet *these* will not convey to Posterity, nor give to Strangers, a just Idea of the real *Worth* and great *Learning* of the *Man.* His *Works* will indeed inform all that read them of his great Knowledge, and singular Piety, his Zeal for God, and Holiness and Truth; and his desire of the Salvation of precious Souls; but it was *Conversation* and Acquaintance with him, in his familiar and occasional Discourses and private Communications, that discovered the vast compass of his Knowledge and the Projections of his Piety; more I have sometimes thought than all his *Pulpit* Exercises. Here he excell'd, here he shone; being exceeding communicative, and bringing out of his *Treasury* things new and old, without measure. Here it was seen how his Wit, and Fancy, his Invention, his Quickness of thought, and ready Apprehension were all consecrated to God, as well as his Heart, Will, and Affections; and out of his Abundance within his *lips* overflow'd, *dropt as the honeycomb,* fed all that came near him, and were as the *choice silver,* for richness and brightness, pleasure and profit.

Benjamin Colman, sermon after
the funeral of Cotton Mather, 1728

# Contents

# Illustrations

# *Preface*

NATHANIEL HAWTHORNE once suggested that although some nineteenth-century writers had portrayed Cotton Mather with considerable accuracy, none had succeeded in treating this remarkable man with the sympathy and love that might make him live on the page as a human being rather than stand there as a phenomenon to be analyzed. I cannot claim to have learned to love Cotton Mather, but I believe I have learned to see why others loved him, and I have come to admire and respect him, both as a writer and as a man. This book represents his life through his first forty years, the period during which he managed, though sometimes with difficulty, to identify his own life with the history and prospects of Congregational New England. The narrative will demonstrate why I believe this identification was not mere megalomania in the years between 1688 and 1693, why it became less complete in the ensuing decade, and why it was virtually impossible thereafter.

Mather's life offers a splendid subject to the biographer, and yet no scholarly biography of him has been written since the early 1890s. Perhaps the abundance and range of Mather's own writing have discouraged prospective biographers as much as his undeserved notoriety for zealous pedantry. In the years since I undertook this biography a number of sympathetic intellectual and literary studies have treated Mather with illuminating respect, and those works have helped me to complete my own chosen assignment. Yet Mather's "Biblia Americana" stands unpublished and virtually untouched in six folio volumes in the Massachusetts Historical Society; his letters to the Royal Society have not been edited and published together; his major medical book was not published until 244 years after his death; and his most celebrated work, his history of New

England, has only now begun to appear in a scholarly edition 275
years after its first publication in London.

The complete biography of Mather must deal with all those
works, as well as with the events of his last twenty-five years, when
his literary reputation flourished even as his political influence continued to decline. Here I have written at length about only one of his
major books, the history of New England, *Magnalia Christi Americana*, for my chief labor has been to re-create the character, to narrate his experience both spiritual and earthly, and to relate his personal experience and the political history of Massachusetts to his
development as a writer, author of the best biographies and the
grandest history written in America before the nineteenth century.
My story begins with his relationship to Increase Mather, the eminent father who gave him the names of the two distinguished grandfathers, John Cotton and Richard Mather; brings him through his
leadership, when only twenty-six, of the Glorious Revolution that
ousted the royal governor of Massachusetts; follows him from that
triumph into direct confrontations with the Devil during the witchcraft crisis, and thence to the writing of his biographies and history
before his spiritual life reached another crisis in the failure of two
divine promises on which he had absolutely relied. It is the unprecedented collapse of these "Particular Faiths" — supernatural promises
that his father would be sent to England on an important mission
and that his own wife would miraculously recover from consumption — that dominates my last chapter and marks the division between Mather's first forty years and his remaining twenty-five.

In an essay years ago about inadequate portrayals of Cotton
Mather's childhood, I remarked that Mather's character and experience challenge the biographical vocabulary of a hostile age. I
resolved then that my own narrative would not condescend to his
religious experience — neither to his conversion nor to his vision of
an angel and his encounters with devils whom he believed to be tormenting some young women under his pastoral care. We need not
believe that an angel or a devil was really there in Mather's study,
but I believe we cannot understand him unless we treat with respect
his own conviction that these beings had really entered his life. My
narrative does not say that the angel was there. I have no doubt that
Mather saw the angel.

I have also tried to resist a natural inclination to conduct the representation of so controversial a figure as if it were a discussion with scholars who have disagreed. My interest in Cotton Mather began nearly thirty years ago, when I enrolled in Samuel Eliot Morison's graduate seminar in American Colonial History and wrote a long paper on the Mathers' influence on the Salem witchcraft trials. For what I learned then and later about Mather and his time, I am immeasurably indebted to Messrs. Morison, Perry Miller, and Kenneth Murdock, and their contributions to this book will be evident to specialists in chapter after chapter. Since I learned so much from these fine teachers, and since I publicly explained my disagreement with them about Mather's childhood while they were all still alive, I have tried to avoid debating with them or other scholars as my narrative proceeds. I have been generally silent about minor disagreements with Sacvan Bercovitch, Robert Middlekauff, and Kenneth Silverman, all of whom have helped this book along in their discussions and correspondence with me and in their published work. Mr. Silverman also did me the great favor of letting me take photocopies of the holographs on which his valuable edition of Mather's selected letters is based, and Ms. Lynn Haims and Professor Michael G. Hall also made materials available to me.

The special collections in which I was allowed to work while preparing this book were of course indispensable, and I am grateful for courteous and generous assistance as well as for permission to quote from unpublished materials. Librarians and staff members at the Boston Athenaeum, the Huntington Library, the Massachusetts Historical Society, the Houghton Library and Widener Library at Harvard University, the American Antiquarian Society, the Boston Public Library, the Alderman Library at the University of Virginia, the Bender Room at Stanford University, the British Museum, and the Royal Society, all have given me valuable help. In the eighteen years since I first committed myself to this subject, I have also received lavish help from several foundations and universities in the form of office space, secretarial help, and time free of teaching and administrative responsibilities. I worked on this book along with other subjects during my year as a Fellow at the Center for Advanced Study in the Behavioral Sciences, and again six years later when a Senior Fellowship from the National Endowment for the Humanities and a sabbatical leave from Stanford University enabled me to devote fourteen months to research in New England

and in London. I am also grateful to the Center for Advanced Study at the University of Virginia, which by reducing my teaching and administrative duties helped me to complete my research. Although I have written parts of the book at different times during this long period, with interruptions for other projects, it was at the Charles Warren Center for Studies in American History, at Harvard University, that I wrote the great bulk of the final draft, while on research leave from the University of Virginia. To all these institutions I am happy to acknowledge my heavy debt.

Besides the teachers and colleagues mentioned above, several other colleagues and friends have given me valuable criticism, information, and encouragement. Oscar Handlin's patient encouragement has helped me immeasurably. At the Behavioral Sciences Center long ago, Erik Erikson, Leo Rangell, and Carl Rogers answered some of my questions about Mather's childhood. Richard Bushman, Robert D. Cross, Michael T. Gilmore, Edward M. Griffin, Alan B. Howard, J. C. Levenson, Stephen Nissenbaum, and G. B. Warden have all read parts of the manuscript, and throughout my year at the Charles Warren Center I have relied on Mr. Nissenbaum for vigorous, instructive debate. Carolyn Billings, Helen Brock, Peter Carlton, Louise Gentry, Alfred Habegger, James Jubak, Louise Lynch, Raymond Nelson, and Roberta Simon have all helped me at various stages in the research. Mr. Carlton also prepared the index.

Patricia Marker Levin, daughter of the Puritans, has criticized the manuscript with the same mixture of grace, self-deprecation, and intelligence that have made the sharing of her household the great joy of my life.

D.L.

Charlottesville, Virginia
January 1978

# COTTON MATHER

## Note on the Seventeenth- and Eighteenth-Century Quotations

The Mathers and most of their contemporaries punctuated rhetorically, using many more commas than even the most conservative modern stylists, and they often used italics to point up rhetorical devices, from simple repetition to parallelisms and puns. Because these peculiarities often make a rhetorical difference, I have preserved them in my quotations, except for some commas between subject and verb or before the beginning or end of a parenthesis. But because I see no value in spelling *he* and *we* as *hee* and *wee*, I have normalized all the irregular spelling according to modern usage, except in the few quotations of verse, where the spelling may occasionally affect meter and rhyme. Irregular capitalization has no consistent rhetorical function in Mather's prose, and it is often impossible to tell whether initial letters in his manuscripts are capitalized or not. For the reader's convenience I have therefore capitalized prose quotations according to modern practice, but have left the poetry in its original form. Readers who wish to sample the actual orthography of Mather's printed works can find adequate examples in my epigraphs.

# I

# *A Covenanted Childhood*

જ્રૂ૭

Cottonus Maderus
Anagram   Est duo Sanctorum
Natus es Doctorum

Cotton Mather
Anagram   [The name] is of two saints
You are a descendant of learned men

Nicholas Noyes, prefatory poem
in *Magnalia Christi Americana*

THE WORLD into which Cotton Mather was born on February 12, 1663, was much larger than the colonial town of Boston. His young father, eleven months married but not yet committed by ordination to any New England church, still dreamed of returning to England, where his excellent preaching had started him on the way to national distinction before the newly restored royal government had forced him to choose between a prosperous conformity and silence. Retreating across the Atlantic to his native Dorchester in the Massachusetts Bay colony, Increase Mather had improved the time during the next two years by assisting his father in the church there, by preaching regularly in the Second Church in Boston (while resisting the call to accept ordination as its Teacher), and by courting and marrying his new step-sister, Maria Cotton.

When they named their first son Cotton, these young parents deliberately set his life in a historical context that began with the founding of Massachusetts Bay. Surely the Harvard official who gave Cotton Mather his baccalaureate degree fifteen years later was not the first person to remind the boy that his two grandfathers, Richard Mather and John Cotton, had been among the strongest leaders of the founding generation. Even if Cotton Mather had not become their biographer and the historian of New England — even if his boyhood stammer had forced him to become a physician rather than a preacher — the history of seventeenth-century Massachusetts would have to be recognized as one of the major influences and one of the major concerns of his childhood. He knew during his earliest years that six of his grandfathers' sons — four Mathers and two Cottons — were ministers. He must have heard often the story of the time his father had fled England and had arrived home providentially on the very Saturday night of Uncle Eleazar's arrival from Northampton. The next day the two brothers had preached in *their* father's church, and (as Cotton Mather described the scene sixty-three years later) "the comforted old patriarch sat shining like the sun in *Gemini*, and hearing his two sons, in his own pulpit entertain the people of GOD, with performances, that made all people proclaim him, *an happy father.*" Surely, too, Cotton heard that eminent grandfather preach more than once in Boston and Dorchester — in a voice whose booming resonance the grandson remembered thirty years later — before the terrible day of the old patriarch's last visit to Increase Mather's house. The biography that Increase Mather published two years after Richard's death can only have served, for a bright young reader, as a literary demonstration that his own blooming life was rooted in the hagiography and the church history of his native land.

Throughout his childhood, moreover, the John Cotton house in which Cotton Mather grew up, the thriving young church in North Square, and the streets themselves were often filled with controversy over threats to the New England Way. In the year before young Cotton was born, his father and grandfather had taken opposite sides in the debate over the Half-Way Covenant (a historical and theological argument over easing the requirements for baptism and church membership), and the issue remained alive throughout the sixties as Increase, who at first had sought to maintain the founders' strict principles, came around to agreement with his congregation and his father. John Norton, his former teacher, led a successful effort to deny young Increase permission to read the synod of 1662 an argument written by the Reverend John Davenport of New Haven against the new covenant. But Increase wrote an approving preface to Davenport's essay, and his very first publication thus appeared as

1. Richard Mather.
Photograph of a woodcut by John Foster.

a defense of the founders' rules in the year of his first son's birth. In-crease accepted the call to the Second Church when the baby was about a year old. As Teacher there, he became an interested partici-pant in the debates over John Davenport's call to the pulpit of the First Church in 1667. Increase himself changed his position on the Half-Way Covenant soon afterward, but he was deeply engaged in the battle over permission to found a third church (the South), formed by discontented members of the First, in 1669.

During Cotton's first six years, then, the traffic was heavy and the discussion intense as the young Mather household sought to main-tain a due place for the old New England Way in modern politics and church government. It was the synod on the disputed founding of the Third Church that caused grandfather Richard Mather to be present in Boston when he suffered his fatal attack of kidney stones. By that time Increase and Richard had reconciled their views on church membership, but Davenport and the leaders of the First Church were hostile to the threat of a synod's authority over an indi-vidual congregation, and as the founding Mather lay dying they revived that old issue of Congregationalism — a recurring trouble for Massachusetts since the days of Roger Williams and Anne Hutchin-son.

The intensity of these disagreements was magnified by the general conviction in Boston that other threats to the old ways were even more serious. With the Act of Uniformity in 1662, the royal govern-ment in England had actually resumed persecution of nonconform-ing clergymen. While the Crown's later insistence on toleration in New England had a liberalizing influence here, the Puritan leaders in Massachusetts, whom we too often regard as mere opponents of progress, genuinely feared the royal government as an aggressive enemy. Even before the new severity drove Increase Mather back to New England and one of his brothers to the Netherlands, it revived alarm in Massachusetts for the virtual independence she had en-joyed during three decades of ineffective or indifferent administra-tion in London. Charles II confirmed the original charter but ex-pressed a new interest in colonial legislation, commerce, and justice. Tolerating a new severity in England, where a former governor of Massachusetts was beheaded and the severed head of another former leader of Massachusetts was displayed on London Bridge, the King commanded Massachusetts not to execute any more Quakers (four men and women had been hanged there between 1658 and 1661), and he insisted that Massachusetts allow Anglicans not only to worship but also, when otherwise qualified, to vote. In the very first months of Cotton Mather's life, Bostonians wrangled over the wisdom and courage of two eminent agents who had returned with only small success from a mission to represent the colony's wishes to the Crown. In the same year there was great talk abroad of renewed persecutions and a new emigration from England. Commissioners apparently hostile to the Massachusetts authorities proclaimed the sovereignty of the King in 1664, demanded that the General Court of the Bay colony do the same, and came to America to attack the Dutch in New Amsterdam, to govern New England, and to lead the unsuccessful search for two regicides who had found shelter in Massachusetts and Connecticut. That crisis passed for a time in 1665, too early for even so precocious a child as Cotton Mather to understand the issues, but the threat was present throughout his childhood and youth, and until the original charter was actually revoked in 1684 the mysterious danger from London formed as real a presence in Boston as the power of the Lord or the Devil.

Providence and Satan established the metaphysical dimension that gave great historical depth to the mere three decades of the Bay colony's experience, and worldwide meaning to the struggle between colonists and Crown. Cotton Mather grew up in an atmosphere charged with bewildering signals of divine promise and threat. The typical Puritan leader in those years was not the self-assured caricature who has figured so prominently in our literature and folklore since the days of Washington Irving, but a hard-working believer struggling to act in the world for the glory of God and to understand the ambiguous Providential messages in historical events. When a Puritan leader strove to maintain the New England Way, he believed he was also defending the primitive Christian churches on which the New England congregations had been modeled. When he heard "rumors of motions [toward conversion] among the Jews in several parts of the world" (as Increase Mather did in 1665), or that the Devil was coming down in great wrath against the covenanted saints, then he looked for the advent of the Millennium, and for the day of doom.

It was this quality that the generation of Emerson and Hawthorne, liberated descendants of these allegory-bound sinners, envied even as they lamented its consequences in their own lives a hundred and fifty years later. "The foregoing generations," Emerson declared, "beheld God . . . face to face," and he tried to rouse his contemporaries to claim their own right to "enjoy an original relation to the universe." That face-to-face relationship was forced on Cotton Mather in all the experience of his childhood: through political institutions, in prayer at home and at school, and above all in the congregation to which his father preached. To understand his life, and even his childhood, we must imagine the profound seriousness and the cosmic significance of that congregation to its members, even as they struggled in the world of business and politics and even as the church's power gradually declined.

Observing his father's elevated place in the meetinghouse gave the child Cotton Mather a sufficiently grand conception of the church's solemnity. From the beginning there were also scenes of individual drama — scenes in which, though comedy might threaten a fallible man's concentration on eternal issues, gravity was sure to prevail. Probably young Cotton sat in the gallery with his mother during one of the most impressive of those scenes, to watch Increase Mather play an awesome role in the drama of John Farnum's salvation. Even if the boy missed the climax of Farnum's excommunication in 1666, it can represent for us the many similar scenes that he did witness in this the only theater permitted in Boston during the seventeen years before Cotton Mather himself became a participant in the last act of Farnum's reconciliation.

John Farnum had been one of the founding members of the Second Church. Long before Cotton Mather's birth, Farnum had stood in the presence of God and the congregation of the First Church in Boston to give evidence of his conversion, to persuade the ruling elders that he genuinely repented of his sins and that he had good reason to believe himself elected for redemption through his faith in Jesus Christ. He had sworn then to give up himself, his family, and his possessions to the true God in Jesus Christ, and "to His people also." In return Farnum's promise to walk with God and with his church had been answered by a solemn covenant from the other church members to accept, protect, and discipline him: "We then the Church of Christ in this place, do receive you in our fellowship, and promise to walk towards you, and to watch over you as a member of this church, endeavoring your spiritual edification, in Christ Jesus our Lord."

The members took this covenant so seriously that they required a formal release — by vote of the congregation — before anyone in full communion could be allowed to join another congregation. Farnum and several other members had gained that permission when they had founded the Second Church in 1650, because the North End of Boston had become sufficiently populous to have a church near the members' homes. As the new congregation had grown during the next fifteen years, they had remained firm in requiring that one of the parents be a church member before a child could be baptized. It was true that only God could know with absolute certainty whom He had chosen to redeem and that some members of His true, "invisible" church might go unrecognized by the faithful in this world. Still, the covenant bound all "visible saints" in Congregational churches to restrict sacred privileges to those who appeared to have good hope of its promises.

John Farnum, meanwhile, had gradually come to believe that no infants at all should be baptized, that baptism must be reserved for penitent sinners who come forward to profess their conversion and join the church. During the winter of 1665-66, Farnum had gone so far as to worship with "censured persons" outside the congregation, and now he demanded that the congregation dismiss Increase Mather and forbid the baptism of infants. The church members had met in March to consider Farnum's behavior, and had decided unanimously "that they must in the fear and name of the Great God and our Savior Jesus Christ proceed unto the sad and dreadful censure of excommunication" — but they had promised "gladly" to forbear execution of "that dreadful sentence" if Farnum should "manifest repentance" by April 22.

With the dramatic scene thus prepared well in advance, the meetinghouse was crowded on the twenty-second. This was living theater. Farnum sat in the highest gallery, visible to only a few members in the pews below, and heard Increase Mather preach for nearly two hours on the eighteenth chapter of Matthew — the church's obligation to be reconciled to erring members, and the eternal recognition of church fellowship or excommunication. As soon as the young Teacher had concluded his sermon, his colleague the aging Pastor, the Reverend Mr. Mayo, summoned Farnum to come down to the main floor of the meetinghouse.

Farnum stayed where he was. "You may speak to me here if you have anything to say to me," he called down. "I can hear you well enough."

At last he was persuaded to come down, but he gave no other sign of yielding. When Mather asked him if he "had an heart given him to repent" his breaches of the ninth and fifth commandments, his breach of the church covenant, and his "schism," Farnum declared himself not guilty of any such evils. The congregation, he charged, was expelling him only for his conscience, because he opposed the baptism of infants.

The debate continued for some time, for the Puritan leaders, like modern authorities conducting trials in the Soviet Union and the United States, used public confrontations as a dramatic means of justifying authority to both church members and the community at large. Neither the child Cotton Mather nor the less intelligent adults attending these compulsory church services could have understood very well the distinction on which Increase Mather insisted in his reply to Farnum: that Farnum might still oppose infant baptism, as other church members did, without suffering any censure for his opinion, so long as he "would walk as did become the Gospel." But even the least perceptive auditors must have felt the solemn importance given to the idea of community, the search for justice, and the individual soul's destiny by the careful attention that authority paid to a defendant's answers. Every observer must also have noticed the threat to a lone individual in such a confrontation, and in this episode the sharp contrast between Farnum's lapses into sarcasm and the two ministers' unbroken gravity. For those who failed to notice, Increase Mather soon made the contrast unmistakable.

Farnum's defense was reduced in the end to anger and laughter. At one point he mocked the Pastor and the church with an ambiguous reminder of their absolute dependence on God's election: "Much good may your baptism do you!" And when Farnum "smiled and laughed in the face of the congregation," Increase Mather pointed up for all observers the symbolic function of the drama.

"What a sad spectacle is here!" the Teacher exclaimed. "A poor creature ready to be delivered up into the hands of Satan, to be bound in heaven and earth, and yet his heart is so strangely besotted and hardened with guilt and sin, and the wrath of God against his soul, that he even laugheth at the calamity which is coming upon him!"

Farnum had had enough. He turned his back on the ministers and smiled at the congregation. "This place is too hot for me," he said; and, as that comment startled many "vain youths into an open laughter in the midst of a work so awful and dreadful," Farnum headed for the door. Mr. Mayo commanded him in the name of Christ to stay. But Farnum executed a perfect conclusion to his part in the ceremony by walking right on out of the meetinghouse. With the greatest possible visibility, a member in full communion had thus abandoned the visible church.

There was nothing left for the Pastor to do then but pronounce the sentence: "in the name of the Lord Jesus (the Judge of quick and dead) [we] deliver this impenitent and profane offender unto Satan for the destruction of the flesh that the spirit might be saved."

Increase Mather's solemn narrative of that scene concludes with a plea that the Lord deliver the poor offender out of the hands of Satan, and the prayer was answered seventeen years later, when Cotton Mather was serving as his father's assistant. It is to the church's credit that old John Eliot persuaded the elders to accept Farnum's penitence and receive him into full communion. The readiness with which Increase Mather and the others received Farnum demonstrates that their most severe punishment really could be directed to what they considered the offender's own good. But of course they seem to have had little hope when they delivered him up to Satan that Farnum would ever be liberated to rejoin them, and although the subsequent church record contains a surprising number of reconciliations after excommunication, surely the main point of such scenes for the child Cotton Mather was to represent the church as a community applying the law of Heaven on earth, to give the individual soul's conduct in that community an eternal significance, and to display the minister — his own father — as mediator and judge, agent of an omnipresent God.

To anyone concerned for the psychological welfare of children, the image of a Calvinist father helping to dispense such justice in the presence of his son must represent a strong argument for clerical celibacy. Yet all the evidence indicates that Increase Mather was a remarkably tender parent who in the religious education of his children emphasized hope much more heavily than dread. The God whom he and Maria described to their first child was sufficiently likable to attract the boy, during an illness at the age of two-and-a-half years, to say "of his own accord": "Father, Ton would go see God." Increase was alarmed not only by the illness but by the words, which might be a Providential hint of an early death. Both the child's temperament, however, and the New England version of covenant theology encouraged the parents to hope. Although the Calvinist doctrine of election left no human being any prior claim on divine mercy, many Puritans believed that the Covenant of Grace gave a redeemed sinner the comfort of Abraham's covenant, a promise that his descendants would also be redeemed. When Cotton fell ill again on September 11, 1665, his father, although frightened, was encouraged by earlier mercies to believe that the Lord would "remember His everlasting covenant towards me and mine."

Within the family there was little experience to contradict such hopes. In the parents' generation, all the siblings on the Mather side and all the surviving Cottons had experienced conversion and had become church members in full communion, and all but one of the sons were ministers. Now young Cotton had begun to pray as soon as he could speak. His father began to suspect that this gifted child was one of the happy few (a tiny fraction of the elected saints) who are given a saving faith and a virtuous character in their very infancy. "He did not know how vile I was," the son wrote fifty years later, but except for that statement itself no specific evidence of vileness has survived him. The only sin of childhood that Cotton could specify for his own son in making this confession so long afterward was the improbable sin of idleness, of which his own testimony plainly acquits him. He learned very early to read and write, long before he began attending school. From both his mother and his father he learned the habit of withdrawing for secret prayer several times a day (his mother did so six times a day). Even before he could read, he was of course attending regular church services, which usually included a pastoral prayer of thirty to sixty minutes and a sermon of one to two hours, twice every Sunday. Before he learned to write fast enough to take notes on sermons in the meetinghouse, as adults commonly did so that they could study God's explicated word at their leisure during the week, he would write a synopsis of what he remembered as soon as he came home. Since the Teacher of the Second Church lived there, too, and took a personal interest in the boy's religious education, we can be sure that Cotton's memory and his capacity to write precise summary — qualities extremely valuable to the historian and the preacher — were immeasurably strengthened during these early years. He learned to live by the word. He wrote, he copied, he read, and he reorganized. Although most of his prayer was extemporaneous, shunning with Puritan dread the insincerity in prescribed forms, he did now and then write out prayers for his schoolmates (when he was about seven or eight years old), and he sometimes "obliged them to pray." For a while he read fifteen chapters of the Bible every day, five in the morning, five at noon, and five at night. He did not need the little grammar school as a motivation to work. When his father kept him at home for a time during the coldest winter months, Cotton read church history and reviewed his Latin in his father's unusually rich library, and waited for the summer weather, during which his father allowed him to return to school and make up in half the time all the work that he had missed.

Similar evidence of hope appeared in the new brothers and sisters born during Cotton's first seven years. Their very survival was a mark of divine favor in a world that gave children less than one chance in two to live beyond the age of seventeen. Maria Mather bore five children in the first eight years of marriage, and they all lived through the deadly smallpox and measles epidemics to become pious adults. The mother admitted to her diary that she had always felt afraid to have many children — not especially because of the high death rate for mothers and children alike, but lest she might "have one more child than Jesus Christ would accept of." As the children grew, however, she found the strength to "believe for them all." None of them died during Cotton Mather's childhood. Katharine, the ninth child, died in infancy when Cotton was twenty.

The Mather children learned to believe that their own lives were exemplary, and to see their father as both the spokesman of God in the pulpit and the imperfect model of a Heavenly Father in his rule over the family. Increase Mather was "a wise and a strict parent," his eldest son wrote long afterward, and a post-Freudian observer can see the value in both his wisdom and his version of strictness. Obliged to teach his children that they were born sinners who could not attain true repentance unless God should give them the unmerited gift of special grace, Increase Mather nonetheless emphasized God's mercy in his teaching and in his own paternal conduct. The Covenant was a great help toward psychological health, for it gave a reasonable basis in hope for moral teaching that did not lay too much stress on telling a child how vile he was. And even if this father had known the full extent of Cotton's vileness, his strictness would have been unusually mild. Ever since an English schoolmaster had beaten Richard Mather into miserable hatred of boarding school, the Mathers had on principle opposed the beating of children (except for extraordinarily grave offenses). In their emblematic lives, the father served more as advocate than as judge. No record of Increase's severity remains, but we have several impressive indications of his advocacy and his support. His children saw him plead with God for them when he prayed with them. He prayed separately with each child for the child's salvation and for deliverance from particular earthly afflictions. In seasons of great danger he brought the whole family together to pray in concert for deliverance. For an impenitent culprit or a righteous dissenter summoned before the congregation, he might seem a strict judge. For a penitent boy he was a weeping advocate, kneeling beside the child to pray for grace.

He was also a resourceful teacher of encouragement. His belief in Cotton's prodigious sanctification tempted the child to "affectations of pre-eminency" in these years and (despite repentance) thereafter. But it also kept Cotton free of excessive self-condemnation and free of especial concentration, in his first few years, on the terrors of Hell. The remarkable spirit of the Mather household in these years is not that of a dynastic political force but of an affectionate family, bound tightly together on earth and in hopes of Heaven. When Cotton, having had some effect on his young schoolmates by "obliging" them to pray, obeyed the biblical command to "rebuke" several boys "for their wicked words and ways," and thereby provoked some verbal and even some physical retaliation, his father rejoiced and tried to comfort him. The child's suffering seemed to fulfill Matthew's description of the world's rewards for faithful Christian service. At the age of seven or eight, Cotton admitted later, he had not understood his father's "heavenly principle," but he eventually came to understand it and even at the time he did not fail to see the great value of his father's worldly response: the strong approval, the affectionate paternal support. If a child, in that newly Copernican universe, had to drag forth and bewail all his little sins under the magnified scrutiny of a perfectly holy Omnipotence, he was fortunate to have a sympathetic father to encourage him.

His mother, too, was not only pious but "loving and tender." She was a rather modest character in a household that soon filled with the ambitious and voluble piety of her husband and sons, but their testimony and the few words of her own that have been preserved, indicate that she wrote, spoke, and acted in harmony with them. She kept days of fasting for the spiritual welfare of her children. She practiced a "sweet authority" over them, read through the entire Bible with them twice every year, and held them firmly to the regular recitation of their catechism. She was a woman who had studied hard, giving "no rest to my eyes, nor slumber to my eye-lids" till she had "great assurance" of her own regeneration, and even as she took much care of her children's bodies — "it is well if not too much care," she wrote — she tried to keep especial watch for the welfare of "their never-dying souls." She expressed "a mighty delight" in her biblical studies and a "very passionate, very rapturous, very marvelous" affection for her eldest son. He seemed to reenact her own best childhood memories by taking what she called "great delight in secret communion with God." As she had lived from the example of the biblical Daniel, Cotton now sought to emulate the piety of both his parents, and he lived in confidence of their love and approval. They knew that straining their authority with harshness and fierceness might discourage their children; their disciplinary practice set an example for the advice that Cotton later gave to parents throughout the community: "Our authority should be so tempered with kindness, and meekness, and loving tenderness, that our children may *fear* us with *delight*, and see that we love them with as much *delight*."

The same emphasis on exemplary delight enlivens Cotton Mather's reminiscences of his most influential schoolmaster, Ezekiel Cheever. He remembered Cheever as a man whose behavior showed that he loved his calling:

> His work he Lov'd; Oh! had we done the same!
> Our Play-dayes still to him ungrateful came.
> And yet so well our Work adjusted Lay,
> We came to *Work*, as if we came to *Play*.

❧

In the affectionate comfort of this family, then, Cotton Mather was initiated into the knowledge of his place in history, the terms of his confrontation with God, and the prospects for his service in the world under the obscure direction of Providence. The Mathers were among the earliest families to teach that the earth was not at the center of God's creation, and of course they taught their children that the end of all life was not the happiness of man but the glory of God. In the Fall of Adam, Cotton Mather learned, all mankind had been corrupted by the first man's violation of the Covenant of Works, a solemn obligation to obey all divine commands, and in consequence he himself and all men were justly liable to eternal punishment for the sins they would inevitably commit. All that could save any one of them was the free gift of grace, by which a merciful Creator had chosen to redeem a few through a second covenant announced to Abraham (Genesis, chapters 15 and 17), and later extended beyond Israel to all nations by the Advent of Jesus Christ and His vicarious atonement on the cross for the sins of true believers. The capacity to repent and to accept the Covenant of Grace through absolute faith in Christ's power to redeem — this was the most precious gift of a merciful (though a justly angry, sovereign) God to undeserving men. Cotton Mather had been baptized as a sign that his parents would do everything in their power to prepare him for the gift, which they and his grandfathers had sealed with a covenant. From early childhood he knew that when the gift came to him he would swear in a written covenant to dedicate his life to the glory of God, in a second covenant with other believers to worship God in a Congregational church, and in a civil calling to perform work that would do some practical good in the world, even while he set aside hours every day for private prayer and meditation. Long before he was ten, he knew that his father had "designed" him for the ministry.

Sketches of the earliest human history came to the boy in biblical stories, which for him were both history and revelation. The compression of historical time, so natural to very small children, was intensified for him by the tradition of typology (which encouraged people to find images of biblical events and characters in historical experience — Moses leaving Egypt foreshadows William Bradford leaving the Netherlands and England), and even more emphatically by the omnipresence and the regular intervention in current affairs of the very Providence that had guided those heroic travelers. The church fathers of the first few centuries would come to seem fairly close because the young scholar looked back to them across

s of Edwards, Mather, and Woolman — and in the lives of less
ordinary Christians — conviction of their own sinfulness came
e childhood or early adolescence with the recognition that their
holiness had been illusory, or at best incomplete. The real cure
e sick soul did not begin until one perceived that one's soul was
usly ill — and that very perception, though it aggravated the
toms, was part of the cure. Meanwhile, it seems, a spiritually
ptible child like Cotton Mather or Jonathan Edwards stored up
apacity for guilt without feeling, or at least without recogniz-
guilt in his first six or seven years.

roughout his first six years, then, Cotton Mather seems to have
secure, promising emotional life. He was also apparently a
thy child. In the spring and summer of 1665 he was sufficiently
awaken his father at night on several occasions, but even so
ously protective a father as Increase Mather was seriously con-
ed on only two of those four occasions. Only twice in 1666 and
in 1667 (a false alarm threatening smallpox) did the anxious
er record any other ailments for Cotton in the years before 1672.
y other indication is that the child was healthy and happy in the
roval of his parents, the pursuit of his elementary religious stud-
the observance of pious duties, and the company of his little
hers and sisters, in whose infantile religious instruction he be-
thus early to take a small part. He must also have felt some jeal-
of them, must have played with them, must have fought,
d, dreamed, imagined, explored. But of all that life his records
almost nothing. We must remember that it existed even though
annot describe or explicate it, or we will be forced to settle for a
nstrous caricature instead of a precocious human child.

he town of Cotton Mather's boyhood was a flourishing capital
port, with two well-fortified, high hills above peninsulas over-
king the harbor and giving the defenders command over any
ship that might try to enter. Most of the town was built on the
e that lay "betwixt these two strong arms" and below the moun-
to the northwest that was higher than the other two. At the top
hat Beacon Hill, above the three small hills that gave its addi-
al name of Tremount, stood a beacon and the most powerful
s in the town. From this height an observer in 1663 saw all the
nds in the bay and all the ships for miles along the coast. He
ld also see the wharves that were built out along piles, "close to-

centuries that were represented to him as
bigotry of antichristian papal rule, which
perhaps now scheming to reestablish in l
founders of New England Congregation;
Reformation, were still visibly present in
John Eliot, Simon Bradstreet, and the bo
father, and Cotton Mather grew to believe
American boys in the next three centuries l
own respective generations: that he lived
history. The first book that his father publi
rael's Salvation (1669), considered signs tha
soon begin. Providence had reserved Mass
by the first modern society willing to live u
of the primitive Christian churches; New E
the honor of becoming the New Jerusalem,
of Increase Mather might be honored with
the service of the Lord during the last year

During his first six years these signs of hop
grandeur outshone the threatening danger
Way in young Cotton Mather's experience, ;
dicates that he was equally hopeful in his pri
he, like his father, did not yet know how vil
common for Puritan children to strive for pie
and to find the meaning of sin and repentar
been living apparently virtuous lives. Surely J
ton Mather, and the Quaker John Woolman
best writers among a large number who later
ence. Mather was taught in his first years to th
ternal love and mercy than of His retributiol
dren in such families concentrated on obedie
tence. Like their parents, they treated God inc
obey Him and love Him even though strict te;
neither obey nor love Him.

Their predicament, even as children, seem
our own because fundamental theory as well a;
experience told them that they could not knc
tion. Even those whose parents did not consid
their very infancy must have believed as chil
achieving some degree of obedience and faith.

2. Bonner's map of Boston, 1722.

gether on each side of the streets as in London." On these wharves stood "many fair shops" made of brick, stone, and lime and "handsomely contrived." Besides the meetinghouses, designated officially by number in the order of their founding, but familiarly known as the First, the North, and when a third was founded during Cotton Mather's boyhood, the South churches, there was a Town House "built upon pillars," wherein merchants could meet and where the regular meetings of the General Court were held. On the south, besides gardens and orchards, the residents and many visitors enjoyed "a small but pleasant common." In the daytime young boys sometimes played at marbles and wickets in the streets. Until the nine o'clock curfew young men strolled there "with their Marmalet-Madams," and thereafter constables patrolled to keep order and "take up loose people." In the northwest and northeast, near the house in which Cotton Mather spent his first seven years on Cotton Hill, two daily markets or fairs prospered and, with the neighboring wharves, gave a vigorous solidity to the life in which some Puritans strove to work out their own salvation and to labor for the glory of God.

In the eleven years between his birth and his admission to Harvard College, Cotton Mather became at least visually familiar with that material life of the town, and although he was generally supervised when out-of-doors some of the scanty evidence hints that he had time to explore the wharves with other children and to play games with them on the large lot that his mother had inherited along with the house from Grandfather Cotton.

❧

ANXIETY CAME at last in shocking catastrophe. Richard Mather had come to Boston for a meeting of leading ministers to consider the dispute over founding the Third Church. He was stricken with "a violent fit of the stone" in the Increase Mather house, and he stayed there overnight, in agony that could not be concealed, until a coach could be hired in the morning to take him home to Dorchester. Within little more than a week this powerful head of the family was dead, and his departure left a serious mark on Cotton Mather. It was bad enough to see the patriarch brought low in such dreadful pain, and then to know that he had died. What hurt even more was the severe disruption of the family's life in Boston, and especially the reaction of Increase Mather.

At first it was only grief, the deep response of a youngest son who had lived in close association with his father, growing closer to him in the last years than he had been able to be as the least important son during childhood. Then, only a few months after Richard's death, Eleazar, the only one of Increase's brothers who had settled in America, died in Northampton at the age of thirty-two. Soon after the bad news itself came a plea from both Eleazar's widow and his congregation, begging Increase to visit Northampton to advise them. He did not want to go, but he felt that after the two deaths this unusual, moving request must represent the will of God. Frankly, he confessed, he did not dare refuse the invitation, "lest He should be angry with me," and he left the Second Church in the care of Mr. Mayo. He also left his family for the first extended absence in Cotton's life.

Just a week after he arrived in Northampton, Increase Mather was "surprised with a violent fever" that nearly killed him. Terrible pains in his side made him think that he could not bear to live, and the effects remained long after "a company of godly Christians" successfully fasted and prayed for his recovery, which may also have been helped by the therapy of a physician who was dispatched from Boston to treat him. Increase Mather was absent from home for nearly three months; when he returned to the household just before winter set in, he was not only weak but gravely depressed. He seemed now to have "the hypochondriacal" affliction, a melancholy so debilitating that during the rest of the winter he could not leave the house at all. He was still weak when he returned to the pulpit in mid-March, and even after he had regained his physical strength he continued to be "very much afflicted with the hypochondriacal vapors." Before that trouble had quieted, he began also to be afflicted with terrifying nightmares (known then as ephialtes).

Like all men of learning who were interested in natural science as well as theology, Increase Mather had read a good deal about the primitive art of medicine, and he remembered now that one of his medical books said the nightmares would lead to apoplexy, epilepsy, or mania. He found the voice of Satan arguing inside his head that mania would be his inevitable fate. He fought back with protestations of faith, but he felt "inexpressible sorrows and fears." At length he remembered that mineral waters were a good remedy for the vapors, and so he went alone to the mineral springs at Lynn for several weeks. There, in the summer of 1671, he began to recover his faith, through powerful assurances from the Lord, that he had indeed been redeemed. The nightmares continued to torment him even after a Providential sign had been brought to him by "a poor godly woman" who had accosted him on his way back from Lynn. She had complained to him of her sinful exaggeration of all her own afflictions, a fault that she said had made her undervalue the many blessings granted to her. Although Increase Mather had seen at once that this woman "spoke to my very condition, as if He that knoweth all things had put words in her mouth," the nightmares and the agony of terror continued long after he had returned to his home in Boston. He began to fear that all his faith would prove to be mere delusion, seventeen years after his conversion and more than a decade after he had begun to preach.

Increase Mather's account of these miseries allows us insight into young Cotton's anxieties and also into the practical discrepancies between Puritan theology and the methods that individual men actually used to survive the warfare waged between God and Satan inside mortal heads. "Full of anxiety and harried with temptation," Increase Mather resolved at one point soon after his return from Lynn to Boston that "if the Tempter" should come to destroy him "he should find me lying at the feet of Christ"—just the kind of resolution that expressed the most a poor sinner could do to set himself in the way of the Lord. If his supposed faith was delusory, he could hardly profess absolute certainty of his election in the very moment that God had chosen to punish his excessive assurance over the last fifteen years. But perhaps God was only testing his faith by allowing the Devil thus to torment him with doubt. In this typical predicament, human nature could hardly rest in the condition of resignation that Increase Mather had resolved to exemplify by lying at the feet of Christ when the Destroyer arrived. Indeed, Mather followed the declaration with a rhetorical question that put the case as an *argument* to convince the sovereign God who had presumably already decided the fate of individual sinners long ago: "Also I promised before the Lord that if he would bring me out of this distress, I would endeavor to carry it better in my family, and in my public relation, and in all other respects."

Great relief came soon afterward for a time, and it is clear (even though the miseries commenced again before long) that Mather wrote the narrative as a kind of manual showing how one might deal with inscrutable majesty. Mather went on arguing with the Lord after the troubles had returned: ready to conclude that mania must soon come, the poor sinner expressed "my humble confidence . . . that it should be otherwise, because He heareth prayer, and because if this evil should come, those truths of His which I have appeared for would suffer, and because I desired to improve my understanding to His glory, therefore He would continue it, though my sins deserve otherwise."

It is this kind of cunning that makes of Hawthorne's Arthur Dimmesdale so excellent a re-creation of the Puritan psyche. Rereading Increase Mather's declaration again and again, one can hardly separate the argument addressed to himself — the reasons why he should retain his humble confidence — from the argument insinuated as a way of placating and (dare one invent new perceptions for the All-Wise?) warning the Lord. But the predicament need not be stated so intricately in order to be recognized. The next day (August 2, 1671) Mather put the question of "sincerity" more plainly: "O my God, If I do not sincerely desire to glorify Thy name then deny my requests, and let me have no answer of my prayers; but if I do in sincerity desire to serve and glorify Thee, then have compassion on me, and deny me not, I pray Thee. Upon these terms let me go either with an answer or a denial." Here, about two years after Eleazar's death, the struggle ended. Confidence returned, and the nightmares did not.

Probably it was in these two years of his father's travail that Cotton Mather's young psyche shaped the anxieties characteristic of his adult life. Cotton Mather observed long before 1669 the eminence of his father and of his own probable destiny. Those affectations of pre-eminence must have had their alarming side, especially for a precocious child. Adoring his eminent father and reassured by his tender instruction, the boy must have been grievously distressed not only by the sudden collapse of Grandfather Richard, but then by the death of Uncle Eleazar, by the long absence and grave illness of his own father (then only thirty years old), and at last by the dreadful change for more than a year after Increase had returned home to the family. Unable to preach, terrified by nightmares and the prognosis of mania, Increase would not have been able to conceal his torment from so perceptive and attentive a son even in a larger house, and even if his own practice had been to shield the children from knowledge of trouble and danger. In fact the routine of explicit, candid family prayer, the close quarters in which seventeenth-century Bostonians dined and slept, and the habit of converting all experience into pious instruction made concealment inconceivable. Surely it was to this time of crisis that Cotton Mather referred in his nineteenth year when he listed among his many blessings the society of a father given to him "as from the *dead*."

With the support of his affectionate household, and by intensifying his prayer and his own academic labors, the boy was able to contain his anxiety. In these years he confirmed his lifelong habit of filling his days with study and meditation, his lifelong resolution to cleave to Boston and his treasured father, and his vulnerability to separation. Not until his freshman year at Harvard in 1674-75, when a crisis at the college involved his own hazing, the dismissal of the President, and an unpleasant defeat for Increase Mather, do we find the first contemporaneous allusion to Cotton Mather's stammer.

## II

# *Harvard College*

❦

Their houses are generally wooden, their streets crooked, with little decency and noe uniformity and, there, neither months, days, seasons of the year, churches nor inns are known by their English names. At Cambridge they have a wooden collidg and, in the yard, a brick pile of two bayes for the Indians, where the commissioners saw but one; they said they had 3 or more at scooll. It may be feared this collidg may afford us many schismaticks to the church, and the corporation as many rebells to the king, as formerly they have done, if not timely prevented.

Undated letter, probably in 1664 or 1665,
from the commissioners of Charles II concerning Massachusetts

WHEN COTTON MATHER enrolled at Harvard College in the summer of 1674, both he and the college were by twentieth-century standards extraordinarily small. He was the youngest student in his academic generation, and almost certainly the youngest in the forty-year history of the college. The entire undergraduate enrollment probably did not exceed twenty-one on the day that Increase Mather brought his prodigious eleven-year-old across the Charles River to be examined by the President of Harvard, the Reverend Leonard Hoar. The entire faculty consisted of the President and two tutors, Samuel Sewall and Peter Thacher, who were themselves studying for advanced degrees; and Urian Oakes, Pastor of the church in Cambridge and Fellow of the Harvard Corporation, did some lecturing at the college. The entire plant in what is now the Yard consisted of one building, which served as dormitory, library, and lecture hall.

A virtually unoccupied building known as the Indian College stood several hundred yards away, expressing the unrealized hopes of converting and training a large number of natives for missionary

work. To the south and east was the President's house with its large
vegetable garden and the beginnings of an orchard that President
Hoar had projected for the college on his accession in 1672. And virtually alone to the north, separated from the college by a quarter-
mile stretch of woods, were the isolated residences of Mr. Oakes and
Captain Daniel Gookin, a friend, protector, and later historian of
the so-called Praying Indians. The town of Cambridge, to the south
and east, had none of the urban character that it has since ac-
quired. Three centuries later, the buildings inside the Harvard Yard
separate a small park, crowded with large buildings and grand old
trees, from the paved streets and traffic of a noisy commercial center. In the summer of 1674, when the Mathers rode across the Dunster Street bridge for Cotton's entrance examination, domestic animals grazed on the Common and around private homes. Captain
Gookin's turkeys moved freely about a fenced section of his property.

The youngest Harvard student was fifteen years old—if Cotton
Mather's classmates had taken up residence before he arrived. What
the boy faced after the triumphant ordeal of his entrance examination was a dormitory life among adolescents and young men ranging
in age from fifteen to twenty-one. He himself was probably smaller
than a sixth-grade pupil in a modern American elementary school.
In a modern high school two of his three Harvard classmates would
ordinarily have been placed in the tenth grade, and the other in the
eleventh. Several of the seniors in Mather's Harvard would have
been seniors if enrolled in Harvard College today.

Yet the new student had some reason to feel at home among his
fellows. Here in the college the concept of the third New England
generation was no mere trope, and the Mather boy was not alone in
bearing an imposing genealogy. Two of his three classmates and
many upperclassmen were ministers' sons. All three of his classmates
were sons of well-known Harvard alumni. Like Cotton Mather himself, John Cotton, his sixteen-year-old classmate and cousin, had
been named for their eminent grandfather and could look forward
with mixed feelings to preaching in his own father's pulpit. On the
maternal side he could claim, in Governor Bradstreet and Anne
Bradstreet the poet, grandparents at least as distinguished as Richard and Maria Mather. Grindall Rawson's father (Harvard 1653)
was Secretary of the colony, and the New England branch of his

family boasted less of its relationship to an Elizabethan Archbishop of Canterbury than of its descent from John Wilson, the founding Pastor of the First Church of Boston, who had labored there with John Cotton. Just as Increase Mather would write the most influential narrative of the war that devastated New England towns throughout Cotton's second year in college, so a proclamation defending the United Colonies' conduct of that war would be signed by Edward Rawson. Urian Oakes, the fourth member of this tiny class of 1678, was the son of the Cambridge minister who became President of Harvard long before the class graduated. In the class of 1677 were John Danforth, son of a powerful minister and grandson of John Wilson; and Edward Payson, grandson of John Eliot, the apostle to the Indians. In the class of 1676 was Thomas Shepard, named for his eminent but short-lived grandfather and father, and famous in childhood for his prodigious ability to remember and recite exact "heads" of long, complex sermons after he had heard them in church.

The entrance examination by the President of the college was a rite that, during Harvard's first hundred and fifty years, impressed many young scholars with the solemnity of their passage into the academic world. In Cotton Mather's day as in John Adams's, no admissions committee was delegated to make the decision. The student presented himself (often in the company of his father) directly to the President, who administered an examination to test his knowledge of the languages of learned men. Latin was the obligatory language for all academic exercises, and undergraduates were even required, though not actually forced, to use Latin as their sole extracurricular language at the college. President Hoar wanted to know first that Cotton Mather was fluent in Latin. He gave the boy some passages from Cicero to be read and translated on sight, and then he gave him some exercises that tested his ability to "make and speak true Latin in verse and prose." Next he made sure of the boy's ability to "decline perfectly the paradigms of nouns and verbs in the Greek tongue," so that he might eventually study the New Testament in the original language. (Hebrew, for the Old Testament and commentaries, was usually reserved for the first or second year in college, but Mather had already begun to study it.)

Cotton Mather had no reason for academic self-doubt. He had already learned much more Latin and Greek than the college re-

quired for admission. Under the private tutelage of his father, and
after a few years in the Free Grammar School taught by Benjamin
Tompson and more recently by Ezekiel Cheever, he had learned to
compose verses and themes in Latin and to take Latin notes on sermons preached at the meetinghouse in English. At school he had
read through the most important Latin authors, including Ovid (*De
Tristibus* and the *Metamorphoses*), Cicero, Virgil, Horace, Juvenal,
Tacitus; he had read the colloquies of Corderius and Erasmus and
had translated some of the Psalms from English into Latin verse. He
had read Homer and Isocrates in Greek, and the New Testament
and Duport's Verses on Job.

Under the firm moral restraint of the legendary Master Cheever,
Mather had been trained to avoid the gravest danger in a classical
education, which St. Augustine had lamented in the account of his
own youth. Mather expressed the key distinction thirty years after
graduating from Master Cheever's school, in a funeral elegy on his
old teacher:

> Young *Austin* wept, when he saw *Dido* dead;
> Though not a tear for a *dead* soul he had.
> Our Master would not let us be so vain,
> But us from *Virgil* did to *David* train.
> Textor's epistles would not clothe our souls;
> *Paul's* too we learnt; *we went to school at Paul's.*

That restriction put a damaging limitation on Mather's literary
taste throughout his life, so that he was capable of preferring Duport to Homer and Castalio to Virgil, but it also helped to establish
a confidence that allowed his faith to be perpetually enriched by
new information which might otherwise have threatened it. As a
boy, he brought to Harvard a scientific book by Pierre Gassendi.
And when he tried, forty years later, to place his church history of
New England in a proper historical context, he declared that the
three great events of the modern age had been the revival of
learning, the Reformation, and the discovery of America. So he had
been taught by Mr. Cheever and Increase Mather, and in his college
days he held in his young mind an odd combination of dogmatic
methods and openness to new scientific knowledge. In the next
twenty years he would praise Francis Bacon, revere Robert Boyle,
admire Isaac Newton; and he would write about devils, angels, and

witches as phenomena no less real than men and the force of gravity. Nor would he give any sign of perceiving a contradiction in these attitudes. He already knew something about the method of Petrus Ramus, which was dogmatic but almost unlimited in its inclusiveness.

Ramus had no heartier defender in New England than Leonard Hoar, but the very letter in which Hoar reveals that allegiance—a letter written two years before he became President—also displays the traits that probably accounted for the mysterious but indisputable failure of his presidency. Of some importance to the early history of Harvard College, that failure had a painful effect on young Cotton Mather.

Before Leonard Hoar became President in the summer of 1672, the college had been declining so noticeably that the Harvard Overseers had written a letter to him and several eminent friends of the colony in England, imploring their aid. Hoping for money and books, the Overseers had even more urgently requested leadership. President Charles Chauncy was old and frail, and a vigorous new President, of unquestionable learning, was needed. Leonard Hoar, who discreetly refrained from signing the English reply to the Overseers, was the man recommended by his friends Robert Boyle and Robert Morison, senior physician to the King. Hoar himself was already planning to emigrate to Boston. In 1660, he had been promptly dismissed from his rectory (Wanstead, Essex) as a nonconformist. He had improved the time by becoming an expert in medicine and botany, and he had become Doctor of Physick at Cambridge in 1670-71. Now he was prepared to preach in the new Third Church of Boston. President Chauncy died while Hoar was at sea, but the cautious Overseers did not act at once upon Hoar's arrival in Boston, even though he brought with him the letter from their English friends that said his impending immigration was a "speaking Providence" in answer to their prayers for aid. Hoar had begun preaching alongside Thomas Thacher at the Third Church, but Providence had quickly spoken again. Within a month of Hoar's arrival in Boston the Harvard President's temporary replacement, Alexander Nowell, had also died, and Hoar found himself elected President of the college in which he had earned his first degree in 1650. He thus became the first of many Harvard alumni to occupy the presidency.

As Samuel Eliot Morison has shown in his excellent history of
Harvard College, the moment of Hoar's inauguration in December
1672 was a fine but painfully frustrated opportunity for hope. Leonard Hoar had greater plans for the college than any of his predecessors had offered, and the letter in which he expressed those hopes to
Robert Boyle seems to have promised a gigantic step toward the
modern university. Hoar proposed a botanical garden and a chemi-
cal laboratory, which Morison says would have been the first in the
British Empire and perhaps the first in the world. Hoar also asked
Boyle to arrange for sending not only Boyle's own books but lists and
copies of the other worthy books being published virtually every day
in London — books which New England's scholars hardly learned the
names of. At the commencement exercises of August 1672 Hoar did
not preside — apparently because he wanted the General Court to
confirm an appropriate presidential salary before he gave up his bar-
gaining power by actually assuming the office. Urian Oakes, said
then and now to have been Hoar's chief rival for the Presidency,
spoke largely in a joking vein and certainly with cordial expressions
of welcome to the newcomer, who twenty-two years earlier had
graduated one year behind Oakes himself.

Under Hoar's leadership, however, the college sank lower and
more rapidly than ever before, and the crisis had severe effects on
young Cotton Mather. Hoar's difficulties had begun almost at once,
while Mather was still a pupil in Ezekiel Cheever's school in the first
months of 1673. The precise origin of the Harvard crisis remains unknown. If Hoar's severe standards were not the main cause, they at
least exacerbated the hostility and suspicion on both sides of the dispute. Hoar was a man who had suffered great pain for his convictions, and who for an entire decade had been forcibly prevented
from following his sacred vocation. He could not smile tolerantly on
young men who wasted their time, and he did not find it easy to forgive. His extraordinary bluntness survives in a moving letter to his
nephew Josiah Flint, a Harvard freshman, a year before his own
emigration from England. Flint had thought one of Hoar's avuncu-
lar letters too severe, but Hoar insisted that instead it had been too
lenient: "and I am sure yourself would be of the same mind if with
me you knew the unutterable misery and irreparable mischief that
follows upon the mispense of those halcyon days which you do yet
enjoy." Hoar told young Flint not to "fence" with honest criticism

any longer, for the "thin-skulled-paper-put-byes" of Flint's defense had been no better than his "empty excuses." Far from satisfying the uncle's high hopes and standards, the nephew's evasions "did but lay upon your own blameworthiness and augment my grief." It was time for the young man to learn that "those unhappy youths" who "elude the expectations of their friends for a little while . . . not only delude, but destroy themselves forever."

Those views were not in themselves unusual among Puritans and Anglicans in the seventeenth century, but with other evidence President Hoar's expression of them suggests that they made him unusually vulnerable to the organized resentment of the young. Somehow a large proportion of the students and the tutors gathered themselves to resist him very soon after his inauguration. Perhaps the rivalry of unsuccessful aspirants to the presidency — Thomas Graves of Charlestown and the Reverend Mr. Urian Oakes, Pastor of the church in Cambridge and resident with his family in the Harvard College Yard — contributed to the hostility.

Certainly Oakes's position did little to bring about peace. Hoar was nearly driven out of office in his first year, when the students and teaching fellows who openly opposed him went so far as to appeal to the General Court. Even the desire of those legislators and the Board of Overseers to support the President and discourage rebelliousness could find no clear division on principles which they could confidently evaluate. They seem to have been as baffled as more recent investigators of the controversy. But for such a body, then as now, the administrator sins as much by failing to resolve a conflict as if he had plainly been culpable on the original issue. In October 1673 the General Court formally concurred in the Overseers' rejection of a petition to remove the President; at the same time they urged the students who had withdrawn from college to return, they admitted that "there may have been some grievances," and they expressed hope that prudent advice from the Overseers would be useful to the President in establishing peace. But by the time Cotton Mather arrived for his entrance examination, the warfare had commenced once again.

Mather's own account more than twenty years later gives us some insight into the nature of the struggle, though not into its causes. Somehow, he says, Hoar happened to make powerful enemies "in the neighborhood," and "the *young men* in the college took advan-

tage therefrom, to ruin his reputation, as far as they were able. . . .
[They] set themselves to *travesty* whatever he *did* and *said*, and aggravate everything in his behavior disagreeable to them, with a design to make him *odious*."

Student rebellion was not unprecedented in seventeenth-century
Harvard, and every president had had some trouble. From vehement
complaints about foul food served by the President in the very first
years of the college, the presidential miseries extended to doctrinal
matters. Henry Dunster, in fact, had been forced to resign because
he could not conscientiously renounce his open opposition to infant
baptism. And in 1671 the future poet Edward Taylor and his classmates had absolutely refused to read a discredited physics textbook.
Their tutor succeeded for a while in reading it aloud to them despite
their objections, just as one of those very undergraduates, Samuel
Sewall, would read a different physics text to *his* students when he
became a tutor three years later; but the rebels eventually prevailed
and the book was discarded in favor of a more modern work. What
made the Hoar controversy unique was the strong alliance of students and Fellows and the absence of intelligible explanation to out-
siders who wanted to know the substance of the dispute.

By the time Cotton Mather enrolled, discipline was surely one of
the issues. The Reverend Mr. Oakes was already convinced that
President Hoar felt too vindictively punitive toward irrepressibly
playful and cruel young men. Some students apparently resented
the severity of Hoar's strictures against dancing and carousing. And
the old Anglo-American custom of fagging, newly forbidden by the
Overseers, was now to be punished more severely: if a defenseless
freshman should be sent on the traditional errands during study
hours by a taunting or bullying upperclassman, "both the sender
and the goer" would be punished. Young Mather, of course, was
universally known to be not only the youngest student but also the
son of Leonard Hoar's most vigorous defender. Age alone would
have made the situation extraordinarily troublesome for the new
boy. The historical and genealogical circumstances made it even
worse.

Although he was destined to lead a revolutionary uprising within
the next fifteen years, he was never a rebel against traditional Puritan authority. He arrived at Harvard with an understandably rever-
ent attitude toward President Hoar and with a habitually evident

desire to please. The sudden change from beloved, prodigious, reliable first-born son to smallest boy in the college made powerful demands upon his need to please and his talent for pleasing. The conflict between college rules and student customs, the warfare between President Hoar and the most powerful students and teaching fellows, and knowledge of Increase Mather's intense desire to see Mr. Hoar prevail—for a few months all these made the boy's life almost unbearably complex.

Even after Hoar's arrival discipline at the college had not been unusually severe. Various forms of hazing had attracted the Overseers' attention over the years, and the right of parents to consider themselves injured by the indignities visited upon their sons at Harvard had been recognized in official documents concerning the class of 1657 (in which one of the aggrieved freshmen was Cotton Mather's favorite uncle, John Cotton). But despite the Overseers' recommendation ten years later of severe, perhaps corporal punishment for hazing, the only penalties recorded are fines. Neither the students who shot and ate one of Daniel Gookin's turkeys in 1673 nor the students who drank too much or (later in Cotton Mather's undergraduate years) caroused and danced with women were severely punished, so long as they found themselves able to repent.

Blasphemy, an outrageous affront to the Lord, would probably have provoked harsh retribution under any administration. Blasphemy against the Holy Ghost was not only thought to be the unpardonable sin; such an enormity might bring divine wrath down upon the entire community if it should go unpunished. Soon after Cotton Mather entered Harvard, the Corporation (with Increase Mather and Leonard Hoar concurring) decided that Thomas Sargeant, a senior who had committed blasphemy against the Holy Ghost, must be whipped at a public ceremony in the college library before all the undergraduates, and that the whipping must be done not by any college authority but by the local jailer. President Hoar opened and closed the grim ceremony with prayer.

That extraordinary scene had the double effect of embittering the opposition to President Hoar and reinforcing Cotton Mather's reluctance to break the college rules. Surely he understood that the new stipulation against fagging might bring punishment on himself—if any upperclassman should presume to send him on an errand "in times enjoined for study."

Parents are explicitly mentioned as sufferers in the Overseers'
1667 prohibition of hazing. Although it is not clear whether Cotton
Mather tattled to his father, or merely consulted him when asked to
run errands for upperclassmen, or whether Increase Mather learned
from someone else about these efforts at fagging, the consequences
can be plainly seen. The boy "received some discouragement" when
several of the students threatened him and accused him of having
told his father of their misconduct. Throughout the remaining
months of Hoar's presidency and for some months thereafter, Increase Mather made the treatment of both Leonard Hoar and Cotton Mather an issue at Overseers' meetings and (after his election as
a Fellow in 1675) meetings of the Corporation. The boy's life was
unpleasantly complicated (while perhaps necessarily protected
against the bullying of much older young men and boys) by his
father's dual role as protective parent and temperamental college
authority. On July 16, 1674, Increase Mather took Cotton home to
Boston. The records, though inconclusive, suggest that Cotton did
not enroll again until nearly a year later.

By October, less than a week before the General Court summoned
President Hoar and the scholars to a hearing, Cotton Mather had
begun to stammer. On the seventh, Increase Mather fasted and
prayed in his study all day, and then called his wife and Cotton to
pray with him for deliverance from the distressing impediment. The
kneeling parents bewailed their sinfulness, asked God's "mercy in
this particular, and solemnly gave the child to God . . . begging the
Lord to accept him." Although this was not the first time the father
wept while praying with his family, the affliction seemed reason
enough for tears. All Boston and Cambridge knew that this boy,
perhaps sanctified from his very infancy, was the hope of his generation. His own consciousness of that very burden contributed to the
tension that his painful experience and the extraordinary circumstances at Harvard had aggravated. And now it seemed that Providence was either punishing the family or at least admonishing them
all not to plan on the vocation to the ministry for which the father
had "designed" his first son. A minister could not preach two long
sermons every Sunday and take his regular turn at the Thursday lecture if he could not speak fluently. And the very ardor of parental
support, the parental hope, the parental entreaty (like the boy's own
eagerness to shine and to please) must have had a choking effect as

Cotton strove to break free into speech. Years later his father remembered having been "much (more than I should have been) exercised in my spirit . . . lest the hesitancy" should prevent Cotton from going on to "the ministry, whereunto I had designed him." Surely Cotton perceived that anxiety.

In the same month "the sins of the country" and other "symptoms of divine displeasure" led Increase Mather to preach and then to publish two sermons on Ezekiel 7:7: "The day of trouble is near." On the thirteenth the deputies in the legislature voted to dismiss President Hoar, but the magistrates, while allowing his salary to be reduced by one third, successfully argued that he should be given until March 15, 1675, to restore order to the college. With Harvard in crisis and the vigor of the Bay colony's religious commitment in some doubt, Increase Mather felt a strong premonition that God would soon punish New England "with the sword."

King Philip's War did not actually begin until the summer of 1675, but throughout the intervening autumn and winter the air of Cambridge was heavy with the conspiratorial chill of academic hostilities. As early as June 5, 1674, Mr. Oakes had warned Samuel Sewall, a teaching fellow, to avoid Oakes's home in the Yard, for fear of being suspected of a cabal against the President. When Sewall had to testify before the General Court in mid-October, he said that the causes of Harvard's "lowness" were external as well as internal. And after all the students had disappeared from the college in November, Thomas Thacher decided that Increase Mather had inconsiderately helped to wreck it by taking young Cotton home; Thacher's son, the teaching fellow, was thus deprived of his students. Even after Hoar resigned on March 15, the bitterness persisted. A number of the students returned to the Yard, but Cotton Mather probably did not join them until June 22, more than a year after his original matriculation. Urian Oakes—protesting great reluctance—agreed to serve as Acting President. By shrewdly emphasizing the relative mildness of his attitude toward extracurricular discipline, he wittily reminded the students and the community of Hoar's severity.

Increase Mather supplied enough indignation to keep both his son and the Acting President from concluding that their life would now be tranquil. Mather was outraged by the cruel treatment of Leonard Hoar in Cambridge. So long as Oakes professed unwilling-

ness to accept the presidency, moreover, Mather himself was a
prominent candidate, and it seems almost certain that he would
have been chosen promptly if he had been willing to give up his residence in the capital town of Boston and his covenanted pulpit in the
Second Church. In May, while Cotton was presumably still living at
home in Boston, someone brought Increase Mather word that Oakes
had accused him of an ambition to become President of Harvard.
Mather rode over to Cambridge at once to confront Oakes with the
charge and an angry denial. Oakes was able to placate him with a
deft protestation that he himself had been misunderstood, but he
could not deny the existence of rumors that Increase Mather "designed" to become president by moving Harvard College to Boston.
As late as the following autumn, Mather, Oakes, and Thacher were
still embittering Corporation meetings with wrangles over the treatment of Hoar, whose death in November moved Increase Mather to
lament that the good man's heart had been broken by his friends in
New England.

Cotton Mather, meanwhile, had returned to Harvard on June 22
to endure the suspicion if not the open hostility of both Mr. Oakes
and the students who believed in hazing. He had escaped a new
flurry of smallpox that had afflicted Boston and two of his own
brothers in April, but he still stammered, he was still only twelve
years old, and his father's ongoing conflict with the new President,
the "wilful and selfish" Fellows, and at least some of the students
made further trouble inevitable. Only three weeks later Increase
Mather found that his labor on a mid-summer sermon was "much
hindered by trouble at Cottons being abused by John Cotton, &
some other scholars at the college." Fagging was again an issue, although as a freshman himself Cousin John Cotton did not have that
privilege of upperclassmen. Increase Mather continued to raise the
issue at Overseers' meetings, and he threatened late in July to remove his son from Harvard once again. When Oakes and Danforth
accepted his reasons he relented, just as he did when on this occasion and several others during the next three decades he threatened
to resign his own office in the college.

※

EXCEPT AS IT coincided with the first explicit allusions to his stammer, this entire controversy during Cotton Mather's freshman year

at Harvard tells us much more about the difficulties he faced than about how he responded to them. The record discloses much about Increase Mather's relations with his colleagues, his solicitude for his son, and his seeming insensitivity to the consequences that his own official behavior would visit upon the boy. Before condemning Increase Mather to the role of overprotective father, one must remember both the comparative ages of Cotton Mather and the other Harvard students, and the possibility that the "abuses" were dangerously severe. The father's willingness to protect him may well have a bearing on Cotton Mather's decision seven or eight years later to refuse a call to preach in New Haven. But there is no way of learning just how Cotton behaved during the summers of 1674 and 1675. Before we make him into the prototype of Sid Sawyer or Master Blifil, we ought to notice that he did not withdraw from the college, that he graduated with his class in 1678, and that after the summer of 1675 the record indicates no further trouble between him and the other students. Surely Increase Mather's diary and the records of the college would provide some allusions if Cotton's suffering had persisted into his years as an upperclassman. Since the only issue that the father continued to press at official meetings was that of fagging, which applied only to freshmen, it seems reasonable to conclude that the son learned to manage his anxieties and his relations with fellow students.

He even learned to control the stammer. It continued to embarrass him during his advanced years in the college, and the thought that it might recur terrified him occasionally when he first began to preach a few years later, but in the meantime an old schoolmaster named Elijah Corlet taught him how to overcome it. Until that glorious day Cotton Mather knew the pain that he described forty years later in a medical book (see Figure 3): the dreadful feeling that God was "continually *binding*" him; the constant anxiety "when every *business* and every *company*" in his daily life put him "in pain, how to get through the speaking part" of the occasion. Next to these the mockery of some heartless classmates seemed at least in retrospect to be unimportant. Before Corlet's blessed visit Cotton was able to take some comfort from a book by Hezekiah Woodward, an English preacher whose memoir in 1640 had described his own impediment and had memorably specified the good that a child might draw from the undeniably miserable affliction.

Cap. LI. EPHPHATHA.

or,

Some Advice to STAMMERERS. ...

There is a great Number of Mankind, that have the unhappy & uneasy Infirmity of STAMMERING, to lay ... upon them.

Sometimes a Weakness upon that pair of Nerves, which give motion and Vigour to the Organs of Speech, may be the Original of this Infir-mity. And hence I have known such a thing as the Spirit of Lavender, or the 2. of Hungary Water, (used both outwardly & in-wardly) still properly & sensibly un-fetter ... one that spoke with difficulty, when the Drinking of Coffee would increase the same.

But with some, there may be a silly Trick of Stuttering, which a little Discretion might reform & relieve to admiration.

My Brethren; Tis a very grievous Humiliation, under which the glorious God has laid you in this Infirmity. Of most merciful Sav-iour beholding one that had an Impediment in his Speech, it is remarkable, He sighed upon upon it. It grieved his merciful Soul, to see such a sad Case, among the miserable children of men. ... All ... that hear the Stammerer, if they have any Goodness in them, employ a Sigh upon the Sufferer. And they that have no Goodness nor Honour nor Breeding in them, are too ready to make him ye Object of an Inhumane Derision. ... Be sure then, the Stammerer himself cannot but fetch many a Sigh, when he finds God continually Binding of him: and when every Business, & every Company, where-with he is concerned, puts him pain, how to get thro' ye Speaking part which lies lies before him. Certainly, ... such a Misery should not be endured, without many Essays, to ... fetch good of Evil. And a prudent Conduct under it, should be mightily laboured for.

whose mocking has indeed been so catching, that we have seen many of these ... Uncivil Creatures, who have in this way Reproached their Maker, by a conspicuous Vengeance of Hea-ven rendred In-curable & con-temptible Stutte-rers all their Days.

3. A page from the chapter on stammering,
in the manuscript of Cotton Mather's *The Angel of Bethesda*.

Especially for one so bright and well-born as Cotton Mather, with his genealogical affectations of pre-eminency, it was excruciating to know that God had impaired one's speech in a way that invited "every prating fool" to assume an attitude of superiority. But the lesson taught by Hezekiah Woodward and Increase Mather was to pray harder, study harder, and "mightily labor" for "a *prudent conduct*" under the affliction. The key to Cotton Mather's developing character is not only the affliction, the anxiety, the incipient neurosis, but the mighty labor to make the most of it. Who can match the determination of the Puritan determinist? If he was to carry about with him a perpetual mark of one whom God would lay low in this world, he would strive to be among those chosen for vessels of honor in the next, and he would "make the experiment," he said, of seeing how far prayer might bring him toward the divine favor. He knew from experience even in childhood that stammerers are likely to "speak ten times more than they need to," and that the "joy and pride of . . . being able to speak *some words* freely" led them to "ostentate this unto all people, at the expense of" revealing "their foible also." With the advice of his elders, then, he resolved to study the discipline of silence and, since stammerers were often of "too choleric a disposition," to control his vulnerable temper and study "the *meekness of wisdom.*" His concern here was prudent as well as spiritual, for he learned that anger would only make his stammer more *"unspeakably"* obvious and ridiculous. He resolved to pray for deliverance and to use his speech in the service of God, for a stammerer would become the most horrid of spectacles if he wasted his speech in sinful words. He based his hope on the example of Moses, who had been chosen by the Lord despite a speech defect, and on the promise of Isaiah: *"The heart of the rash shall understand knowledge, and the tongue of the stammerers shall be ready to speak plainly."* After thousands of prayers to Jesus for "a *free speech,"* he vowed that deliverance would confirm his desire to proclaim his faith in the divinity of Jesus, and then one day, when he was "extraordinarily thus engaged," old Mr. Corlet came to see him in his room at Harvard College.

With Ezekiel Cheever, Corlet was the most respected teacher in the colony. No other schoolmaster in the country had sent so many students to Harvard as Elijah Corlet had sent over from his Cambridge school. Corlet did not temporize. "My friend," he said to

Cotton Mather, "I now visit you for nothing, but only to talk with you about the *infirmity* in your *speech*, and offer you my advice about it, because I suppose 'tis a thing that greatly troubles you." He advised the boy to "seek a cure for it, in the method of *delibera-tion*. Did you ever know anyone stammer," he asked, "in singing of the Psalms?" To answer his own rhetorical question, he began to in-tone the first verse of Homer, drawing out every Greek syllable to demonstrate that even a stammerer could repeat the experiment without faltering. So long as you try to "*snatch* at words," Corlet said, you will try to be too quick and "you'll be *stopped* a thousand times in a day." Develop the habit of "a very *deliberate* way of *speaking*; a *drawling* that shall be little short of *singing*."

Drawling, Corlet argued, would be better than stammering, "es-pecially if what you speak be well worth our waiting for." The point was not to make the drawl permanent, but to encourage confidence and, through deliberation, "a great command of pertinent thoughts." During the period of training the speaker would learn confidence through having enough time to substitute a manageable word whenever "you find a word likely to be too hard for you." Gradually, Corlet predicted, the habit of deliberation would enable Mather to speak without indecent hesitations and his tongue would become "so habituated unto right-speaking, that . . . sooner than you imagine, [you will] grow able to speak as fast again" as ever. But Corlet warned him that he must "beware of speaking too fast, as long as you live."

One could hardly exaggerate the importance of this interview. Even after allowing for the shape that Cotton Mather's own imagi-nation gave to the episode when he recounted it thirty-five years later, one must recognize here exemplary methods that represent the strength of Puritan society — both the kind of support that would help young people to master the anxieties induced by their creed, and the habits of thought implicit in Corlet's argument. The great emotional burden of young Mather's inheritance was alleviated if not balanced by the solicitous and resourceful example of several paternal figures, not only his father and Ezekiel Cheever, but Corlet and old John Eliot, the revered missionary. Within the pious frame-work that saw Corlet's visit as a divine answer to thousands of prayers, these exemplary figures gave Cotton Mather memorable experience of subtle, practical thought, shrewd psychological reasoning, arguments from experience, careful study of evidence, and strong encouragement to live with, while trying always to overcome, one's limitations. In the anecdote as Mather preserved it, Corlet does much more than provide the essential method of overcoming a stammer. He asks a pointed question of the boy's experience: Did you ever know anyone stammer in singing of the Psalms? He exemplifies the method of deliberation by reciting the lines from Homer. He gives two or three ingenious arguments for the value of the proposed method. And he overlays the practical advice with two strong moral admonitions: Make what you speak be worth waiting for, and remember that for the rest of your life you will have to beware of speaking too fast.

One way that the boy prepared to accept his limitations even while he struggled to break through them was in the study of medicine. Among the hundreds of books that he says he had read by the time he was fourteen, the subject that he found himself thinking most practically about after his favorite of church history was medicine. The regular Harvard curriculum seems to have presented no great difficulties for him. He composed systems "both of logic and physics," after the Ramean manner, in what he called "catechisms of my own," and these were passed around in manuscript and copied by other scholars for more than one academic generation. For the periodic "declamations" that were required on Friday mornings, he often chose subjects in science (then called natural philosophy) and thus, as he later advised his son, "contrived to kill two birds with one stone." As he learned about the natural and physiological worlds, he kept a commonplace book—"Quotidiana," he called it —out of which he would draw information for the rest of his life as a prolific writer of sermons and as the author of two large scientific books, *The Angel of Bethesda* and *The Christian Philosopher.*

But in these early years scientific and historical studies were important to him chiefly as they encouraged a way of life that required much solitude along with the conviction of social utility. Even in these studies emotional dangers lurked. Just as the study of St. Augustine (and other pious writers as recent as Thomas Shepard and John Cotton) could provoke doubts about one's own salvation, so the intensive reading of medical texts could induce the illusion of pathological symptoms. Like impressionable medical students everywhere, and after the example of his hypochondriacal father, young

Mather was sometimes "led away with fancies" that he himself had contracted "almost every distemper" that he read about in his studies. Sometimes he was so concerned that he took unnecessary and even damaging medicines to cure his "imaginary maladies." And of course it was in these adolescent years that he began to feel the dreadful guilt that so often precedes religious conversion, the guilt that he seems not to have acknowledged consciously during his childhood. He apparently did not suffer the grave physical illness that would later admonish Jonathan Edwards and John Woolman to repent, but his imaginary ailments sufficed. He fell into a melancholy so depressing that in later years he could not understand why it had not done him more damage.

The remedy was to follow a pattern that he often copied during his adult life. First he consulted his father. Having experienced nothing more than what reflection told him were only "common works" of grace, the good conduct and reputation granted to many of the reprobate as well as the elect, he suspected himself of being only a refined hypocrite. And he found it especially difficult, though at last painfully necessary, to consult his revered father. Not only was the sense of guilt complicated by the bewildering impulses of puberty, which made him suspect he had "apostatised" from God; the paternal image was so strongly associated with the divine that the fourteen-year-old conceived of his own prospective damnation in the language of public reputation and of a confrontation with his earthly father. It was bad enough that "after I had *hoped well* of myself, and many servants of God had *spoke well* of me, I should be a *castaway* after all." The thought that struck him with "a very particular pungency"—though he later decided it had been sent by God—focused on the ultimate judgment by Increase Mather, the parent who did not yet know how vile the boy was: "How shall I be able to look my own father in the face at the Day of Judgment!" It is a tribute to the relationship that the anguish of private prayer during one of these fits of melancholy drove Cotton Mather at last to consult his father about whether Jesus Christ could accept "a vile wretch, that hath been and hath done, as I have." Increase Mather met the occasion with assurances both theological and "experimental": Jesus would accept any truly penitent, returning sinner, and "even among men" one could observe that after a vile sinner's conversion a holy person who had shunned the sinner was now willing to embrace him, acting both in consequence and as an emblem of the Christian spirit.

Cotton Mather experienced the relief, and his first intimations of his own conversion, in explicitly filial terms. He was astonished by the degree to which "these words did *quicken* me!" Soon he began to receive "strange, and strong, and sweet intimations" of his acceptance. "Once especially," after he had heard a sermon on a text from the forty-fourth chapter of Isaiah—"I will pour my spirit on thy seed, and my blessing on thy offspring"—he claimed that promise in a day of sacred meditation, and as he prayed he felt the "Spirit of the Lord wonderfully dissolve" his heart with assurances "that it should be fulfilled upon me." The most important question of his life was thus posed and provisionally settled through an appeal to the covenant of his eminent father and grandfathers.

Disciplined meditation—ingenious and inexhaustible striving for methods of effective devotion, self-improvement, and spiritual usefulness—was the second device in the pattern by which Cotton Mather learned during his teens to dispel his melancholy. He read Henry Scudder's *The Christian's Daily Walk* and especially Joseph Hall's *Meditation*, and he began to keep days of solitary fasting with prayer, sometimes as often as once a week. Although that isolation sometimes increased his melancholy, he learned to concentrate on Hall's advice to make his daily meditations extremely methodical. Because devotional literature provided him with innumerable models of self-abasement, it is always hard to know how vile and how melancholy he really felt himself to be, but there can be no doubt about the intensity of his methodical response. He resolved to begin doctrinally, to instruct himself either by answering a question or explaining a biblical text, according to a strictly categorical method: causes, effects, subject, adjuncts, opposites, resemblances, and so on. Then, by three carefully prescribed steps, he moved "more practically" to stir his own spiritual emotions, from the "expostulation" that would follow self-examination to a new resolution to rely on grace and improve his behavior.

More creatively, but no less relentlessly, he set himself during these years to "aspire after *usefulness*." His best opportunities would come later on in his life. Meanwhile, when he was home in Boston between academic terms and after he had taken his baccalaureate degree, he continued to teach his six brothers and sisters and the servants. He resolved that he would never go out into company without arranging his conversation to the spiritual benefit of his companions. In Boston he soon helped to found societies of religious young men, for evening prayer and discussion. And he decided to fill the tiny intervals of time with what he called daily reflections. Prompted by his reading in William Waller, Robert Boyle, and others, who had based spiritual meditations on the smallest occurrences, he resolved to sharpen his dull wits and redeem the idlest moments of a day with occasional reflections, making the commonest objects in his study, in his social life, and during his travel along a road preach to him. He uttered thousands of ejaculatory prayers, a habit deliberately cultivated in ordinary situations, from attendance at sermons to dining at home. At dinner, watching the gentlewoman who did the carving, he prayed quietly: "Lord, carve of Thy graces and comforts, a rich portion to that person." When he saw a beautiful woman, he prayed: "Lord, give that person an humble mind, and let her mind be most concerned for ornaments, that are of great price in Thy sight." When he saw a tall man walking along the street, he silently wished him the blessing of "high attainments in Christianity: let him fear God above many." When he saw a lame man: "Lord, help that man, upon moral accounts, to walk uprightly"; a man on horseback: "Lord, Thy creatures do serve that man; help him to serve his Creator."

❦

THE HARVARD undergraduate's day, however, allowed few idle moments. Undergraduate as well as advanced scholars were expected to spend long days at work. Although music, skating, and swimming gain some approving reference in official comments of the time, and although John Wise became famous throughout New England as a wrestler, it seems unlikely that many people considered recreation to be a necessary part of the young scholar's life. In the typical working day the only free time seems to have been a portion of the dinner hour, except on Saturday afternoons, and of course Saturday evenings after sundown were consecrated to preparations for the Lord's Day.

The routine of Cotton Mather's life during his residence at the college was established very soon after his arrival. With John Cotton, young Urian Oakes, and Grindall Rawson he was assigned to a tutor when he first enrolled. With them, too, he probably slept in the Long Chamber upstairs in Old College, until all four were assigned individual rooms on entering their second year.

Not even Morison's admirable *Harvard College in the Seventeenth Century*, the indispensable basis for this account, can supply a clear picture of students' dress during the 1670s. We know only that undergraduates were forbidden to leave their rooms without wearing a "coat, gown, or cloak" and that they were forbidden to wear "strange ruffianlike or newfangled fashions." Gold, silver, and other jewelry were also prohibited except on the President's express permission. "Long hair, locks or foretops" were all forbidden, and hair could not be curled, crisped, parted, or powdered. Morison notes that in the days of Sewall and Mather there was a college barber, after some years in which the college printer had been the only hair-cutter. The severity of the proscription against long hair had disappeared even among most Massachusetts Puritans by the time Cotton Mather entered Harvard, and Mather himself was destined to live in our visual memory in the powdered wig that he wore when he sat for his portrait fifty years later. As late as 1672, however, old John Eliot and his fellow townsmen of Roxbury protested to the magistrates of Massachusetts against the Harvard students' lust for long hair.

In spring and summer every student had to attend morning prayers soon after the bell rang at 5:00 A.M., and in the autumn and winter months at 6:00 A.M. Here he listened to explications (by the President or a tutor) of an Old Testament text, which one or more scholars might have to read aloud out of the Hebrew and translate into Latin. Breakfast probably consisted of a pint of beer and a chunk of bread, with butter available for a little more money, and the student was allowed about thirty minutes after prayers to find and consume it. It was for this and the afternoon "sizing" that freshmen were customarily obliged to do the officially prohibited fagging against which Increase Mather and other officials objected. Most students brought their own mugs or tankards, and they consumed these meals in their own rooms or, in better weather, outdoors. During Cotton Mather's years, coffee and chocolate became available in Boston, but there is no evidence of their presence in the Harvard buttery until long afterward. Beer and water, it seems, were the only beverages. A tavern was open near by, wherein students could buy

4. Old Harvard Hall (New College, built in 1677).
From a detail in the Burgis Prospect of 1726.

Ulysses might one day be even braver than his father — a plain allusion to Mather's own heritage and prospects. It seems fair to assume that the boy performed this assignment acceptably before the dread stammer began to afflict him, for Increase Mather's diary does not mention the impediment until months afterward.

Although the curriculum may have been inflated to impress European observers who would see nothing but the program of study, modern observers must recognize what Samuel Eliot Morison said long ago: that Harvard set out to educate Christian gentlemen, not merely to train a few Protestant ministers. By the time they completed their work for the master's degree, as Samuel Sewall and Thomas Brattle did with no intention of becoming ministers, they had studied all of the traditional seven arts except music, and they were reasonably learned in natural and moral philosophy and some classical literature. The students' private libraries (Cotton Mather's was one of the finest) contained books from all over Western Europe, books by pagan and Roman Catholic as well as by Protestant authors: Erasmus, Homer, Milton, Descartes, Alsted, Keckermann, Gassendi.

In a curriculum that tried, "both in content and in method," to "reproduce the major features of the Arts course of Cambridge" University, with one commencement speaker insisting that "gentlemen must be educated like gentlemen," the chief aim was a high conception of utility, *Eupraxia*, or "well-doing." Students developed a mastery of the learned tongues, the rules of logic (as understood by Peter Ramus), the theory and "flowers" of rhetoric, and some polite as well as much theological literature. As Morison points out with characteristic wit, after four years' devotion of every Friday to rhetoric and oratory, a Harvard student ought surely to have formed the seeds of those flowers in his head.

The striking quality of Cotton Mather's English prose, after a reader passes through the early stages of noticing the mannerisms, the word play, and so forth, is its extraordinarily consistent grace and clarity. One groans at the realization that he wrote and preserved so many millions of words; one comes eventually to admire his consistent mastery of his own language. In his Latin training as well as in the occasional declamations given in English as a part of the training at Harvard, he learned a respect for clarity, and a fluency in thought and expression, that New England required not only in preachers but in all learned men. Although apprehensive about pagan authors' moral effect, Harvard teachers required students to learn the flowers of rhetoric from classical authors and especially from phrase books and manuals that quoted them. Among the favorite books, and included in Cotton Mather's private library at Harvard, was the *Colloquies* of Erasmus, more than five hundred pages of "prompt, quick, witty and sententious sayings of certain emperors, kings, captains, philosophers, and orators." Cotton Mather would one day be known for his own mastery of those qualities.

The physics taught at Harvard in the 1670s was transformed after the class of 1671 had refused to read an obsolete, Aristotelian text that the tutor had assigned. Books by followers of Descartes, and especially Adrian Heerebord's *Philosophical Exercises*, became the most popular texts, laying out principles which students could easily memorize as in the old days, but incorporating recent scientific discoveries along with the old principles. It is Heerebord's book that Samuel Sewall read to his students during his teaching fellowship in 1673-74. Charles Morton's unpublished "Compendium Physicae" (1680) was not known in New England until after 1686, when he immigrated from England, but its principle of observing that man establishes "probable opinions . . . by *sense, observation, experience* and *induction*" was well known to Harvard students, who already believed that religious as well as scientific knowledge was essentially progressive. As Morton, who came to New England expecting to become President of Harvard, predicted a continual reformation in scientific knowledge, so Cotton Mather and his classmates knew (before Morton's writing told them so) that scientific investigation was "for the glory of God and our own good."

For divine glory and their own good the students also attended the Cambridge Church every Lord's Day to hear two sermons by Mr. Oakes, whose meetinghouse (built in 1650) was conveniently located on the southwestern corner of the modern Yard. The students walked together to the meetinghouse, where they sat in a gallery that had been especially constructed for them on the east side of the building. The college charged each student three shillings and fourpence "for the use" of the gallery, and thus paid off the mortgage.

ALTHOUGH UNDERGRADUATE students were not conscripted, King

Philip's War affected college life during Cotton Mather's second year almost as markedly as President Hoar's troubles had done the year before. The war began three days after Cotton's first documented return to Harvard in June 1675, and it dragged on through a gloomy summer and, despite some Anglo-American victories, a catastrophic winter and spring. Not until August 12, 1676, did Captain Benjamin Church and a few allies from other tribes drive the Wampanoag prince from his last refuge and shoot him dead as he ran to escape. The body was beheaded and quartered, and the widow and children, captured some time earlier, were sold into West Indian slavery, but it took much more than retributive mutilation to repair the unprecedented damage that the war had done to English settlements. Of course the destruction wrought by English reprisals had a terribly ruinous effect on the Wampanoags and Narragansetts, just as previous encounters had virtually obliterated the Pequots in New England, but the most enlightened cultural relativism can hardly deny that the suffering of the English colonists was real. Beginning in the last week of June 1675, a grand perimeter extending from the towns of Plymouth colony and parts of Rhode Island all the way around through the settlements in the Connecticut Valley was devastated, with more fatalities (in proportion to the population) than in any American war of the next three centuries. One tenth of all the males of fighting age in the colony were killed during the war. In the many towns that were burned, two thousand people were homeless by the time the war ended, and throughout 1675 and 1676 refugees caused embarrassing problems in the towns of Cambridge and Boston. Boston even took some action in a futile attempt to prevent refugees from settling there. In Cambridge, Captain Daniel Gookin, protector of the badly mistreated Christian Indians, had great difficulty (and sometimes failed in) preventing vengeful attacks upon them.

Probably the chief impact of the war upon Harvard undergraduates came from the apparent threat to the Bay colony's existence, the seeming fulfillment of Increase Mather's admonitory prophecy, and efforts to appease the God who had obviously taken up what Michael Wigglesworth called a controversy with New England. As the refugees and news of casualties intruded on Boston and Cambridge, special days of fasting and prayer were appointed, and as these proved ineffective new measures were sought. In one winter

battle, perhaps the major Anglo-American victory of the war because it virtually destroyed the Narragansetts' army, Anglo-American casualties were higher than 20 percent. Many towns, including
Marlborough and Lancaster, were burned. And when a large
enemy force attacked Sudbury on April 20, 1676, in one of the last
large battles of the war, the smoke and flames from grass fires they
had set to confuse the defending soldiers could be plainly seen from
Cambridge and Boston, only seventeen miles away.

Against such grave troubles, the squabbles over hazing and academic administration decreased in significance even for Increase
Mather. Although it permanently weakened Indian military power
in New England, King Philip's War seemed the culmination of a
series of threats and disasters that had begun with the Restoration.
From that perspective the decline of Harvard College was one painful hour in the day of trouble that Increase Mather had prophesied,
and the arrival of Edward Randolph in the spring of 1676, near the
lowest moment of Anglo-American morale, seemed no more coincidental in the Providential plan than it actually was in the minds of
the royal officials who had sent him out to bring Massachusetts into
line.*

From the perspective of the late 1690s, Cotton Mather the historian would add to that incremental series the revocation of the
colony's precious charter, the brief term of Sir Edmund Andros as
royal governor of Massachusetts, the Indian wars of northern New
England in the last decade of the century, and the amazing outbreak of witchcraft near Salem in 1692. But the alternating pattern
that we have already noticed in young Mather's psychic and spiritual
life functioned also in the community and in contemporaneous histories such as Increase Mather's narrative of King Philip's War. Disasters were followed by rescues and victories. After many occasions
for fasting and repentance, there were ceremonies of thanksgiving.
The Devil was let loose among God's people, but then he and his
wicked human servants were defeated.

---

*Randolph's missions to New England will be considered in the next chapter. His assign-
ment in 1676 was to revive the controversy over the colony's duty to the Crown—an issue that
had reached a crisis when Governor Leverett had defied the royal commissioners in 1665. In
the intervening decade troubles at home and international politics had prevented the Crown
from aggressively pressing its claim to authority in Massachusetts.

Only a few months after the war ended, a new shock reminded Boston of the alternating pattern. Increase Mather, who had prophesied the divine retribution in King Philip's War, felt a strong premonition of an unusually destructive fire. For his sermon on the nineteenth of November he chose his text from the third chapter of Zephaniah, the seventh verse: instructions for conduct necessary to forestall divine vengeance upon the congregation's dwelling places. He concluded the sermon "with a strange prediction, that a fire was a coming, which would make a deplorable desolation." He felt the premonition so strongly that he urged his wife privately to find another house for the family as soon as possible. Before the move could be arranged, another Lord's Day came around, and Mather preached on Revelations 3:3, warning those who did not repent and keep faith, that divine vengeance would come upon them like a thief, without their knowing the time.

Before dawn the next morning, a tailor's apprentice neglected to tend properly to his candles and started Boston's greatest fire of the century. A strong southeast wind blew the flames and sparks along so smartly toward the north that Charlestown, on the other side of the river, was threatened by falling ash. Forty-five houses were destroyed in the North End of Boston, and Mather's beloved church in North Square, the very building in which he had warned his congregation of the holocaust, was also consumed. His own house near by, and eighty of his precious books, were ruined, but energetic human action and a steady rain enabled the firefighters to save the other nine hundred volumes in his library.

That loss, Cotton Mather cheerfully reported ten years later, was promptly restored by the generous gift of President Leonard Hoar's library by his widow, and less than two years after the fire the Mather family had a better house than the one that had been damaged. Even the destruction of the meetinghouse had some beneficial results in spreading Increase Mather's "enlightening and awakening ministry" throughout the city as he preached regularly from neighboring pulpits, but of course it was easier to appreciate these hidden signs of Providential blessing ten years later than it was in the weeks just after the fire. Then the only comfort seemed to lie in the merciful rain and in the accuracy of the ministerial warning. Nor was all human animosity restrained during the emergency. Trying to keep his congregation together after their meetinghouse and a large number of their homes had burned down, Increase Mather was not always careful to restrain the family pride. Samuel Willard, one of his colleagues in Boston, was annoyed by Mather's frank statement that he preferred to preach in the afternoon rather than the morning during the temporary loan of Willard's church, "that so he might have a copious auditory." Nor was Willard's temper eased when Mather, offered a chance to keep much of his congregation together by preaching to them as a distinct church in the Town House, replied: "I will not preach in a corner."

Beyond its value as entertaining characterization and as exemplary Puritan effort to interpret and reinterpret New England history, the anecdote of Increase Mather's strange prediction has a special bearing on the development of Cotton Mather's young mind. The father's prediction of the great fire served as a uniquely personal illustration of a phenomenon that would eventually bring the son inexpressible joy and, at two critical moments in his adult personal life, bewildering misery. The great fire is the first recorded example of a phenomenon about which Increase Mather gave his son explicit instruction during these years. Both father and son called the favorable version of such specific premonitions a Particular Faith, a conviction that Providence would allow the faithful believer a particular benefit.

Those who experienced the Particular Faith took pains to distinguish it from more nearly ordinary premonitions or coincidences. In that Providential world the pious observer kept an alert watch for coincidences, and the interpretation of premonitions developed subtle qualities in those who looked for signs of divine or satanic will. Only about two weeks after the great fire, for example, Samuel Sewall recorded a strange anecdote about a young boy named Seth Shove who had come to live in Sewall's house. When Sewall came into the kitchen on the evening of Seth's arrival, he saw a shaggy dog there and spoke apprehensively to a friend: "I am afraid we shall be troubled with the ugly dog." The friend went off in pursuit of the dog, met Seth along the way, mistook him for the dog, "and smote him so hard upon the bare head with a pipe staff, or something like it, that it grieved" Sewall to think anyone might have "struck [even] the dog so hard." Grateful that the welt on Seth's head, "rising almost from the forehead to the crown," indicated God's mercy (for such a blow might have "spilled his brains on the ground"), Sewall observed that "the Devil (I think) seemed to be angry at the child's coming to dwell here."

Such coincidences were more nearly ordinary than the Particular Faith because the events, though perhaps startling, were of no great personal or communal significance, but also because inhabitants of a world subject to both natural and supernatural causes felt obliged to look for signs of God's secret will in events as well as for the operation of natural laws. The death of King Philip, the burning of a Boston church, and the bruising of Seth Shove's head conveyed signs that observers were bound to interpret. A Particular Faith, on the other hand, was an affirmative version of Increase Mather's premonition that fire was acoming to Boston. A Particular Faith gave a faithful believer a rare conviction that his stammer would one day be cured, that his ailing wife would surely recover, that his son, apparently lost at sea, would be rescued. Such a conviction might come not only with an extraordinary light but through the agency of a visible angel.

❧

DESPITE THE menace in Edward Randolph's visit to New England, the balance of Cotton Mather's junior and senior years was reasonably undisturbed by catastrophic events or threats. In 1677 a Quaker woman did blacken her face and burst in upon the Third Church of Boston during worship, thereby causing the greatest uproar that Samuel Sewall had ever experienced. And a number of Harvard students were punished in 1677. In Watertown near by, one young veteran of King Philip's War made a complaint that some authorities considered seditious: Why can't young men meet together with young maids without provoking scandalous reports? Soon, he protested, young men would be required to "pass by the maids like quakers and take no notice of them." For the satisfaction of declaring that "we must serve the country" and that "you can't make an old man out of a young one," this bold speaker was fined forty shillings. Although no Harvard students were involved in the late nocturnal gatherings that were thus expensively defended, some students were reprimanded for excessive drinking and carousing, and in 1678 Samuel Gibson, the turkey-poaching glover of Cambridge, was fined once again for having entertained some students in his house. But turkeys and geese continued to disappear from their proper places throughout the next decade, and even when some dead fowl were found stinking in the chambers of students, the culprits were treated as leniently as those who drank too much, played cards, swore, broke the Sabbath, or roistered at various times during the next twenty years. The records give little reason to doubt either the vitality of Harvard undergraduates or a visiting Friend's observation (twenty-five years later) that Harvard students behaved much "more like Christians" than did undergraduates at Cambridge, Oxford, and Edinburgh.

It was in these years that Commencement Day took on the quality of an annual fair. Not only speeches by students and the President but heavy feasting and hearty drinking at private dinners enlivened the day. With the President's learned address, unusually elegant and witty during Oakes's brief term, the defense of theses in the afternoon by graduate students taking their second degree, and the dinners for family and friends, the ceremony attracted merchants of various kinds, and dignitaries from Boston and the important congregations. Besides Election Day, Commencement Day was the one major annual ceremony that attracted peddlers, hundreds of auditors, and the color and noise of a local fair. Liquor bills as well as food bills were often high at the private dinners. In 1681, for example, the authorities paid grave respect to the late Urian Oakes's memory by restricting the amount of wine that could be provided by the celebrants to three gallons for each graduating student, and one gallon to other students. And William Brattle, in one of the almanacs that were regularly edited by recent Harvard graduates, playfully advised people to stay away from commencement to avoid getting blind drunk:

> Commencement's come, but (friendly) I advise
> All sorts of Rabble now their Homes to prize,
> For if to it they come, so Blind they'll bee,
> That Really no Body will see.

The ceremony began at 11 A.M. in Old Harvard, the new college building completed in 1677. In his elegant Latin President Oakes applied his celebrated wit to each of the four new Bachelors of Arts in turn. To John Cotton he spoke not only of the "sweet and memorable name" of his paternal grandfather but also of Grandfather Bradstreet, in hopes that young Cotton would "not only follow after them . . . but catch up with them." For the second graduate, Cotton Mather, however, Oakes reserved his most elaborate emphasis on names:

> The next is called COTTONUS MATHERUS. What a name! I made a mistake, I confess; I should have said, what names! I shall say nothing of his reverend father, Overseer of the University most vigilant, since I wish not to praise him to his face. But if this youth bring back and represent the piety, learning, and graceful ingenuity, sound judgment, prudence and gravity of his reverend grandsires John Cotton and Richard Mather, he may be said to have done his part well. And I despair not that in this youth Cotton and Mather shall in fact as in name coalesce and revive!

Oakes completed the pattern by alluding to Grindall Rawson's distinguished relatives, including the worthy Archbishop Grindall, and at last by a charming refusal to praise his own son, "already suffering," as Morison notes, from what Cotton Mather later called "a languishing consumption."

The Bachelors' part in the ceremony took up the rest of the morning. They disputed a series of theses in the various subjects — technological,* grammatical, rhetorical, mathematical, and physical. The theses had been printed on the commencement program along with the names of the graduating bachelors (ranked according to the customary seniority). Three of the grammatical theses have been translated thus: "Grammar is the antidote for the confusion of tongues. Quantity and accent are the flavorings (*condimenta*) of syllables. Syntax is the cynosure to direct the reader to the sense of sentences." Under rhetoric one thesis at the 1678 commencement declared that "trope to the learned, figure to the uneducated, is the sweetest part of elocution" — in other words, that the common people can understand only the explicit sense of a sentence, whereas the educated few alone can appreciate subtleties of linguistic allusion. Under logic: "Dialectic [according to the prescription of Ramus] is the art of reasoning." Under physics: "Nature does nothing except by the first cause."

Although Cotton Mather later named the thesis he had defended

---

*Not in our modern sense of the word. The term comes from Peter Ramus's *Technologia*, a scheme for a method of organizing all knowledge in a simpler way than the traditional Scholastic system.

for his A.M. degree in 1681, the assignment of individual parts in these baccalaureate disputations has not been preserved. The disputations presumably involved the four members of the graduating class, with questions from alumni and other scholars generally reserved for the master's candidates in the afternoon. Again we have no indication that Cotton Mather's stammer troubled him during this ceremony, but we may assume that his parents attended it, and neither Increase Mather's nor Samuel Sewall's diary alludes to any difficulty in Cotton Mather's performance.

The master's theses in the afternoon were preceded by a long celebration at dinner. With his parents and perhaps his brothers and sisters present, including the precocious Nathanael, who eight years later would top this performance by giving a commencement oration in Hebrew, Cotton Mather thus achieved the first of many public ceremonies of reassurance. At fifteen he was not only the youngest Harvard graduate of the century but a boy who needed and knew how to elicit public recognition of his value.

# III

# The Call of the Gospel
# and the Loss of the Charter

⁓❦⁓

O Disciple of *Epicurus,* Let not a *Vain Philosophy* tell thee, That such *Heavenly Afflations* are nothing but a *melting of the Brain* by chance happening in a *Warm Temper;* and that they who Speak of GOD *shining out* upon them, only happen to be under *Heats* of the *Brain,* that *rise and flow Copiously* more at some times than at others; and so by Consequence, that the *case of a Troubled mind* Complaining of *Desertions* and *Aridities,* is to be laugh'd at, as the Whimsey of a *Brain* happening to be under a *Cloudy Vapour.* It is true, *Bodily Dispositions* do often affect the mind; and *Ministers* are applied unto, when *Physicians* would be more properly and effectually called for. But they who laugh at all *Spiritual Operations* upon the mind, are Ignorant, and Shortsighted Men, *Sensual, not having the Spirit;* And the many *Volumns* about such things Written by men of Renown in the Congregations of GOD, have not been all thrown away on a meer *Mechanical* and *Chymerical* Business . . .

Cotton Mather, *Parentator*

Proud thoughts fly-blow my best performances.

Cotton Mather, *Diary*

RETURNING HOME to Boston as the youngest Harvard graduate, Cotton Mather soon found himself in the next stage of a dramatic development that would tie his individual life more closely than ever to the fate of New England. There in his parents' new house and in the rebuilt North Church, his father encouraged him both explicitly and by example to identify his own personal, professional, and spiritual life with events in the political world and in the rapidly culminating struggle between Providence and the Devil. Events in New England in the last quarter of the seventeenth century provided good materials for a historical reading shaped in that way, and Cotton Mather had as much reason in doctrine as in myopia or unrecognized pathology for placing Boston, his family, and himself near the center of the drama.

In his personal life the essential question was still his own salvation. The promise that he felt he had received after he had consulted his father was yet to be fulfilled. Until he received grace he could neither join the church as a covenanted member nor pledge himself surely to any Christian calling. He might choose a profession before his conversion, but not strictly as his vocation, not strictly as part of his Christian testimony in the world. On this question as in academic requirements, Harvard's lenient attitude toward graduate students was helpful to the undecided. Candidates for the advanced degree could remain at Harvard or study in absentia, returning only after three years to defend a thesis on the afternoon of Commencement Day and to be certified almost automatically as Masters of Arts. The second degree was not the equivalent of the modern bachelor's degree in divinity. A number of graduates, including Edward Taylor the poet, went off to a lifetime of preaching without formally studying to take the advanced degree, and a significant number (including Samuel Sewall) took the advanced degree without becoming clergymen. One might spend the three years in virtually full-time study, chosen from a variety of subjects with little supervision, or in full-time pastoral or other work. Cotton Mather, like many others, chose to devote himself to church history, homiletics, and divinity as he waited for the critical experience of conversion.

The actual change, when it came over him, was distinctly private. Although absolutely convinced of its reality, young Mather understood as well as any modern skeptic that the experience was inescapably subjective. In writing about it he took care to distinguish his own perception from the objective fact of God's election. The decision itself had been made before time, and even in Mather's young life the effect of the choice could be seen over the years in a variety of blessings ranging from the quality and progress of his education to the alleviation of his stammer and the conversation with his father that had quickened his own assurance of an eventual conversion. What happened now, in the year after his graduation from Harvard, was a fundamental change of perception. In one of those hypochondriacal fits of melancholy that attended his medical reading, Mather once again felt "horribly overwhelmed." As he had often done before, he cried out to the Lord in prayer and cast his "burdens on the care of the Lord Jesus Christ." This time he received more than a promise of eventual relief. He "sensibly felt an unaccountable cloud and load" go off his spirit, and he felt that he was immediately transformed by the experience. He was as much changed "by a new light, and life, and *ease* arriving to me, as the *sunrise* does change the world, from the condition of *midnight*."

Mather knew even then that such language was conventional, and that his spiritual life would continue to move between seasons of great assurance and discouraging self-accusation. He had known for years that an unquestioned assurance of one's own salvation was, in Thomas Shepard's words, one of the easy ways to hell. "Suspect thyself much," Shepard had warned his congregation; and Anne Bradstreet had given her children similarly cautionary advice. Perplexed to learn after her own conversion that a faithful Christian did not feel "constant joy . . . and refreshing," she had learned to comfort herself with the inherent sweetness and the implicit promise in her rare moments of exaltation. "I have sometimes tasted of the hidden manna that the world knows not," she told her children, "and have resolved with myself that against such a promise, such tastes of sweetness, the gates of hell shall never prevail. Yet have I many times sinkings and droopings, and not enjoyed that felicity that sometimes I have done. But when I have been in darkness and seen no light, yet have I desired to stay myself upon the Lord."

Cotton Mather's new perception of the world established the perspective in which his inevitable cycles of self-abasement and self-criticism would thereafter be considered. His father's encouraging counsel and his own knowledge of the literature of conversion helped him to see the intellectual distinction between his obligation to have faith and his duty to suspect himself much. In the periods of sinking and drooping that were sure to follow these exalted days, his melancholy and self-condemnation would have to be real if his conversion had been genuine, for the effect of the new light that made him love virtue and divinity was to make the midnight of his continuing sinfulness all the more appalling to him. Yet the strong memory of his liberation from the spiritual cloud and load, and of having basked in the new light and life and ease, held him as powerfully as Anne Bradstreet's taste of the "Manna" had held her, to stay himself upon the Lord. He learned to perceive his recurring miseries with a double vision. Genuinely painful and frightening, they became, in the context of his periodic escapes from despondency, material for his current enlightenment or his future use. Eventually he was able to preach sermons "which (like the *silkworm*) I had spun out of the bowels of my own *experience*."

In the high moments of these years he rejoiced, occasionally with "raptures almost insupportable." In his community there was little danger that the ravishing ecstasy felt by a pious man in meditation would seduce him from the world into a longing for ever more protracted communion with the Holy Spirit. Cotton Mather learned in his youth that so prudent a governor as John Winthrop had experienced intense moments of rapture during private meditation without losing the commitment to act in political affairs the next day. While still in his teens Mather found a way to bring the two realms of experience together. His methodical determination to string almost every action of his life "upon a thread of religion" brought him the "incredible" experience of "a new life of Soul." When he succeeded for a time in motivating his actions in this way, he felt himself lifted into what he called a high, sweet, heavenly way of living. He felt that he had a new understanding of the phrase "*dwelling in God,* though no books or men on earth had ever instructed me how to do it." And the contemplation of his new way of life "exceedingly ravished" him. This delight he interpreted as God's communication of the "*possession,* which He had long since taken of me." And this experience of ecstasy was complemented by rationally enumerated blessings: his comfortable position in Increase Mather's household ("my father's family," he calls it), his convenient study, the superb family library, his good salary, his success as a teacher, and "a constellation of smiling providences."

But his methodical exercises also obliged him to repent. On one day, for example, he took his private text from the Book of Proverbs (28:13): "He that confesseth and forsaketh [sin] shall find mercy." Arguing from this and similar texts that he himself was probably marked for mercy, he still felt no spiritual quickening "in all this rational way of arguing: None of the *argument* brought unto my soul, that joyful peace which I wanted" (*wanted* here means not only *desired* but *lacked*). Only when he felt the divine spirit come powerfully into his heart with a free offer of Christ's righteousness — "without any *distinct considerations,* on my having these and those *conditions,* wrought in me" — only then could he "*rejoice with joy un-*

*speakable and full of glory.*" And only after that experience had overcome him could he feel "comfortable" in observing in himself "the conditions of a pardoned *soul.*" More than twenty years later, when he copied this passage as a sober father taking a retrospective view of his passionate youth, he added one more refinement for the instruction of his sons: "Nor would I have entertained the afflations and assurances of the persuasion, *that I was pardoned,* if I could not at the same time, have seen these conditions." In the global structure of Puritan logic, the overwhelming experience and the enumerated "conditions" were mutually supportive.

Impossible though it is for any outside observer to measure the intensity of such private experience, we have no reason to doubt the mixed feelings of anticipation and dread with which Mather approached these days of prayer and fasting. His language, though conventional, is strong: grievous conflicts, sorrows, horrors of mind, horrible amazements, agonies. These agonies, he says, "came over me without my calling for them." The "inexpressible bitterness" that came with them made him "dread the repetition of them." It was in just that state of gloom that he had to struggle with "unutterable fervencies . . . to lay hold on the Lord Jesus Christ." A "sweet satisfaction of mind" followed these agonies and struggles so regularly that one may well decide to lay hold on Sigmund Freud or Erik Erikson to explain the repetitive process. But whether or not we read Mather's struggles as (for example) a repetitive search for his father's disapproval, forgiveness, and reassurance, we miss much of their significance if we neglect his self-awareness. The key to the genuineness of these experiences is not only in the perception that the agonies came over him without being bidden, but also in his own recognition of what we might call the compulsive pattern: "Thus I was (while an ignorant youth) strangely led on by the *Spirit* of the most High, to go the whole *work of conversion* often over and over again. And though at the beginning of a day set apart for such devotions, I should even tremble in the thoughts of the *travail* that I foresaw, I should pass through, yet I comforted myself, that my frequent *renewing* of this action, would be my assuring of it."

Even in this spiritual region of Mather's world, moreover, real biographical distinctions did exist. Every saint might at one time or another bewail his own pride; some saints had more cause than others to find pride among the incurable corruptions of their hearts.

From childhood Cotton Mather had extraordinary reason to feel
that he must not bring shame upon either of his distinguished
names, and he displayed throughout his life an extraordinary sensitivity to public attacks upon them. The very vanity that Benjamin
Franklin later placed among the comforts of life was pushing Cotton
Mather to achieve prodigies which inflated his pride and cried out
for mortification. How many other Harvard graduates preached
their first sermon at the age of sixteen? What other eighteen-year-
old preached so effectively in Grandfather John Cotton's First
Church of Boston that some auditors declared themselves hardly
able to forbear crying out aloud during the sermon? Who else was
invited to become Pastor of John Davenport's old church in New
Haven at the age of eighteen? It is not surprising that Cotton Mather's journal records pride as the first of the sins that defied all his
means of mortification, or that he introduced one of his most
powerful statements of self-abasement with the warning that if the
Lord should disown him after all, "I shall be the direst example of a
deluded and exalted hypocrite, that ever was!" He knew that he
must abhor himself even in his "enlargements and attainments,"
and he warned himself to "walk softly and sorrowfully as long as I
breathe on earth." But of course the very love of language that these
lines express, reveals pride as one of the dearest lusts against which
the same meditation inveighs only a few lines later. In one of the few
beautiful passages of these meditations, Mather made a wistful resolution that is the more moving because he could never fulfill it:
"Shame is to be my garment, *grief* my meat, *tears* my drink, and
sighs my language, as long as I am related to this *vile body*!" Recog-
nizing "strength against sin" as a mercy so glorious that Providence
required him to wrestle and struggle before he could attain it, he
wrote down a vow in words more negative, with an emphasis upon
perpetual struggle rather than victory: "*Lord,* I here take my *vow,*
that I will never give Thee, or my own soul rest, until my dearest
lusts become, as bitter as death, as hateful as Hell unto me."

"Proud thoughts fly-blow my best performances." Pride in his
language, his learning, and his name never did become hateful to
him, but he strove to drive that pride in an unflagging parade of
talents expended in the Lord's work. In these early years, as he first
displayed his ability to the community through his tutoring and his
preaching, he also labored to strengthen his ingenuity by inventing

schemes to improve his spiritual behavior. He warned himself, of course, against any hope that he could "*buy off* guilt" with these devices; he intended to make his neglect of religious duties materially as well as spiritually costly. He developed at twenty the kind of scheme that Benjamin Franklin later made famous in "The Art of Virtue." He resolved that he would note every failure to carry out a religious exercise that he had prescribed for himself, and for each omission he resolved to forfeit some money — in addition to his regular tithe — for a gift to the poor. If he noticed that this scheme made his own self-improvement costly to the poor, he did not say so in writing. He simply reported that after two weeks his inclination to be distracted from his religious duties had been "most wonderfully cured." But as he applied the same principle to other matters, and at last to recording in his diary only those actions that he had explicitly dedicated to the glory of God — by saying, for example, "Oh Lord, this is that Thou mayst be glorified!" — he found that the numerical game had become tedious, and he decided that it was useless. Although he preserved a memorandum of his best achievement, twenty piously dedicated actions in a single day, he not only gave up keeping these records but burned the ones that he had written.

That allusion to burned records demonstrates explicitly what many pages of Mather's so-called diaries prove less emphatically: the two fat volumes first published in 1912 as *The Diary of Cotton Mather* are for these early years not a diary at all. Mather himself called these manuscripts his "Reserved Memorials," and the text, beginning in 1681, demonstrates on page after page that the narrative and reflections, though dated precisely, had been copied and revised retrospectively from originals which Mather destroyed. Selected and copied as a spiritual guide for his "little folks" — his sisters and brothers and perhaps some of the other pupils whom he tutored during these years — the Reserved Memorials usually focus on prayers, resolutions, meditations, or other pious expressions, many of them devised for the days of fasting that Mather kept at two- or three-week intervals to prepare himself for worship on the Lord's Day. These papers do not record his daily experience, secular or devotional. They abstract his periodic exercises of solitary devotion and record some of his extraordinary religious experiences.

Mather's dearest lusts in these years naturally included not only pride but sexual desire. Just as his ambitious pride had been harnessed to work usefully in the Lord's service, so his lust would one day find guiltless expression in the marriage bed. Early and late in his Reserved Memorials, apparently guiltless allusions to sexual desire within marriage are as unmistakable as the guilty confessions of adolescent "pollutions." Yet the anxiety that troubled him occasionally in the years before his marriage, found literary expression in two extraordinary passages in the Reserved Memorials, near the end of his twentieth year. In the first of these (November 1683) he takes a typically symbolic lesson from the story of "a very valuable [letter] *seal*" which had been brought from England to be presented to him as a gift, then had apparently been destroyed in a warehouse fire a few months later, but had been "found preserved from the fire" and given to him after all. Mather "prayed herewithal, that by no *fire* of *lust* here, nor the *fire* of *Hell* hereafter, I might miss of the *promises,* which the blood of the Lord Jesus Christ hath *sealed.*" Then, as Satan continued to buffet him with *"unclean temptations,"* Mather resolved to follow the biblical law whose metaphor he echoed, to "pluck out my *right eye,* and cut of[f] my *right hand*" in a battle of prayer and will, including a fortnightly day of fasting and prayer, against his "temptations, or corruptions." And just as he found himself regularly driven by such temptations to secret prayers with fasting, a scandal brought him a powerful message. A respected preacher, "a minister stricken in years, and eminent and remarked all the country over, for a strict profession of holiness," gave "a most infamous wound" to religion by falling into "lascivious violations of the *seventh Commandment.*" With the unerring anxiety that taught every conscientious Puritan youth to refer public events to his own condition, Mather remembered that he, a young and single man who was "strongly haunted by the *evil Spirit*" with similar temptations, might bring as much shame as the old adulterer had brought to religion.

Mather was also led to close self-examination by public transgressions far less specifically resembling any sins to which he himself had been tempted. On September 22, 1681, he witnessed the hanging of a rapist named William Cheny and the burning of two black servants who had burned up some houses and their occupants. Meditating on these gruesome penalties the day before they were carried out, Mather cited Governor William Bradford's custom of regarding any notorious crime as a reminder that his own heart contained inclinations which would make him "as vile as the vilest, if sovereign grace did not prevent it." And in the same private fast that Mather devoted to prayers concerning the minister's adultery and his own unspecified transgressions, he prayed for relief "of this poor country; which is in extreme danger of becoming a prey to *unreasonable men, that have no faith.*"

The danger, of course, was so evidently real that it is easy to see how a very young man could have associated his private struggle with the threats from the government of Charles II, which actually did revoke the precious charter of Massachusetts Bay within the next year. Along with that threat to the entire order on which the eminence of his family and the promise of his life were based, Mather had to endure more subtly painful reminders of the discrepancy between his reputation and his sinful thoughts. Less than three weeks before his twenty-first birthday, the young people in his congregation met to celebrate a day of thanksgiving not only "for the success of the Gospel here," but also for the health and good services of Increase and Cotton Mather. Although this splendid day gave Cotton Mather the confidence to preach a three-hour sermon, his "extraordinary occasion for *fasting* and *praying*" continued so relentlessly that he was provoked to extreme resolutions by the fear that he might disgrace religion. He increased his "macerating exercises" of prayer and fasting, and he resolved to continue crying out for divine help until he should be given so much grace that not even an ugly thought would "once dare to expect any lodging in my soul." His pious aspiration and his remorse over lustful fantasies, wet dreams, masturbation, or merely unexpected erections were so strong that he overdid what he called his mortifications. He broke the sixth Commandment, he said, by wasting his strength, injuring his health, and (he then thought) shortening his life with excessive fasts. "What!" he exclaims as he sees how much "the Devils" have provoked him to risk, "are my very duties now, but murders?"

For this startled awakening he had not only his own "splenetic maladies" to help him but the alarming condition of his brother Nathanael. The third of Cotton Mather's eight younger sisters and brothers, Nathanael (born 1669) was the first brother, and the only sibling precocious enough to emulate Cotton's unique distinction in both scholarship and piety. The prodigious evidence of Nathanael's achievement probably brought mixed feelings of gratification and rivalry to the older brother who had tutored him, and when Nathanael delivered an oration in Hebrew at his Harvard commencement in 1685 those feelings must have revived for the youngest graduate of the century, who had answered his own commencement questions in mere Latin. By that time, strong evidence had also indicated that Nathanael was unlikely to live much longer, and that the strain of emulating the family's piety and learning was helping to ruin his health. *Early Piety*, the memoir that Cotton published after Nathanael's death in 1688, justly celebrates Nathanael's meditations, his piety, and his learning, but it also declares that he killed himself with study. Signs of Nathanael's vulnerability had recurred ever since his first grave illness during Cotton's first year at Harvard in 1674, and although there seems to be no necessary connection between the smallpox that "gently" afflicted Nathanael in 1678 and the cancer that carried him off ten years later, he was obviously frail during his last two years in college, and his rigorously secluded observance of pious exercises combined with his relentless self-criticism and Cotton's own "splenetic" symptoms to warn Cotton against further excess. On one anxious occasion Cotton even admonished himself not to risk falling into "a consumption."

NATHANAEL'S ILLNESS reminds us that as Cotton Mather's spiritual life developed through the experience of his conversion to the point at which he decided that his macerating exercises had endangered his own physical life, events outside his mind and his study also had a major effect upon him. The eighteen years between 1675 and 1693 were probably the most discouraging in New England history before the last quarter of the nineteenth century. Throughout the first fourteen of those years, the energetic figure of Edward Randolph personified the threat to New England's old liberties as he shuttled between London and Boston, lobbied, threatened, commanded, and wrote letters reporting on the latest of the colonists' seemingly inexhaustible evasions, delays, counter-proposals, defiance. But even as that specter of political disaster moved alternately into the foreground and off to London or New York, other calamities—some of them personified, others all but nameless—afflicted New England. The war that had decimated the male population in 1675-76 was hardly over before the great fire destroyed fifty houses and the Second Church in Boston. In September 1678, only a few weeks after Cotton Mather's graduation from Harvard, Boston's worst small-pox epidemic of the century reached its deadliest height, killing as many as 30 people in one day, and 150 in less than a month.

New England had known from the first decade of colonization that this terrible disease, which by the end of the century accounted for about 10 percent of all annual deaths in London, was especially lethal to American Indians, and Anglo-Americans believed that they themselves were more vulnerable to it than Englishmen and Europeans were. Apparently because the American epidemics occurred much less frequently than those in London, large numbers of Bostonians (for example) had developed no immunity during previous outbreaks. When the disease struck one of the larger towns, therefore, as in Charlestown and Boston in 1677-78 after an absence of more than a decade, a large portion of the surviving population, especially the children, had virtually no protection against it. Bostonians dreaded these periodic epidemics because they had no effective treatment, nor any preventative except quarantine of ships carrying infected persons (a method that had apparently succeeded in 1675) and flight from the town once an epidemic had begun. Smallpox, moreover, was not only a nasty and painful infection, but it often disfigured those who recovered. In 1678 as many as 700 deaths were attributed to the epidemic, and the lowest estimate was about 200. In a town of 4000, then, between 5 and 17.5 percent of the entire population died, and probably one person in every four became infected. Adults as well as children suffered. Samuel Sewall was given up for dead, and once actually reported to be dead, but survived. The poet John Saffin's wife and two children died. Thomas Shepard insisted on visiting a sick parishioner who had asked for him, and Shepard caught the smallpox and died.

The emphasis upon quarantine and flight suggested at least the possibility of control, a possibility to which Cotton Mather was to make a major contribution four decades later, but there is no evidence beyond his brother's and sisters' illness (and his own apparent immunity after he himself had caught a mild case) that the experience of 1678 had any bearing on his later thought about infectious diseases. He observed and of course shared the widespread anxiety, the suffering of Nathanael and their sisters, the mild, virtually passive methods of treatment. These were announced with admirable clarity in a broadside by the Reverend Thomas Thacher, which might well have set an example for Cotton Mather's own later medical writings.

Thacher's *Brief Rule to Guide the common-people . . . in the Small pocks, or measels* was probably the first American medical publication outside Mexico. It was also the only advice in English that was available for an American layman to read during the terrifying epidemic of 1678. In a virtual paraphrase of the eminent English physician Thomas Sydenham's advice, which had been published in Latin twelve years earlier, Thacher told people one truth of inestimable value: how they might at least avoid making things worse. At a time when Bostonians could do little more than make rules against careless disposal of the clothing of the dead, Thacher told them calmly and precisely that the disease could be aggravated by too much care: "too much clothes, too hot a room, hot *cordials.*" Bloodletting and purges, he warned, might be equally dangerous. These were among several errors of treatment which might prove deadly "by overmuch hastening Nature beyond its own pace, or in hindering of it from its own vigorous operation."

In that prebacterial time, then, smallpox was considered a disease of the blood. Trying to "recover a new form and state" by "separation" in the first four days of "feverish boiling," the blood went through a second separation during the rest of the illness as pustules formed and eventually dried up. The emphasis on letting Nature keep its own pace was not only a theoretical step toward enlightened science, but good common sense. William Bradford had written a memorable passage about the dreadful suffering of an Indian village in Connecticut, where the smallpox victims lay on their grass mats and died "like rotten sheep," with a whole side of skin flaying off as they tried to turn from one miserable position to another. Thomas Thacher warned Bostonians that staying in bed, especially when the disease struck in summer, would nourish "the feverish heat" and inflame the pox. Sweating, he warned, was especially dangerous to infected children, presumably because they would further inflame the pustules by rubbing or scratching them.

When Nathanael Mather came down with smallpox, his father must have ordered that Thacher's advice be followed: keeping the patient reasonably cool, feeding him "small beer warmed with a toast," and thin water gruel and boiled apples. The parents watched anxiously to see how the pustules developed after the first four days. If the eruptions ripened quickly, if the fever was mild and began to abate on the fourth day, and if the pustules were "red, white, distinct, soft, few, round, sharp topped," then the prognosis would be good — especially if the child bled "largely" at the nose and breathed freely. But if the pustules rose slowly and sank in again, if the fever did not decline when the pustules broke out, if their color was black and bluish green, and if they were hard and "all in one" rather than distinctly separate, then the child was likely to die after suffering fainting spells, "*flux* of the *belly*," and bleeding from the gums and intestines. When the fever began to decline after the fourth day, Nathanael was presumably given a gentle cordial and warm (not hot) milk twice a day until the pustules broke. To prevent the "rotten vapors" from "strik[ing] inward" after the pustules became dry and crusty, he was probably given a temperate cordial twice a day, "four or five spoonfuls of Malago wine tinged with a little saffron." And when the pustules had dried or fallen off, he was probably given a purge.

Cotton Mather himself described the epidemic, in one of the earliest of his surviving letters. In Plymouth for an extended visit to his Uncle John Cotton's family in August, he had dreaded returning to pestilential Boston. And a few weeks after his return he told his uncle that the cemeteries were filling at an unprecedented rate. The bells tolled for burials before sunrise on the Sabbath, and on one Sabbath evening 7 people were buried after the regular services. More than 340 had already died. At first the Mather family seemed to be protected with especial mercy. "First, my brother Nathanael [was] gently smitten, and I more gently than he, and my sister Sarah yet more gently than I. But the order is broken on my sister Maria who, on the same month and day of the month that my father was visited with the same disease 21 years ago, was taken very ill; the symptoms grievous, and our fears great." Sometimes she was light-headed, "but her father prayed down mercy for her and her pox having turned a day or two ago, she is now" so poised between hope and dread that hope seemed likely to prevail. Of the seven Mather children, then, "4 have been visited. God fit and prepare for the three strokes that are yet behind."

Young Mather's letter shows that Thacher's concentration on natural remedies and on empirical observation did not lessen clerical interest in supernatural causes. Although the Mather family survived intact, the epidemic of 1678, killing so many so soon after the war and the fire, helped to persuade New England ministers and the General Court that nothing short of a special synod would suffice to palliate God's controversy with New England. All doubts of the need were resolved in August 1679, when fire again destroyed much of the central section of Boston on the night of August 7-8. The new fire, William Hubbard wrote, "hath half ruined the whole Colony, as well as the town" of Boston. The leading proponent of the "Reforming Synod" was Increase Mather, who wrote the two chief questions that the meeting was called to answer: "What are the evils that have provoked the Lord to bring His judgments on New England?" and "What is to be done that those evils may be reformed?" Only a few days after Cotton Mather and his cousin and classmate John Cotton joined the North Church, the Reforming Synod met in Boston to consider Increase Mather's questions, and Increase Mather was elected to the committee to write a report and revise the church platform.

Looming behind all the actual disasters in Massachusetts, the storm that threatened from London had discharged frightening bolts in 1678 and 1679. A combination of bold shrewdness, defiance masked as obtuseness, and creative transatlantic procrastination had deflected much of the anger thundering from the King's officials. But even while news of the Popish Plot in London brought new fears of persecution to New England Congregationalists during the worst of the smallpox epidemic in 1678, reports from their own agents in London and orders from the Crown showed them that concessions must be made at once and that the precious charter of Massachusetts remained in jeopardy.

As the contending parties perceived the issue, it was a conflict between irreconcilable principles, and each side saw in its antagonists some unprincipled men. While professing loyalty to the Crown, the Massachusetts authorities insisted on gestures that seemed to presume a separate integrity for the Bible commonwealth. To the King's officers Massachusetts seemed to be presumptuously claiming the status of an independent government. Massachusetts even coined money, passed laws concerning legal tender, and made special rules concerning suffrage. Massachusetts had executed four

Quakers, without adequate authority, and in apparent defiance of English laws requiring a limited form of religious toleration. The very term *commonwealth* argued separateness when applied to a mere colony. Massachusetts merchants illegally exported many products, from fish to tar and pitch. Sometimes the elected officials of Massachusetts expressed open defiance: Governor Leverett, rather than apologize during one of Randolph's first visits, kept his hat on and declared that the charter gave legislative power exclusively to the General Court. Sometimes they acted a little more subtly: when they finally did agree to order obedience to the King's navigation laws, they issued an order the same day reviving the law that required "all persons, as well inhabitants as strangers, that have not taken it, to take the oath of fidelity to the country." Randolph and others accurately interpreted this sort of gesture as a challenge to the King's loyal subjects, who (especially if they were Anglicans) might not wish to swear loyalty to Massachusetts even if they could ignore the implication that loyal subjects of the King wanted to subvert "the country." When the colonial authorities did promise obedience, they seemed to hedge by stipulating that they would obey all laws that did not violate the purposes for which their colony had been founded.

Randolph's prejudicial reports of his experiences in Massachusetts did not stress the conciliatory aspects of the colonists' behavior. When the Massachusetts agents charged him with prejudice, he replied that he was well enough liked by the *people* of Massachusetts, who wished to be ruled by the King, but that a small number of powerful leaders opposed the King's interests. On May 16, 1678, lawyers for the Crown recommended that a writ of *quo warranto* be brought against the Massachusetts charter and that new laws be written to replace those that were repugnant to the laws of England. Randolph, then, was appointed Collector of his Majesty's Customs in New England on May 31.

The news of these alarming decisions arrived in Boston during the summer of the smallpox. Governor Leverett immediately took the prescribed oath of allegiance to the King, and ordered that it be administered to all other officials and to the people. The General Court even amended the law of treason to make "printing, preaching, or malicious and advised speaking" against the King's life or his government a capital offense. On the main issues, however, the Bostonian leaders still hoped for delay. They interpreted the criticism of their government as an attack aimed at the basis of their Congregational society as well as their commercial liberty and prosperity, and they remembered that a movement for a writ of *quo warranto* in 1635 had been successfully delayed so that no action had been taken against the charter for forty years. By gradually giving up their claims to New Hampshire, and by purchasing Maine from those who had disputed Massachusetts' claim to it, they hoped to preserve their essential government, and of course their religious autonomy, their covenanted mission. They were newly alarmed when Randolph persuaded the King's advisers, in January 1679, to insist that Anglicans be allowed to hold public office in Massachusetts, that Anglican worship be permitted there, and that the Lord Bishop of London appoint a minister to be sent to Boston.

Meeting in Boston on the tenth of September and for about ten days thereafter, the Reforming Synod agreed to take no formal vote until the churches that had sent only clerical delegates could be advised that ordinary "brethren" would be welcome. More delegates from the various brethren did then appear, and the synod adopted a report, drafted by Increase Mather and published under the title *The Necessity of Reformation*. This document, along with many others of Cotton Mather's childhood and youth, affirmed the continuity between the first New England generation and the third. One of its chief rhetorical claims unanimously commits the brethren as well as the elders to revive the principles of the first Christian churches. The grandeur of God's achievement in bringing New England and her people "to such perfection and considerableness, in so short a time," is celebrated here as a recognition of the founders' loyalty to their errand: "They came not into a wilderness to see a man clothed in soft raiment." But although a few precious souls in every congregation had probably avoided "the sins of the times," too many had forgotten the errand on which the Lord had sent them into the wilderness, and "the present generation" in New England fell "far short" of the founders in the "practice and power of Godliness." Here, as in the indictments by abolitionists nearly two centuries later, New Englanders are measured against a high standard. Their iniquities annoy God more than those of other people, because New Englanders "sin against greater light, and means, and mercies than ever people (all circumstances considered) have done; and therefore the Lord is righteous in all the evil that hath befallen us."

Bringing the churches together for a reaffirmation of faith and for explicit testimony against the sins of the times might revive religion and return the people to first principles. If New England would only "remember whence she is fallen, and do the first works," there was "reason to hope that it shall be better with us than at our beginnings. But if this, after all other means in and by which the Lord hath been striving to reclaim us, shall be despised, or become ineffectual, we may dread what is like to follow." Another biblical parallel was obvious: When "the Jewish Church," like New England's churches, had a chance to reform in Josiah's time but "had no heart unto it, the Lord quickly removed them out of His sight."

The sins complained of in New England, moreover, were often those that had brought biblical prophets to threaten specific punishments, or those that had actually brought down on Israel the kind of retribution that had recently afflicted Massachusetts. In the "visible decay of the power of Godliness" among many church members, for example, New Englanders repeated the very sin that had provoked "the Lord's controversy with His people of old," as abundant citations from the Psalms and from Jeremiah were now given to prove. There was good reason to believe that the Indian warriors—"the wolves which God in His holy providence hath let loose upon us"— had been sent "to chastise His sheep" for their own bickering. And the sin of pride in ornamental dress—especially that of dressing above one's station, but also wealthy Christians' affectation of ornamental clothes in "these days of affliction and misery"—had long ago been singled out by Isaiah for the specific retribution of the "sword and sickness, and . . . loathsome diseases," such as smallpox. Sabbath-breaking had brought "fires and other judgments upon a professing people, Nehemiah 3.17, 18. Jeremiah 17.27." More gravely (for a twentieth-century reader), "inordinate affection to the world," preferring "farms and merchandising . . . before the things of God," had led not only to the settling of plantations without any ministry, but also to the oppression of American Indians, "whereby they have been scandalized and prejudiced against the name of Christ." The Bible demonstrated repeatedly that "the oppressing

sword cometh as a just punishment for that evil. Ezek. 7.11 and
22.15. Prov. 28.8 Isai. 5.7.''

⚜

IN COTTON MATHER's first month as a formally committed Christian, then, his father led an extraordinary session of all the churches in the colony to muster the energy of the entire commonwealth for a revival of the kind of religious faith that issued in public action. Increase Mather's preamble told the General Court that in both Scripture and history a people had rarely succeeded in reforming without help from the civil authorities. The synod's appeal to "every one (both leaders and people) in their proper place and order," to rise "up and be doing" was not lost on a precocious sixteen-year-old whose pious energy needed more expression than in the meditations that he held in secret. The colony languished in crisis, politically and physically as well as religiously. If every person would up and be doing, his father had said, the Lord would "be with us, as He was with our fathers." The jeremiad did go on to focus on the sins of the land, but its great psychological power for Cotton Mather and many others was in its appeal to action, revival, community.

His own contribution to the revival was to found a private religious society, to draw up rules for its government, and, at the first meeting, to preach a sermon on the usefulness of such societies. He hoped that they would be especially attractive to young men, so attractive that young men would form separate societies of their own. In "this projecting age," as Jonathan Swift later called it, Cotton Mather projected one of the first American voluntary societies for mutual aid. He declared explicitly in his founding statement that he expected these little hives of religious and benevolent activity both to "swarm" into new ones as they prospered and to set an example for other groups to emulate. Christians who joined together in private societies would act (in a different image) "like so many *coals of the altar*" to keep one another alive.

It would be hard to overemphasize the significance of this first public work by Cotton Mather. Even if it had not been published for the first time in 1724, the year that young Benjamin Franklin paid a formal call on the eminent author of *Bonifacius*, it would bear clear evidence that the strong link between these two proponents of benevolent ingenuity had been forged at the very beginning of Mather's career, when he was scarcely older than the precocious Franklin who in 1721 wrote the letters of Mrs. Silence Dogood for his brother's newspaper and soon afterward ran off to Philadelphia. The Mather of 1679, thirteen years before the Salem witchcraft trials, must be understood as an impassioned agent of pietism who was already committed to devote his most resourceful ingenuity to organizing ways to do good. He proposes small groups of families, usually no more than twelve, to bind themselves up "in the bundle of Love . . . to be serviceable to one another." Of course they are to pray together, and lovingly to give and take mutual admonitions, activities which will improve their hearts and their conduct. "But also their *abilities* will be thereby sharpened and quickened; they will be rendered more *able*, to serve many valuable interests." They will find "unexpected opportunities to *do good*," especially if the men in the group resolve to spend half an hour together considering the question "What good is there to be done?" with a list of more specific questions laid out by Mather. Here we can see more than a hint of Franklin's celebrated Junto and his Art of Virtue; and in Mather's demand that the young men admit no "taint of *backbiting* or *vanity*" to their discourse, that they confine themselves wholly to "matters of religion, and those also, not the *disputable* and *controversial* matters, but the points of *practical piety*"—here, too, although the context is not Franklinian, Mather foreshadows a major principle of Franklin's cherished Society of the Free and Easy.

More important than anticipations of Franklin here is the inseparable mixture of piety and benevolence. The actual sermon that Mather preached at the society's first meeting in 1679 displays the mixture as Mather tried to sustain it throughout his life. Unusually brief among the shelves full of Mather's volubility, this first sermon also seems more coherent, more carefully controlled than his characteristic later work. As a novice who had reason to fear an attack of stammering, Mather clung to the prescribed form of traditional Puritan sermons, carefully stated questions and propositions, etymological and rational "opening" of his biblical text, and an application of these matters to the particular condition of his auditors. His text was a subordinate clause taken from Luke 19:42: "If thou hadst known, even thou, at least in this thy day, the things which belong unto thy Peace." He asks, methodically, what are the things that belong to our peace, what it is for us to know these things, and "when it may be said, that a day for that purpose is vouchsafed unto us." Declaring that "whatever tends to promote our present and future *welfare*" belongs to our peace, Mather argues that faith, repentance, and holiness are the three qualities most necessary, with holiness of course opening out into benevolent as well as pious action. He concludes that our own righteousness will never save us, but he insists that "the peace of a believer, arises not only from his justification, but from his sanctification also." For the Christian who lives in all godliness and honesty, he declares, "there is a sweetness in the *work* itself; such, that the servants of CHRIST have thought their *work* to be their *wages*." Mather's own work, with a little praise and the yearning hope of more, was his own best wages throughout his career.

Because "ignorance is indeed the *mother of destruction*," the central question here, as in many sermons by Thomas Hooker, Thomas Shepard, and other founders, was the meaning of *knowledge*. It is all too easy to have a superficial knowledge of faith, repentance, and holiness, but the only true knowledge of them, Mather insists, is not only qualitative but "experimental." One must know holy qualities from personal experience, as "the things that are to be prized, valued, esteemed." One must, as Jonathan Edwards would echo in the next century, see "an *excellency* in them. To *know*," Mather said, "is to know the *worth* of them."

The "day" that we are vouchsafed for such knowledge is as long as our lives, Mather says, but of course we cannot have the right kind of knowledge until the Holy Spirit works upon the soul. "The other circumstances give *time* to us; *this* does invest us with *opportunity*." It is in the emphasis on timeliness that Mather makes his application bring together pious duty and public benevolence. Citing Jeremiah (25:5: "Turn ye now everyone from his evil way"), he warns his fellow members of the new society that today is the only day they are sure of. "Lose this NOW, and you shall never have another." They must live in this day as if "today were that which eternity depended on." They must make religion "thy business." And in this day of the new society's founding they must seize their "uncommon *advantages* for the *getting* and the *doing* of *good*" in a strenuous effort to "build up ourselves and one another in the *most holy Faith*" so that at the end "we may be found *so doing*, and hear it said, *Well done, good and faithful servant, enter into the joy of the LORD.*"

In delivering this hortatory message, Mather used a heavy balancing weight of diabolical and military imagery. Sinners, for example, are desperadoes who war against the Lord, and the Lord is so angry with unbelievers that unless Christ's grace intervenes the Father will laugh at the impenitent in the eleventh hour, leaving them "in the dimness of the anguish of death, and the griping talons of a dreadful eternity." But the prevailing tone is unmistakably hopeful and encouraging, inspiriting with a call to communal action.

Among the sins of neglect deplored by the Reforming Synod, abandonment of the traditionally dual ministry—the offices of Teacher and Pastor—was charged against many congregations, which had been willing to support only one preacher. Cotton Mather's first sermon encourages us to see the significance of his eventual service as Pastor in the congregation that his father served as Teacher. As we imagine the sixteen-year-old daring to allude (as he did) to his own stammer near the end of the Application—applying the truths of his sermon to each auditor's heart by spinning them out of the bowels of his own experience—we can see how this prodigy, whom our own century has usually chosen to characterize as a prig, became the cherished favorite of his congregation and, at twenty-six, a popular leader in the revolution of 1689.

❧

DESPITE INCREASE Mather's "very potent sermon," preached when the synod's results were given formally to the General Court on October 15, divine judgments and mysterious signs seemed to continue. In the Mather household itself the patriarch, now nearing the peak of his influence in the community, fell ill early in 1680 with what seemed to be consumption. Old John Eliot came over to the Second Church to lead prayers for the Teacher's recovery, and to preach a sermon on John 11:3: "Lord, behold, he whom thou lovest is sick." Increase Mather did recover, but the consequences of Old Governor Leverett's death in 1679 were now to be painfully felt. Leverett had fought in Cromwell's army during the Civil War, and had served for nearly a decade in the colonial administration of the Protectorate. He had helped to conceal the precious Massachusetts charter from the King's commissioners in 1664-65 and had defied Randolph by appeals to that charter in the 1670s. His even more venerable successor, Simon Bradstreet, was much more conciliatory. Bradstreet's election, along with an expansion of the Court of Assistants (a change ordered by the King and resisted as long as possible by the Massachusetts General Court), gave new strength to those New Englanders who wanted to submit. Although they did not prevail in the debates of 1680 about how the General Court should reply to the King's latest commands, they did have more influence than they had been able to wield during Leverett's administration. Edward Randolph shrewdly identified the leader of this party, Joseph Dudley, later a despised enemy of the Mathers, not only as "a great opposer" of the religious group, but also as a man who, "if he finds things resolutely managed, will cringe and bow to anything. He hath his fortune to make in the world; and if his Majesty, upon alteration of the government, make him captain of the castle in Boston and the forts in the colony, his Majesty will gain a popular man and oblige the better party." In the same letter, moreover, Randolph recommended the arrest of six men who had led "the faction," Randolph's term for "the better party's" opponents, the defenders of the charter and its privileges. That list included Deputy Governor Thomas Danforth, Daniel Gookin, and Elisha Cooke. The same letter attacked Captain John Richards, a member of the Mathers' congregation who would soon be chosen as one of the colony's agents to be sent to London. Randolph called Richards "a man of mean extraction" who had come to New England as "a poor servant, as most of the faction were at their first planting here, but by their extraordinary feats and cozenage have got them great estates in land."

But it was resistance rather than conciliation that brought on new troubles. In the very letter that made some concessions to the King on Maine and civil rights for Anglicans and other Protestants, the General Court not only temporized but defended both the prerogatives given by the charter and the propriety of refusing to allow Quakers to propagate "a multitude of notorious errors and blasphemies." This letter even dared to say that the colony could not afford to send the two new agents whom the King had ordered sent to him at once.

Irritating as it was, the General Court's response only gave a tepid formal expression to the steaming resentment that inevitably found more shrill ways to escape. As John Gorham Palfrey shrewdly perceived a hundred years ago, the recorded complaints of Edward Randolph bring out the irreconcilable issues and attitudes on both sides. Whether or not Randolph was correct in accusing "the Church party" of trying to "debauch the merchants and loyal men," he had striking evidence that those groups united in ways that he and the King were sure to find outrageous. The merchants, he charged, had promised to advance the money for the now forbidden purchase of Maine. And when Randolph proceeded to do his duty as Collector of the Customs, the merchants and the people — ship-owners, courts, juries, and rabble — simply defied him, obstructed him, threatened him. The magistrates refused to assign him an attorney to help him in cases he might have to bring before the local courts. Once when he temporarily left a suspected warehouse in order to find a marshal who could help him in his search, several men beat up the servants he had placed in charge at the warehouse, and anonymous confederates "removed the goods to another place." Again when Randolph and a marshal and six men tried to board a ship in the harbor, "I was threatened to be knocked in the head," Randolph reported, and by the time he had persuaded the Governor to muster enough men to use force against the offenders, "Boston boats" had towed the ship away.

Randolph's own written recommendations demonstrate that the colonists who defied him, and especially the Puritans who suspected his intentions, did not exaggerate his threat to the privileges they had known for half a century. On April 8, 1680, he urged the King to obtain a writ of *quo warranto,* and he made the most extreme summary of all his statements against the colony. "The Bostoneers," he declared, "have no right either to land or government in any part of New England, but are usurpers, the inhabitants yielding obedience unto a supposition only of a royal grant" from Charles I. They had illegally formed "a commonwealth" and, unlike other colonists, had neglected to take the oath of allegiance. They had protected "the murderers of your royal father, in contempt of your Majesty's proclamation of the 6th June, 1660, and your letter of 28th June, 1662." They had coined money, executed British subjects "for religion," violently resisted the royal commissioners in 1665, expelled the King's justices of the peace from Maine in 1666, imposed an oath of fidelity on all inhabitants, and violated "all the Acts of

Trade and Navigation, by which they have engrossed the greatest part of the West-India trade, whereby your Majesty is damnified in the customs £100,000 yearly, and the kingdom much more."

The King, who was about to extend his power to virtually absolute rule by dissolving Parliament, now wrote more peremptorily than ever to the troublesome colony, and while agents were at last elected in Boston and other delays invented there, the English Committee of Trades and Plantations decided that "New England could not be brought to a perfect settlement unless a general governor were sent over, and maintained there at the King's charge."

Against this kind of threat, Massachusetts finally revised some more of the offensive laws. The General Court repealed the law forbidding the celebration of Christmas, along with the law making the return of banished Quakers a capital offense. When Randolph returned to Boston in the autumn of 1681, however, he was armed with new official powers, another indignant letter from the King, and new ways of offending the Puritan colonists whose rule he hoped to terminate. Samuel Sewall reported with disgust that when the Randolphs attended the South Church Mrs. Randolph curtsied every time the Reverend Mr. Willard mentioned the name of Jesus, "even in prayer time." And the Randolphs took up residence in Hezekiah Usher's house, where the Congregational ministers had been in the habit of meeting.

Cotton Mather's contemporaneous reports of these matters consistently bring together affairs in Europe, England, and America. Upon learning that the City of London had been "forced to part with their liberties so far, as to admit sheriffs not of their own, but of the courts' choosing," he exclaimed, "what shall we poor shrubs expect when the stately cedars crack!" And a few weeks later he brought the continent into a similar letter:

> This of public notice: France's persecution; Holland's inundation; England's every way perplexed condition; . . . and the universal combustions of Europe. . . . the persecuted people of God have no place on earth to betake themselves unto. Heaven help them! And now my pen is running, let me add, that as the Lord's people in England are very apprehensive, so we in New England are not altogether unapprehensive.

Besides a drought in the summer of 1681 these troublesome years also brought on New England what seemed an extraordinary num-

5. Portrait of Samuel Sewall in his old age,
by John Smibert.

ber of sudden deaths, which both Samuel Sewall and Cotton Mather recorded. In the unusually cold winter of 1680-81 an Irish woman was found dead on the ground with her forehead in her hands. "Great rumors and fears of trouble with the Indians," Sewall wrote. "Persons to carry a competent number of arms to meeting." Three other Bostonians died suddenly in April, and on the first and second of May two more surprising deaths occurred, one in Cambridge and one in Ipswich. The Cambridge man, on his way home from church, looked in "and smiled on his wife through the window, but sunk down before he got in at the door." On the twenty-fifth of July, "Sabbath-day night," President Oakes of Harvard suddenly died, just a few days before commencement. On December 13, Mrs. Jonathan Jackson hanged herself in her own house. Early in the morning of Wednesday, February 15, 1682, Major Thomas Savage died "very suddenly, having been well at the wedding on Tuesday, and supped well at home afterward, and slept well till midnight or past."

It was in this anxious context that on August 17, 1682, and again the following week Halley's comet—which Increase Mather called "Heaven's Alarm to the World"—startled the entire community, and less than three months later a cluster of sudden deaths within three or four days increased the excitement. The most astonishing of these was the first, on November 9. It remains astonishing not only because it occurred during festivities in a way that twentieth-century medicine still prefers to call a cerebral accident, but also because of the symbolism that Sewall records so faithfully in his brief note. If Nathaniel Hawthorne did not use this incident as the basis for the catastrophic opening of *The House of the Seven Gables,* the coincidence must seem nonetheless eerie to a modern reader of American literature. At the wedding of Daniel Quincy to Mrs. Anne Shepard, Sewall reports, with so many guests present that the bride's uncle Captain Thomas Brattle's great hall was almost full, a young minister had said the concluding prayer after John Hull (a magistrate) had performed the civil ceremony required by Puritan tradition. Sewall and other guests had "eaten cake and drunk wine and beer plentifully," before they were called back into the hall to sing. During the singing Mrs. Brattle suddenly had to leave, and most of the guests quickly departed, "thinking it a qualm or some fit; but she grows worse," Sewall wrote, "speaks not a word, and so dies away in her chair, I holding her feet (for she had slipt down). At length out of the kitchen we carry the chair and her in it, into the wedding hall; and after awhile lay the corpse of the dead aunt in the bride-bed: so that now the strangeness and horror of the thing filled the (just now) joyous house with ejulation:* The bridegroom and bride lie at Mr. Air's, son-in-law to the deceased, going away like persons put to flight in battle."

Two days later a man who was "letting a barrel of cider into a trap-door cellar" was killed outright when "the board he stood on gave way, he fell in, and the end of the barrel" landed on his jaw. Now Sewall remembered two other strange deaths in recent weeks, one in Concord and one in Salem, and commented: "Oh, what strange work is the Lord about to bring to pass." The very next day, Sunday, the mate on Captain Benjamin Gillam's ship drowned, and although the ordination of Nathaniel Gookin on the following Wednesday as successor to Urian Oakes, late Pastor of the Cambridge church, gave Sewall new confidence that "the presence of God seemed to be with his people," another man drowned on Friday the seventeenth. Within forty-eight hours Mr. Edward Winslow, a shipmaster, died on the Sabbath, and an anonymous woman "died suddenly at the North End of the town." On the twenty-eighth, a ship coming from Nevis, having safely made land and stood in, was driven over rocks and shoals by a storm during the night, and stranded on Nahant Beach. Of the thirteen people on board, three drowned and four died of exposure. A few weeks later a day of fasting and prayer was observed at Increase Mather's house.

⚜

THE OCCASION for Cotton Mather's first published allusion to these events was the death of Urian Oakes, only a few days before Oakes was expected to preside, in his witty Latin, at Cotton Mather's second Harvard commencement. Sir Mather, as this candidate for the master's degree would have been called, had prepared to argue the affirmative side of the question, whether the vowel points in Hebrew are of divine origin. Years later, after he had learned to read Hebrew himself without the vowel points, he conceded that they had probably been invented by man for convenience. Meanwhile, in the weeks just after Oakes's death, he found time to com-

---

*An obsolete term for wailing, lamentation.

pose a 430-line poem lamenting that sudden stroke and celebrating Oakes's character. For some reason the printer delayed publication until 1682. By then much of the immediacy that might excuse the passionate clumsiness of an eighteen-year-old's verse had evaporated, as Mather nervously reminded the reader in a few prefatory couplets. This first publication deserves attention both for its substance and for some of its technique, which anticipate characteristic qualities in Mather's later work.

"Grief never made good poet," Mather says, quoting Ovid, and no reader of his tribute to Oakes will disagree. Despite its frequent clumsiness, however, this poem demonstrates Mather's control of the language, his epigrammatic skill, his witty (though of course sometimes tasteless) attachment to wordplay, and his interest in entertaining his audience by wide-ranging allusions. Sometimes his heavy-handed, repeated strokes driving home the significance of Oakes's surname ring as unpleasantly in the reader's skull as if a strong axman were felling a real oak too near by. But when Mather comes to make an anagram of Oakes's name, he triumphs in that favorite game of New England elegiac verse. John Wilson had made of the late John Cotton's name (IOHN KOTTON in an alternate form that was permitted in the seventeenth century's orthography) O HONI KNOTT; Thomas Dudley's death had impelled the anagrammist to exclaim: AH, OLD MUST DYE! Cotton Mather would later call his own biography of Thomas Hooker *Piscator Evangelicus* and would point out that the anagram of John Eliot's name was *Toile*. Here Mather writes:

> Oh! the *Name*
> Of Urian Oakes, New England! does proclame
> SURE I AN OAK was to thee! Feel thy Loss!
> Cry, (*Why forsaken, Lord!*) Under the Cross!

At eighteen, we see in this poem, Mather already knew enough Puritan history to say that many leaders in Old and New England had died (as Oakes did) before reaching fifty, and he had already developed one of the central patterns that would dominate the best biographies of his major work, *Magnalia Christi Americana,* the church history of New England: He mixed the names and deeds of New England leaders, especially those of the founding generation, with those not only of their biblical types but also of classical and Christian history and literature. Here as in the biographies of his

*Magnalia,* Virgil, Homer, Horace, Martial, Socrates, Paul, Moses, Joshua, Solomon, Obadiah, Jeremiah, Chrysostom, Ambrose, Preston, Perkins, and Fuller belong (with about sixty others) to the same world of allusion as the New England founders Wilson, Cotton, Hooker, Norton, Wilson, and Wigglesworth.

Here, too, in the prescribed classical allusions and the thumping rhymed pentameters of the conventional elegy, Mather sounded a major theme of his best mature work: the variety or uniqueness in individual New England lives within the essential uniformity of saintly experience. Oakes does come through here as a unique character — sheltering the college when its "dwindling branches" seem to indicate mortal illness. Mather portrays Oakes's remarkably genial nature, his humility (linked explicitly to his small physical stature):

> A *great Soul* in a *little Body.* (Add!
> In a small *Nutshell* Graces *Iliad.*)
> How many *Angels* on a Needle's point
> Can stand, is thought, perhaps, a *needless Point:*
> Oakes Vertues too I'me at a loss to tell;
> In short, hee was *New-England's SAMUEL;*
> Ah! *graciose Oakes,* wee saw thee *stoop;* wee saw
> In thee the *Moral* of good *Nature's Law,*
> That the *full Ears* of Corn should *bend,* and grow
> Down to the ground: *Worth would sit always low.*

Into this mixture of the classical and biblical with the local, the allegorical with the uniquely historical, Mather also brings specific incidents from the history of New England in his own time. As I have put the comet and the contemporaneous disasters into my biographical narrative, he put them into his elegy:

> The *Earth* was parch't with horrid *heat:* We fear'd
> The *blasts* of a Vast *Comet's flaming Beard.*
> The dreadful *Fire* of Heaven inflames the *blood*
> Of our *Elijah,* carrying him to God.
> Innumerable *Sudden Deaths* abound!
> Our *OAKES* a *Sudden blow* laid on the ground . . .

It is that context, with Mather's awareness of his own place in the third generation, that gives his concluding prayer more than merely conventional meaning. He has already mentioned his hope that

New England might yet become the New Jerusalem. Here he pleads for the college and for worthy successors to the founding generation of ministers:

> Lett not the *Colledge* droop, and dy! O Lett
> The Fountain run! A *Doctor* give to it!
> *Moses's* are to th' *upper Canaan* gone!
> Lett *Joshua's* Succeed them! goes when one
> *Elijah,* raise *Elishas*! *Pauls* become
> *Dissolv'd*! with Christ! Send *Tim'thees* in their room!
> Avert the Omen, that when Teeth apace
> Fall out, No new ones should supply their place!
> Lord! Lett us *Peace* on this our *Israel* see!
> And still both *Hephsibah* and *Beulah* bee!
> Then will thy People *Grace*! and *Glory*! Sing,
> And every Wood with *Hallelujah's* ring.

To keep Harvard College from drooping and dying, the authorities called once again on Increase Mather, whom Oakes had told seven years earlier that he could have the presidency if only he would consent to move to Cambridge. Now again, as in the next decade, residence was the issue. Although a minister who really wanted to accept such an appointment could probably have done so, the very strong bonds of a church covenant obliged one to negotiate a release from one's congregation before accepting another call. Increase Mather accurately predicted, and thereby perhaps shrewdly arranged, that his congregation would not approve his election. He did note in his diary some fear that a vote of acquiescence by his church would consign him to be "voted out of the town" of Boston, but only after he had told Harvard that he could not accept unless his congregation approved.

The congregation emphatically did not approve. In an extraordinary letter to the Harvard Corporation, the church declared that Mather could not be more serviceable to Christ in Cambridge than in Boston, "the Jerusalem of this land," and they refused to "see the ruin of the College wrapped up in our unwillingness that he should remove to Cambridge." The North Church and the North End of Boston, however, would be "a ruined place" if Increase Mather should desert them. The church professed a desire to encourage scholars, singling out Cotton Mather for especial praise:

6. The Paul Revere house in North Square. Built in 1677, probably on the site of the Increase Mather house that was ruined in the great fire of 1676. Painting by Darius Cobb, 1881.

our affections have been, and still are, toward one of them, namely, our reverend Teacher's son, hoping that he may be settled among us with his father; but for the church to give up their interest in their Teacher, is a likely way to be deprived of them both . . . so that though we could be glad to help a sister that has no breasts, yet we see not what rule of charity or reason, requireth us to cut off our own breasts, that our sister may be supplied.

Increase Mather saw Boston not only as his home but as the Jerusalem of the land, the center of action and power, wherein he strongly preferred to abide. His son preferred to live there, too, and that preference brought home one of the few recorded conflicts between the extraordinary father and son who were destined to spend the next forty-three years in close political and pastoral association. Only a very brief passage survives to record Cotton Mather's feelings, and little remains to indicate Increase Mather's motive, but in the context of the father's earlier desertion and collapse after Richard Mather's death (1669-1671), and with our knowledge of a plaintive outburst from Cotton Mather in 1690, we may justly infer that Cotton dreaded being separated from his father.

Here again the community, the church, the family, and the sense of the youth's own identity as well as his professional future come together in a way that allows observers to see how Cotton Mather came to perceive his personal life as an integral part of a vast, complex order. Ever since John Mayo had grown too ill to serve as Pastor, the Second Church had relied solely on Increase Mather for spiritual leadership, even while paying him too little (as he often complained) to keep his family alive without falling into debt. After Cotton had begun to serve the community by founding the religious society in 1679, he had won great applause for his public sermons in the "pulpit of my old Grandfather *Cotton,* in the Old Church of *Boston,*" and he had assisted his father in their own church, which still needed a Pastor. The Reforming Synod, moreover, had admonished every congregation to restore the old practice of supporting two clergymen, a Teacher and a Pastor. Cotton Mather had every reason to hope that he might stay close to his father, his church, and his native community for the rest of his life. He was even chosen to write the Thanksgiving proclamation for the whole colony in October 1681.

But in November and again more insistently the next February, the New Haven church called Cotton Mather to its pulpit. Any New England candidate who had just received his master's degree would have recognized the great honor in being invited to so important a church, and the compliment to an eighteen-year-old was even more gratifying. Well aware of these realities, young Mather evidently drew pleasure from them without feeling the slightest inclination to abandon his secure home in "my father's family," his proximity to his father's library, or the excellent prospects for his vocational life in the metropolis. He must also have felt some hesitation to accept a much greater responsibility among strangers than he was likely to have in his father's church, to which he had been helping to recruit new members and all of whose old members had known him throughout childhood.

He was shocked, therefore, when his father advised him to go to New Haven. Many years later, Increase Mather said that he had been "very backward" about Cotton's proposed election as Pastor of the North Church in Boston, "because of my relation to him," but that he had acquiesced when "the church could not agree on calling any other" candidate. Whether or not Increase saw the New Haven opportunity as a call to more independent service, which would develop the son's talents more freely than life in the father's shadow, Cotton naturally felt the advice as an excruciating rejection. Now that he had to consider actually moving to Connecticut, he thought of the new congregation (in comparison to his own, the largest in America) as "small and mean." Toward the end of December, a month after the first invitation from New Haven, he rejoiced at his own congregation's vote to continue his appointment as assistant to his father, and he noted both their explicit statement that they intended to make him their Pastor, and their award of the handsome salary of £70 per year. Despite that reassuring vote of confidence, it is in these months that the Reserved Memorials record a threatened return of the stammer, which might "render me unserviceable." And when he declined the second New Haven invitation on February 6, just a few days before his nineteenth birthday, he gave a reason that still apparently distinguished between his father's wishes and those of the church members. One might almost infer that he had thought of going over his father's head in an appeal to the congregation: "My reason" for declining, he told the New Haven church, was that "the church of *North Boston* would have entertained uncomfortable dissatisfactions at my Father, if after so many importunate *votes* of theirs, for my settlement here, he had any way permitted my removal from them."

There can be little question about the support of the church. Beginning with its meeting on September 27, 1680, the congregation had unanimously approved Cotton Mather's appointment first as an assistant, preaching at least once every two weeks; then, after several months' experience of his talents, as an assistant who would preach every week; and now, a year later, as the preacher with whose gifts they declare themselves to be so well satisfied that they intend to make him their Pastor. It was in this time, too, that the membership was growing, from 144 in 1678 to 206 in 1682. Surely the colony's troubles, and the campaign for a revival after the Reforming Synod, contributed to this increase, and so, too, of course, did Increase Mather. But since 1681 was the best year of all, with 35 new members, one can at least surmise that Cotton Mather did not drive many prospective members away. By his own account in the next few years, his pastoral efforts were rewarded with dozens of new memberships. Even in the years of his apprenticeship he estimated that 30 new members had joined under his ministry, and an actual membership of 200 probably meant a regular attendance of three to four times that number.

When Cotton Mather told his son about the New Haven offer many years later, he hinted that he might have been mistaken in believing that Increase Mather had advised him to accept. But there can be no mistaking the anxiety that he felt while under that misapprehension, even if his father had merely intended to point out the advantages of accepting. Cotton had been supported by his father at virtually every rite of nurture and passage in his young life — from introduction to the library at home, entry into Harvard College, and blundering intercession in his first difficulties there, to counsel about religious conversion and supervision of his early preaching. His father had presided over his entry into the church, administering the covenant and declaring for the congregation that "we . . . in this place, do receive you in our fellowship, and promise to walk towards you, and to watch over you as a member of this church." His father had even presided at the 1681 commencement, and Cotton had duly noted: "My father was President, so that from his hand I received my degree. Tis when I am got almost half a year, beyond *eighteen,* in my age." He had more than usual reason to add that "all the circumstances of my commencement were ordered by a very sensibly kind providence of God."

The issue was effectively settled by the church's declaration on December 28, 1681, that it intended to call Cotton Mather as Pastor "in due time," presumably after he seemed old enough to accept that formal responsibility. And a year later, on January 8, 1683, the congregation — once again by unanimous vote — formally elected Cotton to the pastorate and asked "the Teacher and himself" to set a day for ordination. But the ordination was delayed by the crisis over the colony's charter until May 13, 1685, more than four years after Cotton had begun to assist his father. That delay offers one more instance of the ways in which Cotton Mather's personal and religious life was repeatedly bound up in the political history of Massachusetts.

❦

IN THE YEARS between 1679 and the final charter crisis of 1684, both Increase and Cotton Mather became more active in the kind of intellectual activity that would later win Cotton Mather election to the Royal Society. Both father and son were already Copernicans, and both insisted that there was no conflict between science and religion. When Cotton wrote some years later about his father's accession to the presidency of Harvard in 1684, he insisted that the college, though it had preferred Ramean to Aristotelian discipline, had not been confined to it. Nor had Harvard students been deprived, he said, "of *Libera Philosophia,* which the *good spirits* of the age have embraced, ever since the great Lord *Bacon* showed 'em the way to *The Advancement of Learning.*" A reading of the Harvard thesis topics, he claimed, would support his interpretation. In 1681, moreover, Increase Mather called on all the ministers and other leaders of New England to send him records of "Illustrious Providences" about which they had any knowledge. The intention here, as the book he published three years later clearly shows, was scientific as well as religious. And in his own treatment of Halley's comet he demonstrated how gracefully, if unconvincingly, a Congregational minister's belief in Providence could absorb new scientific evidence. He had treated comets flatly as Heaven's alarm to the world, in a sermon of that title, preached in 1680. By the time that Halley's comet became visible in New England in the summer of 1682, a good deal of scientific investigation in England and Europe had persuaded advanced thinkers that comets follow predictable laws of nature rather than the arbitrary admonition of Providence. Increase Mather continued to maintain that comets had often appeared just before catastrophic judgments, and he saw a special warning to New England in the fiery August skies of 1682, but in his *Kometographia,* published in 1683, he accepted recent discoveries concerning the regularity of comets' movements, and although he continued to doubt if men could actually predict the exact time of a comet's appearance, he admitted that "some very learned men have supposed the knowledge is obtainable," and that they might be right. He no longer claimed that Providence lights up comets for special occasions, but he saw no reason to deny that comets have actual effects on earth and that Providence can speak to men through events that occur according to natural law.

Both Increase and Cotton Mather participated in the founding of a Philosophical Society in Boston in 1683, and at the same time Cotton inaugurated a Young Men's Association of the kind he had proposed in 1679. No papers read at these meetings exist to demonstrate the level of intellectual interest. Beyond noting that the Philosophical Society met every two weeks, that it lasted for about four years, and that it sent some papers to a professor at the University of Leiden, we can only infer from the essay on comets, from Cotton Mather's praise of Bacon, and from some of his later letters that the Society's interest was serious. Several of the letters that won Cotton Mather membership in the Royal Society thirty years later were based on these early papers of the Philosophical Society — reports of medical phenomena, astronomical peculiarities, and illustrious providences.

By 1712 Cotton Mather was able to smile at people who had read the strange celestial phenomena portentously. In 1685 he and his father had drawn diagrams of their observations showing the sun surrounded by "four mock suns, through which there passed a whole circle; in the midst whereof were two rainbows," and Professor Wolferdus Senguerdius of Leiden had reported those observations in the second edition (1685) of his *Philosophia Naturalis.* Mather told the Royal Society in 1712 that "our people of a more prognosticating and superstitious temper" had tried to make "these appearances . . .

be ominous, of something or other, if they could have told, what! (A learned writer, whom we consulted, said, changes in the Government.) And you may be sure, something did happen after them! However, all the omen that wiser men could find in them, was that of a storm now abreeding, which, I think, always happened." If Mather had applied this critique of fallacious reasoning to all such prognostications in the 1680s and 1690s, his historical reputation would stand much higher than it does. At least his own tendency to make similar prognostications in those early years did not prevent either him or his father from seeing the importance of sending their exact observations to men of science in Europe.

It was in 1682, moreover, that Cotton Mather took his turn as the editor of the annual almanac. Besides advertising his father's history of comets, which was then in press, Cotton's almanac offered a variety of scientific and practical information, carefully blended with religious instruction both scholarly and hortatory. The title page carries a predictable text, "Redeeming the Time," and a concluding address to the reader consists of a miniature sermon on the same subject, in which Mather declares that he would hardly have taken the trouble to prepare the daily and monthly tables if (speaking in the third person) "he had not therein foreseen an opportunity to approve himself a friend to thine everlasting welfare." In frankly seeking to make his almanac do holy service, he remarks that these little books come into almost as many hands as the Bible, and he sees no reason why "every eye" should not be "entertained with what is intelligible, and may be profitable." He includes in the profitable entertainment not only his exhortation to be prepared for sudden death (for twenty of these, he says, have occurred in the last two months) but also a brief disquisition on the chronology of the Bible. "Reader," he says in the blunt voice that will resound through many of his later works, "as one of thy main works in the world is to search like a miner in thy Bible," you may as well consider what "the guesses of the learned" suggest about when the various books of the Bible were written, and when the main figures lived.

For all his emphasis on piety, then, Mather had entered the modern as well as the medieval world before 1683. The biblical dates that he proposes and briefly explains are almost as precise as his tabulated predictions of the sunrises and sunsets, or the time of the one lunar eclipse that will be visible to New Englanders in July

1683. The Exodus occurred in "A.M. 2450," and Moses probably
wrote Genesis "a little before" that time; the book of Numbers is "a
story of 38 years, reaching to 2492." But these are only guesses, and
the reasoning of the learned guessers must be given along with qualifications and sometimes with contrary judgments. Most of the Proverbs of Solomon, for example, "seem to be" written "for the immediate use of his son Rehoboam, about A.M. 2940, though some of
them were collected at sundry seasons after his death." And Isaiah
"prophesied A.M. 3138 and continued at his Master's work, some
say 80 years, though others allow him but 47." Mather also provides
a careful description of Halley's comet, its color, shape, and size,
and its apparent course (given in degrees of latitude) through the
various constellations (against the Bear's tail, head, and so on) on
specific dates of observation. The biblical and spiritual knowledge
imparted in this little book is more important than the astronomical
for a practical as well as an inherent reason: "Alas! there is scarce
one" student of astronomy in a city. But Mather addresses even the
common, practical readers with implicit respect when he assumes
that they may wish to know the conflicting etymological hypotheses
for the word *Almanac,* and for perhaps one other reader in each city
he provides the Hebrew months and dates in a table that parallels
"our *Julian* ones."

The tone of the commentary (as distinct from the exhortation) in
this work expresses a delight in sharing knowledge, as if the teacher's
vanity were almost unrelated to the information he happens to pos-
sess. The young philomath certainly displays his learning, but he
seems almost to be watching it with his readers, as they would observe the comet or any other wonder. Just as Thomas Hooker had
admired that "sweet orderly usefulness the Lord first implanted in
things," so young Cotton Mather delights in showing ordinary Bostonians and farmers how the Hebrew months mesh with the Julian
ones.

⚬❧⚬

SELECTIVE THOUGH Mather's Reserved Memorials naturally are,
they do provide occasional glimpses, in these early years, of his rela-
tionships with other people in the family and the community. His
mother, who bore her last two children—Hannah, 1680, and Katharine, 1682—in Cotton's eighteenth and twentieth years, is never

mentioned in these pages. That silence itself does not invalidate Mather's later declaration that he and his mother were devoted to each other, but it does serve to underline the dominance of Increase Mather in the young man's continuing thoughts about "my father's family." In 1681, as he assisted his father in the church and tried to establish a routine of private devotions, Cotton Mather paid especial attention to exemplary males. He gave particular thanks for the mercy that had given him back his father "from the dead." He said that his grandfather John Cotton had set the only example that he knew for private days of thanksgiving. In the first recorded example of one of his own private thanksgiving days, he saved the last line for "the life and health of my dear *father,* whom I may reckon among the richest of my enjoyments." And at the end of a day of private fasting he concluded a prayer with confidence that the Lord would *"signalize me, as thou hast my father, my grandfathers, and my uncles before me. Hallelujah."*

Earning money of his own for the first time, while living at home, Cotton gave his father some valuable gifts. The most extraordinary of these, especially in light of his later attack upon the slave trade as "one of the worst kinds of thievery in the world," was "a *Spanish Indian,"* whom Cotton bought and gave his father for a servant in the summer of 1681. During this period of relative affluence, Cotton also bought himself a handsome watch, with "a variety of motions in it," of which he became very fond. When he learned that his father wanted such a watch, he gave it to him as a present, whereupon he was quickly and astonishingly rewarded by the gift of an even better watch from a parishioner who (he implies) knew nothing about the matter. Young Mather then resolved to implore his neighbors more urgently than ever to be dutiful to their parents and to *"redeem* the time, which I was helped thus to *measure."*

In tutoring his brothers and sisters and guiding members of the congregation, he combined authority with the tenderness that his grandfather and father had always advocated. When he noticed that the attention of his literate brothers and sisters was wandering during the morning and evening prayers at home, he made them open their Bibles to the assigned lesson and "attentively accompany the vocal reader." He also worked systematically to help educate his sisters. Maria, Elizabeth, and Sarah were all old enough to read by the summer of 1681, and four-year-old Abigail may have been included in their oldest brother's schedule for them. He assembled them for an hour every day and obliged them to divide the time equally between writing and reading about religious matters. Although he had already strengthened the quick wit that one often finds in his later writing, and which his associates noticed in his conversation throughout his adult life, he never did develop a strong sense of humor. One may hope that some playfulness at least entered his relationship to his brothers and sisters, but his resolution (June 1681) to "set a better example of seriousness and gravity" for his sisters probably means only that he feared they did not take him seriously enough as a delegate of the parental authority that ruled the household.

Despite his understandable anxiety lest he seem to be insufficiently grave and mature for his adult responsibilities, he continued to perform creditably both as a spiritual leader and in the large community. Toward the end of May 1681, he drafted the successful resolution for a general fast in which "this nation" of Massachusetts would pray for divine aid against the threatening drought at home and the "deep consultations of the Antichristian party" abroad, consultations designed to subvert "the true Christian protestant religion"—especially by destroying "the Lord's people" in the British Isles and at least harassing them in New England. Within his own church Mather cooperated with a more ambitious series of prayers for the threatened Protestants in England and Europe, a withdrawal from regular business every Monday morning at eleven for an hour of prayer for their liberation.

Long before he was formally chosen as Pastor, moreover, this eighteen-year-old spoke with authority to the individual citizens of Boston. During the spring of 1681 he "lovingly and frequently rebuked" one "honest man in the town" for having neglected to join a church. When the man continued to delay, Mather told him flatly that the God who had been calling the man "by His Word" would now speak to him "by a blow!" Just a few days later the man fell to the street from the top of a house and "lay, for some weeks, as dead." When he regained consciousness he immediately remembered, Mather wrote, "what I had said to him; under the sense whereof, he quickly went and joined himself unto the *South* church." One hopes, even while doubting, that Mather's characteristic underlining of *South* in the concluding line of this anecdote indicates a humorous recognition that, however grateful for his survival and perhaps for Mather's warning, the man preferred to join a church whose young assistant minister would not be so ambiguously related as Cotton Mather was to the nearly fatal blow. Even without the humor, one can easily see in Mather's paragraph that he had already mastered at eighteen the kind of pithy moral anecdote of which he and Benjamin Franklin became the best practitioners in the American colonies.

For Richard Middlecot, a prosperous merchant who was not yet a church member although he owned a pew in the North Church, young Mather chose a less direct approach to reformation. While reading alone in the deserted meetinghouse one day, Mather felt a sudden impulse to enter Middlecot's pew and pray for the conversion of this "gentleman of good fashion and quality" who had too often displayed "an airy temper." Mather asked especially that he himself be allowed to live to see the prayers answered, and eleven years later he solemnly noted in the margin of his Reserved Memorials entry for May 16, 1681, Richard Middlecot's admission to membership in the North Church. Probably Middlecot was one of the merchants whom Mather enlisted in a scheme, designed in 1683, to act benevolently outside the limits of their own community. Mather proposed that these men "single out some godly but needy *ministers* in the country, for the objects of their charity." And a few months later, meeting "an old *hawker,* who will fill this country with devout and useful books, if I will direct him," Mather began his life-long practice of distributing not only pious but otherwise useful books among ministers and others in the smaller towns.

Soon after the congregation formally voted (January 8, 1683) to call him as Pastor and to request him and his father to arrange a date of ordination, Mather increased the rate of his pastoral activities. He instituted in these first weeks of his forty-year collaboration with his father a routine of pastoral visits that became a part of his life throughout his increasingly productive career as a preacher and writer. He set aside one afternoon each week for a series of visits that would bring him into every household in the North End of Boston, whether or not the parents were church members. He intended to "bring all ages and sexes, unto an acquaintance with God," by catechizing the children, reading and assigning scriptural lessons to the parents, addressing little homilies to their individual conditions and needs. He also attended meetings of the religious society, praying and preaching with these brethren, who sometimes met on the day before a communion service to prepare themselves for the sacrament. When he found that he could not persuade enough young men "in the south part of Boston" to form a Young Men's Association there, he recruited a few of them to the Association he had founded in the North End. Soon the number of members from the South grew large enough to justify a separate Association, and Mather preached to them at their first meeting. His pastoral visits to the sick included prayers for their recovery, sometimes with remarkable effect. On September 11, 1683, for example, he prayed "with unaccountable enlargements and expansions of heart over my dear friend, Mr. *Avery,*" who was dying "after long unconquerable illness." But just as Mather was praying above him, Avery "felt as it were a load, or cloud, beginning to roll off his spirits; and from that instant, unto his own admiration, he began to recover; and came abroad shortly, unto the glory of God."

In this twenty-first year of his life Mather regarded all his private and pastoral activities as part of his struggle to attain the scriptural ideal of likeness to God. He meant of course to be "serviceable to God, in being serviceable to man," and one can easily perceive in some of his phrasing, including his "methodizing," a perfectly serious foreshadowing of what old Benjamin Franklin humorously looked back on in his own morally presumptuous youth as "the bold and arduous project of arriving at moral perfection." Actually, however, Mather's pious aspiration in the spring and summer of 1683 is much closer to the youthful resolutions of Jonathan Edwards and to what Edwards later called the nature of true virtue, than to Franklin's bold project or William Ellery Channing's version of "Likeness to God." Taking his instruction from Augustine, from John Howe's *Treatise on the Blessedness of the Righteous* (London, 1668), and from Nathaniel Vincent's *The True Touchstone* (London, 1681), Mather resolved to love human beings, "under whatsoever endearing circumstances they court my affections, with a *love,* not only *less than my love to God,* but also, on the *score,* and for the *sake* of my *love to God;* whose *beauty* or *image* resting thereon, with an *advantage* thereby put into my hands for the glorifying of Him, shall be the *reason,* of my *love* thereunto."

Like both Edwards and Franklin, Mather had an extraordinarily powerful sense of his willing self, which for all his dependence on divine grace he would, when liberated from the chains of sin and the depressing bouts of melancholy, direct in forcible activity. The force of his aspiration and the clarity of his prose bring him as close as any seventeenth-century Protestant came to Edwards' conception of true virtue. One cannot understand Mather's conception of pious action in the world unless one recognizes both the powerful will expressed in the first few sentences of his remarks on likeness to God, and the plea in his last sentence for harmonious acceptance of God's will:

> My highest acquisition, I will reckon to be, a *likeness unto God.* To *love* that which *God* loves, and *hate* that which *God* hates; to be *holy as God is holy,* and like Him, a *great forgiver;* and be His child, as much as may be like the *just at the Resurrection from the dead.* This will I seek, as the noblest *crown,* that ever I can wear; and that which the *thorns* placed upon the temples of the greatest earthly monarchs, were never worthy to be compared with. O that I may be conformable unto the *communicable attributes* of God, and agreeable unto His *incommunicable.*

Edwards would later define true virtue as *consent* to being in general, and God as the essential Being. Mather prayed that his own will might become *agreeable* to the incommunicable attributes of that perfect Being.

Mather's desire to be a great forgiver reflects an unusual emphasis, in his entries for 1683, upon challenges to his capacity to forgive. Evidence from other periods of his life shows that he was extremely sensitive to criticism. From John Corbet's excellent book *Self-Employment in Secret* (London, 1681) Mather copied many passages in June 1683, a heavy portion of them concerned with holding one's temper, avoiding rash words, refusing to bear a grudge against any who might "*despise* thee," bewaring "all secret pleasure, in the lessening of another, for the advancing of *thyself*," avoiding excessive concern about criticism or slander of oneself, refusing to value other men "according to their esteem of *thee*," suppressing the "expectation of hearing thy own praise." All this copying points unmistakably to the pride that we have already noticed, but Mather himself saw that his peculiar "deficiencies" had been enumerated by Corbet. He hoped to convert them into his "excellencies." Probably the occasion for great concern during the summer of 1683 has some connection with Mather's renewed anxiety about his stammer, which he

also mentions often in his Reserved Memorials, and about the exposure of his preaching to general criticism.

On June 11, 1683, Katharine Mather died, at the age of nearly
nine months. She was, Mather noted, "the first of my father's children that have died." She had been ill, apparently with consumption, for nearly half of her brief life, and an autopsy disclosed that
her right lung was "utterly wasted," with nothing "but about three
quarters of a pint of quittor, in the room thereof." This was the first
of Maria Mather's nine children for whom the mother had to sum-
mon the strength she had once found — "to believe for them all" —
for this child alone had not grown old enough to show encouraging
signs of believing for herself. The child's father had once expressed
great thanks that all of the five children born in the first eight years
of his marriage had survived, and he recorded that gratitude in his
autobiography. He did not mention in the autobiography the death
of Katharine, but there is no reason to doubt that his grief was real
or that he regarded this death as a rebuke from Providence. Less
than two months after Katharine's burial Increase and Cotton
Mather went off to Lynn for two weeks, to the very refuge that Increase had sought while trying to fight off the mania that threatened
him after the deaths of his father and brother. Both Increase and
Cotton preached in Lynn on the two Lord's Days of their sojourn,
but the experience near the mineral springs was a happy vacation
for Cotton, one of the few vacations he is known ever to have taken.
Having his father to himself for much of that time, and the opportunity to "enjoy many happy hours, in the country-retirements of
the fields," Cotton Mather must have felt the obvious truth that he
was a blessing to his earthly father. In some of his walks through the
fields near Lynn, he also "received strong and strange *assurances,
that the God of Heaven intended, not only to bless me, but also to
make me a blessing.*" It was soon after this refreshing trip that he
threw his "useless" daily records of piety into the fire.

During this momentous summer, as the movement toward revok-
ing the charter culminated at last in London, Cotton Mather also
began to record some explicit thoughts about the prospect of establishing his own family. He began to feel settled. During a walk
through the North End one afternoon in July, he found himself con-
templating the town from a hilltop and was moved to feel grateful
that he lived "in a place exceedingly populous," whereupon he felt

himself "exceedingly transported" by the desire to see all the souls of Boston converted and saved. On the same day, he recalled, while performing his customary meditations just after he awoke, he had lain in bed going over his prescribed lessons in the Old Testament, one verse at a time. He began to think of "*Isaac* having his happy *consort* brought unto him, *when* and where, he was engaged in his holy *meditations*," and the thought recurred to him. On this morning and others he felt "a strange persuasion" that some day "I should have my *bed* blessed with such a consort given unto me, as *Isaac,* the servant of the Lord was favored withal."

❧

In the fall of 1683, Edward Randolph at last persuaded the royal authorities that nothing short of a writ of *quo warranto,* demanding that Massachusetts surrender the charter and show cause why it should not be revoked, could bring the colony's leaders to submit. Armed with his writ, Randolph sailed for America in October and arrived in Boston on the third of December. He had tried unsuccessfully to arrange that he be brought on this ominous mission in an armed frigate to intimidate the recalcitrant faction in the Massachusetts government, and the official response in Boston gave him more good reason than ever to think that force would be necessary to elicit the charter from the procrastinating and evasive colonists. Although Governor Bradstreet and a majority of the Assistants favored submission and reliance on the king's good intentions, their wishes could not be effected without the consent of the lower chamber, the deputies. Whether the deputies were swayed by the passionate arguments of leading Congregational ministers, among whom Increase Mather was the most eloquent, or by their strong economic interest in maintaining their virtually separate government as long as they possibly could, this group of popularly elected delegates chose after two weeks of debate to withhold their consent from the Assistants' vote of submission.

Cotton Mather kept up with the latest reports from London and relayed the news to his uncle in Plymouth. On December 20, 1683, he reported that many dissenters in England had been "forced to fly. A gentleman, a deacon of Dr. Annesley's church, that is arrived here last week, told me there are warrants out for every nonconformist minister in the city of London." Some "religious noblemen" had also fled, and the Council of London had rescinded its vote of compliance, whereupon the King had revoked the city's charter, appointed a mayor, and replaced the aldermen with "a number of picked justices." The abominations that Boston might anticipate upon losing its charter could be seen in the most recent decree by the Governor's Council in Piscataqua, Maine. There a new law required that no person above the age of sixteen could be denied the sacrament of communion, and that every child must be christened "after the liturgy-way," if the parents wished. If a Congregational minister refused to comply, as his religion and fifty years' practice in New England would require unless strict tests were met, he would be liable to a six-month jail sentence.

Increase Mather's conduct in the crisis gave him for a time the stature of a national hero. Although Cotton Mather did nothing to distinguish himself at the time, his father's achievement here had a major influence on his life. The experience itself, however alarming, was also exhilarating. The young man who had recently been moved to express thanks for living in so populous a town could now feel that he and his family were participants in momentous national events affecting the survival of the Reformation, and perhaps the preparation for the New Jerusalem. It was quite possible that the sixth of the seven vials to be emptied (according to the Book of Revelation) before the Millennium, had already been poured out. Within the next year, as the New England crisis deepened, Samuel Sewall would write to Cotton Mather to ask why the New Jerusalem might not be found in America. The weekly prayers for threatened Protestants in England and France seemed to make New England Puritans participants in the struggle against Louis XIV, Charles II, and an aggressively reactionary Catholicism. And now Increase Mather was called on first to write a learned argument to persuade the General Court, and then in a town meeting to arouse the people, to resist in the name of their religion, the liberties of Englishmen, and the blessed memory of the founders. His behavior set an example that his son would emulate in the political crisis of 1689 and the outbreak of witchcraft in 1692.

In his written arguments for the deputies (December 1683), Increase Mather put the question bluntly: whether the Massachusetts government ought to submit "to the pleasure of the court, as to alterations, called regulations, of the charter." He offered seven arguments to support a negative answer, with heavy emphasis on religious duty. It would be a sin, "great offense to the Majesty of Heaven," to allow an action so "destructive to the interest of religion and of Christ's kingdom in the colony." The royal pretense that the charter would merely be amended or regulated could not disguise the Crown's intention to cancel the essential privileges granted by the charter. And the example of London and other corporations which had submitted to the Crown's varied assaults gave no reason to hope that anything could be gained by submission. The legislature, Mather insisted, had no power to make so grave a decision without explicitly consulting the freemen of the colony, who he declared would never consent.

He was right. After the deputies had withheld their consent, a town meeting of Boston's freemen was called for the twenty-third of January, 1684. In a stirring speech at that crowded meeting, Increase Mather distilled his written arguments. The Scripture, he declared, teaches us not to submit. "We know that . . . Naboth, though he ran a great hazard by the refusal, yet said, 'God forbid that I should give away the inheritance of my fathers!' " The only wise choice was to continue to delay, as the colonists had successfully done in 1638 and 1664 and in the last decade; here again the Bible offered good precedent: "We know that David made a wise choice, when he chose to fall into the hands of God rather than into the hands of men." If we submit, Mather said, "we fall into the hands of men immediately. But if we do not, we keep ourselves still in the hands of God, and trust ourselves with His providence and who knoweth what God may do for us?" As he moved toward his conclusion, he warned that posterity might curse his generation if the vote should favor submission. "I hope there is not one freeman in Boston that will dare to be guilty of so great a sin."

Not one was willing to dare at that meeting. Many of the people wept as Mather was formally thanked for his encouragement, and when a vote was taken not one hand went up in favor of submission. One of the hands raised in support of Increase Mather's arguments belonged to his son. Neither Increase nor Cotton was surprised to learn in the next few weeks that the Boston vote "had a great influence on the country," as many other towns followed the Bostonian example.

In the legal battle in London, it may have seemed for awhile that

Providence was justifying Increase Mather's faith, for the proceeding against Governor Bradstreet and others was successfully challenged on the ground that it was directed against persons rather than the government of the chartered company. The Crown, however, abandoned the suit, in the Court of King's Bench, that would have required Massachusetts to forfeit its charter, and moved instead simply to cancel the charter in the Court of Chancery. This court, as its name implies, had the power to cancel, vacate, annihilate letters patent in which the King had granted a lease or privilege, and possession of the charter in question was not necessary before the court could act. The decree vacating the Massachusetts charter did allow the colony to send an attorney to London to plead its case, but only if he should appear there by the beginning of the next term. News of the shocking decision did not arrive in Massachusetts until too late for an attorney to be appointed and instructed before the new term began. When these obvious difficulties were given as a reason for further delay at the start of the court's new term, the Lord Keeper of the Court ruled that because corporations should always have their attorney present in court, no further delay could be granted, and on October 23, 1684, the court cancelled the charter.

Massachusetts did not hear officially of this catastrophic judgment until the following year, and once again the practical consequences were forestalled by events in England when Charles II, who had recently become a virtually absolute monarch, died suddenly in February. On the very day of the King's death Increase Mather, with no knowledge that Charles was even ill, kept a day of private fasting to pray for the deliverance of New England. During one of his fervent prayers, he suddenly felt himself moved to declare three times aloud, "God will deliver New England!" He described the experience in his diary, where he also reported that after the prayer he had felt "joyful and cheerful." When news of the King's death did come to Boston in mid-April, Increase Mather noted that his prayer had been answered, for the King's death had prevented the actual installation of the man, reputed to be a tyrant, whom Charles had already chosen to become Governor of New England.

The legal and symbolic meaning for Puritans like the Mathers, however, was devastating. The entire basis for their unique civil polity had been destroyed. Grave questions concerning the liberties of Englishmen were of course at issue, as the forthcoming struggle with the royally appointed governor would soon prove, and funda-mental economic questions, including the title to lands granted, bought, and sold under the charter, would be forcibly imposed upon individual citizens. For the Mathers and many other religious people the central question remained the survival of their faith and its institutions in the commonwealth. For more than fifty years their entire way of thinking had depended on assumptions about their established religion which now had to be abolished or revised.

Increase Mather, moreover, found himself in some legal and phys-ical danger. As the author and orator who had addressed strong ar-guments for resistance to both the legislature and the town meeting, he was sure to be marked for some reprisals by Edward Randolph, and in the spring of 1684 a man named George Rosse accused him of a serious offense. Rosse sent Edward Randolph a letter, dated December 3, 1683, and signed with the initials "I.M.," containing libelous statements about Randolph and implicitly treasonous state-ments about the Crown. Parts of the letter were published in Lon-don in November 1684. Mather denied having written the letter, and offered persuasive evidence to show that it must be a forgery, but his liability to criminal arrest persisted for several years.

On the very eve of Cotton Mather's belated ordination, then, the government of Massachusetts and the person of his beloved father stood in jeopardy. The congregation of the Second Church had unanimously voted again on August 31, 1684, that Cotton be or-dained "without further delays" and that Major John Richards ask him to set a date for the ceremony. Unspecified reasons for delay continued to function throughout the autumn and winter of 1684-85, as the charter was canceled and the King died. News of the King's death did not come to Boston until mid-April, and only three weeks before Cotton Mather's ordination in May the new King, James II, was proclaimed in Boston. Old Governor Bradstreet and the faithful Secretary Edward Rawson still survived to lead the grand parade of "a thousand foot soldiers and a hundred horse, with numbers of the principal gentlemen and merchants on horse-back," but now their authority was merely provisional, and Cotton Mather was sure that the beating drums and the trumpets sounded for a Roman Catholic king, an ally of Louis XIV and servant of Antichrist.

IV

# From Vision to Bereavement

⚜

Indeed, as our SAVIOUR has no where promised a *Temporal Prosperity,* unto a Life of *Piety;* but bid us look for the Discipline of the *Cross,* and has told, us, *That through much Tribulation we must enter into the Kingdome of GOD:* So if a whole People were made up of such as led a Life of *Piety,* yet a Promise of all *Temporal Prosperity* could not be claimed for them. If every *Individual Believer* be still Obnoxious to the Things that are *not Joyous but Grievous,* how can a People consisting of such, look for an Exemption from them? It is true, the *Israelites* had a *Promised Land,* wherein they might hope for a *Temporal Prosperity,* while they kept the Condition of the *Covenant* by which they held it. But the *Christian Church,* is got out of that *Minority.* Nor has our SAVIOUR Promised his Church any *Land flowing with Milk and Honey* in this *Present Evil World.* We actually see this, in every Generation; That the most *Reformed People of* GOD (the *Vaudois* for *That!*) have been harassed with *Persecutions,* as well as they that by Sinking into *Criminal Corruptions* have Provoked the Holy JESUS to say, *I have something against thee;* At the same time, they that *Work Wickedness,* have not wanted for *Exaltation.* Yea, let us look where we will at this Day; The People among whom the *Covenant of the Gospel* is most adher'd unto, see much more *Temporal Adversity,* than many People who pay very little Regard unto it.

Cotton Mather, *Parentator*

WHEN THE ANGEL appeared in his study, the intensity of awe and radiant light nearly blinded Cotton Mather. He had given up the debilitating fasts that had threatened his health, but he had decided, shortly before his twenty-second birthday, to withdraw for one more private fast. After he had been praying for a while "with the utmost fervor," he was astonished to see a winged angel, with a face as bright as the sun at noon. The glow of this clean-shaven human face was reflected by a magnificent tiara encircling the head, and the angel stood above Mather in gleaming white raiment — an ankle-length robe, an Oriental belt or sash, unclothed wings growing out of his shoulders.

As Mather looked up from the floor to this splendid presence, he learned that it was not just a vision but an emissary. He heard the angel say so many things he had been yearning to hear, that he later recorded the entire episode in Latin (lest it be read by a young relative too immature to comprehend its potential danger) and concluded the account with a plea that Jesus protect him from the deceptions of the Devil. Some of the angel's words were too extraordinary, Mather decided, to be written at all, but others had to be preserved, if only in Latin. The angel had come as a messenger from Jesus to respond to the young man's prayers and to return with his answer to the Lord. It would be Cotton Mather's destiny to achieve complete expression of his best qualities, and the words of the prophet Ezekiel, which Mather heard the angel repeat, would have especial significance for the young man's future. Those scriptural words Mather wrote in English:

> Behold he was a cedar in Lebanon with fair branches, and with a shadowing shroud, and of an high stature, and his top was among the thick boughs. The waters made him great, the deep set him up on high, with her rivers running about his plants. His height was exalted above all the trees of the field, and his boughs were multiplied, and his branches became long, because of the multitude of waters, when he shot forth. Thus was he fair in his greatness in the length of his branches, for his root was by the great waters. Nor was any tree in the garden of God like unto him in his beauty. I have made him fair by the multitude of his branches, so that all the trees of Eden were in the garden of God envied him.

From that glorious, if ambiguous image Mather heard the angel turn to specific prophecies of the influence and achievement that would be granted to him. His branches would have broad influence. His books would be published not only in America but also in Europe. He would perform great works against sinners and in behalf of Christ's church in the revolutions that were imminent. These specific prophesies, and his concluding prayer, Mather recorded in Latin.

Nobody who reads the entire thirty-first chapter of Ezekiel will be surprised by Mather's prayers entreating Jesus to defend him from the Devil's tricks. The prayer shows, of course, that Mather already

believed the Devil could impersonate an angel of light — a belief that
would be extremely important in the Salem witchcraft trials of 1692.
But the context of Ezekiel's splendid image, which Mather surely
knew as well as anything else in the Bible, gave him additional reason to be wary of a diabolical fate. The grand image of the cedar in
Lebanon describes Asshur, king of the Assyrians, whose fate Ezekiel
holds up to Pharaoh as an illustration of the Lord's power. Cotton
Mather knew even as he transcribed it that the angel's version of
Ezekiel's third verse had substituted the pronoun *he* for the name
Asshur. Mather did not forget what happens in the last eight verses
of the chapter:

> Therefore thus saith the Lord God, Because he is lift up on high,
> and hath shot up his top among the thick boughs, and his heart is lift
> up in his height, I have therefore delivered him into the hands of the
> mightiest among the heathen: he shall handle him, for I have cast him
> away for his wickedness. . . . Upon his ruin shall all the souls of the
> heaven remain, and all the beasts of the fields shall be upon his
> branches, so that none of all the trees by the waters shall be exalted by
> their height, neither shall shoot up their top among the thick boughs,
> neither shall their leaves stand up in their height . . . : for they are all
> delivered unto death in the nether parts of the earth in the midst of
> the children of men among them that go down to the pit. Thus saith
> the Lord God, In the day when he went down to Hell, I caused them
> to mourn . . .

What Mather confronted, then, in this the most extraordinary
experience of his young life, was a prophecy that fulfilled all the
most ambitious hopes he had dared to imagine or to articulate in
prayers — and with apparently specific allusions to the political crises
in Europe, England, and Massachusetts. But the very text that the
angel chose to praise him reminded Mather of his own dangerous
pride, the possibility of eternal retribution, and the political and
economic disaster that threatened New England. He chose to affirm
this vision as a genuinely divine message, and to treasure it above all
his other moments of faith reassured. Yet even as his ambition
soared, even as he would later pray for the death of Louis XIV and
would go forth himself to battle Satan (recently come "down in
great wrath, knowing his time to be but short") — even then Mather
would not confuse himself with any earthly king or with the Master
whom he sought to serve and emulate. He remembered both Satan
and Asshur in the pit.

In the months just before his ordination, Mather continued to refine the schedule for his methodical piety. He now resolved to spend half an hour at noon on every day except Thursday and Saturday in special prayers "for myself, and my flock, and my country," and all of his Saturday afternoons in self-examining preparations for the next day's worship. Like many ministers in the tradition of Martin Luther, Mather felt his self-doubt increasing as the day of his ordination approached, and he had external as well as private reasons for the feeling. Sometimes the destructive gossip of his powerful associates disgusted him. He was vexed to "hear in the most venerable company, for whole hours together, little but the *idle chat* whereby holes are picked in the coats of other, and absent and honest men"; he resolved not to participate in that amusement, and to change the subject when he could. Coming at a time of renewed self-questioning, and increasingly frequent convictions of reassurance from the deity to whom he prayed, such conversations were understandably upsetting to him. Some of his recorded prayers, too, indicate uncertainty about his standing in the community, as if he had been subject to criticism which wounded his feelings. He expresses a conventional willingness (in late March) to suffer if the Lord's name should not be thereby dishonored; what indicates particular anxiety about the disapproval of others at this time is not only the context but the particular language of his prospective suffering: "I am willing to be anything, that God will have me to be.... If *He* will have me rejected, reproached, confounded. . . . And if *He* will have me to be, for the time to come, reckoned as *unsavory salt*."

In the first week of April, moreover, he suffered two disappointments that shook his faith in the congregation's support. His father now was often in Cambridge as President *pro tempore* of the college, since the death of President Rogers. On April 2 someone suggested to Cotton Mather that the political crisis of Massachusetts had made several brethren question whether this would be a proper time for an ordination. Cotton was so upset that in a private prayer at home that night he asked to be taken "out of the world" rather than become a prejudice to God's interest "or a necessary occasion of strife and sin." And three days later, on the very day that the brethren voted after services to set May 13 as the date for his ordination as Pastor, the attendance at the afternoon service was unusually low, whereupon Cotton's "heart began to sink under some foolish discouragements." He calmed himself then by remembering that even on this sparse day he had hundreds of auditors, as many as all but two or three preachers in America, and he had to confess that since he had "heretofore had the temptation of being flocked after," he ought to regard this new test as a reminder: "an affectation of displaying one's gifts before throngs, is too often an abominably proud fishing for popular applause." God's eye, "the *all-seeing eye* of that Majesty," ought to be "*theater* enough."

At this time, one must remember, the suggestion for a delay in ordination may well have had nothing to do with the quality of Mather's performance or with any judgment of his personality. Until the fourteenth of April, everyone in Boston still expected the frightening Colonel Percy Kirke to arrive any day as Governor-General of Massachusetts. When the welcome news of King Charles's death did finally arrive, and when James II was proclaimed so grandly on the twentieth, Cotton Mather did not join in the observance. Instead he "withdrew from the noises of the world," for a day of prayer asking an end to "the confusions with which the Protestant religion and interest were threatened . . ., especially in our own unhappy colony," by James's accession. Two friends joined him in this afternoon of fasting, and in the intervals between their prayers Cotton Mather preached three one-hour sermons to them, extemporaneous homilies on the very first text that he saw after he had let his Bible fall open. The text, he said, was "wonderfully suitable," for verses 19 and 20 of Psalm 109 seemed to refer respectively to New England and Charles II: "Let it be unto him as a garment which covereth him, and for a girdle with which he is girdled continually. Let this be the reward of mine adversaries from the Lord, and of them that speak evil against my soul." At the end of their vigil the three friends resolved to meet again in a few days to consider what special services they would do for the Lord "in case He deliver His people, here (or in England) from the distresses now upon them!" Mather left no record of the proposed meeting, but he had reason to remember this prayer almost exactly four years later, when he himself did help to deliver New England.

THE INVITATIONS had gone out on April 5 to the neighboring churches in Charlestown, Cambridge, Roxbury, and Dorchester as

well as to the First and Third churches of Boston. Each congregation would send messengers to give the right hand of fellowship, and
the other two senior ministers of Boston, James Allen and Samuel
Willard, would join Increase Mather in the ceremony of laying on
hands as Mr. Mather gave his son and colleague the formal charge
to perform his duties under his new covenant as Pastor. The solemnity of this occasion would have been sufficiently impressive if only
the congregation, the neighboring ministers, and (one hoped) the
benevolent eye of Providence had joined the new minister's family as
witnesses to his ordination. Dread of renewed bouts of stammering
intensified anxieties that Cotton Mather had been suffering in
March and April, and of course he became more excited as the day
approached. He knew that the South Church had elected Governor
Bradstreet and Samuel Sewall to accompany the deacons as emis-
saries of that congregation, and that Sewall and the Reverend
Joshua Moody had taken a personal invitation to old John Eliot.
Even Sewall's insistence that Eliot bring along a guest who could
claim no eminence, Eliot's son Benjamin, who was "much touch'd as
to his Understanding," stresses the importance attached to this ceremony, for Benjamin had not been to town for many years.

Cotton Mather found some comfort in his private religious exercises during the week before the ceremony. He kept a private fast,
wrote a new version of his covenant, promised to be a faithful Pastor, resolved to be humble under "whatever *enlargements*," and to
forgive "any *wrong* or *slight*, which any of the church might heretofore have ill-treated me withal." He promised to extend his service,
through writing and preaching, as far as growing capacity and influence might allow, but never to forget his pastoral duties at home
—and all these things he said he would perform with especial dili-
gence if the Lord's people in Massachusetts should be granted deliverance from their miserable predicament. On other days he felt
himself overwhelmed with "melancholy apprehensions" of his unfit-
ness for the ministry, but when he prayed with renewed ardor he was
rewarded with "glorious visions" of God's power and "with a weeping faith" that God would never forsake him.

He spent much of the morning of the great day in solitary meditation on the blessing and the prospects of his vocation—a subject so
moving on this day that he wept several times during his prayers.
Several times, too, he felt himself so close to the source of grace, so

enraptured by "*touches* and prospects," that he was "forced most unwillingly to shake them off." They were too frightening ("they would have been too hard for me"), and they might even leave effects which would be visible at the ceremony. When he made his appearance in the meetinghouse, he still felt that his soul was "inexpressibly irradiated from on high."

Before "one of the vastest congregations that has ever been seen in these parts of the world," this young hope of the third generation was ordained. Neither words nor time was stinted. The Governor and other dignitaries sat as uncomplainingly as the rest of the congregation while Cotton Mather bore verbal witness to his soul's incandescence, first with a seventy-five-minute prayer and then with a sermon that lasted for an hour and three quarters. His text was from the twenty-first chapter of John, Jesus' command to Peter (after repeatedly asking him "Lovest thou me?") to "feed my sheep." Presumably the congregation was then allowed an interval for luncheon on this Wednesday afternoon, before Increase Mather prayed and then preached a sermon on the thirteenth chapter of Acts: "As they ministered to the Lord and fasted, the Holy Ghost said, Separate me Barnabas and Saul for the work whereunto I have called them."

The proud father evidently had some mixed feelings about this consummation of his hopes. He did not resist the inclination to carry his personal observations in the sermon beyond his warm allusion to "my son Cotton Mather." Now almost forty-six, and having been only recently reminded that he was susceptible to grave illness, he struck a valedictory note that he would sound repeatedly during the next thirty-eight years. This ceremony reminded him, he said, of Aaron's "garments being put upon Eleazar"—intimating, Samuel Sewall reported, "that God might now call him out of the world." The accession of the third generation reminded one, more pleasantly but no less emphatically than grave illness, that even at the peak of responsibility and influence the second generation was declining.

The symbolism of the actual ceremony, a tableau that emphasized physical contact as well as visible proximity, brought the three New England generations together. Here again, as in so many of Cotton Mather's rites of passage, stood Increase Mather, blessing the son's ministry by placing his right hand on Cotton's head. James

Allen and Samuel Willard imposed their hands, too. Increase Mather now looked directly at his son and pronounced the charge, which Cotton later pasted (in his father's handwriting) on a page of his Reserved Memorials, and transcribed inside the cover of his Bible:

> Whereas you upon whom we impose our hands, are called to the work of the ministry, and to the office of a *Pastor* in this Church of Christ, we charge you before God and the Lord Jesus Christ and in the presence of elect angels, that you take heed to the ministry which you have received in the Lord, to fulfill it, and that you feed the whole flock of God over which the Holy Ghost hath made you overseer; that you study to show yourself approved of God and a workman that need not be ashamed; that you give yourself to reading and to meditation, to exhortation and to doctrine; and that you endeavor to show yourself an example of the believers, in faith, in spirit, in purity, in charity, and in conversation.
>
> And if you keep this charge, we pronounce unto you that the Lord of Hosts will give you a place among His holy angels that stand by, and are witnesses of this day's solemnity, and of your being thus solemnly set apart to the special service of God, and of Jesus Christ; and if you do thus, when the Lord Jesus shall appear, you shall appear with Him in glory. He, who is the chief Shepherd will then give unto you a crown of glory which shall never fade away.

Then "good old Mr. Eliot" reached across the generations to offer the right hand of fellowship, and assured the people that Cotton Mather was "a lover of Jesus Christ."

IN THE NEXT few weeks the new Pastor savored the privileges of his official status, which allowed him at last to perform sacramental duties. He baptized a child for the first time, and administered his first communion, and on July 2, taking the place of his father, who was occupied at Harvard, he took the North Church's turn for the first time as preacher at the Thursday Lecture. In this summer, too, having resolved to watch continually for new ways to improve his private devotions, he hit upon two innovations that would have considerable importance in his later life. He resolved to read the Bible so attentively that he would "fetch at least one *observation,* and one *supplication,* a *note* and a *wish,* out of every *verse* in all the Bible." Thus began, in his twenty-third year, the most ambitious literary project of his life, his *Biblia Americana,* for which he tried unsuccessfully to find a publisher or sponsor during his last twenty-five years, and which remains unpublished nearly three hundred years after its first conception. As a variation on this discipline he also began to apply it to his private singing of the Psalms. Studying them and insisting on commentary and prayer, he found, made the Psalm singing "a more delicious, entertaining, and profitable exercise." That close study of the Psalms led eventually to his own translation of them in blank verse, which he published in 1718.

To write his sermons, which he was now more and more frequently called to prepare, he devised a procedure that must have been very uncomfortable but that he apparently used often during the rest of his long, productive career. He would prepare while kneeling. On the chair in front of him he would place the book that he called his table-book of slate, a pocket-sized volume in which oiled cardboard pages alternated with sheets of writing paper. Invoking divine aid for his composition, as the designated explicator of God's Word, he would then record the "hints" that occurred to him after a prayer, and he would sometimes "intermingle" his writing and his prayers.

Within three weeks after his ordination he was called on twice for a more painful kind of ministerial duty. Samuel Sewall invited several of the ministers to attend a private fast at his house on May 22, to pray for the recovery of a child who was gravely ill. Both Cotton and Increase Mather attended, along with Messrs. Willard, Allen, John Eliot, Joshua Moody, and the Boston magistrates and their wives. Every one of the ministers prayed in his turn, Mr. Moody for ninety minutes, and both Samuel Willard and Increase Mather preached full-length sermons. After the whole company had sung the seventy-ninth Psalm (the ninth verse of which had been the text for Mather's sermon), Sewall served biscuits, beer, cider, and wine.

Much more distressing was the sudden illness and death of young Thomas Shepard, whom Cotton Mather had befriended and admired in his earliest days at Harvard. Shepard, like Cotton Mather, not only had represented the third generation of New England ministers but also (after his father's death during the smallpox epidemic of 1677-78) had been called to the pulpit of his father's congregation. He suffered an acute abdominal attack on Friday night, June

5, but at first refused to take any medicine because he was hoping to preach and administer communion on the Sabbath. When he saw that he could not preach, he sent for Cotton Mather to take his place at the regular morning service in Charlestown. After preaching there, Mather visited him at noon. Shepard's last words to his young friend declared his faith that if "taken out of the world, I shall only change my place; I shall neither change my company nor change my communion. And as for you, Sir, I beg the Lord Jesus to be with you, unto the end of the world." Mather's account (fifteen years later) of Shepard's life emphasizes the resemblance between Shepard's situation and his own, including both "the obligations laid upon him from his ancestors to do worthily" and his constant awareness of one question as he always kept "the image of his father" with him: "How he might approve himself the son of such a father." Mather also used Shepard's brief life to show that wisdom, gravity, prudence, and temperance are not always confined to older people. In the *Magnalia* he placed Shepard's life next to that of his own brother, and he expressly declared his personal affection for him.

Shepard died later on Sunday night. News of his death circulated through Boston on Monday along with rumors that Colonel Kirke, who was expected soon to descend on Boston as the new governor, had arrived in New York. As if to confirm the truth of the rumor, two newly elected magistrates (Joseph Dudley and William Stoughton) who had delayed taking the oath of office, they said, because they did not wish to suffer the inevitable abuse that their support of the new government was sure to provoke from their fellow magistrates—these two did take the oath. At Shepard's funeral on Tuesday, June 9, with Governor Bradstreet, the Deputy Governor, all the magistrates, and the leading ministers in attendance, both Increase and Cotton Mather served as pallbearers. The cortège was splendid —partly, Sewall suggests, because plans had been made for "a great bustle in training on Tuesday with horse and foot" from Boston as well as Charlestown. Harvard scholars walked ahead of the hearse, and "a pretty number of troopers" followed. Someone had written the customary elegiac verses, but had not followed the usual practice of pinning them on the hearse. As Cotton Mather carried the body of his friend to the grave, he must have noticed that this was the second ceremony within less than a month for which the Governor and other dignitaries had come forth to honor a very young minister. His dead friend had not completed his twenty-seventh year.

Anxious observers like Sewall and the Mathers naturally considered whether the number of such deaths — four ministers in less than eight months — constituted a divine judgment on the land, but their actual political situation was so anomalous in 1685, and the range and number of difficulties so extensive, that no modern inquirer need investigate obscure causes in order to understand the deep perplexity of religious Bostonian Congregationalists. The provisional status of their paralyzed government caused the greatest confusion. Nobody knew exactly when the new royal governor would supplant the elected one, and in the meantime a number of the officials hesitated to take any action, for fear of being judged presumptuous when the new governor arrived. Throughout the year, rumors of that dreaded moment kept stirring the town's circulation, as events reminded citizens of the living connection between some of the most trivial or personal local affairs and the mysterious, bloody drama of English royalty — a drama whose incidents were reported in Boston two months late.

A week after Thomas Shepard's funeral, for example, "a Quaker or two" asked Governor Bradstreet's permission to build a simple commemorative fence to protect the graves of the Friends who had been hanged on Boston Common a quarter of a century ago. Although the Council unanimously advised the Governor to deny the request, this minor annoyance reminded everyone of an action that had done as much as any other to bolster royal agents' claims that Massachusetts had made and executed laws in conflict with the laws of England. When a Quaker warned the Governor on the following day that great calamities of fire and sword would suddenly descend on New England, reports that a French pirate carrying thirty-six guns had been sighted near the coast identified only one of the real dangers that might fulfill the curse. Colonel Kirke was still expected at any time, with perhaps unlimited powers and plans for retribution against people who had sheltered the regicides. When a ship with passengers who were recovering from smallpox took in its colors and dropped anchor near the castle in the Boston harbor, someone spread the rumor that the new governor had actually arrived, and great numbers of people came "flocking to the waterside." Early in

September, moreover, a body of three or four hundred armed Indians was reported on the move near Chelmsford, then near Albany,
and some Indians were blamed for the burning of a mill at Med-
field. To pacify an offended Indian chief, the General Court did
vote to pay him £10 in mid-September, but it also ordered that all
persons be appropriately armed in case of an attack. The regular
training exercises of the Boston and Cambridge artillery companies,
at which Cotton Mather led the morning and evening prayers on
October 5, thus had a more than merely ceremonial meaning.

The guns in that October exercise were divided on the two sides of
the river, and one set was trained "upon the hill in prospect of the
harbor." It was from the direction of the harbor that the most
ominous force and the most sanguinary news came in 1685. In July
the reports said that Titus Oates, fabricator of the counterfeit
Popish Plot, had been "whipt and set in the pillory" on May 19, and
(falsely) that the new governor had arrived. Near the end of August
Bostonians learned that the Duke of Argyll, who had fled an earlier
capital sentence for treason against Charles II, had returned to Scot-
land, led an outnumbered army against King James's forces, and
been defeated and captured. By the time this news came to Boston,
Argyll and the Duke of Monmouth, whose own rebellion was only
now reported with no account of its result, had been executed,
respectively, two months and six weeks ago. News of Monmouth's
execution came to Samuel Sewall on September 22 from "Neighbor
Fifield . . . , who had it from the cryer of fish." Then, as if New England might not feel sufficiently threatened by general reports of
guild halls filled with the political and religious prisoners who were
too numerous for London's jails, a ship brought news on November
13 that Lady Lisle, Mrs. Hezekiah Usher's mother, had been beheaded at Winchester for harboring two fugitives after Monmouth's
defeat. Mrs. Usher was the generous woman who, as the widow of
Leonard Hoar, had replenished Increase Mather's library after the
fire of 1677. Her mother had been sentenced to be burned to death,
but the King had graciously allowed her to be decapitated. More
than the news of Lord Jeffreys' Bloody Assizes, which sentenced a
thousand men to West Indian slavery and three hundred to death,
the execution of Lady Lisle brought home to Massachusetts Puritans
the danger of the new regime. With that deadly news, of course,
came a new rumor that the Massachusetts government would be

replaced during the autumn or winter. By the time Increase Mather told the Thursday Lecture's audience a few days later that New England if "zealous might still save this people," another report from London said Joseph Dudley would be named the new royal governor in the spring. Dudley, as well as the Usher family, who were dressed in mourning, attended Mather's lecture. It would have taken an unusual obtuseness to miss Mr. Mather's political allusion at the December seventeenth Lecture four weeks later, for he preached on Matthew 16:25: "For whosoever will save his life shall lose it."

The known horrors in the news from England and the unknown nature and date of the new Massachusetts government form an essential context for our understanding of concerns in Boston which would otherwise seem amusingly trivial. A hot controversy in midsummer bred "great animosities" when Mr. William Hubbard emerged from a meeting of thirty-one ministers to report that they had decided "the government ought not to give way to another till the General Court had seen and judged" the new claimants' commission. A number of the ministers then denied that Hubbard had been given any authority to represent their views, and a second group insisted that he had indeed been so empowered. The magistrates disagreed among themselves, and the deputies with the magistrates, about how and for how long to adjourn after necessary sessions of the General Court. The Treasurer refused to send out warrants for assessments for taxes unless the General Court would supply him with a special order. Even the usually simple question of declaring a day of thanksgiving became now another occasion for displaying the government's helplessness. Governor Bradstreet and Samuel Sewall feared that printing an order for thanksgiving might offend England. Then the magistrates could not even agree on what to be thankful for. Five days after learning of Lady Lisle's execution, the General Court was disrupted by a vehement battle in which Deputy Governor Danforth, who favored the zealous attitude of Increase Mather, exchanged "extreme sharp words" with Stoughton, Dudley, and others. Sewall argued that there was no point in ordering a day of thanksgiving for "mere generals, as (the mercies of the year)." Governor Bradstreet wanted to limit the proclamation to one article for the peace of England, in line with the King's proclamation, but of course the more zealous group saw more reason for gratitude in the survival of their colony's precarious liberties than in so bloody a peace. No thanksgiving was proclaimed.

The threat implicit in other trivia can be better understood in this perspective. The Quakers defied the government's ruling and built the forbidden fence around the grave of their martyrs. A dancing master named Francis Stepney not only set up classes for "mixt" dancing, which Increase Mather quickly condemned, but also had the impertinence to declare that "by one play he could teach more divinity than Mr. Willard or the Old Testament." A new member of the South Church wore a periwig when he appeared before the members to profess his faith and describe his religious experience. For the first time in the history of Boston (or so Samuel Sewall was told) an infant was left as a foundling by its mother. And on the day after Sewall saw the chestnut coffin of his own infant son set in a grave that a storm had filled with water, some Anglicans insisted on observing the holiday of Christmas, which Mr. Allen denounced as an "Antichristian heresy." Sewall blessed God that Boston still had no authority that could force the people to keep such a holiday.

Beyond their general significance for the colony's history, the particular form in which events of this kind touched the life of Cotton Mather was the murder of Joseph Johnson by James Morgan. In a drunken quarrel on the night of December 10, Morgan had stabbed Johnson in the belly with a spit, and a jury convened before Judge Sewall had indicted him on the fourteenth. Morgan was put in irons and imprisoned for trial before the magistrates. He was convicted on March 3, 1686, on the testimony of several eyewitnesses, although he had pleaded not guilty. On the fourth he was sentenced to be the first person executed in Boston in several years. Increase Mather, whose turn at the Thursday Lecture would fall on the day of execution, was notified at once so that he might compose an appropriate sermon, and both he and Cotton Mather went to the prison to visit the condemned sinner. On Saturday the sixth, although he had previously denied his guilt, Morgan signed a petition admitting the sinfulness of his life and the justice of his capital sentence for the murder of Johnson, whom he now said he had killed without premeditation, in a drunken passion. His petition asked that his execution be delayed so that he might receive the spiritual benefit of

his repentance. The court denied his petition on Saturday, and
Morgan asked that Cotton Mather preach a sermon for his benefit
the following day.

Cotton Mather had been scheduled to preach in Charlestown in
the vacant pulpit of Shepard, but he arranged for his father to take
his place there, and with astonishing speed he wrote a forty-page
sermon on Saturday night. Morgan was brought to the North
Church the next day to hear two sermons, the one he had requested
of Cotton Mather and the other by Joshua Moody. On this Lord's
Day Mather had no reason to complain of a sparse attendance. He
preached before "a vast concourse of people."

He did not know when he prepared this sermon, or when he delivered it, that it would become the first one to be printed over his
name. For modern inquirers, moreover, "The Call of the Gospel applied unto all men in general, and unto a Condemned Malefactor in
particular" has an importance that goes well beyond bibliographical
chronology. It reveals the nature of the teamwork between Increase
and Cotton Mather in a noncontroversial episode six years before
the notorious Salem witchcraft trials. In the execution of James
Morgan it is Cotton Mather who has the more sympathetic role and
his father who appears to be harshly insensitive. In *The Wonders of
the Invisible World,* the book that enabled Robert Calef to tie on
the name of Cotton Mather a tin can that has rattled through nearly
three centuries, it is the son who appears to concede almost no possibility of judicial error, after the father has strongly criticized the
court's procedures. The case of James Morgan should help us to see
not only that, as Increase Mather plainly said in 1692, the two
Mathers emphatically agreed with each other, but also that the
community and the condemned man had a chance to hear and see
Cotton Mather as a man of warm sympathy who could use so grim
an occasion to celebrate divine mercy rather than vengeance.

The two epigraphs on the title page of "The Call of the Gospel"
reinforce the theme of the text that Mather "opens" in the sermon
itself. First he quotes the eighty-ninth Psalm: "I will sing of the mercies of the Lord forever, with my mouth will I make known Thy
faithfulness to all generations." And from Origen, one of Mather's
favorites among the church fathers, he chooses a Latin line declaring that no sin is too wicked for Jesus to forgive. From Isaiah, then,

comes the actual text for the sermon: "Look unto Me, and be ye SAVED, all the ends of the earth."

Both Increase and Cotton Mather, of course, used James Morgan's plight to admonish other sinners. In a way that one can now scarcely read without a cold shudder, both father and son persuaded Morgan himself to participate in that admonition, right down to the moment before the hangman turned him off the ladder. From outside their system one might understandably suspect them of cynically exploiting the condemned man. One shudders again, however, on perceiving that within its limits their sympathy was genuine. They really believed Morgan's eternal welfare coincided with the use to which they and the community were putting him. The whole grisly drama was performed as a trope that explicitly reminded the community of every sinner's progress to the critical moment of Judgment. This condemned sinner was encouraged, pitied, warned, interrogated, comforted, and at last told to consider the nicest of theological distinctions, just before the Pastor reminded him at the foot of the ladder — as the Teacher had reminded him in the meetinghouse — that they could do no more than pray for him, he no more than throw all his hopes on his belief in Jesus Christ.

As Hawthorne shrewdly suggested with a shining suit of Puritan armor that dwarfs the image of Hester Prynne behind her magnified scarlet letter, this process led the community to magnify the typical nature of sin in a way that tended to conceal the poor human sinner. But Hawthorne also saw with mixed horror and admiration that the same system gave potential dignity to every person's conduct, for its effect on the moral instruction of the community and for its claim on the attention not only of the Governor but of the Lord. Increase Mather actually believed that the civil government could not safely fail to execute a murderer, for the Bible explicitly commanded (Numbers 35:16): "the murderer shall surely be *put to DEATH*." In their exploitation of the condemned murderer's feelings, moreover, the Mathers did to his private experience just what they and many others were willing to do with their own, both in the sermons that they spun out of their own experience and in the diaries that they reserved for their children and friends to read. Before turning to Cotton Mather's sermon, one shudders again.

Preaching four days before the execution, Mather used "The Call of the Gospel" to celebrate the glory of divine forgiveness, and he took care to address Morgan sympathetically, as soon as he had admonished the congregation to consider what good the murderer's story might do them. "Poor man," he said to Morgan, who sat in irons before him, "do *you* hearken, I'll study to make this whole hour very particularly suitable and serviceable to *you;* and methinks a man that knows himself about to take an eternal *farewell* of all sermons, should endeavor to hear with *most earnest heed.* The God of Heaven grant, that *faith* may *come* unto *you* by your *hearing.*" Later on in the sermon Mather gave Morgan and the congregation the prescribed Calvinist warning that they could not genuinely look to Christ until unmerited grace had enabled them to "*see* that you cannot look . . . with any abilities of your *own.*" But he struck his main theme, and the dominant tone, in his second and third propositions: that "SALVATION will most undoubtedly be the fruit of a believer's *looking* unto the Lord Jesus Christ," and that Jesus "in His Gospel does *graciously and earnestly* INVITE all men thus to *look* to *Him* and be *saved.*" For James Morgan the essential news declared that the God who "once said unto *upright* man, *Obey* and *live,* now saith unto lapsed man, *Believe and be saved.*" Nor had Jesus made the invitation quietly. It was a "loud and loving outcry — O Never, never was there an Oyee's vouchsafed unto the world like to this! — in Isai. 55.1. *Ho, every one that thirsteth let him come* and partake hereof." "*James,*" Mather said to "the poor fettered prisoner"; "thy name is not excepted in these INVITATIONS."

Even in the Application addressed specifically to Morgan (after a perfunctory warning that sinners in the congregation who did not look to Christ would themselves burn in Hell), Mather used the inevitable moment of execution more for its possibilities of mercy than for its horror. He warned Morgan not to wait till the executioner put "the cloth of death over your eyes," but urged him to look on Jesus now as not only able but willing to be his Savior. And he frankly invited him to use his last days and minutes to warn others: "Even after your eyes are so covered as to take their leave of all sights below, still continue LOOKING unto Him whom you have heard saying, *Look* unto Me." He concluded with a prayer asking Jesus to give this "extraordinary sinner, a place among the wonders of free grace."

The excitement that accumulated in the days before the hanging on the eleventh caused great confusion, and a nearly fatal panic, on Thursday morning. Soon after an immense crowd had been packed into the First Church to hear the Lecture by Increase Mather, "a crazed woman" rushed into the building and started to beat some of the women who were already there. Someone screamed that the gallery was collapsing, and people rushed wildly to get out to safety. They did slowly reassemble after they had been calmed and the woman subdued, but John Eliot was still concerned for their safety in the old building, and he asked Samuel Sewall to join him in persuading the Governor to move the meeting to the newer South Church. The tension thus had time to grow even more taut during the delay, as the crowd moved slowly from one meetinghouse to the other. Gathered inside at last, the congregation sang the first part of the fifty-first Psalm, in which David asks mercy for his iniquities. Then Increase Mather began to speak.

His tone was much less personal and warm than his son's had been. The climax toward which Increase Mather moved was the actual moment at which Morgan would "hang between Heaven and Earth, as it were forsaken of both, and unworthy to be in either," and he was obliged to explain the basis for the death sentence as well as its monitory significance. He cited the biblical command of death to murderers; distinguished between murder and justifiable killing on the one hand, manslaughter on the other; and vehemently applied the lesson of Morgan's rash murder to those who fell into drunkenness or other passionate anger, including revenge. He denounced those of his auditors who had sold liquor to Indians; soon they "must answer for the blood of souls and bodies too." He denounced more emphatically than his son had deplored the sinners who, like Morgan, had absented themselves from sermons. And in Morgan's presence he declared that a murderer's "soul is filled with hellish horror of heart; so that he is as it were damned above ground, and in Hell whilst he is yet alive." Perhaps bearing the mark of Cain, with "a ghastly guilty *countenance,* that . . . had *Hell and horror*" in it, the murderer, unless he could become truly repentant, would suffer an "eternal curse, a weight of everlasting vengeance, heavier than mountains of *lead,* that shall press his soul to *death,* world without *end.*"

When Increase Mather turned to address his final words to Morgan himself, he again spoke more sternly than Cotton had done, al-

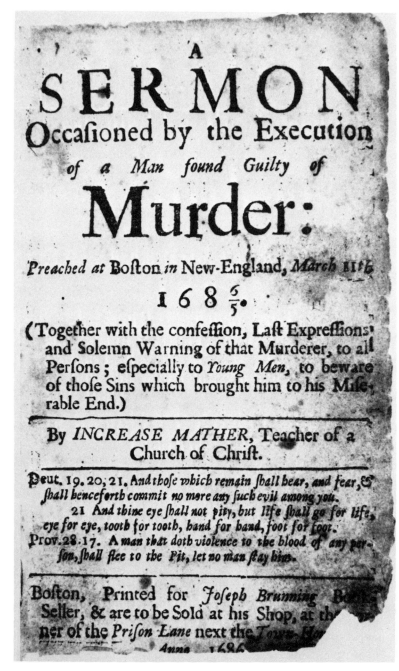

A
# SERMON
Occaſioned by the Execution

*of a Man found Guilty of*

# Murder:

*Preached at* Boſton *in* New-England, *March* 11th

# 1 6 8 $\frac{6}{5}$.

(Together with the confeſſion, Laſt Expreſſions,
and Solemn Warning of that Murderer, to all
Perſons ; eſpecially to *Young Men*, to beware
of thoſe Sins which brought him to his Miſe-
rable End.)

By *INCREASE MATHER*, Teacher of a
Church of Chriſt.

Deut. 19. 20, 21. And thoſe which remain ſhall bear, and fear, &
ſhall henceforth commit no more any ſuch evil among you.
　　21 And thine eye ſhall not pity, but life ſhall go for life,
eye for eye, tooth for tooth, hand for hand, foot for foot.
Prov. 28. 17. A man that doth violence to the blood of any per-
ſon, ſhall flee to the Pit, let no man ſtay him.

Boſton, Printed for *Joſeph Brunning* Book-
Seller, & are to be Sold at his Shop, at the
ner of the *Priſon Lane* next the *Town-Ho*
　　　　　　　*Anno* 1686.

7. Title page of Increase Mather's sermon
before the execution of James Morgan.

though his goal was the same genuine penitence that "The Call of the Gospel" had sought to provoke. He reminded Morgan that this was the last sermon he would ever hear, though now (he said) Morgan belatedly wanted to hear the preaching that he had so often avoided. Mather even gave him three subjects to consider in the brief minutes between the sermon and the execution: all his other sins, including that of lying since his condemnation; the misery that he had brought upon his body, upon his children, upon "your never-dying soul"; and finally, in the last minute, a word of hope. "Consider 3. *There is a possibility that your soul may be saved.* Notwithstanding all that has been spoken to you, don't despair; repent but do not despair."

Here Increase Mather's voice must have risen to express the faith that lay at the heart of Puritan doctrine. As in Cotton Mather's sermon, but now much nearer to death, the murderer stood before the community to exemplify the drama of conversion. Just at the moment of any sinner's greatest self-condemnation, on the edge of despair, he had to remember that, as Increase Mather now fairly sang: "Though men cannot forgive you, *God* can; and he *will* do it, if you unfeignedly repent and *believe* on the *Lord Jesus.* There is infinite merit in the death of *Christ:* if your bloody soul be washed in *His blood,* it shall be made whiter than the snow." Mather reminded Morgan that God had forgiven other murderers, including Manasseh, who had "filled the streets of *Jerusalem* with *innocent blood.*" As Cotton Mather had done before him, then, Mather warned Morgan to be sure his repentance was sincere, to beware of letting his fear deceive him, and to rely not on his confession of sin or on the fact that "good *men* have *prayed* for you," but on Christ alone. "And I pray the Son of GOD," Mather concluded, "to have compassion on you."

When the service had ended, Morgan asked Cotton Mather to accompany him to the gallows, and the young Pastor agreed. In thanking him, Morgan expressed wonder that any servant of God would take notice of so miserable a criminal. Everyone present must feel compassion for the condemned man, Mather replied, and human compassion is nothing in comparison to that of Jesus. As they walked along the muddy street, Morgan asked what Mather could do for his soul; Mather told him that his worst sin had been despising Christ and that sincere repentance would have to include a desire to be sanctified as well as justified. When Morgan said he had given up all his sins, Mather rebuked him for having expressed "unruly passionateness" just last night in complaining about the place assigned for his burial. "Sir, I confess it," Morgan replied, "and I was quickly sorry for it." Mather told him he would have to abandon his grudges against those who had convicted and condemned him, and Morgan declared that he heartily wished them all well.

At this point Morgan stumbled and someone in the crowd mocked him. Mather explicitly asked the Lord to forgive "that hardhearted creature," and as the muddy way became more difficult he himself kept silent. Morgan asked him to "speak to me. Do me all the good you can." All Mather could offer was another injunction to call on Christ, whereupon Morgan asked him to "show me then again what I have to do."

Now Mather seems to have noticed that the best he could do for the poor man was to keep on paying attention to him by talking. "Christ wants to know if you'll accept him," he said. "Are you willing?"

"I hope I am."

"Do you value His grace and opposition to sin above all?"

Again Morgan had the right answer. "I think I do," he said, and then he thanked Mather for his help and comfort.

At the foot of the ladder, Mather stopped and explained the final difference between private and public roles: "When up this ladder my last service will be to pray for you, but I will say my personal farewell now. Oh that I might meet you at the right hand of the LORD JESUS in the Last Day! Farewell, poor heart, fare thee well. The everlasting Arms receive thee! . . . The great GOD who is a great Forgiver, grant thee repentance unto Life!"

On the ladder itself Morgan had a speaking role to perform before his body was suspended between Heaven and earth in the way that Increase Mather had foretold. Morgan's words were preserved, and undoubtedly edited into rhetorical correctness, in Cotton Mather's shorthand, but there is no reason to doubt their substance or their tone. Even if we did not know that Cotton Mather has an excellent record for accuracy as a factual reporter, we would have to notice, as he surely did, that other people near the scaffold had heard Morgan's last words. With many of the auditors, moreover, he gave unusual respect to the words of a soul that would appear, as

Morgan said, before the Lord in a few minutes. "I pray God," Morgan said in Mather's version, "that I may be a *warning* to you all, and that I may be the last that ever shall suffer after this manner." He admonished the people to avoid profanity, drunkenness, and murderous anger, and begged God to have them take especial notice of his words because he was about to appear before the final Judgment. He then began a kind of joint prayer and exhortation:

O that I may make improvement of this little time . . .
O let all mind what I'm a-saying now I'm going out of this world.
O take warning by me, and beg of God to keep you from this sin
which has been my ruin.

When the cloth was put over his face, he performed exactly as Cotton Mather had requested. "His last words," Mather wrote, "were, O Lord, I come unto thee O Lord; I come, I come, I come."

No contemporaneous report describes the crowd's reaction after Morgan dropped from the ladder, but it would be hard to imagine a more complete enactment of an exemplary execution. A London publisher and bookseller named John Dunton, who happened to be visiting Boston at the time, saw at once the great prospective value in bringing out an edition of the Mathers' sermons that would communicate the thrill of Morgan's dreadful consummation. He arranged with a Dutch bookseller named Joseph Brunning to share the first edition, with Dunton's copies to be sold in London. That printing quickly sold out, and the printer, Richard Pierce, got out another version in 1687. In his announcement of this second edition Pierce confessed that he had used an *"innocent wile"* to procure — "utterly without" Cotton Mather's knowledge — a true copy of Mather's conversation with Morgan during the walk to the gallows. Mather did not object. Although he had not submitted the transcript for the original edition, he had shown it to some friends, and he did reprint it more than once when it seemed useful to do so in his later works.

⁂

THAT FIRST experience beside the gallows was not to be Cotton Mather's last. A few weeks after Morgan's execution, however, Mather's concern with judgment was brought closer to his personal life. On April 7, he was obliged to sit in judgment on the sins of another young man, a minister in Malden whom he had known as an undergraduate at Harvard. The shame of Thomas Cheever, accused by his congregation of both adultery and obscene speech, reminded Cotton Mather of his own vulnerability to sexual temptation. The pathetic plea of Cheever's father that the ministers allow the accused man to defend himself provoked Cotton Mather to remember (if he had ever forgotten) his own father's central position as moderator of the council. And the suspension of Cheever from his ministerial duties led young Mather to meditate on the question "What if God should single me out now to be so publicly loaded with shame for sin?"

By that time, his own sexual future had been settled. He had been thinking seriously again about his prospects for marriage and had set aside a day of prayer on the subject in November 1685. With the characteristic indirection that he had learned to use in ordering his prayers, he had asked not simply for a wife but only that God smile on him in "the ordering of my single or married estate, unto His glory." Indirectly again, his prayer reminded the Lord of a promise in the eighty-fourth Psalm: "no good thing will He withhold from them that walk uprightly." Mather disclaimed any presumption that he himself was worthy to receive such a "good thing," and promised to do nothing about the matter that might displease the Lord. If choosing a wife might obstruct his main purpose—which remained the glorifying of God—then he asked Providence to "hinder me from having that [thing], whatever my misguided appetites might plead to the contrary: . . . if He would have me embrace a celibacy, I would evermore take a contentment in it." But of course he admitted that his own inclinations, as well as some unspecified invitations, "did now seem to recommend a married estate," and he promised that if granted the privilege of a good marriage he would join his wife twice every year in a special day of thanksgiving for that blessing. A number of times thereafter, and long before her final illness, he referred to his first wife, in these papers and in his prayers, as his "good thing."

Probably his visits to Thomas Shepard's pulpit in Charlestown had some effect on his eventual choice, for Abigail Phillips, the fifteen-year-old daughter of Captain John Phillips, attended that church, and Mather met her during the winter. In those days of January and February 1686 he was working extraordinarily hard, preaching as many as five sermons a week, once five on five successive days, and another time five sermons in only two days. Surely Abigail heard him preach during a part of this strenuous schedule. Details of the courtship cannot be inferred from the record, which only says that on January 23, 1686, Mather kept a secret fast, lying on his study floor "with my mouth in the dust," to lament the unspecified "follies" that might ruin his hopes. "I judged, I loathed, I hated myself, because of those *accursed things*," he said, and begged not only divine forgiveness but also, "notwithstanding all my miscarriages," success in his quest for "*a companion for my life*, by whose prudence, virtue, good nature" he might be assisted in the service of his Master. This time his plea was direct. He claimed that marriage was God's own ordinance and that God had "promised, no *good thing* should be withheld from me." The rest of his language here and later suggests that he did not single out Abigail Phillips as the object of his courtship until a few weeks afterward. In courting her, Mather wrote years later, he tried to make his conduct analogous to the sacred methods by which he thought Jesus "engages the hearts of His elect unto Himself . . . But, alas," Mather conceded, "I am foolish and sinful in all my undertakings."

Beyond the obvious respectability of her prosperous father,* and the fact that she married Mather a month before her sixteenth birthday, we know almost nothing about Abigail Phillips. Throughout the sixteen years of their marriage, this young woman followed the widespread custom of referring to her husband as Mr. Mather. Considering their respective ages and positions at the time of their wedding, we may infer that she held him in some awe and that he became her teacher in other matters than spiritual ones. The scant evidence that survives seems clearly to show that he took great delight in her and that he loved her as well as he could. Long after the death of their own son, for whom Mather had composed the first part of his "Paterna," Mather scrupulously crossed out the identifi-

---

*John Phillips was elected in 1685 to the rank of captain in the Ancient and Honorable Artillery Company, and elected or appointed to several other important offices during the next thirty years: the Committee of Safety and the Governor's Council in 1691; Treasurer of the Province of Massachusetts in 1692 and 1693; Judge of the Court of Common Pleas for Middlesex County, 1702-1715; and commissioner to negotiate with the Indians in 1698 and 1701. See Thomas J. Holmes, *Cotton Mather: A Bibliography* (Cambridge, Mass., 1940), III, 1003, n. 1.

cation of this first bride as the mother of the new son to whom "Paterna" was addressed, for this surviving son was the child of the
second Mrs. Mather. But with equal scrupulosity Mather left un-
changed in his manuscript the language that praised Abigail Phillips Mather not only as "a lovely and worthy young gentlewoman,
whom God made a comfort and blessing to me," but also as proof
that "never anybody saw more sensible answers of prayer in a *marriage*, than your poor father did in his."

Their wedding on May 4, 1686, was a splendid affair. In the
weeks before the ceremony, Mather had been characteristically afflicted with a number of doubts and anxieties: fears, prompted by
Cheever's disgrace, lest his own name should cause dishonor to religion and his family; intimations that some people in the town dis-
liked him; resolutions to pity those who were prejudiced against
him. But the wedding itself brought on him a period of joyous celebration. On the morning before the ceremony he felt his prayers rewarded with "celestial and unutterable satisfactions," assurances
that his marriage would be blessed. And later on, in the Phillips
family's garden in Charlestown, as he waited for the guests to appear, he read over the story of the wedding in the second chapter of
John, wherein Jesus turns the water into wine. Now Mather felt another surge of divine reassurance. He was married by Major John
Richards, a member of his own congregation whose relationship to
him would become important during the witchcraft trials of 1692.

The effect of Mather's new status can be seen in the sermons that
he preached on the two Sabbaths after his wedding. On the ninth he
preached in Charlestown on the Psalmist's warning to those whose
"portion is in this life" only, and he conceded (at least in his diary)
that he himself feared being put off with only a worldly portion—
"now that I had received so good an one, *in*, as well as *with*, my consort." And on the sixteenth he preached in Charlestown again, on
*divine delights*. His bride, her dowry, his ministry, and his apparent
spiritual condition all gave him occasion to rejoice. Not even the
unexpected birth of a child (May 11, 1686) to his father's unmarried
housemaid, a member of their church, restrains the joy in these
pages.

THE POLITICAL ORDER, however, had gone through what appeared to
be its final change, with ominous meaning for the Congregational

churches. For months the Massachusetts government's difficulties and quarrels had increased. On May 12, the authorities held their annual election, once again without legal basis in any valid charter. Samuel Shrimpton had dared to say publicly that the Governor and Company of Massachusetts no longer existed, and Governor Bradstreet's furious response, though it did belatedly lead to an indictment charging Shrimpton with sedition, only underlined the essential truth of Shrimpton's declaration. Before Shrimpton could even be tried for an offense that in earlier days would have brought swift punishment, the long-awaited royal emissary did arrive with a commission for the new government. Bearing the commission in the frigate that arrived on May 14 was not the dreaded Colonel Percy Kirke but the despised Edward Randolph. And the temporary President of the new government was to be Joseph Dudley, who had failed only two days earlier to win reelection as a magistrate.

The new government had a completely different form from the old. It would contain no house of deputies, and none of its officials would be elected by the freemen. Not only the President and the Deputy President but all sixteen members of the Council were to be appointed. They could not enact any laws or collect any new taxes. Both Joseph Dudley and William Stoughton, the new President and Deputy President, were well known to have favored submission to the Crown since the days of Charles II, and to have hesitated to accept their election as magistrates in 1685, after the charter had been revoked. Both were from good Congregationalist families, however, and Stoughton had taken both a first and a second degree at Harvard. Within a few years his all too selectively orthodox readings of scriptural law would help to destroy the convicted witches at Salem. Now he seemed to defenders of the old charter to be willing to acquiesce in the destruction not only of Congregationalists' privileges but of Englishmen's liberties.

During the first week some individual and concerted gestures in Boston expressed the passionate intensity of the continuing desire to resist. Samuel Willard omitted from his May sixteenth service his customary prayers for the Governor or government, but "spake so as implied it to be changed or changing." Willard, John Phillips, Increase Mather, and others tried to dissuade Dudley and Stoughton from accepting their new offices. Apparently preferring a militant protest, Willard, both Mathers, and John Richards stayed away from a prayer service that Sewall had proposed as a moderate gesture of concern. Even at the grand scene of the old government's demise on May 17, when Dudley brought the new commission before the magistrates—brought it to them expressly as leading citizens rather than as an official body—signs of resistance abounded. The very gathering of the General Court seemed to say that the old government still existed, and in the crowded room members of the General Court gathered on one side, leaving the new officials to the other. After Joseph Dudley had presented his commission and explained his inability to treat the old government as a corporate body any longer, Deputy Governor Danforth responded by saying he assumed that Dudley would give the General Court some time to draft an appropriate answer. Dudley insisted that he could not recognize the General Court's existence, that he "could no way capitulate with them," whereupon Danforth kept silent. Three days later, however, when the old government finally did dissolve itself "provisionally and under protest," it unanimously adopted a reply to Dudley which upheld the right of colonists to English liberties.

Since this document lays the foundation for the political activity of Increase and Cotton Mather in 1688 and 1689, it ought to be reprinted here:

Gentlemen,—We have perused what you left with us as a true copy of his Majesty's commission, showed to us the 17th instant, empowering you for the governing of his Majesty's subjects inhabiting this colony, and other places therein mentioned. You then applied to us, not as a Governor and Company, but (as you were pleased to term us) some of the principal gentlemen and chief inhabitants of the several towns of the Massachusetts, amongst other discourse saying, it concerned us to consider what therein might be thought hard and uneasy. Upon perusal whereof we find, as we conceive,—First, That there is no certain determinate rule for your administration of justice; and that which is, seems to be too arbitrary. Secondly, That the subjects are abridged of their liberty, as Englishmen, both in the matters of legislation and in laying of taxes; and indeed the whole unquestioned privilege of the subject transferred upon yourselves, there not being the least mention of an Assembly in the commission. And therefore we think it highly concerns you to consider whether such a commission be safe for you or us. But, if you are satisfied therein as that you hold yourselves obliged thereby, and do take upon you the government of this people, although we cannot give our assent thereto, yet we hope we shall demean ourselves as true and loyal subjects to his Majesty, and humbly make our addresses unto God, and in due time to our gracious Prince, for our relief.

The tone, of course, though outwardly polite, was calculated to offend. The authors did not even concede that the document purporting to be a true copy of the royal commission was genuine, and at the end they warned that they would continue to seek relief from the King. But the central point for the political future of Cotton Mather is the articulation of English liberties.

Ceremonies of loss and of token resistance did continue throughout the spring and summer, for even those old magistrates who, like Samuel Sewall, saw no alternative to submission could not easily abandon the institutions and the hope of half a century. On May 21 the magistrates had to give up the keys to the fort. Old Samuel Nowell, who was now to head a small private committee charged with preserving records of Indian treaties and other records concerning land title and the charter, led a prayer for forgiveness and "thanked God for our hithertos of mercy 56 years later, in which time sad calamities" had done greater damage to other peoples. When Nowell also thanked God for what good might be expected "from sundry of those now set over us," Sewall felt himself moved to sing the seventeenth and eighteenth verses of the last chapter of Habakkuk: "For the fig tree shall not flourish, neither shall fruit be in the vines: the labor of the olive shall fail, and the fields shall yield no meat: the sheep shall be cut off from the fold, and there shall be no bullock in the stalls. But I will rejoice in the Lord: I will joy in the God of my salvation." Many men wept during the prayers, and the Marshal-General wept as he declared the Court in adjournment until the second Wednesday of October.

Some of the artillery companies indicated varying kinds of reluctance or opposition to participating in ceremonies proclaiming the new government. When Randolph sought permission for the Anglican minister to conduct his services in one of the three meeting-houses, all that was granted was permission to use the east end of the Town House. Nobody that Samuel Sewall knew of went out to meet President Dudley when he made his first formal entry into Boston, but Sewall and others, including most of the ministers, did agree to meet with Dudley and the Council. Sewall did take the oath of allegiance on June 11 as captain of the artillery company, but Captain Hutchinson and others refused to take the oath, and Sewall himself insisted on the Puritan way of swearing. He would not kiss the Bible; he held it in his left hand and raised his right hand toward Heaven.

Sewall was also distressed at the command to return the cross to his artillery company's flag. Ever since John Endicott and Roger Williams had provoked anxious anger in the 1630s by cutting out the cross as an idolatrous image, a compromise had allowed the artillery companies to march under ensigns without the cross, whereas the cross did fly in the flag over the castle. On August 23, Sewall tried to resign his commission, but was refused.

Resentful Congregationalists were further irritated by customary actions of the invaders which were more insistently obtrusive than the performance of Anglican liturgy. A raucous group, "inflamed with drink," not only sang lustily as they rode home to Boston from a party in Roxbury one Friday night, but also stopped to "drink healths, curse, swear, talk profanely and bawdily to the great disturbance of the town and grief of good people." And on Saturday, September 25, the celebrants of the Queen's birthday, having obeyed an old ordinance against beating drums and building bonfires in the town, fired their ships' guns in the harbor during the day and built a great fire on Castle Island that night, profaning with their loud huzzahs what the Puritans still regarded as the first hours of the Sabbath. Drums and guns sounded again on the King's birthday in October, the day after the Wednesday on which the defunct General Court had planned, but had proved unable, to meet.

Toward the end of December, then, the final indignities appeared. Sir Edmund Andros, the new royal governor of the Dominion of New England, arrived in a laced scarlet coat and was greeted ceremonially by President Dudley and the guards of the eight military companies. He took the oath as Governor, announced that his commission gave him power to appoint new members of the Council, and declared that one of the Congregationalist meetinghouses might well serve for Anglican worship. Increase Mather did attend a dinner for the Governor that night and did ask the blessing before the meal, but on the next day both Increase and Cotton Mather joined with the elders and leading brethren of all the congregations in declaring that they could not conscientiously allow Anglican services to be held in their meetinghouses. On Christmas Eve a company of sixty redcoats, the first that had ever been settled in Boston, landed and marched through the town to Fort Hill. And on Christmas Day Sir Edmund Andros, the first governor who had pointedly neglected to attend the Thursday Lecture in Boston, marched through the town twice to attend the Anglican services. Samuel Sewall noted with some satisfaction that most of the shops were still open, but the sight of the Governor, flanked by a redcoat and a local captain, marching to worship in the Town House led Sewall to read the chapters in Isaiah that promise destruction of Babylonian idols and the deliverance of God's people.

THROUGH ALL this trouble Cotton Mather made common cause with his father and the other ministers, but a variety of circumstances led him for a time to concentrate more on piety than on politics. Once Dudley and Stoughton were in office, however strongly one might have preferred that they refuse to serve, the only hope for the righteous was to exert what influence one could here while hoping that some relief would eventually come from abroad. Mather was convinced that New England would be delivered before the Millennium, which he soon began to calculate for 1697. He continued to devote all his public energy to a heavy schedule of preaching, to a steady round of visits to all the households in his neighborhood, and to a new kind of teaching. During these months his personal life was so happy and his pastoral work so successful that for the first time in several years he was able to separate them from the kind of emotions brought on by the apparent fate of the colony. He did of course complain about the institution of Anglican services in Boston, and in September he did preach a sermon on military duties to the Middlesex County Artillery Company, whose invitation he understandably interpreted as an unusual compliment to a young minister from outside the company's own boundaries. But he concentrated his greatest attention on his new duties as a husband and the new religious opportunities that his marital status offered him.

At first his residence with his bride's family in Charlestown, which he left only on Lord's Days to preside at services in his church in Boston, helped to influence this division, but even after he and Abigail moved into the house that Increase Mather had occupied for two years after the fire of 1677 his domestic and pastoral concerns predominated. A heavy cold in September caused him so high a fever that he thought he might die. Since the cold came on during a nightmare in which Mather saw his dead friend Thomas Shepard alive in the room, he thought he had foreseen his own death. In the dream Mather had tried to "slip out of the room" because he knew Shepard was dead, but Shepard had "nimbly" followed him, had taken his hand, and had said, "Sir, you need not be so shy of me, for you shall quickly be as I am, and where I am." Mather felt that the nightmare itself had nearly killed him, but during the illness he felt himself much less afraid of death than he had been before. When he recovered, he held a day of thanksgiving for all his blessings, especially the divine gift that Providence had made him of "a good thing, a meet help, an extremely desirable companion for my joys and griefs." He was delighted to be settled in a family of his own, where he felt that he was "surrounded with all the blessings of goodness." In return he promised to do what he could toward his "dear consort's" salvation, praying daily with her as well as for her. At morning prayers with her, he read a chapter or part of a chapter in the Bible, and in the evening he gave a short meditation, for their mutual benefit, on a text from the Bible or "a head of divinity."

The house, too, was a great comfort to him. Any house of his own would have given him some satisfaction. The spacious building in which his father had lived with a large family made Cotton Mather's sense of independent maturity at twenty-three all the more gratifying. He now began to receive neighbors there at an open house every Lord's Day evening, for an hour of prayers and Psalm singing and a repetition of the main points of the day's sermons. At this regular meeting, he said, the wholly voluntary attendance usually exceeded one hundred.

He also used the house as a meeting place for the new seminar that he had begun in 1685. This was the occasion for his new method of teaching. He chose a number of recent Harvard graduates and invited them to meet with him once a week in his study for "a course of disputation upon the body of divinity." They took up a number of the central controversies that had been debated in the church over the centuries. Mather himself always served as the moderator, until the final minutes, when he concluded the discussion with a decisive argument that "established the *truth*, defended by the respondent." Although it is hard to imagine that these discussions were entirely free in the range of speculation, Mather did distinguish between the major questions disputed and the "multitudes" of minor questions. The minor ones he "laboriously gathered up" and distributed at meetings, so that the scholars as well as he himself could come to the next meeting "prepared with *brief*, but *strong* and *proved* answers to them." He apparently shared equally with them in these assignments, and despite his belief that true answers could eventually be proved, his attitude toward the mutual benefit of these meetings is admirable. "It is incredible," he said, "how much we advantaged ourselves by these exercises."

It was in this house, too, that he established the practice that he and Abigail observed for the rest of their life together. After the hours of communal reading or private study that followed evening prayers, they met again to sing a verse or two of a Psalm before going to bed, and they always ended with one variation or another of the last verse of the fourth Psalm, sometimes in Mather's own version:

> In peace with God, and far from fear,
> I'll now lie down to rest;
> My God, in thy kind love and care,
> Safe and forever blest.

In January 1687 he learned that Abigail had conceived a child. Not only one but many good things seemed to have been reserved for him in that house. In one of his meditations on a private day of thanksgiving, he had gone from room to room of the "richly furnished" building, reminding himself that although an owner he was really a steward. "With a ravished soul," he wrote later, he "gave everything back to God, variously *contriving*" and promising ways by which he would make it all serviceable to God's glory.

Before twelve more months had passed he was given sad reason to remember that he had given everything back to God. His first child, Abigail, "perhaps one of the comeliest infants that has been seen in the world," was born on August 22, 1687, but at the age of five months she had a sudden, fatal attack of convulsions. She was only the first of thirteen children whom this affectionate father would survive. At her funeral, as at many others that would later oblige him to speak within a day or two after a child, a wife, a mother of his had died, he managed to apply a strong measure of divine meaning to the occasion, but he remembered years later that her death had been "a particular trial" for him. Writing for his son in that reminiscence, he said that he had often resisted invitations to notice little Abigail's "lovely features and actions . . . 'No,' " he now said he had usually replied, " ' 'tis mortal, and I will not entangle my affections with it!' " His rationalizing memory told him that God had enabled him to "reap the benefit of this disengagedness" by giving him the strength to preach a sermon comforting his wife and teaching his neighbors. Even in retrospect, however, as he remembered that he had striven to have "right thoughts in sad hours," he could only hope that he had actually glorified the Lord as he had kept repeating to himself, "God will never hurt me! My God will never do me any harm!"

The sermon itself, one of the best he ever wrote, indicates clearly enough that his affections were still entangled with the child as he sought to explain the meaning of afflictions on the very afternoon of her death. He chose his text from Jacob's lament in Genesis 42:36: "Me have ye bereaved of my children; Joseph is not, and Simeon is not—all these things are against me." Although Mather (quoting Chrysostom) said these words gave fit expression to "the relenting bowels of a parent," he denied that they "so well become the grace, the faith, the patience of a Christian." He analyzed Jacob's lament in the plainest of modern paraphrases to show that

> the happy event proved him egregiously *mistaken* here; "Joseph is not," said he; yet, *he was;* and his father had no cause to be sorry that he was *what he was:* "Simeon is not," said he; yet *he was,* and his father might have been starved, if he had not been *where he was.* Those things, which he so fondly counted *against him,* were the very things that not only tried his *grace,* but also saved his *life.* Let us admit the deplored *child* [Joseph] himself to correct the sad *mistake;* he said afterwards, in Gen. 50.20. *God meant it unto good.*

The people of God, Mather insisted, too often conclude erroneously that God's "afflictive dispensations" toward them are harmful "or but a little to their benefit." As the typological descendants of Jacob, he said, all Christians "must even in a peculiar manner" expect to be like him—along with Timothy, Lazarus, Elijah, David, Job, and Paul. "The Christian that promises himself an immunity from afflictions in this evil world, is indeed a *Christian* only in the *Italian,* wicked, scoffing usage of the word, that is, a *fool."* We are promised a quiet haven, he conceded. "But where? But when? Truly, this *Bliss-land* is not on this side the water; it is a *land afar off,* and we shall not see it, until we put ashore at the *land flowing with milk and honey,* beyond the stars."

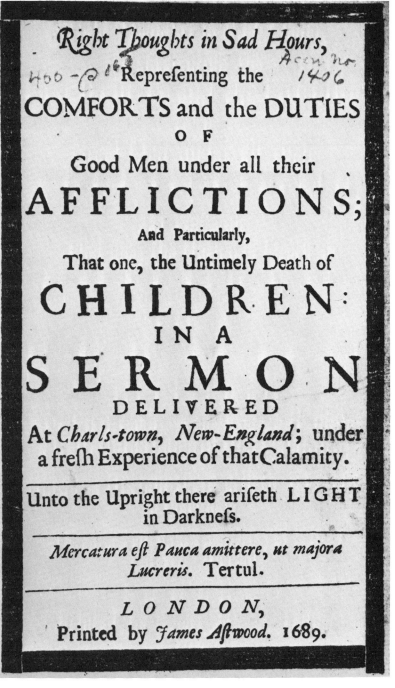

*Right Thoughts in Sad Hours,*
Reprefenting the
**COMFORTS** and the **DUTIES**
O F
Good Men under all their
**AFFLICTIONS;**
And Particularly,
That one, the Untimely Death of
**CHILDREN:**
**IN A**
**SERMON**
DELIVERED
At *Charls-town*, *New-England*; under
a frefh Experience of that Calamity.

Unto the Upright there arifeth **LIGHT**
in Darknefs.

*Mercatura eft Pauca amittere, ut majora*
*Lucreris.* Tertul.

*L O N D O N,*
Printed by *James Aftwood*. 1689.

8. Title page of *Right Thoughts in Sad Hours,*
Cotton Mather's sermon on the death of his daughter.

The argument that this young father brought to bear a few weeks before his twenty-fifth birthday so that his wife, who was not yet eighteen, might rise to her duty of acquiescence begins, then, in Genesis, but its main roots are in the Book of Job. All griefs, Mather says, even those that come to you by way of Satan, are ordered by the very God who numbers the hairs on your head. "Not so much as the *tongue* of a *dog* will ever stir against thee, unless managed by the *Hand* of the Lord." We misunderstand because our flesh "cannot forbear to shriek, I am hurt," and because God's methods for our good, though glorious, "are also very *obscure*." We must never forget the Devil's power to deceive. "The *Accuser of men* to God, is also an *accuser of God* to men." Satan will claim that your God has forgotten you, and you will often "give that mean, that shameful, that pitiful account" of yourself that is found in the second verse of the seventy-second Psalm: "In the day of my trouble, my soul refused to be comforted." If like Jacob (or the chastened Job) we say all these things are against us, rather than (Romans 3:28) "all things shall work together for good," we wrong both God's kindness ("Whom I love, I rebuke and chasten," Rev. 3:19) and His wisdom ("What I do, thou knowest not now, but thou shalt know hereafter").

The first use of these doctrines — that of due faith and patience — obliged Mather to make one of his few allusions to his own grief: "I am this day visited myself with the *sudden death of a dear and only child*." To edify his auditors, most of whom he was sure had experienced the same kind of affliction, he offered to consider the very thoughts with which "I would this day quiet my own tempestuous rebellious heart." Perhaps one purpose of his own affliction had been to enable him "more feelingly [to] speak a word in season" to other afflicted people. With Jacob's example before him, he exhorted all the people to refuse to assume that any affliction was "utterly against us." To the "talking sorrow" of people who would not be comforted, he requested one commanding answer: "Eternal *silence* unto thee now, O thou inordinate *passion*, before the Lord."

But there were a dozen comforts as well. No better than Jacob, who would have starved had Joseph the Provider not been absent in Egypt, could Mather's auditors know what was best for themselves; even in their worldly affairs the very things they lamented losing might have been the worse for them. The living child might have

grown to suffer and to bring them even more grief, and to go to per-
dition rather than to the Heaven that the covenant gave good reason
to hope for. Affliction, moreover, forces us to know God better,
forces us to see His sovereignty; and to know Christ better, because
we may be reminded in our grief that our afflictions are less than
those He suffered: "Bad weather in the world makes afflicted men to
keep their eyes much upon the *Light shining in a dark place* unto
them." Affliction teaches us to know ourselves better: "*A wound*
will convince an *Emperor* that he is a *man.*" It also teaches us what
religion is: "The fear of the Lord is the beginning of wisdom." Affliction teaches us to wean our affections from the wrong objects, for
(as Tertullian long ago warned us) idolatry is "the grand crime of
mankind: Affliction mortifies that *rebellion*; therefore, *David*, are
thy children cut off; therefore, Jacob, is the wife of thy bosom
snatched out of it." God will "cause creatures to be our *grief* that
they may not be our *god.*" By afflictions He "is as it were pounding
or grinding of his rare spices in your souls, the scent of them will
now become very fragrant, very glorious."

Mather's general advice, then, urges repentance, patience, faith:
"Though He slay me, yet will I trust in Him." (Job 13:15) And in the
special case of the dead child he reminds himself, his wife, and other
bereaved parents that they must be "believing parents." In an image
used by Ben Jonson in a splendid poem on the death of his own son,
Mather insists that "our children [who were on loan] are not lost,
but given back." To Cotton and Abigail Mather the loss of the child
is "like the tearing off of a limb," but they must remember their obligation to pluck out an eye for sin. Was the infant "very pretty"?
Well, "at the Resurrection we will see the dear lambs again." Since
the promise of the covenant gave the child a place in "the sweet
Bosom of Jesus," Mather said he heard the spirits of all such children "crying aloud unto us, 'As well as you love us, we would not be
with you again. . . . Count not yourselves at home till you come to
be, as we, forever with the Lord." In conclusion he said that "the fit
epitaph of a dead infant" ought to be an adequate "*solace* of a sad
parent, *Of such is the Kingdom of Heaven.*"

Beyond saying that he took his wife with him to his study for the
day of fasting and prayer that he observed soon afterward, Mather
does not say how she expressed her grief or responded to his arguments and consolation, but we have good evidence of Samuel Sew-

all's response to this sermon. Sewall, whose diary had already criticized some of Mather's pulpit rhetoric, found *Right Thoughts in Sad Hours* so appropriate for his own condition that he financed its publication, and both he and Mather had the satisfaction of seeing it reprinted more than once. Sewall himself had lost two very young sons in the mid-1680s, and Mather noted in the preface, which dedicated the book affectionately to Sewall, that those boys had died of the same affliction that had killed his Abigail. Sewall, moreover, added at the end of the 1689 edition an excerpt from a letter of consolation by Edward Taylor, the poet and preacher of Westfield, Massachusetts, consoling Sewall on the death of one of the sons and concluding with some lines from the poem that has been often reprinted in our own day as *On Wedlock and the Death of Children.*

With *Right Thoughts in Sad Hours*, Cotton Mather appeared before the community in the most attractive, the most sympathetic position of his life. He had already warmed the community's attitude toward him by his compassionate yet unequivocal participation in the drama of James Morgan's execution, and in the witty self-deprecation with which he had introduced his sermon to the artillery company. Now he appeared as the bereaved young father addressing the traditional arguments of Jewish and Christian wisdom to his own grief and that of his very young wife. We can be sure that his grief showed in his presence and his voice as well as his language on that winter afternoon, and that the tough vigor of his relatively plain, epigrammatic sentences seemed to at least some of his auditors a proper vehicle for the sad wisdom of their creed. Two other crises in the summer of 1688 brought him to the eminence at which he could speak credibly as the voice of the people in Boston's version of the Glorious Revolution.

# V

## *Witchcraft and Revolution*

This Week, dream'd, that being left alone, I was putt upon preaching a Sermon publickly, for which I had no Time to prepare aforehand. I dream'd, that being driven to this extemporaneous Extremity, I preached a Sermon upon those Words, *I will never leave thee, nor forsake thee.* The Thoughts, which I had upon this Text, in my Sleep, were so proper and so lively, and I could, after I awoke, remember so many of them, that indeed, I preached the *Lords-Day* following upon that very Text.

Cotton Mather, *Diary,* April 1688

COTTON MATHER had to face these new challenges without the support of his father. In earlier years the absence of Increase Mather for more than a few days might have constituted a crisis by itself. Even now the emotional cost, which became evident in a letter written by the son after his father had been in London for two years, was magnified by a much larger burden of work. But the comforting support of Abigail and the still novel pleasure of acting on his own and receiving the brethren in his own household combined with a sense of patriotism, and with thanksgiving for his father's narrow escape, to help him accept that deprivation as a necessary sacrifice.

Increase Mather's celebrated escape from New England gives an ironic balance to his reluctant departure from England in 1661. Forced to leave Restoration England rather than take the oath of conformity or give up his vocation to preach, Mather had often dreamed during the next quarter century of returning one day to perform valuable services for the Lord in a theater worthy of his gifts. Since the publication of his actual letters defending the old charter in 1684, and of the forged letter printed over his initials, he had been marked as an enemy of the Crown by Edward Randolph,

who once called him "the bellows of sedition and treason." In complaining to Joseph Dudley about the forged letter, Increase Mather
had now imprudently declared that the forger was Randolph himself, whom he denounced as "a great knave." Soon after the congregations of Boston voted in October 1687 to send an agent to London, Increase Mather was chosen, his church granted its unanimous
consent, and (on Christmas Eve) Randolph had him arrested and
charged with defamation. A Boston jury acquitted Mather on January 31, and he was now free, he believed, to sail for England. Randolph, however, tried to have him arrested a second time on what
one must presume was an additional pretext of defamation. For several days Mather avoided receiving the new warrant, as rumors of
his actual arrest were accepted throughout the town. Warned by
friends on Friday night, March 30, that he would be arrested if he
tried to preach on the Lord's Day, he put on a disguise, walked past
the agent who was watching his house, took refuge in the Charlestown home of Cotton Mather's father-in-law, and the next night
made his way to Rumney Marsh, where he hid until his sons Cotton
and Samuel joined him the following Tuesday. They helped him to
keep a rendezvous with a fishing ketch, which at last (April 7) got
him and thirteen-year-old Samuel safely onto Captain Tanner's ship
*The President* — just in time, Cotton Mather claimed, to escape the
vessels that Randolph had sent out to prevent them from getting
aboard. Fleeing his native Massachusetts in the night, Increase
Mather thus went to seek redress from the Roman Catholic brother
of the king whose oath of Anglican conformity had driven him back
to Massachusetts in 1661. And his ostensible message was a letter,
unanimously approved by his congregation, thanking the King for
his willingness to "promise us the free exercise of our religion."

The escape of Increase Mather also served to liberate his eldest
son. Left alone with the responsibilities of his large congregation,
Cotton Mather was now ready to take his own place in the great
world. Besides serving his long novitiate in his father's church, he
had been conducting church affairs alone during his father's extended absences in Cambridge, and of course he and Abigail had
been entertaining large groups at their weekly open house. That
amenity had to be given up some time after Increase Mather's departure, because the double duty of Teacher and Pastor demanded
so much of Cotton's energy, but it had given him valuable experi-

9. Portrait of Increase Mather in London, 1688.
From a photograph of the painting by Van Der Spriett.

ence in his new role. During the summer and autumn of 1688 he
found himself comfortable as representative of the family and the
church at the tables of Governor Andros, Samuel Sewall, and a representative of the Duke of Albemarle, whose yacht visited Boston
harbor early in September and provided dinner and music for Sewall, Mather, and other guests. With Increase Mather absent it was
Cotton Mather who went to Sewall's house in mid-April with the
news of two new appointments to the Governor's Council. It was
Cotton Mather alone who presided in the North Church at the first
service attended by the returning hero William Phips, discoverer of
one of the richest treasures ever raised from a sunken Spanish galleon.

Throughout the summer and autumn of 1688, moreover, Mather
was also deeply concerned in the town's responses to political, military, and religious dangers. The Anglicans had managed after all to
intrude temporarily into the South meetinghouse, sharing it impatiently between the morning and afternoon services of its owners,
whose morning service occasionally droned beyond noon. Mr. Willard and his congregation (apparently with some help from Joseph
Dudley) resisted Governor Andros' threats and demands after inevitable conflicts between Congregational and Anglican practices had
enraged the Governor. Mather was also outraged by the new government's assaults on colonists' title to their lands, challenges that
obliged faithful subjects like Samuel Sewall, for example, to petition
for patents for land they had held for forty years. Mather deplored
the new government's insistence on arresting and fining conscientious Puritans who, though perfectly willing to be sworn in court,
would not place their hands on the Bible when they took their oath.
And of course Mather participated in the fast called on August 23
after an Indian attack on Northfield had killed "5 English persons."
Mather and others suspected the new governor of deep complicity in
the Indian and French attacks upon Maine that began what Mather
later called the grievous decade. At the mustering of some conscripted men to fight in the autumn of 1688, he preached a sermon
on the distinction between just and unjust wars.

Yet the two crises that made the greatest demands on him in that
important year touched him much more personally than did the
political events after his father's departure. Each of these crises led
him to publish a book in 1689, and his conduct in both of them

strengthened his growing reputation as a mature young preacher. The book that he published about one of them helped to ruin his reputation for nearly three centuries. He would not have been greatly surprised by this misfortune, for before he had completed his manuscript he and several bystanders plainly heard the demons who "possessed" a young girl threaten him with disgrace if he should persist in his efforts to publish the book.

The witchcraft case began in midsummer. Four children of John Goodwin, a God-fearing mason from the neighborhood of the South Church, were afflicted with "strange fits," more extreme than epileptic or "cataleptic" seizures. Thirteen-year-old Martha, the eldest daughter, had offended the family's laundrywoman by asking her about some missing linen. The laundrywoman's mother was an Irish widow named Glover, whose husband had sometimes called her a witch. In defending her daughter, Goodwife Glover had cursed Martha Goodwin, whose fits had come on almost at once. Soon the malady infected three of the other five Goodwin children, and all four victims were periodically tormented by a variety of strange symptoms:

> Sometimes they would be deaf, sometimes dumb, and sometimes blind, and often, all this at once. One while their tongues would be drawn down their throats; another while they would be pulled out upon their chins, to a prodigious length. They would have their mouths opened unto such a wideness, that their jaws went out of joint; and anon they would clap together again with a force like that of a strong spring-lock. The same would happen to their shoulder-blades, and their elbows, and hand-wrists, and several of their joints.

Sometimes they would be completely numb. Then their extremities would be drawn together as if the poor children had been tied neck at heels. Suddenly again they would be stretched out and bent backward so far that the adults who came to observe them "feared the very skin of their bellies would have cracked." The children would cry that they were cut with knives, and beaten with clubs. Their necks would appear to be broken, so limp that the *"neck-bone would seem dissolved"* to the adults who anxiously tried to feel it; *"and yet on the sudden, it would become again so stiff"* that the adults could not make the head move at all.

Bostonians, as Cotton Mather would say later, had as much mother wit as any other people. As soon as the physician, Dr.

Thomas Oakes, was called in to examine the children, the adults did what they could to make sure that the children were not dissembling. Although nothing would have been "more unreasonable than to imagine" that any pretense could cause such extreme fits, Dr. Oakes and the ministers of the town, whom he promptly advised the children's father to consult, contrived to arrange some "experiments" which made it "perfectly impossible for any dissimulation" to hoodwink them. The first, obvious requirement was to separate the children from one another. Then, even when unable to see or hear one another, the children were all afflicted at the same time and, respectively, in the same part of the body. Their "pains and sprains were swift like lightning," but when "the *neck,* or the *hand,* or the *back* of one was racked, so it was at that instant with t'other too." The diagnosis was bewitchment.

Long before autumn, the Goodwin house became a kind of medical theater. There the curious might observe mysterious phenomena which were at once frightening, pathetic, edifying, and (one could notice without meaning to exploit the poor children) entertaining. The children, so obviously tormented during the day, were fortunately able to take good nourishment and to sleep after about nine or ten o'clock at night.

Nobody knows exactly how the magistrates were informed of the witchcraft, but especially in that time of political and military trouble no specific complaint against Goodwife Glover was needed before the judicial authority could act. One of the main arguments for the existence of witches in the world was the express command in Exodus (22:18): "Thou shalt not suffer a witch to live." Ignoring the evidence might well bring more trouble on the colony. Whether or not Cotton Mather was accurate in saying that the magistrates heard about the witchcraft case and inquired into it, the accused woman would sooner or later have been brought before them. John Goodwin, Mather was careful to report, "had no proof that could have done" the woman "any hurt," but when she was brought in to be interrogated she found herself unable to deny her guilt.

Here, as in the Salem trials three years later, the magistrate's role resembled that of a modern police interrogator or a district attorney before a grand jury, so that wide-ranging questions designed to elicit the defendant's attitude, and perhaps to induce confusion and therefore a confession, were generally accepted even by those who, like Cotton Mather, saw a clear distinction between being disagreeable (or wicked) and being guilty of witchcraft. At this distance one cannot tell any more clearly than Goodwife Glover's interrogators could tell how much of the proceedings (beyond her obvious peril) the defendant understood. When asked whether she believed in God, she gave what was considered a blasphemous answer—presumably in English, although later on she was able to participate only through two interpreters who understood some of her Gaelic. A Roman Catholic, she also had great difficulty reciting the Lord's Prayer, stumbling again and again when "the experiment" was made during her interrogation, although "clause after clause was most carefully repeated unto her."

Experiments of this kind were admittedly dangerous to both the defendant and the community, as Increase Mather had plainly warned in his chapters on witchcraft in *Illustrious Providences*. The Devil, after all, might tie the tongue of a defendant who had never been a witch. The Lord's people were expressly forbidden to use the Devil's charms for any purpose, good or evil. Papists, Increase Mather had said, might use such devices, just as they would keep urine in a bottle, or nail horseshoes over doors, or "stick the house round with bays" to ward off evil spirits. Obedient Christians should know that such methods sought to heal with the Devil's, and not God's, aid. Throughout the summer the pious Goodwin family had rejected all such superstitious remedies. The only way to get rid of witches was to pray and to hope. The four leading ministers, Cotton Mather among them, held a day of prayer at the Goodwin house; the youngest child, aged four or five, recovered at once. But the magistrates and Cotton Mather apparently believed in the autumn of 1688 that the Lord's Prayer test was a justifiable experiment if confined to the preliminary examination and if not used formally as evidence against the defendant—if, in other words, its sole legal function was to induce the sort of confusion that might make the defendant confess. The desire for knowledge about the Devil's powers and limitations was another matter. It was that temptation—mixed of course with what he took to be his scholarly and Christian duty—that led Cotton Mather into practices which have damaged his reputation among nineteenth- and twentieth-century readers.

At the trial in November, soon after her indictment, Goody Glover was now able to answer only in Gaelic. At first her interpreters said that she was unable to enter a plea at all; when she did plead, she apparently confessed. In a search of her house several rag puppets, "stuffed with *goat's hair* and other such ingredients," were found. She apparently admitted in court that she had used these to torment her victims, by wetting her finger with spittle and stroking the little dolls. During the first part of the trial she had seemed to stoop and shrink down as if "almost pressed to death with a mighty weight," but when one of these dolls was given to her she immediately straightened up and took it, whereupon one of the Goodwin children "fell into sad *fits,* before the whole assembly." This "experiment" was now repeated, with the same predictable result.

From the skeptical distance of three centuries, Goody Glover's answers at the actual trial seem to be ambiguous, not necessarily a confession of guilt. When asked whether she had anyone to stand by her, for example, she at first said that she had, but then, "looking very pertly in the *air,* she added, 'No, he's gone,'" whereupon she "confessed, that she had *One,* who was her *Prince,* with whom she maintained" what Cotton Mather called "I know not what communion." Her auditors and judges seem unanimously to have interpreted these statements as a confession of her guilt during the trial, and some of them heard their judgment confirmed the next night. In the prison itself they overheard her "expostulating with a *Devil,* for his thus deserting her; telling him that *because he had served her so basely and falsely, she had confessed all.*" Five or six physicians then examined her to see whether "*folly* and *madness*" had mistakenly brought her the "reputation of a *witch.*" When several hours of such interrogation elicited only "pertinent and agreeable" answers, she was doomed. Tales about her past conduct began to circulate after she was sentenced to be hanged, and one dreadful incident in the jail seemed to Cotton Mather to confirm her guilt.

A six-year-old boy who had been afflicted, complained to his parents that "the shape of a black thing with a blue cap" had tormented him, and had thrust a hand into his bed in an effort to pull out his bowels. The boy's mother went to the jail to ask the convicted witch why she had tormented the child. The condemned woman not only gave a reason ("because of wrong done to herself and daughter") but also said, "I was in your house last night." When the afflicted boy's mother asked in what shape she had entered the house, Glover replied, "As a black thing with a blue cap." She admitted that she had tried to disembowel the boy, but she agreed to wish him well when the mother brought him to see her in jail, and after she kept her word, he recovered.

When Cotton Mather interviewed Goody Glover in jail, she did not deny her guilt. Mather recognized the linguistic difficulties, even the alleged use of a single word "in Irish" to signify both *spirits* and *saints*. But he could not mistake the interpreter's statement that Glover had four confederates, nor could he mistake the names. One major difference between this case and the Salem outbreak four years later is that Mather alone (and the anonymous interpreter) knew the names of Glover's alleged confederates, whereas the first witch accused in Salem Village in 1692 not only confessed in open court but publicly accused two women of collaborating with her.

Mather insisted on praying for Goody Glover despite her protest that she could pray for herself, and when he told her that he had to pray for her because he pitied her, she thanked him "with many good words." On her way to the execution she told him that her death would not relieve the Goodwin children's affliction, because others were also guilty. This time she named only one confederate, and Mather never revealed the name, although he did imply in the book he published the following spring that she had accused her own daughter. Nothing was ever done to accuse or interrogate the women Glover accused. Not even an "*ob*noxious woman in the town" who was "very credibly *reported*" to have received an actual wound when an adult struck with his sword at the place where one of the Goodwin boys cried that he saw a tormenting specter — not even that woman, whose name Mather refused to expose for fear of harming the innocent, was charged with any offense.

Goody Glover's prediction proved to be correct. Her execution on November 16, 1688, did not cure the Goodwin children. They barked like dogs and purred like cats. As Mather and other neighbors came in to observe them, the children were struck by invisible cudgels, and the observers noticed with mixed amazement and satisfaction that red streaks quickly appeared where the invisible blows had landed on the children's skin. One boy apparently felt the devils run a spit through his mouth and out at his foot, and on that invisible spit he rolled and roasted on the floor, crying that he was being cooked by an invisible fire. Later his head was nailed to the floor by invisible nails. All the children went limp, then stiff. They flew like geese about the room, "carried with incredible *swiftness* through the *air*, having but just their *toes* now and then upon the ground," and flapping their arms. When they were taken to the house of Mr. Willis, who had a twenty-foot room on the first floor, one of the children *"flew* the length of the room" and — "as it is affirmed," Mather reported — landed securely in an infant's highchair, "none seeing her feet all the way touch the floor."

Repeatedly the skeptical questions that must be asked of such reports did occur to Cotton Mather, but always within a context dominated by two overwhelming arguments from his own experience: the reality of the angel of light who had appeared to him, and the "experiments" in which precautions had been taken to forestall collusion among the afflicted children. Mather frankly saw that denying the existence of devils would threaten one's belief in the existence of angels and perhaps of God Himself. Both his conversion and his angelic vision might have deluded him, he knew, but he felt absolutely convinced that they had come from either God or the Devil. When he noticed that the Goodwin children, who seemed constantly in danger of drowning themselves or falling into the great open fireplace, always avoided serious injury, he no longer thought of suspecting the validity of the diagnosis. He reasoned instead that they must have their good angels as well as bad, to prevent what the devils were trying to do to the poor victims. And when he took Martha, the thirteen-year-old, into his own household, his explicit purpose was not only to cure her but also, without the slightest skepticism about the nature of her affliction, to observe her symptoms and the devils' powers at length, and to accumulate "*evidence* and *argument* as a critical eye-witness to confute the Sadducism of this debauched age."

The seven days following the twentieth of November 1688 were the strangest of Cotton Mather's life. He probably brought Martha Goodwin into the household just after Goody Glover's execution. For the first few days Martha seemed to have recovered so well that she was not only calm but able and willing to pray. On the morning of the twentieth, however, she suddenly cried out, "Ah, you have found me out! I thought it would be so!" and her fits immediately came over her again. One can hardly imagine how Abigail Mather coped with this wild intrusion of an adolescent only four or five years younger than herself, but her husband left a clear record both of what he saw and of what he failed to see. He found himself in the awkward position of trying to do three incompatible things at once. He had to fight the devils who possessed Martha, he wanted to study their behavior, and of course he wanted to cure the afflicted child. His fascinated curiosity and his desire to confute skeptics led him to overemphasize his study of the devils' behavior. His relative neglect of the other two purposes prompted him to concentrate on one of them when he did recoil from the temptation to follow his curiosity recklessly. The sexual implications of Martha's behavior, and occasionally of his own unconscious responses, seem obvious now, but except for one or two hints that his vanity had been teased, he seems to have been completely unaware of them. He was preoccupied with scientific observation, medical and spiritual therapy, supernatural warfare.

The strange behavior of Martha and her devils kept the household and Cotton Mather's mind in such a turmoil that one might well understand an utter failure of coherent analysis. On the first day of her renewed fits Martha coughed up a "ball as big as a small egg," choking on it until stroking and drinking brought it down again. As a new fit came on, she would rush to the fireplace and look up the chimney in a strange way, but when asked what she saw there she would be unable to say. Mather told her to cry to the Lord Jesus for help, but as soon as he uttered those words her teeth were set. She could not open her mouth or speak through them. "Yet, child, *look* unto Him," Mather cried, echoing the text of one of his first sermons. Again, as if the devils heard and thwarted him, "her eyes were presently pulled into her head, so far that one might have feared she should never have used them more." When Mather began to pray, her arms were "clapped upon her ears" with great force. Mather stepped forth boldly to engage with the devils — only the first of many times that they or the infatuated, hysterical girl contrived to involve him in physical contact with her — and he violently pulled her hands away from her ears. It was no use. She cried out that the devils made "such a noise, I cannot hear a word!"

These brief periods of torment were followed by extended "frolics," during which Martha spoke for hours with a liveliness and wit beyond her ordinary powers, but at first Mather himself became an actual participant in her struggles only during her afflicted times. She flew — not without touching the ground now and then, but beyond the "ordinary power of Nature, in our opinion of it" — and then dived toward the floor, "on which, if we had not held her, she would have thrown herself." Cotton and Abigail Mather held her back when Martha said that the demons had ordered her to go to the bottom of the well and fish out some silver plate. (A former owner of the house later told the Mathers that there was indeed some plate at the bottom of the well.) When Martha complained of an invisible chain that had been fastened to her, Mather himself knocked it off with his hand. Later, both he and Abigail had to struggle to keep the girl from being pulled into the fire, but even these efforts to help were dangerous. Once when she was being dragged, in a crouching position, from her chair, Mather "gave a stamp on the hearth, just between her and the fire," whereupon Martha "screamed out (though I think she *saw* me *not*) *that I jarred her chain, and hurt her back.*"

During some of her frolics, then, Mather experimented, often with witnesses from outside the house. He demonstrated with some satisfaction that she could not read the Bible; her neck went limp and seemed to be broken when he asked her to read it. Even when someone else in the room tried to read the Bible silently and in a place hidden from her view, she was "cast into very terrible agonies." Once she did read the fifty-ninth Psalm, but then suffered a fit, and Mather walked right into the trap that curiosity set for him. "Poor child," he said to the other observers, "she can't now read the Psalm she read a little while ago."

"But I can read it," Martha said, and she read it when Mather showed her the place.

Totally engaged now, Mather asked her to say "Amen" to it, "but that she could not do." Triumphantly, then, he asked her to read the next Psalm, "but nowhere else in the Bible could she read a word." Now he brought her a Quaker's book, in which she could read everything but the names of God and Christ. Further inquiry showed that she could spell the word *God* but could not pronounce it; that she could read jest-books, the *Oxford Jests* and *Cambridge Jests,* but could not read "good books"; that she could read "very well" a book which tries "to prove, *that there are no witches*"; that she could read "popish" books but not works by Increase Mather, Samuel Willard, Joseph Glanvil. Mather saw that he might now be going too far — especially after Martha suffered "hideous convulsions" when she saw John Cotton's catechism, *Milk for Babes,* and when the mere opening of Increase Mather's book about faith and repentance and the Day of Judgment struck her down "backwards as dead upon the floor"—but he could not resist showing "multitudes of witnesses" that she could read the Book of Common Prayer with ease. (If this experiment seemed to be an insult to the Anglicans whose way of worship had so recently intruded on Boston, Mather advised them, in the book that he finished the following spring, not to blame him but the devils. "I make no reflections" on the phenomenon, he protested ironically, but only report the facts as "a faithful and honest historian.")

The most spectacular of the devices by which Martha and her demons transfixed the attention of the young minister and his fellow observers was an invisible horse. Invited guests came in to stand beside Mather as Martha mounted and rode all over the downstairs. Mather still had some restraint left. When Martha asked him for a knife so that she might cut off the horse's head, he gave her only a sheath. Slashing at her own throat with it as she rode past him, she complained that Mather's "knife" would not cut. But Mather did join other observers in asking her questions about the companions who "rode" with her, and once he became so engrossed that he said, "Child, if you can't tell their names, pray tell me what clothes they have on." Once again she was immediately "laid for *dead* upon the floor."

One of the spectators eventually asked Martha whether the horse could mount the stairs. She immediately rode up to the second floor, followed by several of the observers, and was thrown from the horse when it shied (as she later reported) at the door of Mather's study. The demons, she declared, could not enter the study of a man of God. Once again Mather took the bait, with appropriately modest disclaimers. Whenever the horse and the companions returned to take Martha riding, Mather offered to take her into the sanctuary of his study, where she was (as a skeptic might have predicted) at ease. But she did not go there easily, or without Mather's physical aid. His very invitation sent her into such dreadful fits that

it gave me much trouble to get her into my arms, and much more to drag her up the stairs. She was pulled out of my hands, and when I recovered my hold, she was thrust so hard upon me, that I had almost fallen backwards, by their compressions to detain her . . . With incredible forcing (though she kept screaming, "They say I must not go in!") at length we pulled her in; *where* she was no sooner come, but she could stand on her feet, and with an *altered tone,* could thank me, saying, "Now I am well."

After a minute or two of faintness, she was able to "attend any devotion."

Mather's observation of the poor girl was so solicitous, and so evidently genuine in its several concerns, that one need not suspect her of dissembling in these literally escalating demands on his attention. It is the uncanny blending of pathology, demonology, wish fulfillment, and therapy that gives the episode its human richness, comical though that mixture must now appear to be. When Martha, riding about with her companions after the great struggle that ended in Mather's study, told Mather that her companions wanted to hurt *Mrs.* Mather but that they could not, she rejoiced. Then she revealed to Cotton Mather alone the names of her three tormentors, names which (again) he never disclosed. She reported that her tormentors had admitted she would recover after the day of prayer that was scheduled for November 27 in Mather's house. They were unable to hurt Mr. Mather, she said. But they predicted she would become very ill before she recovered, and they said they would kill her "tonight if I went to bed before ten o'clock, if I told a word."

The day of prayer broke the Enemy's power. Messrs. Morton, Allen, Moody, and Willard joined Mather in trying to pray over the noisy sufferings of the afflicted children, all of whom had been reunited for this concerted assault. Within a little while after the prayers, the children were all perfectly at ease. Martha did have a few more seizures during the winter, most severely in the two days of Mather's preparations for a sermon on witchcraft. But Mather saw that the devils had evidently conspired "to distract me in what I was about," and he wrote his sermon bravely under almost impossible conditions. Martha became saucy and impertinent toward him. She threw things at him — "small things" that would not harm him, he noted — and she got hold once again of his narrative. Although she had often read it, she was now unable to do so. Instead she made an incredible travesty of it, and it was now that she warned him he would "quickly come to disgrace by that history."

During these last "frolics," Mather tried one or two more experiments. He spoke Latin to some Harvard scholars who had stopped in to observe Martha, and they were not surprised to learn that the devils understood that language. He also demonstrated that the *silent* reading of Greek in the New Testament or Hebrew in the Old, an experiment tried more than once, would bring on Martha's fits. Mather asked her if she desired the mercies of God. She was dumb. He asked her to lift her hand if she wanted those mercies. She went stiff. Mather then lifted her hand and asked her to let the hand drop if she wanted God's mercies. Her hand went stiff and remained where he had placed it. Then she began to beat and kick a man who prayed for her, and at last she fell senseless on the floor, her "belly swelled like a drum," as the men prayed above her.

From that time on she grew steadily better, despite one or two possessions each week, until she was completely cured in the spring. In her very last fit she did seem to be dying, and Mather believed that the attack actually was going to kill her. She said "something about the state of the country, which we wondered at"—for it was just about, or soon after, the uprising that overthrew Governor Andros—and "anon, the fit went over." Martha recovered completely. She left the Mather household in June.

Mather did not give his manuscript to the printer until after the governmental crisis had passed, and he bolstered the account with two sermons he had preached on witchcraft, along with an affidavit from John Goodwin which briefly described the main events. Both of the most important truths that Mather said he himself had learned from this amazing experience came to public attention during the Salem witchcraft trials of 1692, and although many historians have understandably remembered only the first of them, both need to be remembered by anyone interested in a fair reading of that catastrophe. Having written nothing but what he judged to be true, and having been with others an eyewitness to many of the events, Mather resolved that from now on he would never "use but just one grain of patience with any man that shall go to impose on me, a denial of *Devils,* or of *witches.*" That purpose, in the lurid context of 1692 and of his experimental curiosity, has been remembered. Less often noticed has been his declaration that *"prayer and faith,* was the thing which drove the *devils* from the *children.*"

※

THE SECOND personal crisis that Cotton Mather had to endure in 1688 was the death of his brother, whose final illness came on in the midst of the excitement about the Goodwin children. Nathanael had moved to Salem to assist in the church there. Although the malignant tumor that was discovered and "opened" late in the summer of 1688 probably had no connection with Nathanael's childhood illnesses, Cotton became convinced that this prodigious youth had killed himself with study. Nathanael had devoured books, Cotton said, and then books devoured him. Born in the miserable summer of Richard Mather's death, when Cotton was six years old, Nathanael had always revered his older brother and had striven to emulate him as well as their illustrious father and grandfathers. Nathanael had been one of Cotton's own pupils after Cotton had graduated from Harvard, and he had copied a number of Cotton's favorite pious devices — meditations, secret days of thanksgiving, the ambitious project of deriving a note and a prayer from every verse of the Bible. He had even joined one of the Young Men's Associations that Cotton had founded in North Boston. Now, in the absence of their father, it was Cotton who had to preside at his deathbed and then to console the family and arrange for the funeral.

Cotton visited him a number of times in September and October and was surprised at first to learn that Nathanael, whose exemplary piety had been evident since he had joined the church in 1683, was unable to express any joy at the prospect of going to Heaven. Nathanael was resigned and calm, and of course he was suffering physical pain. But unlike Thomas Shepard, who had died full of a glorious assurance, Nathanael refused to express any conviction of his own salvation. "Never did I see more caution against hypocrisy," Cotton wrote about him in October. Nathanael would talk to only one or two ministers about such matters, and then only in Latin if others were present — apparently for fear of making an unseemly display. When Cotton sought to console him by asking rhetorically whether he did not think his faith sincere, Nathanael only replied, "I should think so, if it were not for the seventeenth of *Jeremiah,* and the ninth." (Both the ninth and the seventeenth chapters of Jeremiah warn against those who put their trust in man, and against the deceit in man's heart, but the reference may be specifically to the ninth verse of chapter 17: "The heart is deceitful and wicked above all things, who can know it?")

Nathanael held to this position for the rest of his brief life. Cotton found him to be dejected but not despairing, and gracious though not joyful. "He was all made up of longings and breathings after all the *fullness of God,* when he could not or would not pretend unto any confidence of his *acceptance* with the Lord." Cotton sat up with him throughout the night before his death, read him the song of Simeon when Nathanael requested it, and stayed with him during the day rather than attend the ordination of Nehemiah Walter in Roxbury, one of the great social events of the year. In the morning Nathanael seemed to express a little more confidence. "I have now been with Jesus Christ," he told his brother. But when Cotton—always pressing curiously in these months for knowledge of the other world, whether diabolical or heavenly—asked him to explain, he refused. Christians generally believed, of course, that the approach of death gave one a privileged view of the spiritual world, and the Puritans' emphasis on faith also made last-minute declarations especially important, as signs of the soul's condition just before the moment of Judgment. A moment before Nathanael died, another minister therefore asked him whether he could not find comfort in Jesus. Nathanael's "discreet and humble answer" showed that he was consistent to the end: "I endeavor to do those things which will issue in comfort." His brother, moved by those cautious last words, was there at the end to close Nathanael's eyes.

Within twelve days Cotton not only preached a memorial sermon called "The Duty and Interest of Youth; or, the *Thought* of an *Elder,* on the *Death* of a *Younger* Brother." He also wrote and sent off to his father in London the little book that was printed the following spring, with a brief preface by fourteen-year-old Samuel, as *Early Piety, Exemplified in the Life and Death of Mr. Nathanael Mather.* As Cotton went through his brother's papers, he was moved by the discovery of how thoroughly Nathanael had worked to follow his own example, and he was astonished to see how painfully Nathanael had suffered in secret. Nathanael had signed his covenant and joined the church at the age of fourteen, and although the family had noticed some slackening of intensity in his piety a year or two later, nobody had suspected that his soul was enduring "sore terrors and horrors." Much more diffident and reticent than his older brother, he had kept his troubles to himself. Only on his deathbed had Nathanael confided to Cotton that "blasphemous injections" had struck "like fiery venomous darts" to inflame his soul. "Horrible conceptions of *God,*" he had confessed, had buzzed about in his mind. Now that Cotton read his papers, it was clear that those miseries had been much more painful than the virtuous youth's self-accusation on his deathbed had allowed Cotton to believe. Now Cotton saw Nathanael's extraordinary humility in a different light. He decided to praise the courage with which Nathanael had fought off "these fiends" of blasphemy and despair—the exemplary piety, the splendid meditations, and the persistent humility of Nathanael's final days and hours. But now he also used the gloomy side of Nathanael's experience as an admonition to young Christians. In this respect as in neglecting his physical health, Nathanael would be represented in the book less "as a *pattern*" than "as a *caution* to young students; for it may be truly written on his grave," as Cotton wrote in his little memoir, "Study killed him." The melancholy and the aches and pains that Cotton Mather attributed to Nathanael's excessive work had become chronic by 1685, but Cotton remembered how strongly Nathanael's earlier illnesses, a fainting spell at the age of six and then the milder smallpox, had warned Cotton to temper his own self-punishing devotions at a time when he too had been in danger. While he was able to say, then, that Nathanael had attained "as high a pitch of Christianity, as any that I have known," he did seem to imply that the example set by Nathanael's older brother and their eminent progenitors had served the poor lad as a blessing that was emphatically mixed.

Besides humility and piety, the most attractive quality in Nathanael is one that Cotton communicates with particular force in the memoir because he too strove to exemplify it: a "delightful and surprising way of thinking" which constantly directed ingenious attention to bringing common experience into touch with the divine. Having resolved to praise God in every act of his life, Nathanael reflected, as his brother and biographer had taught him, "that the whole *Creation* was full of God; and that there was not a leaf of *grass* in the field, which might not make an observer to be sensible of the Lord. He apprehended that the *idle minutes* of our lives were many more than a short liver should allow." Fragments of hours, like filings of gold, were too precious to be wasted. Nathanael resolved to devote otherwise idle moments to the service and worship of God. His readiness to let every leaf of grass make him sensible of the Lord leads him, in Cotton Mather's version of his life, to notice that a kettle of water taken from the fire in his cold room is quickly "seized with lukewarmness." Soon cold too, he observes, are Christians after they have been warmed by some awareness of God's glory. When Nathanael jumps from his "bed of security," braving the cold to put on "Christ's garments" and walk to the fire, both he in his meditation and his surviving brother in the memoir make the lesson characteristically explicit. Thus they establish a base from which lines extend through American literary history, to Jonathan Edwards, Benjamin Franklin, Emerson, Thoreau, and even Whitman.

In *Early Piety,* and in a group of sermons on practical godliness which he also published in 1689, Cotton Mather established a clear relationship between redeeming the time and doing methodical and ingenious good. Just as Henry Thoreau would later tell New England's time-passing knitters that one cannot kill time without injuring eternity, so Mather warned his congregation that God would "find an *eternity* to *damn* the man that cannot find a *time* to *pray*." He urged the people to be *"zealous of good works, work for God.* Let even your *eating,* your *trading,* your *visiting,* be done as a *service* for the Lord, and let your *time,* your *strength,* your *estates,* all the *powers* of your spirits and all the *members* of your bodies be ingeniously laid out in that *service*." He urged them even to "court, and hunt advantages to be serviceable." As a very young man, then, he established once again the basis for a work with which his name would be associated decades later, after a major publication of his middle age.

Samuel Mather's preface to *Early Piety* is dated February 5, 1689, and when the book was published a few weeks later it became the first of Cotton's works to be published in England before it appeared in America. It received unusually wide distribution because a wealthy minister who had lost two of his own pious children bought up a large supply to be given away, and it was reprinted in London before the first American edition was published in Boston the next year. Cotton Mather's name and his efforts at "the *plain style* of a *just historian*" thus began to become known in England just as he was preparing to take an active part in overthrowing the royal government in Boston. Since his father's departure a year ago, Cotton had helped Nathanael to fight off the Devil in the sickroom at Salem, and he had taken on the devils in both physical and spiritual combat during the worst of Martha Goodwin's afflictions in his own household. Now, while Martha was still suffering attacks once or twice a week in his house, he would engage the tyrant Sir Edmund Andros.

☙

IT WAS THROUGH his writing that Cotton Mather participated in the Glorious Revolution. Ever since he had first written a thanksgiving proclamation at the age of eighteen, he had been gaining experience as a writer of public documents. Now, with his father absent in London, he inherited the duty not only of scribe but of spokesman.

Once again, though separated this time by the ocean, and though forced by that distance to work separately in ignorance of transatlantic events, Increase and Cotton Mather performed complementary duties in a single cause, the restoration of the colony's "ancient privileges." With the aid of two other agents from Massachusetts, Increase Mather had tried to maintain a consistent position since his arrival in London, but revolutionary events there had forced him to change both the substance and the audience of his appeal. At first — risking his neck, John Cotton of Plymouth believed — he had boldly approached King James II with the letter of thanksgiving that he had brought with him from his own church. Here he had argued that the King's Declaration of Indulgence was a welcome decree of toleration which his grateful subjects in the Bay colony would have liked to see the new dominion government respect. The misdeeds of Governor Andros and his agents appeared in this argument within the context of the colonists' gratitude to the King. After James was overthrown in the autumn of 1688 and replaced by a Protestant king and queen who promised to restore all the charters of English corporations that had been arbitrarily or illegally revoked, Mather felt obliged to appeal not only for the restoration of the Massachusetts charter but also for the liberties of Englishmen.

From the perspective of Massachusetts Puritans, these liberties coincided with the civil liberty that Governor John Winthrop had celebrated and briefly defined in a speech to the General Court in 1645. If an antagonist had argued in 1689, as some historians have recently done, that Mather's tardy discovery of English liberties came only after his church had been disestablished in Massachusetts, and after Anglicans and Quakers, previously denied the status of freemen (and sometimes even the right to live at all), had become free to worship there, Mather might have pointed accurately to civil liberties that Congregationalists, at least, did actually exercise in Massachusetts until the old charter was revoked: town meetings, an elected assembly to levy taxes and enact other laws, trial by jury, secure title to land and other property, and annual elections of the Governor and magistrates. Neither the Puritans' earlier appeal to the laws of God nor the new timeliness of Whig principles meant that the founders of New England or their descendants had ever given up their belief in English liberties.

Before the overthrow of Andros in Boston, Increase Mather had published two pamphlets in London within the relatively brief period of his agency there. In both of these, the grievances he stressed were virtually the same as those Cotton listed in his own writings. But of course the circumstances differed sharply. Increase perhaps contributed to the overthrow of Andros by persuading the new King to delay sending Andros any instructions or any confirmation of his authority. Far from scheming for a revolution in Massachusetts, as Edward Randolph later charged, Mather had also persuaded the new House of Commons to include New England in the Corporation Bill that in January 1689 had seemed likely to restore all the city and borough charters. Until weeks after the revolution in Boston was an accomplished fact, Increase Mather had good reason to hope that the old charter might be restored, and Andros and his crew removed, by administrative means. Whether or not Mather worked secretly (by correspondence that has disappeared) to foment the uprising in Massachusetts, his activities in London were restricted to lobbying and diplomatic pleading.

Cotton Mather's duties were necessarily more secret, and his published words, when at last they appeared, had to sound much more emphatic. The delay of all instructions from the King to Andros left Massachusetts open to rumor and speculation, including some indications that Andros himself knew his power was in jeopardy in London. Puritan fears that Andros was somehow in league with the French were magnified by King James's arbitrary acts to strengthen the position of Catholics in the English government, by news that the Catholic king had prosecuted Anglican bishops in England for seditious libel, and by rumors of William's plans to invade England from the Netherlands. When Governor Andros made what seemed an ineffective response to French and Indian attacks on English settlers in Massachusetts and Maine, just at the time that King James was reported to be taking refuge with Louis XIV in France, the evidence seemed very strong.

Even if the Puritan "faction" had been willing to listen to refutations of the kind that Edward Randolph did send to England some months later, pointing out Andros' military responses to particular Indian raids, his efforts at a general conciliation of outraged Indian victims of English assaults, and the unjust English provocations of some Indian belligerence, it would have been too late to establish any basis of trust. Andros had alienated not only the group that Randolph had once called the church party, nor only the wealthy merchants whom Randolph said that party had seduced. Now William Stoughton, Samuel Shrimpton, and other members of the Council who had favored submission in the battles over the charter had also turned against him. They had come to see that the Governor's arbitrary ways of ruling, however understandable from the perspective of a soldier who had come out to establish a new central policy in His Majesty's Dominion, were disastrous. When Andros was forced to surrender on April 18, William Stoughton was there to tell him that he had only himself to thank for his fall.

Besides abolishing the colonial legislature, challenging the validity of title to real estate, and trying to enforce the navigation acts, Andros had struck at a number of practices which many people in Massachusetts felt extremely reluctant to give up. When he prosecuted men who would not use Anglican gestures as they swore on the Bible, for example, he changed the basis of eligibility for jury duty, so that the chances of acquittal by sympathetic Puritans were virtually killed. He also saw to it that a group of defendants, including the Reverend John Wise, were not tried in Ipswich, where their alleged crime had been committed, but in Boston, and before a jury chosen in the new way. He canceled the time-honored tax for the support of Congregational ministers, which even Joseph Dudley had supported during his brief term as President. Andros forbade proclamations of thanksgiving and days of humiliation. And he forbade the regular town meetings at which Massachusetts freemen had always considered such local problems as the use of their common lands. When members of his own Council opposed these measures and others, he often seemed to pay no attention. Sometimes he

simply acted in defiance of a majority vote against a proposed measure, and sometimes he contrived to avoid taking any vote at all
within the Council.

As the late New England spring began, all this bubbling discontent and uncertainty threatened to erupt in Boston. Andros, who
had already drawn his full year's salary in advance, reported on
April 16 that he sensed "a general buzzing among the people." Secret
meetings among the leading opponents of the dominion government
must also have occurred, and Cotton Mather must have attended at
least one of them. Not even he, with all his facility as a writer, could
have dared to compose the *Declaration of Gentlemen and Merchants* on the morning of the uprising if he had only begun to consider writing it after a spontaneous revolution had begun. But except for Mather's refusal to deny authorship of the *Declaration*
when it was attributed to him later on, none of the conspirators ever
admitted planning the revolution. Their shrewd emphasis in the
document itself, and in all the subsequent reports that survive, fell
on the outrages committed by the "crew of abject wretches" that
Andros had "fetched from New York," and on their own role in restraining the spontaneous popular eruption from flowing destruc-
tively over any property or threatening the principle of royal authority.

The eighteenth fell on a Thursday, Lecture day, but it became
clear in the morning that there would be no Lecture this week. By
eight o'clock the general buzzing that Governor Andros had heard
among the people was beginning to sound like a roar. People in the
North End, Cotton Mather's neighborhood, began to assemble in
the streets as they heard rumors that their fellow townsmen in the
South End were up in arms. At the same time the people in the
South End were being told that the North End was "all in arms."
Captain John George, commander of the *Rose,* the twenty-four-gun
frigate in the harbor, was taken prisoner as soon as he stepped out of
a boat that had brought him ashore, and by nine o'clock members
of the local militia were beating drums throughout the town to muster all the available men. While some of the leading citizens—
including Thomas Danforth, John Richards, and several members
of the Council—were being escorted to the Town House by some of
the anonymous leaders of the insurrection, others were efficiently
arresting the chief partisans of Andros, including the jailer, the

sheriff, and Edward Randolph. Having replaced the jailer with a trustworthy Congregationalist, one "Scates the bricklayer," the rebels locked up their large company of dignitaries in the jail.

By noon, a great crowd of participants and observers had filled and surrounded the Town House, cheering when old Governor Bradstreet appeared, and Cotton Mather's *Declaration of Gentlemen and Merchants* was soon read aloud. The leaders who had met there, ostensibly to prepare that document, now sent a message to Governor Andros, who prudently kept out of sight at the fort on Fort Hill. They told him that in their best judgment the only way to quiet the rebels and secure both his own safety and that of the people would be to surrender the fort and the government, "to be preserved and disposed" according to orders from the Crown. They promised that neither he nor any of "your gentlemen or soldiers" would be harmed or robbed.

Andros at first refused, but by two o'clock in the afternoon the armed militia in Boston had been reinforced by twelve other companies from the surrounding towns, and reports said that another 1,500 men were ready in Charlestown but unable to get across the water. Some of the militia, marching on the fort at about four o'clock, intercepted a boat that had been sent from the frigate to the fort with ammunition, and Captain John Nelson, commander of the Boston militia, demanded that Andros surrender the fort. After some more hints of resistance, Andros saw that he had no choice. Some reports say that his outnumbered redcoats refused to fight even after he had beaten some of them. He came out of the fort with his entourage and allowed himself to be led to the Town House, where he received William Stoughton's rebuke and Simon Bradstreet's promise of safety. He was held captive at the house of John Usher that night, and then imprisoned in the fort under the command of Captain Nelson. A few days later Andros was transferred to the fort on Castle Island in the harbor.

Captain George later claimed that his ship's carpenter had absconded a few days before the eighteenth and had spread the rumor not only that Andros intended to "deliver this government to the French," but also that Andros and George were going to set fires at opposite ends of Boston before they left. Whatever the truth of these contradictory charges on both sides, there is evidence of a mutiny aboard the frigate after the troops had begun to assemble in Boston on the eighteenth, and one man testified later that Captain George, on learning that King James had been deposed, had said he would take the frigate to France but had been opposed by some members of his crew.

Even today, in reconsidering the revolutionary events that have been so well narrated in several nineteenth- and twentieth-century histories, one is surprised by the powerful evidence of the colonists' restraint and coordination. It would be condescending to attribute the restraint wholly to the gentlemen and merchants, as some historians have done, for even under the wisest anonymous leadership the "inhabitants of Boston, and the country adjacent" would have been an extraordinarily self-controlled mob of revolutionaries. It is true that they luckily encountered no violent resistance from the naval and military commanders, and one imprisoned supporter of Andros did claim that a Congregational minister had said all the Anglicans in Boston would have been slaughtered "if any blood had been spilt." Besides luck or Providence, however, the organization, the character, and the aims of the Boston rebels must be given much of the credit for both the decision of the British not to fight and the fact that nobody on either side was killed or seriously injured. The frigate might have fired on the town if its captain had not been captured and (later) if superior fire-power from the town had not been trained on the fort and then the frigate itself. One does not need to be so filiopietistic as Cotton Mather or George Bancroft to acknowledge the unusual importance of "the people's" behavior in this uprising, and its exemplary value in the bloody revolution that began in Lexington and Concord precisely eighty-six years later. It was Cotton Mather who wrote the two most important printed versions of that example.

He probably wrote at least a draft of the first version before the revolution that erupted on April 18, 1689. Friends of Andros later claimed that Bostonians had been planning the revolution as early as January, but mid-April seems a more likely date. On April 4, a copy of William's proclamation, issued before his departure from the Netherlands in the autumn of 1688, had arrived in Plymouth. It gave an excellent pretext for ousting Andros, for it asked all those English "magistrates who have been unjustly turned out" of office to resume "their former employments." No record supports the testimony of one Andros partisan that a committee of rebels met at Cotton Mather's house on the night of the seventeenth, but one can safely assume that after broadside copies of William's proclamation had been distributed soon after the fourth, Mather and a group of collaborators met to consider a draft of the declaration that might have to be issued if Andros should be overthrown. They quietly assumed what few English Tories or Whigs had been willing to assume during Increase Mather's frustrating negotiations, that William's appeal to English magistrates included the magistrates in English colonies, even those in a colony whose charter had been revoked before the accession of James II.

⌘

*The Declaration of Gentlemen and Merchants* gives that assumption some plausibility by beginning with an elaborate allusion to the Popish Plot. Bostonians had long known that Titus Oates had been convicted and whipped for perjury, but Cotton Mather's *Declaration* now represented the mistreatment of New England throughout the 1680s as part of "the great Scarlet Whore's" bigoted conspiracy to destroy Protestantism. Even this effort to implicate the two last Stuart kings in an antichristian conspiracy may be said to have some parallels in the charges against George III in 1776, and other grievances and language in Mather's *Declaration* come much closer to anticipations of Thomas Jefferson's in the Declaration of Independence. In the first of the twelve articles, for example, Mather insisted that the people of New England had been remarkably patient while enduring the consequences of the tyrannous plot. The old charter, he said, was revoked "with a most injurious pretense (and scarce that) of law, . . . before it was possible for us to appear at *Westminster* in the legal defense of it: and [then] without [granting] a fair leave to answer for ourselves concerning crimes falsely laid to our charge," a commission put Massachusetts "under a *President* and *Council,* without any liberty for an Assembly which the other American *plantations* have." That royal commission, moreover, "was as illegal for the form of it, as the way of obtaining it was *malicious* and *unreasonable;* yet we made no resistance thereunto as we could easily have done; but chose to give all mankind a demonstration of our being a people sufficiently dutiful and loyal to our King: and this was yet more satisfaction because we took pains to make ourselves believe as much as ever we could of the wheedle then offered unto us; that his Majesty's desire was no other than the happy increase and advance of these *provinces* by their more immediate dependence on the *Crown* of *England*."

Mather did not achieve the splendid phrase "a decent respect to the opinions of mankind," but he certainly thought of setting all mankind an example and of appealing to mankind's sense of duty, loyalty, and forbearance. The New England people as he described them here were a people of law who wanted to retain their ancient liberties. They were also, as Jefferson and others would echo even more stridently in the 1770s, a people with their own implicitly political as well as religious identity. In one of his thanksgiving proclamations, Mather had referred to Massachusetts as a nation, and he knew that the colony had been rebuked in London for calling itself a commonwealth. In *The Declaration of Gentlemen,* he did not call Massachusetts a state, but his reminder that *we* could *easily* have resisted the King's illegal commission, but *chose* to give mankind a demonstration of loyalty, is unmistakable. The patient New Englanders' response to the King's wheedle, moreover, anticipated the strategy of Jefferson's claim after 1774 that the American colonists had appealed trustingly but unsuccessfully for their King's protection against a usurping Parliament.

Once he had exposed the former King's wheedle, Mather shifted attention to Sir Edmund Andros' arbitrary power, which Andros had assumed barely six months after the King's first promise. Andros, Mather said, had claimed the power not only of unlimited conscription but also "to make laws and raise taxes as he pleased. And several companies of *redcoats* were now brought from *Europe,* to support what was to be imposed upon us, not without repeated menaces that some hundreds more were intended for us." Even worse than the redcoats were the "horse leeches" to whom public offices and employments had been given — "strangers to, and haters of the people," Mather called them. It is the corruption and arbitrariness of this "crew of abject persons fetched from New York" that form one of the strongest links between the grievances of 1689 and those of 1776: "what laws they made it was as impossible for us to know, as dangerous for us to break; [Andros] would neither suffer them to be printed nor fairly published." Whereas New England had once been ruled by men of virtue, the wicked now walked on every side, and "the vilest men [were] exalted."

Mather's *Declaration* also anticipated the rhetoric of slavery that was to be so prominently displayed in the Declaration of Independence and other tracts of the Revolutionary period, and he was able to attribute that language to a defender of the Crown. Saving the rhetoric of slavery for his sixth article, the one that gives the most detailed grievances, Mather declared that after the Andros regime had been established, "it was now plainly affirmed both by some in open Council and by the same in private converse, that the people of *New England* were all *slaves* and the only difference between them and *slaves* is their not being bought and sold; and it was a maxim delivered in open court unto us by one of the Council, that we must not think the privileges of *Englishmen* would follow us to the end of the world: Accordingly we have been treated with multiplied contradictions to *Magna Carta,* the rights of which we laid claim unto."

Mather's appeal to the liberties of free speech, habeas corpus, and trial by a fair jury anticipated the diction and parallel structure of charges that would one day be laid to George III in the Declaration of Independence, and his words must have stirred the hundreds of people who assembled to hear them declaimed from the gallery of the Town House on the day Andros was overthrown:

> Persons who did but peaceably object against the raising of taxes without an assembly have been for it fined, some twenty, some thirty, and others fifty pounds. Packed and picked juries have been very common things among us, when under a pretended form of law the trouble of some perhaps honest and worthy men has been aimed at: but when this gang have been brought upon the stage, for the most detestable enormities that ever the sun beheld, all men have with admiration seen what methods have been taken that they might not be treated according to their crimes.

Under the pretense or the genuine fear that Andros had planned to turn New England over to "a foreign power," Mather claimed that the overthrown officials were being held for what orders justice, the King, and Parliament might direct. He did not hesitate to appeal, moreover, to the example of the Prince of Orange who had so recently gone to England to replace James II: "in compliance with which glorious action, we ought surely to follow the patterns which the nobility, gentry and commonalty in several parts of the kingdom have set before us." Here Mather could not resist pointing out that the English people had taken such action chiefly "to prevent what we already endure."

To the people who heard Mather's *Declaration* in Massachusetts it was probably important that he also dwelt heavily on threats to land title and on dubious charges that Andros was in league with the French and Indian enemies of New England. That emphasis helped to justify the concluding plea of the merchants and gentlemen "to all our neighbors, for whom we have thus ventured ourselves, to join with us in prayers and all just actions, for the defense of the land." In the strategy of the leaders and in the establishment of a precedent for a later generation, however, the key points were not only reliance on ancient liberties but also moderation, the restoration of a government that had been illegally supplanted, and the patient resolution to wait "humbly" for further orders from London. Mather's second version of these events, which he published in narrative form in his biography of Sir William Phips several years later, memorialized those very qualities in a context that set Phips's virtues against the cupidity of Andros and his abject crew. Phips, the "Knight of Honesty" whom Mather himself welcomed into the church covenant a year after the revolution, had converted "the old *heathen* virtue of . . . *LOVE TO ONE'S COUNTRY* . . . into [a] *Christian*" virtue. Even after the overthrow of Andros, Phips had turned down the governorship of New England because, he said in Mather's paraphrase, "a government without an assembly [is] treason." Here, too, Mather was able to cite an English attorney general's opinion that the King "could no more grant a commission to levy money on his subjects [in New England] without their consent by an assembly, than they could discharge themselves from their allegiance to the *English* Crown." Thus Mather's life of Phips coupled together, eight decades before the American Revolution, the unthinkable outrage of independence and the enormity of taxation without representation.

Surely the anonymous gentlemen, merchants, and ministers gave at least some thought to their own safety when they represented themselves as a Committee of Safety to preserve order and wait for royal instructions after the allegedly spontaneous revolution had begun. They could not be sure that King William would approve of an armed rebellion by colonists. Even the document that many of them signed, the request drawn up at the Town House on April 18, asking Andros to give himself up for the sake of restoring order, insisted that "we were wholly ignorant" of any revolutionary plans for "the present accident," and that they had been "surprised with the people's sudden taking of arms." Besides portraying themselves as a restraining influence, this language strengthened their connection with the Puritan tradition that would add moral force (for the middle classes, at least) to the American Revolution. Like their Puritan ancestors and other Protestants before them, they claimed to restore traditional principles that had been betrayed by corrupt authorities. The "principal gentlemen of Boston," as Mather later portrayed them, constituted the prudent center between a king who wanted to foist discontented Irish Catholics on New England "to check the growing *Independents*" there, and the threat of bloody insurrection "by an ungoverned *mobile.*" Of all the revolutionary movements in the American colonies in the 1670s and 1680s, the "accident" in Boston and the language in which it was represented set the most useful example for the American Revolution. Cotton Mather later described the spirit of Bostonians on the eighteenth of April 1689 as "the most *unanimous resolution* perhaps that ever was known to have inspired any people," and he praised the leaders for having "managed" the affair "without the least *bloodshed* or *plunder,* and with as much *order* as ever attended any *tumult,* it may be, in the world." He praised them, too, for having taken no revenge on their oppressors, and for their prudent care as they considered "into what form they should cast the government." Their decision to restore old Governor Bradstreet and the other magistrates who had held office "before the late usurpation," reinforced Mather's emphasis on moderation — and so, too, of course, did their request for further instructions from England.

In the spring of 1689, then, Cotton Mather had reached the highest popular recognition and public usefulness of his young life, and he was probably happier in these weeks than he would ever be again. Without direct help from his father, he had fought successfully against both the Devil and the Pope. At the age of twenty-six he had used his best talents to represent the wishes of his people, whom he now saw more completely united than he had ever known them to be. With Simon Bradstreet back in the governor's chair, and with Increase Mather apparently getting a sympathetic audience in London, it must even have seemed likely that the best hopes of New England's founders might soon be realized. Abigail, moreover, had conceived another child, to be born in September, and the affairs of the Second Church were in excellent order despite the continued absence of Increase Mather.

VI

# *Struggling toward the Millennium:*
# *War, Smallpox, Witchcraft*

෩

If the Blessed God intend that the Divel shall keep *America* during the Happy *Chil-iad* which His Church is now very *quickly* Entring into, . . . then our Lord Jesus will within a few months break up House among us, and we go for Lodging either to *Heaven* or to *Europe* in a very little while. But if our God will wrest *America* out of the Hands of its old Land-Lord, *Satan,* and give these *utmost ends of the Earth* to our Lord Jesus, then our present conflicts will shortly be blown over, and something better than, *A Golden Age,* will arrive to this place, and this perhaps before all our *First Planters* are fallen asleep. Now, 'tis a dismal *Uncertainty* and *Ambiguity* we see ourselves placed in. And indeed our *All is at the Stake;* we are beset with a Thousand Perplexities and Entanglements. The Question which we have now before us, in short is this, *Whether we will venture All, with an Hope to Preserve All, or Whether we will keep All, with an Assurance to Loose All, by doing so.*

Cotton Mather, *The Present State of New England,* 1690

SAMUEL PRINCE, who wrote one of the earliest and best accounts of the revolution, predicted that "settling things under a new government" might "prove far more difficult than the getting from under the power" of Andros' dominion. He was right. Not until several weeks later did the leaders take formal action to establish a provisional government and ask the Crown's approval of it, and nearly three more years passed before a new royal charter did issue from Increase Mather's protracted negotiations in London. By the time Mather arrived in Boston with the new royal governor, whom the King had graciously allowed him to nominate, Massachusetts was suffering not only from renewed Indian attacks on the eastern frontier but also from political dissension, severe economic troubles, and the most demoralizing outbreak of witchcraft in American history. These three years were the critical years in Cotton Mather's experi-

ence as a leader of his people and in the development of his commitment to write their history.

The cosmic range and the peculiar intensity of Cotton Mather's
experience during these years cannot be explained solely by emphasis on pathology or on his affectations of pre-eminence. Coincidental experience, the actual achievements of both Increase and
Cotton Mather, and actual events in the great world of English and
European politics gave a strong plausibility to interpretations that
might ordinarily be attributed chiefly to Cotton's peculiar reading
of his private spiritual life or to the bias in Puritan interpretations of
history. Consider the young man's position in May 1689.

At the age of twenty-six he found himself in charge of his father's
large family as well as of his own household and of the very large
congregation. He was preparing his wife and two of his younger sisters, along with twenty-three other young people, to become covenanted members in full communion, and of course he continued to
observe his schedule of private meditations, pastoral visits, and sermons for his own congregation and others. Within the past year he
had engaged and vanquished both the Devil and the agents of James
II. His father, meanwhile, was being received sympathetically by
the Queen and sometimes by the King, whom both father and son
regarded as the chief defender of Protestantism in a world that was
gravely threatened by the power of Louis XIV. Hopes for a restoration of the old charter, with all the special privileges of Congregationalists intact, remained strong in Boston and in London. Cotton
Mather himself had been chosen to write one declaration addressed
to the new royal champion of Protestantism in England, and now
the Committee of Safety had asked him to write two other major
documents, a formal address to their majesties and a sermon (the
regular Thursday Lecture) addressed to the delegates who had been
called to a convention in Boston for the establishment of a new provisional government. In his father's absence he was the sole spiritual
adviser to Sir William Phips and Major John Richards. His studies,
meanwhile, gave him strong reason to believe (as Sir Isaac Newton
coincidentally believed) that the Millennium would begin in his own
lifetime, and reports from the province of Dauphine in France suggested an exhilarating context into which to fit his own experience
of the Goodwin witchcraft case.

Not even the terrible new edicts against French Protestants had been able to silence the devoted peasants who insisted on singing the Psalms in the vernacular, and now Mather read reports of invisible angels singing identifiable Psalms "with a ravishing melody" in the heavens above Dauphine. Peasants were speaking with tongues. The most extraordinary of these people, Mather believed, were the young. He noted that French children and youths between the ages of six and twenty-five had rebuked notorious adult sinners with what seemed remarkable perspicacity. Secret sinners themselves had often been astonished by the children's accurate insight and language, so startled that the children had persuaded some of them to confess. The reports of one ignorant shepherdess reminded Mather of Martha Goodwin, for they said that the shepherdess had suddenly found herself in command of enough Latin to refute "Romish superstitions" in the priests' own language. Along with the deliverance of New England, these mysterious signs persuaded Mather that "the day" might be "at hand, when the kingdoms of the world, shall be the kingdoms of our Lord, and of his Christ." A revolution more violent than the recent earthquake in southern Europe was likely soon to overthrow the Pope, Mather believed, and Reformed Christians might soon find themselves in the City of God on earth.

As his own books began to appear in London and Boston with the frequency that would characterize his productivity during the next three decades, Cotton Mather had reason to believe that the unforgettable angel's prediction was coming true. His own branches were spreading across the ocean, his influence reaching to London, his actions having effect not only in the salvation of souls and of the old charter in New England, but also in the ultimate battle of the Lord's people against the Devil and the Pope. In the very years that saw Massachusetts fail to escape her provincial destiny as merely another royal colony, Mather came closest to fulfilling his most ambitious hopes. He was acting near the center of history's last battle.

Of course he knew that he could not be absolutely certain. Just as he had seen reason to question the origin of his own angelic vision, so he now saw that prodigious signs and historical events were ambiguous. Later in the year he warned a thanksgiving-day audience not to put absolute faith in the French phenomena, or in the completeness of New England's deliverance. Most of the Protestant princes who had reigned in Europe sixty years ago, he remembered, had been replaced by Catholics, and "we do not certainly know what changes may yet come upon us, nor how far the clouds may return after the rain." But the note of foreboding only qualified his thanksgiving celebration. Even if more catastrophes were coming, the Lord's people must be "found *singing to the Lord*." If they were going to sink after all, Mather declared, they must "*sink* and *sing* both at once, and keep *singing* to Him that has done excellent things, while we have any breath."

Mather's sermon to the convention on May 23, 1689, was designed to resolve in pious allegiance the inevitable disagreements of factions that had achieved unanimity in opposition to Governor Andros. He chose his text from the second book of Chronicles, the ringing assurance at the beginning of the fifteenth chapter that "the Lord is with you while you are with Him." In the familiar pattern of the jeremiad, Mather emphasized the qualifying clause and recited a litany of ways in which the people of New England had *not* been with the Lord. The worst "of all our errors," he declared, was "the contention which we are too prone to break forth into." He warned that a "divided and quarrelsome people" would drive God away, and he observed ironically that while debating about political "*submission* and regulation in our various revolutions," Bostonians had obeyed "the tyranny of our own *passions*." He pleaded for "a public spirit in us all, for the good of the *whole*." William the Silent, Mather said, had exemplified that noble spirit by using his last breath to ask God to pity "this poor people" as well as his own soul, after the assassin's bullet had struck him down. "When he had but one breath to draw in the world, his *poor people* had half of it! O let this poor people [of New England] have no less than half our cares," Mather echoed, "half our prayers."

Mather's praise for the Dutch national hero had special value in the first year of his descendant's reign in England, and so too did Mather's elaborate allusion to the contemporaneous exemplar, Increase Mather. Cotton Mather's plea for a public spirit did more than remind the delegates of New England's national covenant. It asked them to trust Increase Mather, the self-sacrificing negotiator struggling for the public good in the Court of St. James. Although the Mathers still hoped that the old charter would soon be restored, they were already feeling some of the tension between two opposing groups who would deplore Increase Mather's new willingness to compromise: those who suspected him of being too submissive in

London, and those who wanted to reduce the power of Congregationalism and the clergy in New England. The convention's decision
to restore the old government of Simon Bradstreet brought unity for
several more months, until a new series of catastrophes in 1690 —
and intimations from London that Increase Mather was willing to
settle for the best he could get — revived the controversies.

For the rest of 1689, the news was good. Sir William Phips had
sailed for London in October 1688 after Andros had frustrated his
effort to act on his royal commission as high sheriff in New England
— and after someone had tried to assassinate Phips on Phips's own
doorstep. Now he returned on the twenty-ninth of May with the first
official word of the new king and queen. The proclamation of the
new regime set off the most splendid celebration in Boston's young
life: a long parade of mounted dignitaries and marching militia,
great crowds of people from the countryside, a grand dinner at the
Town House, wine distributed freely to the celebrating people in the
streets, and singing and cheering into the night, until the nine
o'clock bell sent people back to their homes.

Phips immediately began to attend the Second Church, and as
Cotton Mather encouraged this fat, choleric hero to think about
confessing his sins and entering a church covenant, Phips remembered that it had been Increase Mather's *The Day of Trouble is
Near* that had begun to awaken his religious conscience fifteen years
ago. As the summer passed and the King endorsed the provisional
government, pending his decision about the charter, Phips accepted
Cotton Mather's argument that he must beware the trap of having
his portion only in this world. Mather's power and influence approached their greatest strength in March 1690, when Phips and
more than twenty others increased the Second Church's membership by almost 10 percent. Although the Mathers had for years accepted the Half-Way Covenant, their church had not accepted half-
way members, and Cotton Mather did not persuade his congregation to do so until 1693. Phips and some members of the congregation had scruples about his eligibility, because this twenty-first son of
an almost incredibly durable mother had not been baptized during
his childhood on the frontier in Maine. At last Mather persuaded
him to submit to adult baptism and to submit a relation of his private religious experience and a declaration of faith. The salty hero
addressed this declaration to Mather himself rather than to the con-

The Prefent state of the

# New-Englifh Affairs.

This is Publifhed to prevent Falfe Reports

*An Extract of a Letter from Mr. Mather, To the Governour, Dated Sept.* 3. 1689 *from Deal in Kent.*

THe Houfe of Commons Ordered a Bill to be drawn up for the Reftoration of Charters to all Corporations. Some Enemies of *New-England* did beftir themfelves on that Occafion. But it has pleafed God to fucceed Endeavours and Sollicitations here fo far, as that N. E. is particularly mentioned in the Bill.

It has been read twice, and after that referred unto a Committee for Emendations. What concerns N. England paffed without any great oppofition. The Bill has been in part read the third Time, and the Charters of N.-Eng. then alfo paffed without Objection. Only fome Additional Claufes refpecting Corporations here, caufed Debates; fo that the Bill is not as yet Enacted.

In the latter end of *June*, a Veffel from *Mount Hope* arrived here, which brought your Declaration of *April* 18. with an account of the Revolution in *New-England*. The week after I went to *Hampton Court*, and had the favour to wait on His Majefty, who told me, *That He did accept of, and was well pleafed with what was done in* New-England, *and that he would order the Secretary of State to fignifie fo much, and that His Subjects there fhould have their Ancient Rights and Priviledges reftored to them.*

The King has fent a Gracious Letter (which was delivered to me, and if I return not my felf, I fhall take care that it be fent to you) bearing Date *Auguft* 12. *Wherein He fignifies His Royal Approbation* of what has been done at *Bofton,* and affures you that the Government there fhall be fettled, fo as fhall be for the Security and Satisfaction of His Subjects in that Colony, and in the mean time bids you go on to Adminifter the Laws, and manage the Government, according as in your Addrefs you have Petitioned.

My Lord *Mordent* ( now Earl of *Monmouth* ) bade me affure you that He would be your Friend, and he bade me tell you from him, *That your Charters fhould be reftored to you by Act of Parliament.*

I have been with moft of the Kings moft Honourable Privy Council, who have promifed to befriend *New-England* as there fhall be occafion for it. The like I may fay, of all the Leading-men in the Parliament.

I have been in the *Downs* a fortnight, and Aboard Mr. *Clark*, feveral Nights, but the Wind has been againft us. And we now hear that the *New-found-Land* Convoyes ( on whofe Affiftance we had a Dependance) are gone.

*Superfcribed To the Honourable*
Simon Bradftreet, *Efq;*

*Governour of the Maffachufets Colony in N-England.*

*A Paffage extracted from the publick News-Letter, Dated* July 6. 1689.

The people of *New-England* having made e thorow Revolution, and fecured the publick Criminals. On *Thursday* laft, the Reverend and Learned Mr. *Mather*, Prefident of the *Colledge*, and Minifter of *Bofton*, waited on the King; and in a moft Excellent Speech laid before His Majefty, the State of that People; faying, *That they were fober, and Induftrious, and fit for Martial Service; and all with their Lives and Interefts were at His Majefties Command, to tender the fame unto His Majefty: That they defired nothing but His Majefties Acceptance of what they had done, and His Protection; and that if His Majefty pleafed to encourage and Commiffion them, He might eafily be Emperour of America.* His Majefty affured him, that He was pleafed with what was done for Him, and for themfelves in the Revolution, and that their Priviledges and Religion fhould be fecured unto them.

*Extracted from a Letter of Mr.* Mather, *to his Son, Dated Sept.* 2. 1689.

On *July* 4. The King faid unto me, *That He did kindly Accept of what was done in Bofton. And that His Subjects in* New-England *fhould have their Ancient Rights and Priviledges Reftored and Confirmed unto them,* Yea, He told me, *That if it were in his power to caufe it to be done it fhould be done,* and bade me reft affured of it.

The *Charter-Bill* is not finifhed, becaufe fome Additional Claufes refpecting Corporations here in *England* caufed a Debate; and the Parliament is for fome weeks Adjourned.

Befides the Letter from the Kings Majefty, whereof we have notice as above; there is now arrived, an Order from His Majefty to the Government, bearing Date, *July* 30. 1689. Requiring, *That Sir* Edmund Androfs, Edward Randolph, *and others, that have been Seized by the people of* Bofton, *and fhall be at the Receipt of thefe Commands, Detained there, under Confinement, be fent on Board the firft Ship, bound to* England, *to anfwer what may be objected againft them.*

Bofton, Printed and Sold by *Samuel Green*, 1689.

10. *The Present State of the New-English Affairs.*
Facsimile of a broadside reporting Increase Mather's letters
to Governor Bradstreet and Cotton Mather about negotiations
to restore the old charter.

gregation. The document, Mather said when he printed it in his biography of Phips, was written in Phips's own hand, and there is no reason to doubt his word. By the time Mather printed it in his biography of Phips, however, its prose style resembled Cotton Mather's more than Phips's extant letters on other subjects. If Mather did not touch it up before printing it in the biography, he had already helped Phips to compose it before Phips wrote out the final copy.

In this brief narrative Phips cast himself as a man whose biography might well bear the title that Mather later gave it, *Pietas in Patriam,* love of country. Phips was a man whose perseverance, courage, and leadership had brought him from poverty to extraordinary wealth. After he had discovered the wrecked Spanish treasure ship in the Caribbean, he had been knighted, celebrated, and tempted with several "great offers" in England. But now, less than a year after their own Glorious Revolution, the members of Mather's congregation heard this "Knight of Honesty" say that as soon as he had found the treasure he had solemnly vowed to serve the Lord's people and churches in New England. "I knew," he said in Mather's version of the document, "*that if God had a people anywhere, it was here:* And I *resolved to rise and fall with them.*" Phips apologized for having waited so long to seek formal permission to join the church. He mentioned his scruples about baptism, pointed out that he had refused several invitations to be baptized in Anglican churches, confessed his fears lest the great blessing of his accession to wealth "should not be in mercy," and asked to be admitted as a member of the church. Cotton Mather baptized him on March 23, 1690, and happily admitted him to membership along with Elizabeth and Sarah Mather.

The timing of Phips's admission to the church was fortuitous. The French and Indian attacks on English colonies had begun to cause great destruction again in the new year. They had destroyed Schenectady, New York, on the night of February 8-9, killing sixty men, women, and children. News of that catastrophe had arrived in Boston on the day of a grand dinner party given by Samuel Sewall to celebrate his safe return from London. Cotton Mather, who had attended with his mother and his sister Maria, had "returned thanks in an excellent manner" before the dinner, and had led the singing of part of the fifty-sixth Psalm — which seemed appropriate both because of the Psalmist's allusion to wandering and because it declared his faith that God would protect him against his wicked, destructive enemies. On that afternoon, as the dinner was about to begin, the Governor, who was also present at Sewall's dinner, had approved an expedition against the French in eastern Canada, and Sewall had subscribed £100 to help finance the New England troops. On March 21, then, just two days before Sir William Phips's admission to church membership, news had arrived of another French raid at Salmon Falls, with eighty to one hundred English colonists killed or taken captive, and on March 22 Phips had volunteered to lead the expedition against the French. He was made a freeman by the General Court, and immediately sworn in as major general on Saturday afternoon, the day before he joined the church.

Phips's expedition against Port Royal was a glorious success, accomplished so easily that it encouraged the colonists to plan the conquest of Quebec. It is true that after Phips and his fleet of eight small ships had sailed in the last week of April a large force of French and Indians had destroyed the English fort on Casco Bay. But the quick, virtually bloodless capture of Port Royal seemed likely to put an end to some of the worst raids from Acadia, and the spoil that Phips and his men brought back along with the prisoners and pledges of allegiance from the inhabitants near Port Royal, gave many colonists hope that they might do Massachusetts immeasurable good by mounting an expedition against Quebec. If they could succeed there, they could put an end to the French-Indian menace on their frontiers, they could silence at last the blasphemous libels of French Jesuits,* and of course they might give the new rulers of England more reason than ever to treat Massachusetts with special favor.

Even during the spring and summer, however, Cotton Mather began to see less encouraging evidence. Smallpox had broken out again in Boston, in what would become by the end of autumn the

---

*In 1690 Mather wrote a preface in French to Ezekiel Carré's *Enchantillon*, an exposé of misrepresentations allegedly foisted upon the Iroquois by French Jesuits. Carré was a French Protestant minister who had recently emigrated to New England with forty-five families in his congregation. He said the Jesuits had taught some Iroquois that Jesus was a Frenchman, Mary a French lady, and the English their murderous enemies. Mather hoped that the exposé would move his readers to destroy popery and work harder to spread the true faith. See Ezekiel Carré, *Enchantillon* (Boston, 1690); and Thomas J. Holmes, *Cotton Mather: A Bibliography* (Cambridge, Mass., 1940), II, 831.

worst epidemic of the century except for the all too memorable one of 1678. Now there were also indications that, just as the war against antichristian forces seemed likely to be decisively won, New England's exemplary unity was dissolving. Some leaders had become suspicious of Increase Mather's willingness to compromise in the negotiations for restoring the old charter, and the General Court decided to send two more agents, Dr. Thomas Oakes and Elisha Cooke, to London to strengthen his resolution against modifications. Plymouth, meanwhile, had asked to be kept separate from Massachusetts in the new charter arrangements even though it now seemed likely, as Cotton Mather warned the Governor of Plymouth, that Plymouth would soon be annexed to either Massachusetts or New York. In a letter to Governor Hinckley with which he forwarded some letters that Increase Mather had entrusted to him, Cotton Mather protested that his father had tried to save Plymouth's Congregationalist integrity by asking that it be included in the Massachusetts charter after the Governor of New York had apparently been granted authority over Plymouth. If annexation to New York should bring "manifold miseries" on Plymouth, Cotton Mather warned, "you have none to thank for it but one of your own"—the Plymouth agent who had insisted on striking out Increase Mather's request.

Caught between the different factions as he tried to defend his father and maintain unity in the colony's complex struggles, Cotton Mather also had to contend with his father's volatile temperament. He did so by bringing his own into action against a frightening threat. After eighteen months in London, Increase had planned to sail home with Samuel Sewall and Thomas Brattle in the autumn of 1689, but young Samuel Mather had contracted smallpox just before sailing time and had thus forced his father to stay in England. By the time Increase sent Cotton the letters announcing that a new charter, the best that could be obtained, was ready for the King to sign but with Plymouth in danger of annexation by New York, the hypersensitive father had received indications that his service was not much appreciated by his fellow countrymen. He had received no new money for his inevitable expenses, and the General Court's reported dispatch of two new agents to keep him in line seemed now to confirm an English friend's warning that the people of New England were always ungrateful to their public servants. When some English friends suggested that he settle permanently in England, Mather apparently wrote to his son about his hurt feelings and his intention to consider the invitation seriously.

Whether or not this suggestion was a petulant echo of earlier threats to resign as Fellow and as President of Harvard College, Cotton Mather treated it seriously. In the most vehement letter he ever wrote to his father, he flatly called the intention dishonorable. He did try to soothe his father's vanity by declaring that nobody else in New England had received such respect and esteem as their countrymen had shown to Increase Mather. But he insisted that "the *slights,* which you have thought cast upon you" were *"imaginary,"* and although he briefly reminded his father of his evident duty to "the country, the college, your own church," he reserved his most powerful statement for the Mather family, and especially for himself. He was sorry, he said, for all these institutions that his father seemed about to desert, and he was sorry, too,

> for myself, who am left alone, in the midst of more cares, fears, anxieties, than, I believe any one person in these territories; and who have just now been within a few minutes of death, by a very dangerous fever, the relics whereof are yet upon me. But I am sorry for my dear father too, who is, *entered into temptation,* and will find snares in his resolutions. May the God of Heaven direct you; and prevent every step, which may not be for the honor of His blessed name!
>
> I confess, that I write with a most ill-boding jealousy, that I shall never see you again in this evil world; and it overwhelms me into tears, which cannot be dried up, unless by this consideration, that you will shortly find among the spirits of just men made perfect,
>
> Your Son,<br>C.M.

The son had learned well from the father both the language of self-pity and the tactics of premature valediction to this world, but the genuineness of his anxiety and the forcible tone of his rebuke seem none the less remarkable. The most rebellious letter that he ever wrote to his father begs him to come back home before it is too late to help his desolate son.

Three days after Mather wrote that letter, he was again reminded of his place among the New England generations, by the death of John Eliot. The eighty-six-year-old patriarch had been active in Roxbury and outspoken in Boston for nearly sixty years. Mather did not forget that Eliot had given him the right hand of fellowship at his ordination, and some unsolicited, forthright advice about his preaching. In this critical spring, while the smallpox epidemic took more and more lives and the war continued, with news awaited daily from the Phips expedition against Port Royal, reflections on Eliot's long life and on the new accumulation of New England's troubles led Mather to think of composing a biography. This new book, *The Triumphs of the Reformed Religion in America* (1691), would be considerably more elaborate than the memoir of Nathanael Mather. Whereas Nathanael's life had exemplified early piety, Eliot's would be represented as the fulfilled experience of the complete evangelist.

The term "evangelist" was no mere synonym for "missionary." Eliot had earned the title by extraordinary service as one of the earliest bearers of the Gospel into the wilderness of America. Besides translating the Psalms, with Richard Mather and others, in the first book published in New England, Eliot had produced the first Bible published in North America, his translation in the Algonquin tongue. He had founded the Roxbury Latin school and had worked among Christian Indians, training some of them as preachers, for half a century. Mather saw him as an antitype of John the Baptist, fulfilling in modern history—perhaps just before the Millennium—the promise implicit in that original evangelist's preaching of the good news in the wilderness. Eliot's fulfillment of that promise included, in Mather's biography, a wholeness that his saintly predecessor had lacked. Mather constructed his life so that the reader might see it opening outward, from Eliot's own religious conversion to his expanding action for the glory of God—in the choice of a wife, the discipline and education of their family, the teaching of his congregation, and finally the conversion and nurture of the native Americans.

In creating this typical saint, the first figure in what was soon to become a New England hagiography, Mather established a fundamental quality of his very best historical work. Eliot, like Mather's other Puritan saints, would represent both a kind of Puritan character and an antitype to predecessors in biblical typology. But while he stands forth in Mather's pages as the evangelist, he is also a memorably unique historical figure, both in the achievements for which he is best known and in several anecdotes with which Mather skillfully dramatizes a unique character's action and speech. In one incident, for example, Mather describes Eliot's habit of commenting critically on sermons. A young minister, who bears a close resemblance to Cotton Mather himself, has just finished preaching an excellent sermon, and old Mr. Eliot greets him in the moment of his triumph with a helpful admonition: "Study mortification, brother."

Mather had reason to study mortification in 1690. As he wrote the biography during the summer, evidence of disaster continued to accumulate in Boston, and his emphasis on the triumphs of his religion in America became an almost desperate affirmation of faith. The cheering confirmation of Phips's easy victory at Port Royal did reach Boston in May, two days after Eliot's death, and the consultation with New York and Connecticut authorities on a plan for invading Canada did lead to a grand expedition that Mather hoped would not only eliminate the French menace but also open the whole northern country for Protestant evangelism. Mather had some good reasons, too, for personal satisfaction. Besides the publication of his 1689 sermons and a new *Companion for Communicants,* he was honored by his election as a Fellow of Harvard College on June 12, and by the special attention paid him by Sir William Phips. But along with the happy news of Port Royal in May came reports of a disaster at Casco Bay and reports that Joshua Moody had come down with smallpox, which also ran through the Sewall family. In June Dr. Wait-Still Winthrop's wife died of the smallpox, and Mather was called to pray with Samuel Sewall's dying cousin, Daniel Quincy. Mather computed the fatalities in this epidemic at 320. Less than a week before Phips's grand fleet sailed for Quebec early in August, an extensive fire damaged many houses in the South End, and in mid-September a smaller fire destroyed five houses and was barely kept from ruining the South meetinghouse. A fast was held at Mather's house the next day, September 17, but the bad news continued to flow in.

Under the heavy pressure created by the conflicting signals from Providence, Mather began in the summer and autumn of 1690 to respond in two ways that have virtually dominated his characterization by historians ever since the end of the seventeenth century. In a period of dreadful uncertainty, this man who had recently resolved to be found singing the Lord's praises even while sinking, began to write biographies that emphasized New England's triumphs, the golden age, the lives of the finest saints. In the very summer during which Indians joined French raiders in renewed attacks on New England towns, Mather wrote of Eliot's evangelical success among other Indians. And although the representation in this biography and Mather's later narratives was consistently ethnocentric, Mather expressed a degree of compassion for all "savages" during this year in which he was more firmly convinced than ever that the Indian allies of the French were the Devil's dupes as well as the Pope's. The biography calls the Indians of North America "the veriest ruins of mankind." "Stone was instead of metal for their tools" before the English arrived, Mather says, and their term for an Englishman at first was the equivalent of "knife-man." They had to be made men, Mather says, before they could be made Christians. Eliot's achievements and those of some missionaries on Martha's Vineyard became in this biography all the more praiseworthy because of the extreme difficulty of the challenge.

In the first year of the new decade, Mather's imaginative representation of glorious achievements was not yet what some scholars believe it became a few years later — an escape from a gloomy present into an idealized past. The Book of Revelation and other biblical prophecies had prepared him at least theoretically for the coincidence of glorious wonders and terrifying upheavals in the time just before the Millennium. Besides the prodigious Psalm singing in France, Mather also considered the scientific discoveries of the dawning Enlightenment among the wonders that supported his chiliastic hopes. In his Thanksgiving sermon "The Wonderful Works of God" in 1689, he had urged New Englanders to become "citizens of the WORLD" in their grateful awareness of God's splendid creation "in every corner of it." "There are above six thousand *plants* growing on that little spot of the world, which we tread upon," Mather had told them, in a modernized version of the old argument from design:

> and yet a learned man, has more than once, found *one* vegetable enough to make a subject for a *treatise* on it. What might then be said about the hundred and fifty *volatils,* the five and twenty *reptiles,* besides the vast multitudes of *aquatils,* added unto the rich variety of gems and minerals, in our world? Our own *bodies* are, to use the phrase of the Psalmist, *so fearfully and wonderfully made,* that one of the ancient heathen at the sight thereof, could not forbear breaking forth into an hymn unto the praise of the great Creator; 'tis impossible that anything should be better shaped! Indeed, all the things that we have every day before our eyes, have a most charming prospect in them; and the very deformities which the Flood has brought upon this terraqueous globe, are made *beauties,* by the disposals of *the Lord*

*that sat upon the Flood.* There is not a *fly,* but what may confuse an *atheist.* And the little things which our naked eyes cannot penetrate into, have in them a *greatness* not to be seen without astonishment. By the assistance of the *microscopes* have I seen *animals* of which many hundreds would not equal a grain of sand. How exquisite, how stupendous must the structure of them be! The *whales* that are sometimes found more than a *hundred* foot in length, methinks those moving islands, are not such *wonders* as these minute fishes are.

But alas, all this *globe* is but as a pin's point, if compared with the mighty *universe.* Never did any man yet make a tolerable guess at its dimensions: but were we among the *stars,* we should utterly lose sight of our *earth,* although it be above twenty-six thousand *Italian* miles in the compass of it.

The extraordinary flexibility of Mather's perspective here did not always please his auditors. (As late as 1714, Samuel Sewall, who had taught physics at Harvard, complained that he found it "inconvenient" of Mather to declare that the sun was in the center of the solar system.) But Mather felt impelled to follow the celebration of God's glory, wherever it led. Moving in this passage and the next few lines from the miniature worlds so recently opened by the microscope to the cosmic spaces from which even a telescope would not be able to make the earth visible, Mather suggested that in the world of the new order men would need such flexibility. They might have to think of the stars themselves as worlds, he implied, and he hoped that men would one day be better able to travel physically over the world than they now could travel in fantasy. As if he perceived how unsettling these new perspectives might be, he remarked that gazing at the sun had blinded him to further examples, but he had already gone far enough to anticipate (once again) a problem that would command the attention of American writers as diverse as Jonathan Edwards, Benjamin Franklin, Herman Melville, and Henry Adams.

In a year of great troubles, it was easier to accept the theory of such affirmations than to acquiesce with appropriate resignation when the troubles struck oneself, one's father, one's chosen associates. Ill-tempered sensitivity to criticism is the second response to great pressure that helped Cotton Mather fashion in 1690 the image by which he would be known in later centuries. He had always been eager to please, and anxious about the family name and his own. Now, as a famous and influential young man trying to sustain his share of the Lord's work at a time when the fluctuations between good and bad omens seemed as extreme as the different perspectives required for looking through a microscope and a telescope, he began to sound irritable, sometimes petulant.

The provocation in these months usually concerned somebody else with whom Mather identified himself, or whom he chose to defend, but he attracted the opponent's fire to himself, and he sometimes took it personally even when it was more generally directed. From a vehement argument with the Quaker George Keith, who had challenged Puritan ministers to a debate and had accused Increase Mather of lies and slander, these encounters extended to his defense of his father against political critics (as in the letter to the Governor of Plymouth), to the defense of a would-be publisher named Benjamin Harris, and to the defense of Sir William Phips.

Benjamin Harris, for example, published a newspaper in Boston on September 25, 1690, probably the first newspaper in North America, under the title of *Public Occurrences*. He obviously had the support of Cotton Mather, and the rumor that Mather had actually written the paper (as he had written several other anonymous documents in recent years) gained some acceptance, although it was probably inaccurate. Certainly Mather approved of the three chief purposes announced in Harris's first and only issue: to record memorable providences, to encourage citizens to be properly informed on public affairs "both abroad and at home," and to cure "the spirit of lying, which prevails amongst us." On the third point, Harris even promised to expose the name of any rumormonger whose false witness could be traced to its source.

Governor Bradstreet and the Council immediately suppressed the paper. Harris had not requested a license to publish it, and he had published offensive material about the Mohawks (allies of the English colonies in their campaign against Quebec) and about Louis XIV. The Mohawks, he had intimated in one article, had not behaved so loyally as to allay doubts about their opposition to the French; Louis XIV had provoked his son to parricidal rebellion by seducing the son's wife. The entire item about Louis XIV was plainly identified as an unsubstantiated rumor, and the paper contained nothing else that could justify the Council's charge that it was scandalous, but the authorities must have anticipated the inconvenience that might be caused by a monthly paper whose editor interpreted his obligation to cure the spirit of lying in these ways.

Mather's reaction was swift and, in Samuel Sewall's judgment, sharp. The proclamation to silence the paper was issued on October 1, and Mather objected angrily in a letter, since lost, that Samuel Sewall read the next day. Two weeks later, Mather protested that he had only helped Harris to compress some of the narrative about the military expedition into Canada, and he was still obviously irritated by the Council's allusion to *"some,* that had published that scandalous thing." He did defend the comment about the Mohawks as a hard truth with which they deserved to be confronted, and he ridiculed the notion that Massachusetts should fear offending Louis XIV with a newspaper "when we are taking from him the best *country* he has in *America.*" But he concluded that the real purpose of the proclamation — "to make me odious" — had been achieved, and he predicted that "a few such tricks" would "render me uncapable of serving either *God* or *man* in *New England.*" He also alluded vaguely and miserably to "the calumnies of the people against poor me," and even when he insisted that he was not one of the three or four honest and ingenious men who had sponsored the *Occurrences,* he whined that before attacking such men the paper's critics "might do well to endeavor themselves to do something that may render them worthy to be accounted *serviceable.*"

The collapse of the assault upon Canada shortened many tempers along with Mather's. Phips's fleet had sailed splendidly on a fine day in August, but had unaccountably taken nine weeks to reach Quebec. The army that had been expected to march with Indian allies from Albany to Montreal, to create an essential diversion there while Phips invaded Quebec, never did get far enough to trouble Count Frontenac's small garrison of defenders. Smallpox and other pestilence virtually ruined Phips's army while the men were still crowded into their ships, and the onset of cold weather combined with the smallpox, storms, and inadequate supplies to raise the mortality rate to disastrous heights before the miserable survivors found their way back to Boston. Soon after portents of catastrophe arrived there on November 8, with the report that sixty corpses (mostly Indian warriors from Plymouth) had been buried from one ship at sea before it had returned from Quebec to Salem, critics began to suggest that Sir William Phips's indecisiveness had kept him from seizing Quebec at the very time it was most likely to fall. Soldiers at the Boston fort began to die of smallpox in mid-November, and reports that others had drowned on the way back from Quebec were received while Bostonians arranged funerals for those who had died after their return. At Major Samuel Ward's burial on November 22, with Governor and Mrs. Bradstreet present, only one volley was fired in salute, because powder was now scarce. The colony had lost between £ 40,000 and £ 50,000 in the misadventure.

Cotton Mather was outraged by Phips's critics. The chief objection that was officially laid to Phips was his alleged fleecing of the captured governor of Port Royal, one Meneval, whom Phips had brought to Boston. Meneval had charged Phips with dishonorably confiscating a trunkful of his personal effects, which Meneval had entrusted to Phips upon surrendering. It seems likely that some of Meneval's best clothes had been disposed of at the sale of the New England soldiers' plunder in mid-June, for when Phips at last (in January 1691) obeyed Governor Bradstreet's command to return the trunk, Meneval protested that his money and much of his finery were missing. Meanwhile, Phips had "very fiery words" with a member of the Council during a meeting on this general subject on November 29, and as he rushed from the room he seemed to say not only that he would never come there again, but also that if the Council did not defend his honor against the insulting member, Phips would defend it himself. Mather felt sure that Phips would never have been so badly treated if he had not suffered the recent defeat at Quebec. Mather saw more reason to blame the defeat and the small-pox on the Lord's anger over the construction of an Anglican church in the heart of Boston than to criticize Sir William.

Both Mather and Phips were so upset by the Council's response to the Meneval charges that, although Mather was reported to be ill and Phips to have sprained his ankle, their mutual absence from the services on the Fast day December 17 indicates that more than Phips's ankle was "out of joint." Phips was apparently still sulking or steaming on the twenty-ninth, for when Samuel Sewall called at his home in one of several attempts to mollify him, both Cotton Mather and Joshua Moody were already there. In the "very sharp discourse" of the four men, Mather "very angrily said that they who did such things as suffering Sir William to be arrested by Meneval, were Frenchmen, or the people would say they were." Apparently the anger had some effect, for Sewall and the Council voted the next day to annul the writ that had been entered against Phips, but the squabble was protracted by an order for the return of Meneval's chest and clothes.

Conflicts and anxieties of these trivial and more serious kinds per-

sisted throughout the next year as the war continued and Increase
Mather's negotiations dragged to a conclusion. Sir Edmund Andros
and Joseph Dudley had returned to London and had made a strong
case before the Lords of Trade against the Puritan colonists and the
defiant merchants. The news that the King's advisers were insisting
that he appoint a royal governor came to Boston along with rumors
that Andros might once again become the royal governor of New
York. Joseph Dudley returned to Massachusetts in January 1691,
and the gravity of the potential danger was underlined by the
news—first reported in Boston on May 21 by the frustrated newspaper publisher Benjamin Harris—that Jacob Leisler, the rebel
governor of New York with whom Massachusetts had cooperated in
the unsuccessful invasion of Canada, had been executed by order of
his royally appointed successor. Even after Increase Mather cited
the King's promise to appoint a governor who would be acceptable
to the people of Massachusetts "and recommended by their agents"
in London, some Bostonians understandably suspected that the
elder Mather had been seduced by aristocratic and royal guile, and
perhaps by the virtual invitation to name the new governor by himself. Mather declared that the King had promised to restore the
colony's "charter and privileges" and that he had insisted on appointing a military man as governor-general only during the temporary crisis; but the King had gone to Holland the day after giving his
ambiguous order, and his Council had ordered the Attorney General to draw up a charter providing for a royal governor with veto
power over all acts of the colonial legislature. Mather's subsequent
protests went unanswered, and the King eventually signed the new
charter after his return.

Bostonians, of course, received this information in painfully separate installments. Cotton Mather learned in mid-September his father's version of the King's instructions, and transcribed it in a letter
to his uncle in Plymouth. He even quoted Increase Mather's version
of the King's ambiguous sentence about a temporary general or governor. He reported happily that the officials' efforts to distort the
King's intention had been foiled, although he did not suggest how
the remaining ambiguity might be resolved when the King should
return from Holland to sign the completed document. He emphasized the inclusion of Maine in the new charter, the annual election
of the deputy governor and the General Court, and the King's agreement that—although he reserved the power to send "a general, for

all the united colonies"—such an official would "have no power to do anything in our colony without the concurrence of our own magistrates; nor can any laws, be made, or taxes levied, without a General Court." As late as December 8, however, Cotton Mather felt obliged to deny the persistent rumor that his father had sent for his family in order to emigrate to London. The reason for the alleged plan was said to be the predicted return of Sir Edmund Andros to New England. Should that dreaded prediction be accurate, Cotton Mather said, at least ten of the "most considerable persons in the country" would immediately "strike into England; and they will not go, unless I accompany them." That exodus would not be a retreat, Mather declared, but a boldly calculated entry into a theater "where our Tories would be loath to have them go." By going directly to London, he implied, they would interest William and Mary in their plight. Less than three months after rejoicing in the prospects for the new charter and in the likelihood that his father would be allowed to nominate Sir William Phips as general or governor of the united colonies, Mather was so serious about the prospect of having to emigrate that he not only wrote about it in a private letter but also spoke to his congregation about the possibility of requesting the necessary release from his covenant as Pastor. Before he mailed this letter, he learned that the King had returned to England, giving Puritans "cause to hope that our adversaries are still clogged. God clog them a little further," he concluded, "and all will be well."

It is these kinds of polarized expectations that dominated Cotton Mather's thoughts about political and religious affairs during the months and weeks before a vast conspiracy of witches was discovered near Salem Village in the winter of 1692. Mather's ordinary life in the family, the church, and the community continued to take much of his time during 1691. He published the biography of Eliot and a number of other works: a catechism; two counter-attacks on George Keith and other Quakers; a chiliastic sermon preached before the artillery company on June 1, the day of their annual election of officers; and a defense of the value of bills of credit, the paper money that had been issued (and almost immediately depreciated by about 25 percent) after the financial disaster of the Canadian expedition. He also preached a sermon against hypocrisy, in which he offended Samuel Sewall by citing objection to periwigs as an example of how self-righteous men, willing to swallow a camel, might strain at a gnat. He stood in his father's place at the plain wedding of his sister

Sarah to the Reverend Nehemiah Walter on October 22, with his own father-in-law, John Phillips, performing the ceremony. He presided at the very large funeral of Mrs. John Richards early in November. And he wrote the report for a council of congregations called to mediate a religious dispute in Lynn early in November. But his deepest concern focused on signs of the approaching Millennium in the affairs of his church as well as those of the state.

One major sign that became apparent to Bostonians during the winter of 1691-92 was the "Blessed Union" (as Mather called it in a sermon) joining the English Presbyterians and Congregationalists under the name of United Brethren. Cotton Mather was proud of his father's participation in the articles of agreement that joined the two denominations in England. In his own church he worked hard throughout 1691 and into the spring of 1692 to persuade the congregation to accept a formal ceremony re-owning the covenant. He saw this personal campaign as his own reaction to the "awakening" that he believed Providence was evidently trying to effect by the strange political, ecumenical, medical, and military events. He now calculated that the reign of Antichrist would probably end, according to the prophecy in the Book of Revelation, in 1697, and he saw the Glorious Revolution of 1689 (now nearly three years in the past) as a major signal of the divine intention. New England must respond by doing something "remarkable about returning to God." A proper awakening required the Lord's people to know the time, and a minister who knew history as well as typology felt obliged to explain "what peculiar things there are in this time, that are for our awakening." Mather did not preach the sermon called *A Midnight Cry* until April 10, 1692, when he had at last persuaded his congregation to hold a special Fast day, but he had been pleading for more than six months that something unusual must be done to awaken sleeping Christians. They must be committed to the imminent "NEW REFORMATION . . . ; a REFORMATION more glorious, more heavenly, more universal far away than" the Reformation of 1517. Mather felt convinced that "we are got into the very dawn of the day, when God will vouchsafe a marvellous effusion of His own *Spirit* upon many nations, and REFORMATION, with all *piety,* and *charity,* shall gain the ascendant, over those men and things, that for many ages have been the oppressors of it." All the peace of New England, he declared, "lies in her being, *a wise virgin,* that shall go forth to meet, *this blessed Reformation.*"

In the winter of 1691-92 Mather also "amplified and fitted" for publication a sermon of Samuel Lee's called *The Great Day of Judgment,* and Mather wrote an extended preface. Here his arguments ranged all the way from traditional doctrines concerning the Judgment to specific mathematical computations. Besides some ingeniously contrived examples to impress on every sinner the true magnitude of an eternal punishment, he demonstrated (even as he scorned the skeptic's demand for such proofs) that England alone would be large enough to provide ample standing room after the Judgment for every human being who had ever lived or would ever be born. For this computation he allowed a world population of one billion every fifty years, he said, and he allowed the world what he considered the incredibly long existence of ten thousand years from the Creation to the Judgment. But he knew in the winter of 1691-92 that the Judge was "at the door; I do without any hesitation venture to say, *The Great Day of the Lord is near, it is near, and it hastens greatly.*" Going forth to meet the Bridegroom was a matter of prudence as well as duty.

To encourage that voluntary encounter as history approached its culmination, Mather spent much of his energy during the winter of 1691-92 on a new campaign to persuade his church to accept the Half-Way Covenant. His father had accepted it twenty years ago, and had defended it against Solomon Stoddard's still more extravagantly liberal practice ever since the celebrated Mather-Stoddard debate during the Reforming Synod of 1679. But several leading members of the Mathers' church persisted in believing that the Half-Way Covenant violated one of the first principles of covenanted Congregationalism. They could not accept the "half-way" compromise that allowed the children of covenanted members to have their own infants baptized even though these parents themselves—the intermediate generation—had never experienced the conversion necessary for full membership. Cotton Mather resolved that his own special duty, in a time when churches must "do some remarkable thing," required him to bring as many new people as possible into his church. Convinced that the Devil would be more active as the Millennium approached, Mather also believed that many children of the covenant had failed to come forward as prospective church members because they feared being presumptuous. He wanted to encourage them by offering baptism to any person who was "instructed and orthodox in the Christian religion." Full membership, of course, would still require evidence of a genuine conversion, but the church's gesture and the experience of re-owning the covenant might encourage the timid to go forth and meet the blessed Reformation.

This was no time for open controversy in the church. Nor did Mather forget that among those old members who opposed the innovation stood Major John Richards, a magistrate, a wealthy merchant, formerly the colony's agent in London. Mather wrote to him personally on February 13, 1692, to request his approval of at least a ceremony in which all those reared in the covenant would renew their commitment to it, and the church would acknowledge the ways in which its members had fallen short. Richards apparently did not acquiesce. With considerable adroitness, then, Mather proceeded to gain the approval of at least seventy-five church members, including three magistrates. He preached a sermon on the Half-Way Covenant during a church meeting, after which he forbade public discussion of his arguments. At Mather's instigation, several influential members introduced a resolution containing Mather's own "sentiments and purposes," and asking Mather to "act accordingly." By behaving "peaceably, and obligingly, and yet resolutely towards" the few members who still opposed the innovation, Mather eventually won his way with them, too. That process took almost another year, during which Mather held off the actual change out of respect for the scruples of Richards and others. But both Mather's effort and the position of Richards in mid-February establish an important part of the context in which the Devil's attack upon Salem Village engaged the attention of Cotton Mather. Mather told Richards that the design was close to his own heart, and that he was sure the entire church would immediately concur if Richards should approve. That action, he concluded, "would be as great a compliance with the loud calls of God, as any that I am capable of devising; and *I think also, that I am somewhat awake.*"

⁓⧉⤙

THE FIRST warrant was issued in Salem on February 29, 1692, to arrest a woman named Sarah Good. Several young girls, including the Salem Village minister's daughter, had come down with fits that closely resembled the symptoms of the Goodwin children in Boston, and those of some Swedish children who had been afflicted in 1669. A physician in Salem had diagnosed bewitchment. Several of the girls, who had been dabbling in fortune telling and other minor forms of the occult, had cried out upon Sarah Good and the minister's West Indian slave, a woman named Tituba. At her examination before the magistrates on the first day of March, Tituba had confessed to witchcraft.

Except for the afflicted children's implication in guilty play with diabolical materials, this new case would thus far be perfectly familiar to any observer who remembered the Goodwin-Glover case. Not only the children's symptoms, but the prompt confession by a foreign woman whose comprehension and powers of resistance might have failed her under the magistrates' aggressive questioning even if she had not been guilty, followed the Bostonian pattern. Tituba, however, did not confide the names of her confederates to the discretion of a minister. She named two of them in open court, confirming the afflicted girls' accusations against Sarah Good and Sarah Osborne, and she swore that those two had forced her to serve the Devil and hurt the girls. Long before Cotton Mather had a chance to suggest that the afflicted girls be separated from one another and that he be allowed to take at least one of them into his home to be treated as he had treated Martha Goodwin (who by now belonged with her parents to Mather's church), the opportunity to limit the investigation, if not the witch hunt, had been lost.

Salem Village, moreover, was not Boston. An anomalous entity, an extensive parish that had a meetinghouse and a minister but few of the other institutions or privileges of the usual New England town, Salem Village had no clear relation to the town of Salem. Even the village church, covenanted only three years earlier, had come into being against the opposition of the town, and the village had become notorious in recent years for unusually bitter disagreements involving its ministers. Since October 1691, the minister of the Salem Village church had been obliged to subsist without the customary funds collected by local taxes, for an explicit vote of the village had denied him a salary for 1692. When the girls became afflicted, two of them in the minister's household and others in the family of one of his chief supporters, the minister did try to cure them in the way that Cotton Mather had prescribed, by fasting and prayer, but evidence and suspicion of terrible malice in the community were overwhelming. When members of the minister's own household tried to cure the girls by making a hellish witch-cake out of excrement, the fits grew worse instead of better, and the distraught adults concentrated more intensely than ever on discovering who the tormentors were.

The exact date of Cotton Mather's offer to "scatter" the possessed girls "far asunder" and to take personal responsibility for six of them cannot now be determined. He said later in the year that he had made his proposal "at the beginning" and that it had been rejected —probably to the great relief of Abigail Mather, his silent partner in the exhausting therapy of Martha Goodwin. It seems inconceivable that the Mather household could have provided "singly" for six of the possessed, but Mather's behavior in the Goodwin case suggests that he would have tried to avoid publicizing the names they cried out. Since both Sarah Good (who did not confess) and Tituba publicly accused other people on the very first day of official questioning, it seems likely that at best Mather's plan might have limited the girls' powerful effect on one another, and perhaps the spectacular effects of a new name upon the girls when a magistrate or one of the afflicted herself called it out in open court. The rejection of Mather's offer left the girls free to appear regularly before the magistrates in terrifying scenes of possession and accusations. Sometimes the girls' fits were almost unbearably affecting for adult observers, and sometimes the entire room would vibrate with noisy excitement as an afflicted person claimed to see a diabolical specter or a grotesque familiar on a beam, or coming through a window.

Besides the social conditions in Salem Village, about which Mather knew virtually nothing, the rapid multiplication of accusations and arrests during March and April seemed then as now to depend heavily on the astonishing number and quality of actual confessions. Even Sarah Good, at the very first examination by John Hathorne and Jonathan Corwin, had admitted knowing more than an innocent bystander ought to have known about who was afflicting the children, and she herself seemed to impeach her evasive claims that she had been thanking Mr. Parris—no, saying her commandments—or no, a Psalm—when the girls had heard her muttering as she had left the minister's house one day, after a quarrel. Besides what the prejudiced court reporter called "the many lies [Good] was taken in," and her own husband's declaration that "she is an enemy to all good," the elaborate confession of Tituba must have been extremely impressive to anyone who heard about it in

Boston. Tituba's answers may well have been prompted by a canny recognition of what her examiners wanted to hear, but they were so elaborate and circumstantial that nobody who believed in the world of spirits could easily have dismissed them. After denying that she had hurt the children, she quickly admitted that the Devil had threatened her, that Good and Osborne had forced her to hurt the children, that she had flown to Boston with them on sticks, and that a tall man of Boston was in league with the witches. She said that she had seen on four different occasions a creature "like a hog and sometimes like a great dog," which threatened her, and that when the dog had turned into a man who kept a yellow bird with him, the spectral man had offered her pretty things in return for her agreement to serve him. She spoke of having seen two rats, one black and the other red, and of having been pulled and hauled to Thomas Putnam's house and forced there to hurt the children again. She said that Sarah Good had a yellow bird as a familiar that sucked between Good's fingers, and that Good had offered to give her such a bird for herself. Sarah Osborne, Tituba swore, had a yellow dog and "a thing with a head like a woman with 2 legs, and wings," and one of the afflicted girls confirmed that description. Tituba swore that she had heard Osborne and Good confess that they had hurt a child named Corwin, and that she had seen Sarah Good set a wolf on Elizabeth Hubbard last Saturday. She spoke of a tall white-haired man in black clothes, and of a woman in a white hood and a black hood with a topknot.

Perhaps the most powerful confession besides Tituba's was that of Deliverance Hobbs, who broke down under examination on April 22. At first she emphatically denied her guilt, and when the magistrate asked whether she had given the Devil permission for the appearance that had undoubtedly taken her shape, she replied: "No in the sight of God, and man, as I shall answer another day." But soon she began to describe the strange sights she had seen—birds, cats, dogs—and the voice she had heard urging her to come away. She had seen specters, she said, but they had not threatened her or asked her to sign the Devil's book. When two of the afflicted girls suddenly cried out that they saw Goody Hobbs herself on a beam above the examination room, the magistrates tried again to persuade her to confess, and Tituba's husband and two others were convulsed in apparent fits when Goody Hobbs looked at them.

"Tell us the reason of this change," said a magistrate. "Tell us the truth. What have you done?"

"I cannot speak."

"What do you say? What have you done?"

"I cannot tell."

"Have you signed to any book?"

Innocent or guilty, Hobbs could hold out no longer. "It is very lately then," she said. And the story came forth readily as she answered leading questions. Now she contradicted her denials of having been threatened, she gave several names of people who had threatened her, and the name of a child she had afflicted, and she said she had seen a "tall black man with a highcrowned hat" among the other witches. In prison a few days later, she said she had attended a meeting with many other accused witches in the minister's pasture near Salem Village, and that the Reverend George Burroughs, a minister who had formerly preached in the Salem Village church, had administered the Devil's sacrament and urged his followers to "bewitch all in the village, . . . gradually and not all at once, assuring them they should prevail." A man in a long crowned white hat, she said, had sat next to Burroughs.

Abigail Hobbs had already testified on April 20 that she too had attended "the great meeting in Mr. Parris's pasture when they administered the sacrament and did eat of the red bread and drink of the red wine at the same time." No modern inquirer will fail to notice with a healthy skepticism the coincidence of names, dates, and descriptions. "Flashy people," Cotton Mather foresaw when he wrote about these matters a few years later, might "*burlesque* these things," but here as in 1688 he believed that the authorities had used their mother wit to screen out evidence of fraud and delusion. They checked for teeth marks in spectrally bitten arms, they sometimes separated the afflicted from one another, and sometimes made sure that the afflicted could not see or hear what a defendant did before their reaction was observed. For a minister receiving news in Boston in March and April 1692, the central question could not have been — although perhaps it ought to have been — whether the entire complex of afflictions, accusations, and confessions was a delusion. Before the autumn of 1692, nobody in Boston suggested publicly or in any surviving private record that the entire outbreak was a delusion. Before twenty people accused of witchcraft had been executed that summer, nobody in New England wrote so often as Cotton Mather wrote to warn the authorities against evidence that might convict the innocent.

Yet the record will not allow even the most sympathetic biographer the pleasure of casting Mather as a defeated hero in this tragic affair. One major reason for granting this episode the dignity of tragedy is that all their wisdom, skepticism, and respect for human liberties did not prevent Mather and his fellow ministers from acquiescing in some of the executions and vigorously endorsing others. Although it would be as unjust to blame the entire "delusion" on the clergy as it was convenient for Mather to blame it chiefly on the Devil, the point of a sympathetic analysis is not to deny that Mather had any responsibility for what happened. The student of his life hopes rather to understand how Mather could have come to allow the witch hunt to continue with his approval despite his clear warnings, issued before the first trial began and repeated before the first execution, against the judges' fatal error.

Before examining Mather's judicious warnings, consider the negative side of his behavior, his fierce encouragement of retributory justice. Ever since his own life had been splendidly irradiated by his vision of the angel, he had lived with the threatening knowledge that the Devil has power to assume the shape of an angel of light, and this experience of his personal vision had given additional force in his life to the logical corollary available to any student of theology: denial of the Devil's power in this world implied the denial of other spirits, including angels, and perhaps of still greater supernatural powers and actions that were described as unequivocally in the Bible as the command (Exodus 22:18) to execute witches. Whether or not it was consciously articulated, this line of personal and theological reasoning helps to explain the triumphantly derisive tone in which Mather resolved after his experience in the Goodwin case to have little patience with anybody who might question the existence of witches.

The chiliastic and military context must also be prominently remembered. The four or five jeremiads that Cotton Mather preached between December 1691 and August 1692 deplored New England's sins in the context of the seemingly endless French and Indian wars, the cycle of other catastrophes, and the approaching Millennium. In two of these sermons, one on the cause and the other on the cure of a wounded spirit, Mather conceded that suicide was a major problem in New England, and he blamed it on "a more than ordinary impulse of the Devil, whereof I have seen most prodigious evidences." One overconscientious Puritan had resisted all of Mather's pleas for trust in God's mercy and had gone away with these parting words, *"Well, the Devil will have me after all!* And some company just then *hindering* me from going after" the poor man "as I *intended,"* Mather said, "ere I could get at him, he was found sitting in his chamber, choked unto death with a *rope,* which *rope* nevertheless was found, not about his neck, but in his *hand* and on his *knee."* This *"unnatural execution"* and others Mather attributed to those devils who had "dogged the *swine* into the deep of old, . . . the same that compel persons to be so much worse than *swine,* as to kill themselves."

Similar devils also roamed at large in human form along the eastern frontier. In writing about devils, Indians, and the King of France during wartime, Mather used invective that released much of the powerful anger he had long ago resolved to convert into prayers for the personal enemies who might strive to injure him. In the sermon published as *Fair Weather,* a jeremiad warning Bostonians against unwarranted discontent in their adversity, Mather associated the dragoons of King *"Louis Le Loup"* with fierce dragons, and he declared that the "tawny pagans" who had left their "inaccessible kennels" to raid the settlement at York, Maine, on January 25, 1692, were among the worst "devils incarnate upon earth!" The "tigers that were preying upon the *sheep* of York" murdered the local shepherd, the Reverend Shubael Dummer.

These sermons, preached before the first witchcraft accusations of 1692, could hardly have affected anybody in Salem Village until the irrevocable crying-out had resounded through the village and the town for many weeks. The value of the sermons here is to establish an essential part of the attitude with which Cotton Mather received the news from Salem. His extremely important *A Midnight Cry,* preached in April on the day that his congregation unanimously acknowledged sins and agreed to stay awake in preparedness for the Bridegroom's imminent arrival, warned that the sleep of sin makes a man "prey to all his internal and infernal adversaries." In such a war, Mather reasoned, the Lord might well act like a great general who, on finding a sleeping sentry, had immediately run him through, "saying, *Dead I found thee, dead I leave thee.*" Mather's hope that all the churches would awake and join the concerted battle against the world, the flesh, and the Devil was disappointed. Most of the other churches had neglected to approve his call for a general confession of New England's sins that would echo the Reforming Synod of 1679. All the more reason for the intensity of his call to seize this moment "by the *forelock*; . . .our *sleeping* in it," he warned again, "may cause our *slipping* in it forever. Every sand of this *time* is more precious than dust of *gold*." He laid no heavy emphasis on witchcraft in this sermon. His hope in preaching it was to achieve the function that a special impression of divine assurance actually gave him on the day the book was published: to be used by God as a John the Baptist, as a "herald of the Lord's Kingdom now approaching and *the voice crying in the wilderness*, for preparation thereunto." In *A Midnight Cry* the attack of the devils is only one of the many calamities and other signs by which the Lord has recently sought to awaken New England to prepare for the ultimate Reformation.

On August 4, however, when the deadly process of that demoralizing summer approached its culmination in the multiple executions of mid-August and mid-September, Mather brought out his most extreme rhetoric in a sermon prepared for the special day of fasting. On that very morning Boston had received word of an earthquake in Jamaica in which thousands of people had died. Now Mather, preaching on a chiliastic text — "the Devil is come down unto you, having great wrath; because he knoweth, that he hath but a short time" — spoke forcibly of the earthquakes that would increasingly convulse the world in the years just before the Millennium, and of the Devil's war against the Lord's people. Although Mather came back repeatedly to the court's difficulty in trying to punish the guilty without injuring the innocent, he brought out his most vehement rhetoric against the "high treason" that had "been committed against the most high God, by the witchcrafts in our neighborhood. . . . O 'tis a most humbling thing, to think, that ever there should be such an abomination among us, as for a crew of human race, to renounce their *Maker*, and to unite with the *Devil*, for the troubling of mankind, and for the people to be (as is by some confessed) *baptized* by a *fiend* [and] afterwards . . . communicating in an Hellish *bread* and *wine*. . . . It was said in Deut. 18.10, 11, 12. *There shall not be found among you an enchanter, or a witch, or a charmer, or a consulter with familiar spirits, or a wizard, or a necromancer; for all that do these things are an abomination to the Lord, and because of these abominations, the Lord thy God doth drive them out before thee.* That *New England* now should have these *abominations* in it, yea, that some of no mean *profession*, should be found guilty of them: Alas, what humiliations are we all hereby obliged unto? O 'tis a *defiled* land, wherein we live; let us be humbled for these *defiling abominations,* lest we be driven out of our land."

The critical spring and summer of 1692 brought to a powerful climax Mather's lifelong habit of converting political and religious conflicts into personal battles. His religious vocation, his conscientious dedication to New England's covenant, and his genealogical obligation to emulate the Mathers and the Cottons—all these intensified the habit. And in the peculiar year of 1692 objective evidence accumulated to reinforce his private judgment—just as his vision of the angel had been given an objective counterpart in what Mather called the "miraculous" cure of his stammer, the affliction that had long ago disappeared from the pages of his Reserved Memorials. Now Mather's father had been granted the privilege of nominating both the new royal governor and the entire council of magistrates, which included Abigail Mather's father. The governor would be Sir William Phips himself, and Phips and Increase Mather were bringing home the new charter in the spring. Cotton Mather was thus obliged once again to defend his family, himself, and his own congregation in a debate over fidelity to New England's original errand in the wilderness. He argued that the new charter was in some ways even better than the old. To quiet his own doubts about the Crown's power to appoint the governor, he had not only the comforting reality of Phips's incumbency but also the many signs that the ultimate Reformation would soon begin. As Cotton Mather found himself advising Governor Phips, the other ministers of Boston, and Judge John Richards about procedures in the witchcraft trials, it seemed perfectly clear that Providence had fulfilled his hope of being chosen for a singular commission in the last wars against the Devil. The innocent must not be mistaken for the guilty, but the human enemies in those wars would not be treated with the same compassion Mather had expressed toward James Morgan and other murderers.

⚬❊⚬

BY THE TIME Increase Mather and Governor Phips arrived on May 14, they found "the prisons full of people committed upon suspicion of witchcraft." More than fifty people were in jail. Because it was a Saturday night, time for Christians to prepare for worship on the Lord's Day, no cannon were fired in salute, and the celebration was put off until Monday. The North Church, however, was filled the next morning with joyous people to see the new native governor and their long-absent Teacher, and Cotton Mather delivered a hastily prepared sermon on the fourteenth chapter of Matthew, "Our Lord's *passing over the water.*"

Phips had to act quickly on both the witchcraft and the military campaign. Despite grave questions about his authority to act before the first meeting of the new General Court, he soon learned that relatives and friends of the afflicted were demanding action. Deputy Governor William Stoughton and many others, probably including the Mathers, advised Phips to create a Special Court of Oyer and Terminer, to hear and determine cases. The only immediate hope of reducing the great flood of accusations seemed to lie in prompt legal action. Phips appointed the special court, with William Stoughton as chief justice, on May 29.

Cotton Mather was pleased to see that John Richards was one of the seven judges. Explaining that he felt too ill to attend the first trial, which was to be held in Salem on the second day of June, Mather set his inexhaustible pen in motion. On May 31, he answered Richards' request for advice, in the first of two extraordinarily liberal statements that Mather issued in defense of human rights before any convicted witch was executed.

The tone of the letter to Richards contains none of the fierceness that characterized Mather's militant statements about devils and witches. Even in the fiery "Discourse on Witchcraft" that Mather had appended to his *Memorable Providences* in 1689, he had taken care to warn the congregation against accusing anybody "*wrongfully . . .* of this horrid and monstrous evil. . . . An *ill-look,* or a *cross word,*" he had warned, "will make a witch with many people, who may on more ground be counted so themselves." Now, after a rather perfunctory recommendation of a fast as a means of encouraging Providence to expose the guilty, Mather opened the central discussion of evidence with a warning against spectral evidence. He begged Richards not to put "more stress upon pure specter testimony than it will bear." Even after good legal evidence shows that the afflicting demons "do indeed represent such and such people to the sufferers," he warned, "though this be a presumption, yet I suppose you will not reckon it a conviction that the people so represented are witches to be immediately exterminated. It is very certain that the devils have sometimes represented the shapes of persons not only innocent, but also very virtuous. Though I believe that the just God then ordinarily provides a way for the speedy vindication of the persons thus abused."

Mather's warning against relying on spectral evidence did not stop with the virtuous. Ordinarily malignant, envious, or malicious people, he said, "may unhappily expose themselves to the judgment of being represented by devils, of whom they never had any vision, and with whom they have much less written any covenant." With a clear-headed warning that was soon to sound like accurate prophecy, Mather said that if the court should rely on spectral evidence "a door may be thereby opened for the devils to obtain from the courts in the invisible world a license to proceed unto the most hideous desolations upon the repute and repose" of people who had not yet committed any witchcraft. "If mankind have thus far consented unto the credit of diabolical representations the door is opened!" Wise and good men might call Mather a "witch advocate" for insisting on this caution, he said, "but in the winding up this caution will certainly be wished for."

Certainly it was wished for in October, when there was no chance of reviving the innocent who had died along with the (probably) guilty. In May and June, when absolute condemnation of spectral evidence might have affected the court, neither Mather nor the other ministers could make the caution unequivocal. In the letter to Richards, Mather even acknowledged that the devils might be moved by the imminence of Christ's ultimate Reformation to attack loyal Christians *without* using witchcraft. Yet the difficulty of learning who was guilty could not erase Mather's indelible impression that the evidence showed witchcraft was involved in the troubles at Salem Village. Witchcraft, he conceded, was a crime "very much transacted on the stage of Imagination," but here as in treason "the business thus managed in Imagination yet may not be called imaginary. The effects are dreadfully real. Our dear neighbors are most really tormented." Both the Bible and human law required that those who tormented others with witchcraft must be punished.

In the rest of his letter to Richards Mather recommended the search for a credible confession—"I say a credible confession, because even confession itself sometimes is not credible"—as the best way of apprehending the guilty. He approved of "cross and swift questions" as an appropriate way of trying to throw the guilty into such confusion that a genuine confession might be provoked. He also gave a qualified endorsement to one "experiment," the effort to see whether the defendant could recite the Lord's Prayer. Such tests, he insisted, must not be used as evidence, but only as a means of "confounding the lisping witches to give a reason why they cannot, even with prompting, repeat those heavenly composures." Here Mather gives no indication of remembering the gloomy occasions on which he himself had nearly choked in anguished efforts to break through a stammer into free speech. For the same purpose of confusion that might induce a confession, he also suggested a search for puppets in the defendant's lodgings, and a search by physicians for a witch's teat, the excrescence between a witch's fingers or legs whence a familiar was believed to suck for spiritual nourishment.

Despite these frightening concessions to loose investigative practices, Mather concluded by suggesting that, since many fools fall easily into witchcraft through the Devil's threats, some punishment far short of execution be found to reenlist the dupes in the wars against the Devil. If linked to public, "explicit renunciation of the Devil," relatively lenient punishment of "some of the lesser criminals" might provoke the devils to "cease afflicting the neighborhood." They might either go elsewhere or begin attacking the former witches themselves.

Here, in venturing some "free thoughts" to a member of his church who faced a difficult assignment, Mather inadvertently anticipated the crazy logic by which Satan, fear, or zeal did actually throw the court and Essex County into confusion. Although some confessed witches were condemned to death, none of these sentences was ever carried out; nobody who confessed was ever officially punished. Only those who insisted on their innocence—and one heroic old man who refused to plead guilty or not guilty before a tribunal that was sure to convict him and confiscate his property — were killed. The court was dominated by Chief Justice Stoughton's insistence that the Devil could not, or at least rarely did, take the shape of an innocent person when afflicting somebody else. Richards and Samuel Sewall, as well as Nathanael Saltonstall, who resigned after the first verdict was declared for conviction, may have argued for Mather's caution against opening a door for the Devil, but the court as a whole continued to take spectral evidence seriously throughout the summer.

The second of Cotton Mather's remarkably liberal statements in the midst of the witchcraft crisis was addressed to the newly constituted legislature on the day of its first meeting, which happened to fall on Thursday, June 9. This Thursday was not only the regular Lecture day but also the eve of the first convicted witch's execution. Mather's subject on this occasion — the greatest day in the history of Massachusetts, he said — had nothing directly to do with witchcraft. This was a time for speaking of good men rather than witches. Four days earlier, he had preached a sermon "directed unto the GOVERNOR," which he called *Good Men Described*. Now he spoke to the legislature on "good things propounded," advice on public attitudes and behavior to enhance the well-being of the newly chartered province. The most memorable passages in this sermon concern religious liberty. Even when one remembers that the new royal government required religious toleration in Massachusetts, Mather's statement to the legislature seems remarkably strong, an echo of Roger Williams, John Milton, and John Locke. Mather reminded the legislators that their King had recently said, "I will not be obliged to become a persecutor," and that every magistrate in Massachusetts was only a civil officer concerned with the citizens' behavior in human society. Political officers must leave the judgment of a man's religious behavior to religious societies. A Christian who fails to conform "to this or that imposed *way of worship*," Mather said, "does not break the terms on which he is to enjoy the benefits of *human society*. A man has a right unto his life, his estate, his liberty, and his family, although he should not come up to these and those blessed *institutions* of our Lord." In virtually the same language that Thomas Jefferson would use in Virginia, Mather told his fellow Puritans that forcible action to make people conform would be self-defeating: "*Violences* may bring the erroneous to be *hypocrites;* but they will never bring them to be *believers;* no, they naturally prejudice men's minds against the *Cause,* which is therein pretended for; as being a weak, a wrong, an evil cause." For his exemplary authority in these matters, Mather appealed not to John Milton or Roger Williams but, as many Puritans had done before him, to "the primitive Church." For the first three hundred years of Christianity, he said, that church had "cut off a thousand new *Hydra's* heads, without borrowing such *penal laws* as have since been used; it was by sound preaching, by discipline, by catechizing, and by disputation, that they *turned to flight the armies of the aliens.*"

In his account of this sermon in his Reserved Memorials some months later, Mather noted privately a motive that he had not mentioned to the General Court. On the eve of the first execution at Salem he had spoken for religious liberty at least partly because he "feared, that the zeal of my country had formerly had in it more *fire* than should have been; especially, when the mad *Quakers* were sent unto the *gallows,* that should have been kept rather in a *bedlam.*" He never did concede that all the condemned witches should have been reprieved, but he soon came to see, and within a few years he publicly acknowledged, that some innocent people may have been executed in Salem for witchcraft.

The conviction of Bridget Bishop on June 2 provoked Judge Nathanael Saltonstall to resign from the special court because he deplored either the verdict itself or the court's methods, or both. Governor Phips then asked the ministers of Boston to advise him and the Council about procedures in witchcraft cases. "The Ministers' Return" in answer to Phips's request was another of those anonymous documents that Cotton Mather wrote for a committee or informal group. Its arguments against the reliability of spectral evidence, and its warnings against the dangers of trusting such evidence, sometimes paraphrase Mather's letter of May 31 to John Richards. But now the condemnation of spectral evidence and other "things received only upon the Devil's authority" was even more emphatic. The ministers briefly expressed sympathy for the afflicted, and gratitude for "the assiduous endeavors of our honorable rulers to detect the abominable witchcrafts" in the country. But even here they subtly suggested that the methods of discovering "these mysterious and mischievous wickednesses" needed to be "perfected." They devoted the bulk of their advice to five numbered paragraphs warning the Governor and Council of "the need for a very critical and exquisite caution, lest by too much credulity for things received only upon the Devil's authority, there be a door opened for a long train of miserable consequences, and Satan get an advantage over us, for we should not be ignorant of his devices." They recommended "an exceeding tenderness towards those that may be complained of; especially if they have been persons formerly of an unblemished reputation." Instead of encouraging the authorities to try to confuse the defendants (as Mather in his private letter had advised Richards to do), the ministers now urged that those interrogations be conducted with "as little as is possible, of such noise, company, and openness, as may too hastily expose" the defendants. They asked the authorities to refrain from using any test that might be of doubtful validity "among the people of God." They insisted that not only convictions but even original arrests on suspicion "ought certainly to be more considerable, than barely the accused person being represented by a specter unto the afflicted," for they called it both "undoubted" and "notorious" that a demon might appear in the shape of innocent and virtuous people. They insisted that one other kind of circumstantial evidence was similarly fallible because it was "frequently liable to be abused by the Devil's legerdemains": the startling changes that were apparently wrought upon "the sufferers, by a look or touch of the accused." And they suggested that by "our disbelieving" those kinds of testimony, "whose whole force and strength is from [the devils] alone," the whole community might give the devils "remarkable affronts" and thus stop the dreadful proliferation of accusations.

In this penultimate article Mather and his colleagues had moved a long way from their opening paragraphs. They had begun by deploring the suffering of the afflicted. Now they focused on a different problem as a "dreadful calamity": the progressive "accusation of so many persons, whereof we hope, some are yet clear from the great transgression laid unto their charge." The ministers were undoubtedly alarmed by the arrest of John Alden. A respected Boston merchant, Alden had gone to Salem Village on May 28, had been accused by the afflicted girls, had then apparently induced new fits by merely looking at them, and had been arrested on May 31, the very day of Cotton Mather's letter to Richards. Alden was the first Bostonian of excellent repute to be summoned before the magistrates in Salem. His arrest, the execution of Bridget Bishop, and the resignation of Judge Saltonstall apparently persuaded Mather and his colleagues that the door was already open, not because they doubted Bridget Bishop's guilt but because there now seemed almost no way to stop John Hathorne and Jonathan Corwin from haling into court and packing off to jail any respectable person whose name the devils or any other informant might whisper to the afflicted girls.

Had the ministers ended their "Return" with the seventh of their eight articles, their reputation in the next three centuries might have been as humane as Cotton Mather tried to make it when he omitted their eighth article from his summary of the document in his biography of Phips. Even if their admonition had failed to check the progress of the dreadful calamity, then, its import would have been much less ambiguous, much more emphatic. After only one execution, and as soon as their advice was requested, they would have had the honor of an unequivocal declaration that the galloping witch hunt was a calamity as bad as the afflictions of the possessed. But of course they did believe that the Devil was using witchcraft in his assault on the Lord's people in New England, just as he was assisting the French and Indians to whom the afflicted girls had accused John Alden of selling powder and shot. Cotton Mather wrote, and the other ministers endorsed, the eighth article with an explicit recognition of its contrast to the preceding five: "Nevertheless, We cannot but humbly recommend unto the government, the speedy and vigorous prosecution of such as have rendered themselves obnoxious, according to the direction given in the laws of God, and the wholesome statutes of the *English* nation, for the detection of witchcrafts." A sharp eye might notice that the laws of God offered some protection in capital cases, as well as a flat command to execute witches, and that the ministers did not endorse any *un*wholesome English statutes or folk practices, such as ducking. But the door was open.

❧

NINETEEN MEN and women were hanged before the end of September. Cotton Mather did not attend the trials in Salem. He kept in close touch with their progress, and his few contemporaneous letters indicate that the dozens of confessions, and other amazing events, reinforced his belief that a massive campaign of witches endangered New England. On August 5, the day after the whole town of Boston had "turned the Lecture into a fast, kept in our meeting-house," he wrote to his Uncle John Cotton not only about the earthquake in Jamaica that had killed seventeen hundred people in a town he considered "a very Sodom for wickedness," but also about other miraculous signs. "Our good God is working miracles," he said. Five witches were hanged on July 19, after they had "impudently" demanded that God give "a miraculous vindication of their innocency." But immediately after the execution, "our God miraculously sent in five Andover-witches, who made a most ample, surprising, amazing confession, of all their villainies and declared the five newly executed to have been of their company." All five confessors had agreed, moreover, that George Burroughs, formerly the minister at Salem Village, had been their "ringleader." Mather wrote this letter on the day of Burroughs' trial in Salem, to which Increase Mather and "a vast concourse of people" from Boston had gone. Along with the new confessions that now seemed to be coming in every day, the conviction of this minister seemed to be irrefutable evidence of the Devil's use of witchcraft in his last war. Mather had been praying secretly for a great number of confessions to ruin the evil strategy, and he believed that the answers to his prayers had been so nearly miraculous that he must not risk recording them.

On August 17, two days before the next group of executions, Mather answered an inquiry from John Foster, a member of the Governor's Council who wanted to know whether he had changed his mind about the unreliability of spectral evidence. Mather repeated in stronger terms than ever his conviction that the devils have "a natural power" to assume "what shape they please," and he predicted accurately that they might one day assume the shape of Cotton Mather himself. "All Protestant writers," he insisted, believe "that the Devil may thus abuse the innocent," and some Catholic writers concur. Mather expressed confidence that "our honorable judges" were too "eminent for their justice, wisdom, and goodness" to "proceed capitally against any" defendant on a contrary principle, even if some of the judges individually disagreed with the prevailing religious judgment. Yet Mather did defend the court's "very great use . . . of the spectral impressions upon the sufferers," for he claimed it might justly initiate an inquiry and "strengthen other presumptions." Virtually no defendant, he declared, had been tried by the court without "more human and most convincing testimonies" than merely spectral ones. He added quickly, however, that if any of the judges felt uneasy about guilty verdicts that had already been declared, the condemned persons in question ought to be given at least a temporary reprieve, and he even suggested that people arrested on wholly spectral evidence ought to be granted bail.

The society's proper interest in any defendant's behavior must be restricted to what Mather called "a suspected and unlawful communion with a familiar spirit." It was perfectly possible, he said, for "the communion on the Devil's part" to be proved while, "for aught I can say, the man may be innocent; the Devil may impudently impose his communion upon some that care not for his company." Mather even warned that the Devil might behave consistently in nineteen cases only to deceive "us at last if we thence make a rule to form an infallible judgment of a twentieth." Whether from prudence or conviction, Mather continued to insist that "we are blessed with judges who are aware of this danger."

Protecting the innocent was a difficulty so troublesome that Mather at last ventured a suggestion which he hoped might "cleanse the land of witchcrafts" without destroying innocent lives. He proposed some form of exile—"transportation," he called it—for any person who should have the misfortune to be represented by a specter molesting the neighborhood. Since Mather volunteered to undergo the transportation himself if his own person should be counterfeited in this way and if his neighbors' affliction could not be relieved without his actual departure, one must assume that he thought of the measure as a temporary expedient. He suggested vaguely that the Governor's power of commuting sentences, or a law passed by the General Court, might accomplish the innovation.

This letter to Foster shows clearly that by mid-August Mather felt troubled by the growing complaints against the court's procedures and judgments, even though he himself had been the first to articulate some of the most telling of those objections. Two days later he went to Salem and joined the very large crowd observing the execution of George Burroughs, John Proctor, and three others. That dramatic event brought the protests toward a crescendo, and one belated report of it made Cotton Mather into a specter of vengeance that has haunted his name ever since. Among the five persons who protested their innocence to the end on the nineteenth, Proctor and Burroughs were extraordinarily persuasive. Proctor had brought great trouble on himself in the spring by threatening publicly to whip the devil out of his housemaid when she turned out to be one of the afflicted girls. Thirty-two of his neighbors respected him and his wife so highly that they took the risk of signing a petition denouncing the accusations against the Proctors and affirming the superior value of the charitable judgment required by their own personal acquaintance and observation. Late in July Proctor had also addressed a moving petition from Salem prison to the ministers of Boston (with "Mr. Mather" heading the list), denying the accusations of the five Andover witches whose miraculous confessions Cotton Mather had cited, and complaining that Proctor's son William had been tortured in an effort to make him confess.

It was Burroughs, however, whose valedictory words made the greatest impression at Gallows Hill. A little man whose boasts of prodigious strength had played a major part in bringing him to the gallows, Burroughs, the only minister tried and convicted, bore the sensationally symbolic responsibility of antichristian leader, celebrator of the Devil's sacrament in the Reverend Samuel Parris's pasture in Salem Village. Pious observers had every reason to hope that the Devil might desert such a man in the minutes just before he went to Judgment, but Burroughs, like Proctor, behaved with such dignity and prayed with such apparent sincerity that his protestation of innocence "did much move unthinking persons," some of whom complained against his execution. Cotton Mather said that all five of the condemned people had died by a righteous sentence.

From the different verb tenses in Samuel Sewall's account in his diary, it seems reasonable to infer that both Mather's observation and the complaints against Burroughs' execution were made after Burroughs had been hanged. Sewall was a remarkably precise writer in the abbreviated scale of narrative that he usually chose for his daily entries. Here is the entire entry concerning the executions on August 19, 1692. Sewall himself had not been present in Salem, but had spent the day in Watertown.

> This day [in the margin, Dolefull! Witchcraft] George Burroughs, John Willard, Jn⁰ Proctor, Martha Carrier, and George Jacobs were executed at Salem, a very great number of spectators being present. Mr. Cotton Mather was there, Mr. Sims, Hale, Noyes, Cheever, &c.

1692.

Augt. 19th 1692. This day the Lieut Gour
Major Phillips, mr. Russel, Capt. Lynde
& my self went to Watertown. Advis'd
ye Inhabitants at yr Town-Meeting to settle
a Minister; and if coud not otherwise
agree, shoud first have a Town-Meeting
to decide where ye Meetinghouse shoud
be set: Many say Whitney's Hill
woud be a convenient place.

This day George Burrough, John
Willard, Jno Procter, Martha Carrier &
George Jacobs were executed at Salem
a very great number of Spectators be-
-ing present. Mr. Cotton Mather was
there, Mr. Sims, Hale, Noyes, Chiever
&c. All of ym said they were inocent,
Carrier & all. Mr. Mather says they all
died by a Righteous Sentence. mr. Bur-
-rough by his Speech, Prayer, protestati-
-on of his Inocence, did much move un-
-thinking persons, wch occasions yr speaking
hardly concerning his being Executed.
Augt 25. Fast at ye old church respecting
ye Witchcraft, Drought &c.

Augt. 27. abt 4 p m Cous. Fissenden
comes in & tells ye sad News of Simon
Gates being dead of ye ~~~~~~~~ Fever
died yesterday & is burried to day. I
heard not a word of it, & so neither
saw him sick; nor was at his Burial.

Dolefull!
Witchcraft.

Simon
Gates m.c.
Dies. at
muddy River

11. A page from Samuel Sewall's manuscript diary, reporting the
execution of John Proctor and George Burroughs, August 19, 1692.

> All of them said they were innocent, Carrier and all. Mr. Mather says they all died by a righteous sentence. Mr. Burroughs by his speech, prayer, protestation of his innocence, did much move unthinking persons, which occasions their speaking hardly concerning his being executed.

Because of Cotton Mather's other statements about the trials, commentators have unanimously assumed that the Mr. Mather to whom Sewall attributes the statement about Burroughs was Cotton Mather. Although the inference is reasonable, Increase Mather, who expressed precisely the same judgment of Burroughs in a postscript to *Cases of Conscience*, may have expressed it to Sewall in Boston on the evening of the nineteenth, after Sewall had returned from Watertown, and while Cotton Mather was still in Salem, thirty miles away.

One does not need to accept Robert Calef's improbable charge, published eight years after the event, in order to see the effect of that scene upon Cotton Mather's contemporaneous reputation. The drama that nobody but Calef described makes a stirring scene: the speeches of the convicts so moving that the crowd threatens to block the execution; Cotton Mather, mounted on a horse, haranguing the crowd and demanding that the executions proceed as a recognition of divine justice. Although there is no evidence besides Calef's belated account for Mather's addressing the crowd, and although it seems inconceivable that Sewall would have failed to mention both the crowd's action and Mather's speech if they had actually occurred, Mather could well have provoked adequate resentment by the more probable (because more characteristic) conduct that Sewall's brief note seems to indicate. By telling a few associates in private or in public that the sentences were just, Mather would have said what he was already known to have written several times during the summer, and the unique fact of his attendance at this one execution would have sufficed to remind unthinking people that he was determined to side with the court and oppose the devils.

No record summarizes discussions that must have occurred between the two Mathers, but it is clear that Increase Mather, having attended the trial of George Burroughs, agreed with the verdict of guilty. Before the first day of September, both Increase and Cotton Mather began, independently of each other, to write books about the witchcraft crisis. All the remaining evidence of their own writings suggests that they worked here in complementary ways, as they had done in the sermons preceding James Morgan's execution, but now with their roles reversed. Increase Mather chose to concentrate exclusively on "cases of conscience," a rational and scriptural demolition of the kinds of evidence and procedures that had troubled the ministers since before the first trial. Cotton's assignment was at once more complex and more dangerous to his reputation. There is no reason to believe he wrote disingenuously when he told Chief Justice Stoughton on September 2 that he considered the Salem outbreak "as wonderful a piece of devilism as has been seen in the world." Having invested an immeasurable quantity of feeling and belief in the millennial significance of both the new government and the wonders that had recently entered New England from the invisible world, Cotton Mather chose to demonstrate in his new manuscript that witchcraft had actually been practiced on a wide scale in Salem Village and that the government and the court had acted properly.

The coordination of the two Mathers' books was very important. In so poisonous an atmosphere, the antidote to the court's worst procedures concerning reputations might impassion "the rashest *mobile*" to attack the judges. Cotton Mather feared that if his father's argument should appear alone, it might enable "our witch-advocates very learnedly to cavil and nibble at the late proceedings against the witches, considered in parcels, while things as they lay in bulk, with their whole dependencies, were not exposed." He wanted not only to defend his friends, as he said later, but to avoid the fatal dissension that he eventually came to believe had been the Devil's main goal from the beginning. The judges need our prayers, Mather had said in August, but meanwhile the Devil "improves the *darkness* of this affair, to push us into a *blindman's buffet,* and we are even ready to be sinfully, yea, hotly and madly, mauling one another in the *dark*." On September 2, therefore, Cotton Mather wrote Chief Justice Stoughton an extremely delicate letter asking approval of his plan to publish a work, already begun, that was designed to "flatten that fury which we now so much turn upon one another." He asked permission to write a narrative of several trials, in order to "vindicate the country, as well as the judges and juries." In the section already composed, he said, he had "set our calamities in as true a light as I can," and he offered to submit for Stoughton's correction one or two passages in which he had alluded to "the jealousies among us, of innocent people being accused."

Some time before the twentieth of September, Governor Phips apparently added his command to the Mathers' agreement that Cotton Mather would write a narrative of the Salem trials. On that day Cotton Mather repeated an earlier request that he had sent to Stephen Sewall, the court's recorder, for a factual narrative of the evidence in six or more of the trials. He asked especially, too, for evidence of the juries' attitude toward spectral evidence, about the confessors and their credibility, and about any facts "evidently preternatural in the witchcrafts." He asked Sewall to write to him as if to an obstinate "Sadducee and witch-advocate . . . that believed nothing reasonable; and when you have knocked me down, in a specter so unlike me," he promised, "you will enable me to box it about among my neighbors, till it come, I know not where, at last."

By the time Mather wrote that letter, he admitted, he was already being pestered by "objectors" to the court's procedures. Accusations against respectable men and women worked from opposite directions to intensify public criticism of the trials. The escape of John Alden from Boston jail, and the authorities' reluctance to arrest prominent citizens who were cried out upon, persuaded some critics that the law was being applied unequally. Friends of the court, on the other hand, became alarmed by accusations against some of the most respectable names in Boston, probably including that of Lady Phips herself, who had allegedly signed a warrant releasing an accused woman from jail. The mother-in-law of Judge Corwin was accused, but never arrested. While Cotton Mather waited impatiently for the narratives that he had asked Stephen Sewall to prepare, the last executions were carried out. Old Giles Corey was pressed to death with heavy stones on August 19, as the sheriff, in accord with an old provision of common law that was never enforced in this way in any other part of English America, tried to force Corey to plead guilty or not guilty to the indictment. And three days later the last and most numerous of the multiple hangings took the lives of one man and seven women, including Martha, the wife of Giles Corey. Mary Easty, one of those executed, wrote perhaps the most moving declaration of innocence to the court. While those eight people were being hanged in Salem, Cotton Mather was meeting at last with Stephen Sewall at Judge Samuel

Sewall's house in Boston. There Chief Justice Stoughton and John Hathorne, a Salem magistrate who had conducted some of the most aggressive preliminary examinations of the defendants, joined in the discussion of Mather's plan to publish his narrative of some of the trials.

It was the return of Governor Phips from his summer campaigns, and the completion of Increase Mather's manuscript, that finally brought respectable authority to acknowledge what many thinking and unthinking people had recognized for some time: the court must not be allowed to order any more executions. If Lady Phips had not been formally accused, her husband could at least see both the reason why she had ordered the release of a woman from jail, and that her action had caused considerable resentment against her. Increase Mather, moreover, had now completed his *Cases of Conscience concerning Evil Spirits Personating Men,* which he read to fifteen ministers of Boston and other towns on October 3. Mather's argument was devastating to the court's procedures. The heart of his objection to spectral evidence had been perfectly visible in Cotton Mather's letter to Richards, in the ministers' "Return" of June 15, in Cotton Mather's Fast-day sermon on August 4, and in Cotton Mather's letter to Foster in mid-August. Now, however, there was no equivocation. Increase Mather denounced both spectral evidence and inferences drawn from the behavior of afflicted persons. The "Father of Lies," he said, "is never to be believed: He will utter twenty great truths to make way for one lie: He will accuse twenty witches, if he can thereby bring one honest person into trouble: He mixeth truths with lies, that so those truths giving credit unto lies, men may believe both, and so be deceived." Nor did Mather fail on this belated occasion to utter a definitive corollary that called upon Christians to act on a principle opposite to the Devil's: "I had rather judge a witch to be an honest woman," he declared, "than judge an honest woman as a witch." He said it would be better for ten suspected witches to go free than for one innocent person to be condemned.

In their approving preface to *Cases of Conscience,* the fourteen ministers who endorsed the book made an even more inclusive statement about evidence and charity. They appealed to the good sense of Puritans who had always known that God's purposes in historical events were difficult for human minds to perceive. The same God who had ordered men not to suffer a witch to live had said (Numbers 35:30) that nobody should be put to death on the testimony of only one witness. God, they said, had "never intended that all persons guilty of capital crimes should be discovered and punished by men in this life, though they be never so curious in searching after iniquity." It was true that "the most shining" of professing believers might secretly be "a most abominable sinner," they conceded; "yet till he be detected, our charity is bound to judge according to what appears: and notwithstanding that a clear evidence must determine a case; yet presumptions must be weighed against presumptions, and charity is not to be foregone as long as it has the most preponderating on its side." If the evidence does not "infallibly prove the crime against the person accused, it ought not to determine him guilty of it; for so a righteous man may be condemned unjustly."

Cotton Mather did not sign this preface. His own book, hastily completed, was now in press, and he apparently felt that its intended effect—to "vindicate the country, as well as the judges and juries"—might be weakened if he explicitly endorsed his father's book. *The Wonders of the Invisible World* was supposed to placate the militant defenders of the court at home, and Mather had hoped that concurrent publication of his own book and his father's would forestall "a public and open contest with the judges" and protect them from the anger of the mob that the separate publication of his father's book unintentionally risked. Because his father had read and approved the manuscript of *Wonders,* and because he himself had repeatedly (if sometimes equivocally) warned against spectral evidence and other threats to the liberty of innocent people, Cotton Mather could not understand the "raging asperity" with which people treated him after he had refused to sign the preface to *Cases of Conscience.* In answer to the ministers who expressed their criticism directly, he successfully asked that they "find the thousandth part of one wrong step taken by me in all these matters, except it were my use of all humble and sober endeavors to prevent . . . a bloody quarrel between Moses and Aaron." But the bitterest result for him was "the great slander" circulated through New England: "*that I run against my own father and all the ministers in the* country." All he had done, he said, was to "run between them when they are like mad men running against one another." The injury of that slander, he said, could not be repaired in this world, but he did persuade his father to add a postscript to *Cases,* explicitly denying any disagreement with Cotton Mather on the issues in the witchcraft cases; to make the note even more emphatic, Increase Mather said that if he had been a judge at the trial of George Burroughs — the only trial he had attended — he "could not have acquitted him." Increase also reminded people who had "taken up a notion" of his disagreement with *Wonders,* that he had read and approved it before its publication, and that he and Cotton had both signed the ministers' "Return" in June.

For once Cotton Mather's gloomy assessment of his public image seems to have been justified by evidence more lasting than the anxiety brought on by a temporary disagreement with members of his congregation. The "crafty, busy, prevailing Devil" had succeeded in virtually ruining Mather's "opportunities of serving my neighbors." Throughout the summer Mather had attracted blame to himself because of his insistence on fighting prominently against the devils and defending the character of the judges even while he repeatedly criticized spectral evidence. He insisted that even those judges with whom he disagreed, deserved always to be treated honorably and compassionately — both because their task was extremely difficult and because they were much more judicious than "most other people, whom I generally saw enchanted into a raging, railing, scandalous and unreasonable disposition, as the distress increased upon us." Understandably, but with a selective memory that tended to overlook his encouragement of aggressive tactics to confuse the defendants, Mather found it hard to believe that people should come to revile him "as if I had been the doer of all the hard things, that were done, in the prosecution of the witchcraft." The price that he paid for his sometimes almost desperate efforts to counter-attack against the Devil and to avoid at all costs any dissension between Moses and Aaron, the price of trying to stand as John the Baptist, was identification with the oppressors. His declaration in the preface to *Wonders* did not help to dissociate him from the court, although he repeatedly mentioned even in that book the defects of spectral evidence. "I have set myself to countermine the whole PLOT of the Devil, against *New England,* in every branch of it," he wrote in the preface, "as far as one in *darkness* can comprehend such a work of Darkness." That resolution, along with his decision not to sign the preface to his father's book, left him almost alone with his countermining equipment after the most militant part of the Lord's army had retreated. He himself could remember proudly that, besides speaking out to protect the innocent against deceptive evidence, he had even gone to the jail and preached to the defendants there on the unjust accusation and imprisonment of Paul. Others would remember his defense of the court and the fierce rhetoric that he had used against devils and the witches he considered guilty.

In the book itself both the forcible quality of his prose and the impossibility of achieving his entire purpose tended to make him more vulnerable. He did succeed in getting out a book that placated the Chief Justice and thus perhaps helped to prevent the absolute ruin of Governor Phips's administration. In his account of the trials of Bridget Bishop, Sarah Good, and George Burroughs, Mather showed that incriminating evidence beyond the spectral had been sworn against them. Both Bishop and Good had been caught in explicit lies and contradiction during their examinations before the magistrates, and puppets with pins stuck in them had been found in a wall of Bishop's house when she had been accused in 1680. Burroughs had been named by several confessed witches as the celebrant of a black mass, and several other witnesses had sworn they had knowledge of superhuman strength that this "very puny man" had demonstrated on various occasions. Yet everybody in Boston soon learned that defendants whose behavior had been equally suspect, and many who had actually confessed to witchcraft, were eventually released from prison without any apparent increase in diabolical injury to the community. As Mather's pithy summaries showed believers and skeptics how the people of Massachusetts could have been brought to execute nineteen men and women for witchcraft, they inevitably revealed as well that much of the evidence had been inconclusive. Spectral testimony about George Burroughs' alleged mistreatment of his wives, long before the year of the trial, might not have played a major role in bringing the jury to convict him, but Mather's scrupulously accurate summary of that testimony served as an unforgettably damning comment on the fairness of the court that admitted it in evidence against the defendant. As Thomas Brattle pointed out in a letter dated October 8, the court had admitted evidence far from relevant to the specific indictments.

Ever painfully sensitive about his reputation, Mather consoled himself by defending his behavior in a retrospective account for his Reserved Memorials, and by mentioning William Stoughton's approval of *The Wonders of the Invisible World.* When he reviewed his private papers some time later, he wrote in the margin: "Upon the severest examination, and the solemnest supplication, I still think, that for the main, I have, *written right.*" He continued to take comfort, too, in thanksgiving for his private blessings: his father's health as well as his own, his wife, his library, his freedom of speech — and "my unblemished reputation."

His most significant consolation, however, entered these pages in his reflections on a peculiar fact he had noticed in the testimony about witchcraft. This was the year in which he came to his greatest power both as a political figure and as a herald of the Millennium, only to lose much of his power and virtually the last of his hopes that he might unite political and religious action in a unified commonwealth prepared for the coming of the Bridegroom. To conclude his Reserved Memorials in this thirtieth year of his life, he thought again about his enemy, the Devil. Now Mather remembered that he had distributed throughout the country copies of his little books concerning "the *New Covenant* formally drawn up" for his neighbors. The specters, he perceived, had repeatedly offered the afflicted people books, soliciting them "to subscribe unto a league with the *Devil* therein exhibited" — and tormenting them if they refused. Mather modestly denied that he was the first to notice the connection; others, he said, had suggested that "this assault of the *evil angels* upon the country, was intended by *Hell,* as a particular defiance, unto my poor endeavors, to bring the souls of men unto *heaven.*" He resolved to write more evangelically than ever about the Covenant of Grace. He entered private resolutions in his Bibles to defy the Devil's book-signing tactics. And at last he renewed his private resolution to "deny myself of my humor, my esteem and anything in the world," rather than ever to mention any of his personal quarrels with other people. His reason for that resolution, he tried to believe, was that no man could manage a personal quarrel without losing a great deal of time, which might better be used in the service of Christ and His church. Anyone likely to live "so little a time, as I," he wrote, "had need throw away, as little of his *time,* as ever he can."

Mather had a long time to live, and he was not yet through with with either the Devil or personal quarrels.

# VII

# *Two Brands, Two Deaths, and a Sadducee*

❦

It may be no man living ever had more people under Preternatural and astonishing Circumstances, cast by the Providence of God, into his more peculiar care, then I have had; but the *Name* of no one Good person in the world, ever came under any *Blemish,* that I know of, by means of any *Afflicted* person, that fell under my particular care; yea, no Man, Woman or Child, ever came into any trouble, for the sake of any that were Afflicted, after I had once began to look after them.

> Cotton Mather, letter printed
> in *Some Few Remarks,* edited by
> Obadiah Gill and others (1701)

These are some of the destructive notions of this Age, and however the asserters of them seem sometimes to value themselves much upon sheltring their Neighbours from Spectral Accusations, They may deserve as much thanks as that Tyrant, that having industriously obtained an unintelligible charge against his Subjects, in matters wherein it was impossible they should be Guilty, having thereby their lives in his power, yet suffers them of his meer Grace to live, and will be call'd gracious Lord.

> Robert Calef, *More Wonders
> of the Invisible World* (1700)

NOT UNTIL the autumn of 1693 did Mather meet the man who was to become his chief human antagonist, but the Devil required his immediate personal attention in Boston within a few weeks after *The Wonders of the Invisible World* was published on October 15, 1692. Mather had learned during the summer about the affliction of Mercy Short, a seventeen-year-old who had been ransomed from Indian captivity after surviving a frontier raid in which her parents and a brother and sister had been killed. Brought back from Canada to live in Boston after Phips's expedition against Quebec, she had been sent to the prison on an errand one day in June 1692.

There she had provoked a curse from Sarah Good by throwing some wood shavings at the suspected witch, instead of the tobacco that Good had requested, "and poor Mercy was taken with just such, or perhaps much worse, fits as those which held the bewitched people then tormented by invisible furies in the County of Essex."

Along with some of the confessions at Salem, the explicit reports of afflictions in Essex County, and his own previous observation of Martha Goodwin, it was the undeniable genuineness of Mercy Short's suffering that kept Mather from doubting whether Satan's minions were really attacking New England. Mather did not know the modern diagnoses of hysteria or anorexia. The choking sensations, the swollen belly, and Mercy Short's refusal to eat for twelve entire days seemed to him unquestionable evidence that "the immediate efficiency of some agent, . . . rational or malicious," was causing the misery. Prayers did apparently cure Mercy Short for several months. On November 22, however, she fainted and "lay for dead for several hours together; and it was not long before the distinct and formal fits of witchcraft returned upon her." Cotton Mather's help was requested, and he soon took a personal interest in her case, returning to the methods he had used to treat Martha Goodwin but without bringing the patient to his own house. He arranged a day of prayer at Mercy Short's own lodgings, to which he "took a little company of his praying neighbors." During that entire day, the afflicted girl gave no indication of perceiving that any human beings were in the room. She apparently saw, heard, and felt only "the cursed specters."

Mather decided to preach to the little company on a text from the ninth chapter of Mark, in which the people ask Jesus why they themselves cannot cast an unclean spirit out of a possessed person, and Jesus replies: "This kind can by no other means come forth, but by prayer and fasting." In the midst of this homily, Mercy Short suddenly leaped from her bed, attacked Mather, and tore a page of his Bible, right against the text that Mather had chosen. Later on that evening, Mather recorded both the text and the date in his Bible, with a brief note of the remarkable: "Nov. 29, 1692. While I was preaching at a private fast (kept for a possessed young woman)—on Mark 9.28, 29.—the Devil in the damsel flew upon me, and tore the leaf, as it is now torn over against the text."

For the next nine days the poor girl ate virtually nothing. Her miseries abated during the first three days of December, however, and she ate a little food, enough to gain the strength to attend services on the Lord's Day in the North Church, half a mile away, on December 4. Now again she saw only the specters and heard them rather than the preacher, and at the end of the service her fits came on so powerfully that several strong men could take her no farther than a house near the church. The family took her in and nursed her for several weeks as she suffered great torture and "entertained" the neighborhood both as a medical curiosity and as the precious human soul over whom Mather fought one more extended battle with the Devil.

Except for some weeks of remission, Mercy Short's affliction lasted through most of the winter. During these very weeks the discredited Special Court of Oyer and Terminer was transformed into a new Superior Court, created by the legislature. The judges were not personally discredited—not only were four of them reappointed to the new court, but all were reelected to the Governor's Council at the next election—but their punitive authority in witchcraft cases had disappeared. In more than fifty new trials early in January, the only defendants convicted of witchcraft were three people who confessed, and when William Stoughton sentenced them to death along with five other people convicted in previous sessions but for various reasons reprieved, Governor Phips reprieved them all indefinitely. Stoughton walked out of the courtroom in fury when he heard the news.

While the drama of the court's loss of authority thus came to its sudden dénouement, Cotton Mather, though of course not indifferent to these events, was preoccupied with the kind of witchcraft case that he would always have preferred. He did not yet doubt the reality of a witches' conspiracy against New England, but he was more interested in treating the afflicted, and in studying and counteracting the Devil's powers, than in hunting witches. His prolonged encounters with diabolical antagonists over the souls and bodies of Martha Goodwin and Mercy Short did more than increase his hunger for knowledge about medicine and the invisible world. They also gave him the one other kind of knowledge for which he felt an even deeper craving. He had long ago described religious conviction as a special form of knowledge. The radiant vision of his angel, and the "afflations" that he sometimes felt in answer to his prayers, represented the highest form of knowing. Actual engagement with the Devil in defense of a human soul confirmed his deepest faith in the same way, though of course in a lower register. "A Brand Plucked out of the Burning," his unpublished narrative of Mercy Short's ordeal, made a powerful argument for the reality of supernatural agency. His experience itself needed no argument. It filled his consciousness with the essential knowledge beyond articulation.

During these long sessions in the girl's room, Mather and other observers not only saw the evidence of her torment. They became participants in her resistance. They saw her jaws forced open to receive invisible poison, and they saw her belly "swell prodigiously," just as if she had been "poisoned with a dose of rats-bane." They saw the bloody evidence of invisible pins with which she said the specters had afflicted her. They saw the blisters and smelled the brimstone when "Hell-hounds" scalded her for nearly fifteen minutes. They heard her argue defiantly, even sarcastically, with the Devil, and Mather kept a record of her statements, many of which he insisted were beyond her ordinary powers of both discourse and comprehension. As many as seven witnesses at a time heard "the scratches of the specters on the bed and on the wall." They observed with mixed wonder and satisfaction that the bloody marks and the blisters were "cured, perhaps in less than a minute" — Mather noted that this was "a strange property of most witch-wounds." What was most convincing as well as most exciting, however, was participation. Some of the pins were clearly visible, and when the observers saw that the invisible specters were trying to force the girl to swallow real pins, "the standers-by would by some dexterity" pull the pins out of her mouth "before they were got into her throat." Again, when Mather and the other observers understood that one protracted torture the specters used was to sit on the girl's chest and pull open her jaw so that she seemed virtually unable to breathe, they decided to resist "with main force." When they lifted the girl into an upright position, they felt that she was much heavier than her ordinary weight and that they had to exert extraordinary force to right her, whereupon "the specters would immediately . . . so fall off, that her breath returned unto her." The specters apparently not only stole apples that had been given to the girl, but pinched and scratched bystanders, some of whom reported partial success in retaliating against them by laying hands on the "palpable" but invisible forms.

Mather himself participated in less physical ways. He tried to get through to the girl by devising an effective code of letters, words, and gestures when her tormentors apparently deafened her to all religious words and sentiments. During one of these assaults, for example, she shouted an appeal to Mather for advice on how to answer "*Them*" (Mather's designation for the specters). "Mercy," he replied, "tell 'em that the Lord Jesus Christ has broke the Old Serpent's head."

"What do you say?" she asked.

"I say, Tell 'em that the Lord Jesus Christ has broken the Old Serpent's head. —Can you hear?"

"No. I can't hear a word."

"Well, then; mind me and you shall know what you can't hear. —A Snake. —Mercy, can you hear?"

"Yes."

"Well, —An Old Snake. —Can you hear?"

"Yes, —well, what of an old snake?"

Mather struck his forehead with his finger. "Why, his head broke. D'ye hear?"

"Yes; and what then?"

Mather pointed up to heaven. "Why, who broke it? D'ye mind?"

"Oh!" Mercy answered. "I understand. —Well, what else shall I tell them?"

In this new case, moreover, Mather saw that he was able to control some of the publicity as well as the means of resisting the Devil. Some people in the town were "scoffing, railing, raving" at his special days of prayer, he complained, but good Christians in the neighborhood did attend them; these Christians kept on "praying, fasting and believing." When the specters began appearing to Mercy Short in the shapes of identifiable Bostonians, Mather succeeded in keeping the names secret, as in the good old days of 1688, and in his unpublished narrative he made the comparison explicit. "The methods that were taken for the deliverance of Mr. Goodwin's afflicted family, four years ago, were the very same that we now followed for Mercy Short; and she would herself most affectionately express her own desires, that none but such might be taken. Had we not studiously suppressed all clamors and rumors that might have touched the reputation of people exhibited in this witchcraft, there might have ensued most uncomfortable uproars."

Once again, as in the Goodwin case, Mather was drawn into other experiments that tested the Devil's powers, and this time the most perplexing results gave him the most flattering evidence he had ever known that the Devil's concentration on books in New England bore directly on the library and person of Cotton Mather. The lore of the Book moved to Cotton Mather's study in three steps. First Mercy Short, on Mather's advice, asked the Devil's permission to read one of the three books that had been offered to her, in order to decide whether to sign it. She then told Mather that she had been allowed to read the details of the chief rituals performed in the great witch meetings, the methods used to seduce people into covenants of witchcraft, and the names of witches and their various terms of supernatural powers. On the night of March 9, then, in her most dramatically prepared revelations thus far, she brought the lore of the Book nearer to Mather himself. She summoned him and Governor Phips to her room and told them that the specters had been forced to drop one of their precious books in a neighbor's attic. Although sympathetic toward the poor girl's sufferings, Mather doubted there was any corporeal book, but he decided a few days later to send "a discreet servant privately" to investigate the neighbor's attic—presumably with the owner's permission. That poor servant was frightened away from the attic when a "great black cat, never before known to be in the house," jumped over him.

Mercy Short then completed the second step by summoning Mather and reprimanding him for his neglect of the book. The specters, she said, had informed her that by extraordinary pleading they had persuaded the Devil to let one of them assume the shape of a cat "and fetch the book away; which was done (she said) just as the servant had almost laid his hand upon it." The attendants in Mercy Short's room told Mather that no human being had ever told her a word of what had happened.

Mather was now perfectly set up for the third step. Despite the coincidences, he still felt that these phenomena had "much of a diabolical delusion in them." He refused to venture his own opinion about the nature of the cat. Other people, he said, believed that devils had power to "attract suitable matter out of all things for a covering or body," but he himself could only venture the hope that someone might state the theory clearly and then "prove" and "apply" it. Now that he was set up for the clinching argument, secure in the reassertion of his prudent skepticism of diabolical delusions, he did not have to wait long. Mercy Short reported that the specters had shown her yet another book—this one taken from Mather's own study!

The ignorant girl described the book so exactly that Mather recognized it quickly and brought it to her, whereupon she confirmed its identity. She had already told him that the book had been brought by specters who had attended meetings with French Canadians and Indian sagamores "to concert the methods of ruining New England," and Mather had marveled at the way this story echoed a Salem witch's confession about which Mercy Short "had never heard, as far as I have learned." Now she reported that the witches relied on this book for "their directions for devotions performed at their meetings"; it was a book of what Mather called idolatrous devotions, *Les saints devoirs de l'âme devoté*. Mather found one page folded down in the book. Two days later he left the book on a table in his study with no pages folded down, but when he returned he found three pages "unaccountably folded." Mercy Short reported the specters' boast that they had stolen the book and turned down three pages in it. They had also turned around another French book in his study, she said, so that the binding faced the wall, and she described that large gray book to Mather. He said their alleged theft of the book was probably a lie, but he was both astonished and gratified to find another French Catholic book, a gray one on the offices of Holy Week, turned backward on his bookshelf.

These wonders "very naturally" reminded Mather of "the proper *enchantments,* whereby *popery* was at first begun, and has been maintained," and he reasoned that the devils must be suffering new confusion caused by the imminent destruction of all the charms that "have hitherto intoxicated the nations in that superstition." In his own family, however, the consequences of all this excitement were less comforting. Abigail, who was expecting a child at the end of March, was terrified by the vision of a horrible specter as she stood on her own porch—so frightened that she felt her bowels turn within her. Before the child was born, Mercy Short told Cotton Mather that the specters had boasted of the fright they had given his wife— "in hopes, they said, of doing mischief unto her *infant* at least, if not unto the *mother.*"

Before that infant son was born, Mercy Short had been delivered from her torture. Mather had brought into action in mid-February a new squad of spiritual militia, the neighborhood societies of "Young Folks." These adjourned their weekly meetings to the girl's "haunted chamber," where special prayers were said by some vigilant Christians every night for a month. Marvelous evidence of response to these prayers indicated that an angel was watching over the young woman, for she not only responded effectively to the Devil's inaudible arguments. Now she began to cite relevant answers from her Bible, in a way that struck Mather and the other observers with awe. When the specters urged her to sign their book, she picked up a Bible and, without even looking at the text, flipped through scores of pages and turned down the corner of one to Revelations 13:8: "All that dwell upon earth shall worship him, whose names are not written in the Book of Life of the Lamb." Then, without looking at the text, she held it up for the specters to read, and she declared that since her own name was already written in the Book of the Lamb she would not sign their accursed book. With at least two other texts that were similarly apt replies, the angel apparently guided her to answer other diabolical arguments in the same astonishing way. And on Thursday the ninth of March she announced that she would be "gloriously delivered" at about nine or ten o'clock on the evening of the sixteenth. She asked Mather to bring his brother Samuel with him on that night.

Mather suspected that the mystical number three had special value in these dark matters; he remembered that Mercy Short's first remission had come after three days of fasting and prayer had been kept in the neighborhood. There was no longer any hope of persuading the church or any other group to keep three whole days of fasting and prayer for Mercy Short, but he himself had kept two private ones. Believing that "the Lord must be again besought thrice," and remembering the girl's own prediction, he fasted for the third time on the sixteenth. When he and Samuel Mather went to her room that night, they noticed at once that she seemed to be free of all torment. She told them that the specters had been trying all evening to torment her but that they had been unable to touch her. The "Black Man," she said, kicked, struck, and mauled the specters to punish them for their failure. Then she began to mock her former tormentors: "Well, I see you are going; what good counsel have you to give me before you go?" And before they could finish their answer, she begged them passionately to resist the Devil and repent. When they apparently persisted in damning her, she explicitly refused to wish them damned in return, but commanded them "in the name of the Blessed Lord Jesus Christ, be gone, and let me be no more troubled with you." They immediately flew away, she said, but as they did so a young woman who had been watching was struck down senseless on the floor.

Presumably the young woman who fainted was revived, and it is certain that Mercy Short was cured, but Cotton and Abigail Mather had to endure further grief. Their infant son, born Tuesday, March 28, lived only until Saturday night, for he suffered from what appeared to be a fatal obstruction of the bowels. When the child died, Mather had ready the two appropriate texts on which he would preach the next morning and afternoon. The one that he took from Job offered one more pointed answer to the grieving of Abigail Mather, the afflicted Job's reply to his wife's advice that he give up righteousness, blaspheme God, and die: "But he said unto her, Thou speakest like a foolish woman: what? shall we receive good at the hand of God, and not receive evil? In all this did not Job sin with his lips." No autopsy could be performed on the Lord's Day, but before the child was buried on Monday an examination revealed "that the lower end of the *rectum intestinum,* instead of being *musculous,* as it should have been, was *membranous,* and altogether closed up."

Besides Abigail's frightening vision of the specter, Mather had other reason to believe that witchcraft had destroyed his first son. One of the suspected women whose names he had refused to publicize wrote his father an angry letter very soon after the baby's birth. The letter, "full of railing" against Cotton Mather, warned vaguely that "he little knew, what might quickly befall some of his posterity." Mather made "little use" of this information beyond recording it in his diary, along with his recollection that Mercy Short had told him the specters in her room had boasted of their plans to injure the child. Whether "little use" includes some effort to investigate the chances of prosecuting the woman who had threatened him, one cannot now learn. In the spring of 1693 a successful prosecution for witchcraft in Boston was probably unthinkable. Mather decided that he could not risk publishing his superb narrative of Mercy Short's affliction, and he would not even trust to unpublished paper his reflections on "the true nature and meaning of these preternatural occurrences." The atmosphere in Boston was so soured, he said, and the people "enchanted" with so proud a humor, "that no man in his wits would fully expose his thoughts unto them, till the charms which enrage [them] are a little better dissipated." He began another sentence, but broke off his narrative in the middle of it, and he never did publish "A Brand Plucked out of the Burning."

As HIS ACTIVITY in the Mercy Short case may suggest, Cotton Mather's brief career as a powerful force in Massachusetts politics virtually ended in the autumn of 1692. *The Wonders of the Invisible World* did not strengthen his political influence, but the problem was not that he lost favor with the Governor. Phips himself encountered and provoked strong opposition during his remaining two years in office, and both Increase and Cotton Mather, still proud to be identified with him and to rebuke his detractors, shared the criticism. Now that his vigorous father had returned to Boston, Cotton Mather was no longer the sole clerical adviser to Phips, nor the only minister in the Second Church. He would probably have slipped back into a subordinate political role even if the defense of the witchcraft judges had never been associated with his name. Surely the witch hunt did become more and more closely attached to his name during the ensuing decade, as many people identified not only him but the entire Puritan clergy with the prosecution. Vehement opposition to both Phips and the Mathers came also from the outraged group, led by Elisha Cooke, that believed Increase Mather had betrayed his covenanted duty by accepting a charter providing for a royally appointed governor. Cooke felt convinced that the precious tradition of town meetings had been jeopardized by the new charter, and it seemed to him and other Bostonians that Mather had packed the Governor's Council with men from North Boston, in a bid for personal control. In many ways, moreover, the society was moving beyond the control of the people who called themselves the Lord's. Yet the central fact that marks 1692-93 as the end of Cotton Mather's most effective political action is the separation of the political world from the world of spirits.

For more than fifteen years threats to the independent action of Puritan leaders in Massachusetts had issued from officials who were not only imperial but Anglican. Randolph, Andros, and the two Stuart kings had embodied a political enmity that unquestionably threatened the power of covenanted Congregationalism. For the history of Massachusetts the new charter itself, by establishing a royal governor and enfranchising men who were not Congregationalists, became the most effective wedge that divided secular and religious affairs. For the life of Cotton Mather, the critical moment of change was the autumn of 1692. Battles in which the Lord's people had defended themselves against human antagonists in the 1680s had been joined for a few months in the spring of 1692 by the Devil himself, at a time of renewed French and Indian attacks and lingering uncertainty about the new provincial government. Cotton Mather had hailed the inauguration of that new government in June 1692 as the greatest day in the history of Massachusetts, for now the government itself, reconstituted under a national hero who was also a member of the Second Church, had been freed from all conflict with the Crown and could join in the apocalyptic war against the French, the Indians, and the Devil. When Governor Phips overruled the Special Court of Oyer and Terminer in October 1692, that exhilarating union of issues was permanently dissolved. Mather was still challenged to fight the Devil, and Phips and the militia still had to fight the human enemy in Maine, but the government of Massachusetts no longer fought against the legions from the invisible world. The religious issues that did survive in Massachusetts politics divided the Congregationalists from one another, in largely recriminatory debates over Increase Mather's acceptance of the new charter, or the procedures of the witchcraft court. In 1693 only eight of the twenty-three men whom Increase Mather had chosen for Phips's Council were reelected. Even if Cotton Mather had never been blamed for his conduct during the witchcraft trials, the glorious union of his political and spiritual action could no longer have been maintained after 1692.

In 1693, then, his undiminished energy was forced back into less political and in some ways more private forms of expression. He took a secondary place in the bitter wrangling between his father and Elisha Cooke. When Cooke gave a banquet to celebrate a day of thanksgiving for his safe return from England in November 1692, Cotton Mather's absence was noted along with that of his father — either because they were not invited or because they both chose not to attend. Having recorded their absence, Samuel Sewall immediately asked "the good Lord [to] unite us in His fear, and remove our animosities!" But when Cooke was elected to the Council in the spring of 1693, Governor Phips vetoed his election, and that decision was generally blamed on Increase Mather. Cotton certainly stood by his father, but was not mentioned as a political influence. He put through the Second Church's adoption of the Half-Way Covenant in 1693, he wrote a letter to King William about the condition of Massachusetts, and in mid-July he opened a meeting of the Governor's Council with a successful prayer for rain that brought the first relief from that summer's unusually bad drought. Again at the Council meeting four days later, he opened the morning session with a prayer, but there is no evidence to suggest that he played any part in Governor Phips's abrupt, angry decision to dissolve the assembly that afternoon.

Mather addressed himself with new intensity to his pastoral duties in both the neighborhood and the larger community. Soon after Mercy Short recovered, he began a new round of pastoral visits throughout the North End, and in May and the first week of June he spent many hours in the prison trying to bring two condemned young women to a saving repentance. Both of them were to be hanged for murdering their newborn illegitimate children. Although Mather did not feel so hopeful about the results of his ministry to them as he had felt about the soul of James Morgan, the first murderer he had accompanied to the gallows, he did elicit from one of them a "pathetical" written statement of her misdeeds and a warning to "the rising generation." He read that admonition as a part of his sermon on the day of the execution, June 8, 1693, before a Lecture-day audience that both he and Samuel Sewall considered extraordinarily large. That sermon, "A Holy Rebuke to the Unclean Spirit," was quickly bound with an earlier one Mather had written on a similar occasion. Benjamin Harris published them as *Warnings from the Dead,* and Mather was gratified to see that the book was "greedily bought up."

Less than a week after the execution, he had a chance to extend his pastoral influence far beyond his usual range, but was prevented in a way that he could only regard as a good angel's intervention. A large expeditionary force had been sent out from England in the Crown's first major effort to invade Canada with regular troops. The 4500 sailors and soldiers had attacked Martinique before heading north, and a deadly fever (probably yellow fever) had killed

3100 of them before the fleet arrived in Boston on June 11. Unaware of the fever, Mather accepted an invitation to preach to the troops on shipboard on the Lord's Day, June 18, and he set out in Governor Phips's barge for one of the ships anchored near Noddle's Island. He soon became so miserably seasick, however, that he had to be brought back to shore, where he recovered fast enough to be able to preach that afternoon before the admiral and the senior officers in the steady, familiar pulpit of his own North Church. The fleet fever, as it was called, spread through Boston in July, killing more people that summer than any epidemic since the smallpox of 1678. Mather felt sure that he too would have caught it if he had actually reached the crowded ship on which he had been invited to preach; the first death Samuel Sewall reported, on June 26, was that of a servant who was said to have visited the hold of one of the ships in the fleet.

Mather also preached a number of sermons in other places outside his own church during the summer. At a special Fast day held in the First Church on the day after the Harvard commencement in July, he preached two sermons, and he was invited later in the month to preach at a special day of prayer for the rising generation in Reading. Toward the end of the summer he went to preach at Salem. Later in the year, he revised the rules for the Young Men's meetings and preached to one of them, and he spent an afternoon praying and preaching for the poor and old people in the almshouse. "A company of poor Negroes, of their own accord," asked him in October to help them organize a special society "for the welfare of their miserable nation that were servants among us." He attended one of their evening meetings and preached to them on the sixty-eighth Psalm: "Princes shall come out of Egypt; Ethiopa shall soon stretch out her hands unto God."

For this society of black Christians Mather wrote out a series of eight rules according to which they "freely resolve[d]" to "join together in a company." These rules obliged the members never to meet "without the leave of such as have power over us," and to meet only with people who had "sensibly *reformed* their lives." Besides inviting good English neighbors (including preachers) to visit them and "do what they think fitting for us," the rules obliged the members to admonish and, if need be, punish by exclusion or suspension fellow members who stole, swore, lied, fornicated, got drunk, or disobeyed their masters. All members were obliged to "do all the good we can to the other *Negro-servants* in the town," but to give no shelter to runaways and to expel any member of the group that should be "found faulty in this matter." Mather even required them to agree to inform the owner of any member who had pretended to come to a meeting but had used the time to go elsewhere. Mather did not publish these rules until 1706, when he added a ninth which required every member to learn the catechism. Strict and condescending though these rules unquestionably are, and although they carefully anticipate virtually every objection that an anxious owner might conceive against such a society, they do constitute the first basis for a voluntary congregation of black Christians in New England. That principle of free resolution and voluntary association was eventually as important as the obvious paternalism.

The Reserved Memorials for this year also mention a special request for "angelical communications" for the first time since 1686. Although he was far from withdrawing from the world, Mather had more time now, and felt a stronger need, for private transcendental experience than when his consciousness had been filled with the assurance that comes of acting near the center of momentous events. In the spring of 1693 he asked that angelical kindnesses be given him "in a manner and measure more *transcendent*, than what the great *corruptions*" in most good men would allow them to receive. He promised never to let angelical communications delude him into forsaking "the Lord's *written Word*"; they would only lead him back to it with new devotion. And he promised once again to "be continually *contriving* how to glorify God, in being eminently serviceable."

The contrivances that he settled on in this extraordinary year were the three or four major literary and intellectual projects of his life. First he began to collect a number of the best remedies he could find for all diseases, so that he might "publish them unto the world; so, by my hand," he said, "will be done the things that the *angels* love to do." Not until thirty-one years later did he finish the manuscript for this book, *The Angel of Bethesda,* but he began to work on the immense project within four months after he completed *The Wonders of the Invisible World.* He regarded it from the beginning as a part of his renewed efforts to do good in the world in emulation of angelic models, and in special charity toward the poor and the sick. Despite all his efforts, this book was not published until 244

years after his death. Although some of its bizarre and lethal remedies have provoked scorn from nineteenth- and twentieth-century
commentators, it remains the only work of its kind and scope produced in North America before the Revolution, and many of its
medical ideas reflect the most advanced theory and practice of the
time.

The second major work that Mather conceived in 1693 was his
"church history of this country," the *Magnalia Christi Americana,*
for which he began a broad outline in July. He completed the history about five years later, and it was published in London, in a
folio volume of about eight hundred and fifty pages, in 1702. He
frankly intended this work to be useful both in New England and in
Europe, "especially at the approaching *Reformation.*" He had not
lost his faith in the imminence of that glorious change; he was now
transferring into literary action the passionate energy that he had
recently been expending in political and spiritual conflicts. He consulted his colleagues in Boston about the proposed history, and
treated their approval of it as an indication of its social usefulness.
One cannot now learn whether he knew so early as 1693 that his
memoir of Nathanael Mather would be included in the history, but
he must have known that he would reprint his biography of John
Eliot and that the lives of a number of other ministers would form a
major section of the book. He did not actually begin to work on the
history until September.

In August, moreover, he began to think of both harvest-time and
(wishfully?) winter. He resolved to "contrive . . . with as charming a
mixture of *religion* and *ingenuity,* as I could," to encourage readers
to "improve the leisure of *winter,* for the *glory* of God, and their
own spiritual and eternal *advantage.*" He composed a little book
called *Winter Meditations,* which he published in October. That
book, along with the sermon *The Wonderful Works of God,* antici-
pates the major work of Mather's meditations on Nature, *The Christian Philosopher* (1721).

The most elaborate of all Mather's projects, which still remains
unpublished in six folio volumes of manuscript, is his cherished
"Biblia Americana." Both he and Nathanael had recorded their
independent designs to "fetch a lesson" out of every text in the Bible,
but in August 1693 Cotton Mather actually began to collect commentaries on every verse of Scripture, and not only to illustrate every

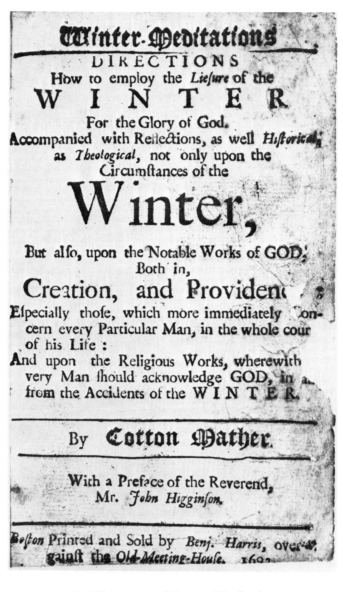

# Winter-Meditations

## DIRECTIONS

How to employ the *Leisure* of the

# WINTER

For the Glory of God.

Accompanied with Reflections, as well *Historical*,
as *Theological*, not only upon the
Circumstances of the

# Winter,

But also, upon the Notable Works of GOD,
Both in,

## Creation, and Providence:

Especially those, which more immediately Concern every Particular Man, in the whole cour
of his Life :

And upon the Religious Works, wherewith
very Man should acknowledge GOD, in a
from the Accidents of the WINTER.

By **Cotton Mather.**

With a Preface of the Reverend,
Mr. *John Higginson.*

Boston Printed and Sold by *Benj. Harris*, over ag
gainst the Old-Meeting-House. 169

12. Title page of Cotton Mather's
*Winter Meditations.*

verse with what was known about it but also to add appropriate
meditations at times about relevant events and phenomena in modern experience. Once again he resolved to apply a "laborious ingenuity" to a pious task. He would work on one text each day, and he
calculated that he might finish the entire work within seven years. It
took him nearly three times as long as that, and although he adver-
tised it with various kinds of enticements during the last fourteen
years of his life, he never did succeed in finding someone to sponsor
or risk its publication.

MATHER BELIEVED that these abundant opportunities to do the
Lord's work were "unquestionably" thrown into his hands "by
*angelical* operation," but before the middle of September he was
forced by a series of wonders into his last contest with the Devil.
Having arranged to preach in Salem so that he could do some research there for his church history, with a special eye to preserving
records of the witchcraft episode, Mather lost the notes for the three
sermons he had prepared. "Circumstances" that he did not specify
persuaded him that specters or other devils had stolen the papers,
and in October he received evidence to confirm that view. He managed to remember much of what he had written, and to fill up the
sermons with new material, "so that the Devil got nothing!"

In Salem, moreover, he met a Mrs. Carver, who professed to be
the recipient of secret information from some good angels. She confided several of these secrets to Mather, who did not record them,
and she also told him that "a new *storm* of *witchcraft* would fall
upon the country" as divine chastisement for the "iniquity that was
used in the willful smothering and covering of *the last*." Many
"fierce" opponents to the exposure of the Salem witchcraft, she said,
would now "be convinced."

Although Mather was careful not to endorse Mrs. Carver's assurance that the *"shining spirits"* who had visited her had actually been
good angels, he was astonished, when he returned to Boston, to
learn that another young woman in the North End had been "horribly arrested by *evil spirits*." Caught between fear and what must
have been a dreadful hope that Mrs. Carver's prediction might
prove true, Mather immediately arranged for extraordinary prayers
for Margaret Rule's deliverance, and he firmly ordered her (during

an interval of calm) not to accuse any of her neighbors. This time, too, he forbade the observers at her sickbed to ask her any questions.

He himself, however, did ask her the usual questions, and this time in the presence of a human antagonist who would use ridicule, sly misrepresentation, and powerful argument to do Mather more damage than Satan alone ever managed to inflict on him. Robert Calef was a forty-four-year-old merchant — Mather called him a weaver — who had emigrated from England some time before 1688. He apparently made no objections in public during the Salem trials of 1692, although he did later say that he had attended the execution of George Burroughs and John Proctor. By the middle of September 1693 he had decided that witches have no ability to use or command the Devil's supernatural powers to injure other human beings. He did not deny the existence of the Devil or of witches; he only questioned the witches' power to use supernatural means for serious harm, and he was prepared to demand that those who believed in this power show him biblical authority for their belief. When he heard that Cotton Mather, just returned from Salem, would visit Margaret Rule's room on Wednesday evening, September 13, the fourth night of her affliction, he resolved to be present, too, as an observer of both the patient and her healers.

Calef was appalled by what he saw and heard. The seventeen-year-old patient seemed to be healthy and reasonably calm as she lay "very still," and when she did speak she seemed to him only "light-headed." When Increase and Cotton Mather arrived, with a retinue of thirty to forty persons, and established themselves at the bedside for the interview — the son seated on the bed and the father on a stool — Calef stood in the crowded room, ready to describe their behavior in language that emphasized only what he saw and heard. The notes that he wrote down soon afterward do not say, as Mather said of both Mercy Short and Margaret Rule, that the afflicted girl was struck deaf or dumb when Mather asked the first question about her condition, but only that there was "then a pause without any answer." Calef's account represents both the Mathers as indulging in leading questions which bring on a fit. Calef does not describe the fit, but when Cotton Mather lays his "hand upon her face and nose" and, "he said," perceives no breath, Calef chooses graphic, damaging language to describe what happened next:

then he brushed her on the face with his glove, and rubbed her stomach (her breast not covered with the bed-clothes) and bid others do so too, and said it eased her, then she revived. . . . Then again [after another two leading questions] she was in a fit, and he again rubbed her breast, etc. (about this time Margaret Perd an attendant assisted him in rubbing of her. The afflicted spake angrily to her saying don't you meddle with me, and hastily put away her hand) he wrought his fingers before her eyes and asked her if she saw the witches? *A*. No. *Q*. Do you believe? *A*. Yes. *Q*. Do you believe in you know who? *A*. Yes. *Q*. Who is it that afflicts you? *A*. I know not, there is a great many of them (about this time the father questioned if she knew the specters? An attendant said, if she did she would not tell; the son proceeded) *Q*. You have seen the Black-man, ha[ve]n't you? *A*. No. . . . She turned herself and a little groaned. *Q*. Now the witches scratch you and pinch you, and bite you, don't they? *A*. Yes. Then he put his hand upon her breast and belly, *viz.* on the clothes over her, and felt a living thing, as he said, which moved the father also to feel, and some others; *Q*. Don't you feel the live thing in the bed? *A*. No. *Reply,* that is only fancy. *Q*. The great company of people increase your torment, don't they? *A*. Yes. The people about were desired to withdraw. One woman said, I am sure I am no witch, I will not go; so others, so none withdrew.

After some more leading questions, more rubbing, and some prayers and admonitions by the Mathers, Calef's brief account ends with the Mathers' departure and Margaret Rule's subsequent declaration that the remaining women must leave, the remaining men stay: "and having hold of the hand of a young man, said to have been her sweetheart formerly, who was withdrawing; she pulled him again into his seat, saying he should not go tonight."

When Cotton Mather got to see this account, which Calef circulated in manuscript, he was outraged — not only because it implied that he and his father had pruriently gratified the girl's wanton desire to be stroked by male hands, but also because it plainly represented the Mathers as gullible or cynical accomplices in a fraud. Not until the winter of 1693-94 did Mather reply in any detail to Calef's misrepresentations, but of course he allowed unnamed friends to speak in his defense as Calef's "libel" spread through Boston as fast and as ominously as the fleet fever, causing "paroxysms" of ridicule and indignation against the Mathers.

Chadwick Hansen has recently shown that in the complicated exchange of letters with Cotton Mather in 1693-94 Calef at best distorted the facts and at worst lied about them. Any reader of the Mather and Calef narratives about Margaret Rule's affliction can see without special assistance that Calef's distortions are the reverse of Mather's interpretations. Calef's description begged the question by assuming the girl was dissembling, and by omitting every plausible reason (besides leading the girl on) for the Mathers' questions and circumlocutions. Pointing out Calef's inaccuracies or falsehoods could do Mather's reputation no more good than suing for libel. In Margaret Rule's nine-day fast (except for a little rum), her fits of rigidity, her alleged levitation from the bed (confirmed by a number of witnesses), her screaming efforts to avoid having her distended jaws violated by the invisible liquid that the specters apparently tried to feed her, the inexplicable pins in her flesh, her black and blue marks, her periodic deafness, her coy preference for the comforting guidance of her minister — in all these Mather saw evidence of symptoms exactly like those of Martha Goodwin and Mercy Short. He, like Calef, recognized that young women seemed especially susceptible to this kind of affliction, and neither Mather nor Calef knew of any earthly illness that would produce these symptoms.

But of course Calef assumed from the start that the answer was not in bewitchment. Perverse sexuality and a desire to be led by the ministers whose prayers brought her so much extraordinary attention — these seemed to Calef a much better explanation than diabolical affliction. Mather's furious protestations that he and his father had never sought to induce the girl to name her tormentors in public, that she had really been deaf to some of their questions and prayers, that the name of God or Jesus had thrown her into fits, that Calef had repeatedly misquoted the questions, and that neither of the ministers had felt either the girl's bare breast or a palpable but invisible imp on her belly — none of these discredited the Sadducee, who took some ironic delight in further quibbling. In 1693 and 1700 as in the centuries that have intervened, one was likely to react to these explanations and observations according to one's assumptions about the Devil's powers and the Mathers' motives.

For his brave, persistent attack on superstition and injustice, Calef deserves the honor that historians have generally accorded him. In the best tradition of protestants before and since, he dared (though tardily) to ask believers in a dogma to risk an open discus-

sion of their biblical and rational authority for it. At a moment
when he could not be sure that a new witch hunt would be avoided
— when Cotton Mather himself obviously feared the same catastrophe, though Calef did not trust Mather's motives or judgment
enough to see that fear in him — Calef demanded that New England
authorities take a much more candid look than they had ever acknowledged at the doctrines and practices followed during the Salem
trials in 1692. The magistrates and ministers, he said, had never
adequately lamented the chief errors that they knew had brought "a
stain and lasting infamy . . . upon the whole country, . . . endanger-
ing the future welfare not only of this but of other places," and "a
bigoted zeal" had stirred up "a blind and most bloody rage, not
against enemies, or irreligious profligate persons, but (in judgment
of charity, and to view) against as virtuous and religious as any they
have left behind them in this country." Of course he ignored the
strongest of the ministers' criticisms of the witchcraft court, and he
scornfully dismissed their efforts to protect their neighbors against
spectral accusations. These efforts, he said, were hardly better than
the arbitrary mercies of the tyrant who chose to let his subjects live
after he had "obtained an unintelligible charge against [them], in
matters wherein it was impossible they should be guilty."

Yet Calef in his own way was as interested a party as Cotton
Mather, and his version of Mather's words and motives in 1693 deserves only a little more credence than Mather's repeated declaration that Calef himself was guided by the Devil. When Mather made
no direct reply to the scandalous misrepresentations in Calef's narrative of September 13, Calef pursued him with a letter on the
twenty-ninth, challenging him to what now sounds like an intellectual duel. Calef acknowledged that some of Mather's friends had
denounced the narrative and that it had offended Mather; he invited Mather "and any one particular friend" to "meet me and some
other indifferent person" at the bookshop of either Benjamin Harris
or John Wilkins, where Calef would read Mather his narratives of
events in Margaret Rule's bedroom on both the thirteenth and the
nineteenth, "and let deserved blame be cast where it ought."

Mather apparently agreed to meet Calef, but meanwhile both Increase and Cotton Mather had him arrested on a charge of scandalous libel. One must assume that Cotton Mather had no intention of
meeting Calef at the bookshop, or else that his father's determina-

tion to prosecute overruled him. In retrospect Cotton Mather did concede that he had probably resented Calef's slander more bitterly than was good for his own spirit, and when Calef actually appeared before the regular session of the court in December, as he was bound to do, neither Increase nor Cotton Mather was there to bring any charges against him. In the first week of October, however, Cotton Mather had quite a different kind of reason for neglecting the proposed debate.

For the second time in less than six months Mather's involvement in a witchcraft case coincided with the fatal illness of one of his own children. Margaret Rule did not report any threat of the specters against Mather's children, as Mercy Short had done. This time, moreover, the blow struck the Mather family before the bewitched girl had been cured, and Margaret Rule only reported having heard the specters boast that they had stolen the notes for Mather's missing sermon, which she said they had confessed they would be unable to keep from him. Every page of the missing notes, eighteen quarter-sheets that had been scattered about the streets of Lynn, was accordingly returned to Mather on October 5, but by that time his two-year-old daughter Maria had been ill for two days, with a fever, vomiting, and worms. She had been stricken while visiting her grandfather Phillips' house in Charlestown, and it was there that she died early in the morning of the sixth.

During the first two days of her illness, Mather had found himself "hindered from importunate prayers" for her life, but on the evening of the fifth he had gone to his father-in-law's house and had felt his "heart wonderfully melted" in prayers there. He did not demand the child's life in these prayers, but in emulation of Abraham "resigned it unto the mercy of God, in Jesus Christ." His answer, he wrote several months later, came to him in "such rapturous assurances of divine love unto *me* and *mine*, as would richly have *made amends for the death of more children, if God had then called for them*." In the midst of this prayer that released much anxious emotion about other matters as well as Maria's danger, Mather felt a strange, overwhelming assurance "not only that this *child*, shall be happy forever, but that I should never have *any child*, except what should be an *everlasting temple* to the Spirit of God: *Yea, that I and mine* [like Abraham and his covenanted descendants] *should be together in the Kingdom of God, world without end*." At the funeral in Boston the day after the child's death, Mather declared her epitaph, "Gone, but Not Lost," and at the regular communion service in his church the day after the funeral he preached on the biblical verse (Genesis 22:12) in which God releases Abraham from the command to sacrifice Isaac, because the father's willingness to obey has demonstrated his fear of the Lord. Mather was determined once again to show his neighbors by his own conduct how to behave under affliction.

With Maria dead, only one child remained alive in the Mather household. The precious name of Mather, so often the object of Cotton Mather's entreaties for divine protection from ridicule or shame, now suffered "cursed reproaches" from "unworthy, ungodly, ungrateful people"—reproaches heaped not only on Cotton Mather but on both Increase Mather and John Phillips, a loyal member of Phips's Council. Some of Cotton Mather's friends advised him to rebuke the partisan supporters of Calef, many of whom attended the First Church, by refusing to take his regular turn at the Thursday Lecture there. But Mather resolved to try, at least, to forgive his critics, to seek forgiveness himself through a private day of fasting, and to continue his secret prayers for the family name. Under the pressure of such constraints, holding in or reserving for his diary the angry words that would betray his resolution to forgive his enemies, he found once again the "great assurance" that he sought: "particularly," he said, that God "would make *my name* and the *names* of both my *fathers* also, to become honorable among His people: that He would support us, comfort us, and at last, *requite us good,* for all the evil that we meet withal."

Nor did he abandon his efforts to cure Margaret Rule by prayer. On the evening of October 10, his private Fast day, he went to visit her again. He had prayed for her during the day, remembering that she had been the occasion for some of the miseries that had led him to keep the special fast. Having resigned his own daughter to the Lord, he now "wrestled with God" for Margaret Rule, insisting that this young woman wanted to profess her faith and join the church but that the devils were blocking her. Mather argued in his prayer that, as the minister who had invited her into Christian service, he "had a sort of *right* to demand her deliverance from these invading devils, and to demand such a *liberty* for her as might make her capable of glorifying my glorious Lord." Before the day was over,

Margaret Rule told him, a spirit in bright white raiment had appeared to her "with a *face unseen*," had told her of Mather's special fast for her, and had ordered her to "count me her *father*, and regard me and obey me; and she should now within a few days be delivered."

"It proved," Mather said, "accordingly." After Margaret Rule found angelic assurance of her duty to obey him as a surrogate father, after he found some comfort in the opportunity to cure one more surrogate daughter, and after he had kept his third day of fasting and prayer for her, she recovered. Although Mather said she had never heard the terms in which he had prayed for his right to save her for the church, she began to address him as Father on the night of October tenth. She predicted that she would be cured on Saturday the fourteenth, and that the specters would then be unable to torment her. On Saturday she was able to insult them with what Mather called "a very proper derision" when their pins would (she said) no longer enter the bodies of their puppets, whom they tried to use to torment her in the customary way. Like Mercy Short, she argued with the specters after she had mocked them, and she reported that they warned her she would not be the last person afflicted. Finally, she said, they told her to go, "and the Devil go with you," and they "flew out of the room." Margaret Rule returned "perfectly to herself" and "most affectionately gave thanks to God for her deliverance." Except for some fainting spells, which Mather attributed to her weakness, and some occasional spells of mental confusion, she appeared to be permanently cured.

"Another Brand Plucked out of the Burning," Mather's brief narrative of her affliction and apparent cure, is much more defensive than any of his previous writings on witchcraft. Having observed the victim's behavior for more than five weeks, while "some of our learned *witlings* of the *coffeehouse*," fearing his "proofs of an *invisible world*," were ready to "turn them all into sport," Mather wrote his account essentially for them. He paid especial attention to the possibility that Margaret Rule might have dissembled, but even though he conceded that there might be some question about her earlier reputation, his repeated observations and inquiries convinced him that her sufferings had been genuine. He insisted that "if the most suspicious person in the world had beheld all the circumstances of this matter," instead of the two brief evenings of observation that Calef had chosen, "he would have said [Rule's behavior] could not have been dissembled."

Mather also felt insulted by the criticism that blamed him for spending so much time on the case. In less than six months he had plucked two brands out of the burning. Far from soliciting names to accuse of witchcraft, he had concealed the four names that had been disclosed only to him. He had prayed for Margaret Rule at a time of renewed grief in his own family, and had fasted and prayed to rescue her "from the lions and bears of *Hell*." He was outraged by the complaints that seemed to blame him for visiting and giving counsel to the afflicted people in his own congregation. As the passion flowed, he wrote not only an extended defense of his criticisms of spectral evidence during the Salem trials, but also an attack upon Calef's "sly, base, unpretending *insinuations*" implying Mather had behaved immodestly in Margaret Rule's bedroom. Mather even hinted that he was about to take Calef into court for the libel.

After the effort to prosecute Calef had been abandoned, Cotton Mather's debate with him dragged on into 1694, with both men circulating their writings among their respective partisans. Calef answered Mather's narrative about Margaret Rule with another letter addressed directly to Mather on January 11, and Mather at last sent him an extensive reply on the fifteenth. Unaware that Calef would eventually publish the whole exchange, including Mather's narrative about Margaret Rule, Mather sought to expose the inaccuracies and distortions in Calef's first notes reporting the scene in Margaret Rule's bedroom, but of course the name of Mather continued to suffer ridicule.

One threatened disgrace does seem to have been forestalled. During the winter another young woman was diabolically possessed for one day, and she cried that the specter who tormented her appeared in the image of Cotton Mather. She began to complain that it was Mather himself who threatened and molested her, but when she recovered from a fit she would immediately insist that her tormentors had been unable to make Mather's "dead shape" do her injury. As soon as a fit had passed, she was able to ask Mather himself to pray for her. Mather expressed a mixture of horror and pride at this new threat. Although naturally anxious about the way the story would be used against his name in "a malicious town and land," he saw here new evidence of the Devil's singular plot against him. Once again he cried out in prayer "for the deliverance of my *name,* from the malice of Hell," and he felt sure that his prayer was answered when the afflicted girl quickly recovered.

In mid-January, moreover, just as Calef had renewed the debate, Mather's household was afflicted with new misery when Katharine, the last surviving child, became so ill that her parents felt sure she would die. Once again Mather decided he must resign one of his children to the Lord, but when he sought for a biblical passage to comfort him he was "amazed" to find that he had opened his Bible "accidentally" to the eighth chapter of Luke (verses 49-56) — Jesus' revival of the daughter of the ruler of the synagogue after she had been given up for dead. Since Jesus in that passage insists that the parents have faith in the child's recovery, Mather, already in tears over the amazing "pertinency of this place," not only resigned the child's life to the Lord but also begged for her life in this world. He promised to bring her up for the Lord, and that he himself would soon do some special service for the rising generation in Massachusetts. Katharine "immediately . . . fell into a critical and plentiful *bleeding,* and recovered from *that hour,* unto the admiration of us all."

On the day of Katharine's recovery this inexhaustibly resourceful believer prepared a hopeful sermon on II Chronicles 25:9: "The Lord is able to give thee much more than this." Despite the dreadful personal cost to himself and his family, he insisted, the recent witchcraft crises had humiliated the Devil and increased church membership in the North End of Boston. "The Devil got just nothing," Mather had said in his narrative on Margaret Rule, "but God got praises, Christ got subjects, the Holy Spirit got *temples,* the church got *addition,* and the souls of men got everlasting benefits."

Yet the most practiced resignation could not conceal the evident signs that Mather's great political strength had virtually disappeared. The very fact that he found himself reduced to exchanging letters with a Robert Calef, fencing over such trivia as whether they should meet in Cotton Mather's study or in John Wilkins' bookshop, signified a decline from the great days of 1689 and 1692, when his antagonists had been Governor Andros and the Devil. By the end of 1694, moreover, both of Mather's strongest political allies had also disappeared. John Richards died suddenly of an apoplectic stroke on April 2, just after he had furiously rebuked a servant. Gov-

ernor Phips, increasingly irascible and controversial during the
summer and autumn of 1694, left for England after a series of furious confrontations and a pointed absence not only from a party
given in his own honor on November 9 but also from the Lecture the
following Thursday. Two days later he sailed for England in hopes
of successfully answering charges made against him there, but soon
after his arrival he had to post bail against a £20,000 suit brought
against him by Joseph Dudley and another plaintiff, and Phips died
in London on February 18, 1695. Samuel Sewall, alert for Providential signs, noted that Phips had arrived in Boston on a Saturday
night to take up his governorship and had left in the dark of another
Saturday night, both the arrival and the departure "uncomfortable,
because of the Sabbath."

Increase and Cotton Mather had both stayed away from the dinner Phips had snubbed in November. Even if Cotton Mather had
not explained that his own absence had been caused by "a grievous
pain in the face," it would have been clear that his special influence
in the Town House was gone. He would continue to be respected
and invited by political officials to preach, but he was now freer
than he had ever been to devote his mind to history, and the death
of Phips underlined the obvious truth that at least for a while
Mather's best chance of influencing political thought in Massachusetts was to write church history and political biography.

# VIII

# The Lord's Remembrancer:
## The Value of Historical Uncertainty

❧

If ever I have deserved well of my Country, it has been when I have given to the World the Histories and Characters of Eminent Persons, which have adorned it. Malice will call some of those things Romances, but . . . I do here declare, Let any Man living evince any one *Material Mistake* in any one of those Composures, it shall have the most Publick Recantation that can be desired. In the meantime, while some Impotent Cavils nibbling at the Statues which we have erected for our Worthies, take pains to prove themselves, *The Enemies of* New England, and of *Religion,* the Statues will out-live all their Idle Nibbles; *The Righteous will be had in Everlasting Remembrance,* when the Wicked who see it and are grieved, shall *gnash with their Teeth and melt away.*

Cotton Mather, *Magnalia Christi Americana*

MATHER WROTE between 1694 and 1698 almost all of the church history that was finally published in 1702 as *Magnalia Christi Americana.* He published parts of it under separate titles as his composition of the "rhapsody" proceeded, and before he sent the entire manuscript to England in 1700 he incorporated works that he had published before he had even recorded his intention to write the *Magnalia.* He even reprinted in Book VI a sermon he had preached in 1694, *Brontologia Sacra: The Voice of the Glorious God in the Thunder.* He had published that sermon anonymously in London in 1695 from notes taken by one of his auditors, for he had never written it out himself before he preached it. "A strange and strong impression upon his mind," he explained in the preface, had moved him to lay aside his prepared sermon during a thunderstorm that had broken while he was praying at the meetinghouse just before preaching. Obeying the commands of this "impression," which had offered him "assistances" if he would preach an extemporaneous sermon on God's voice in the thunder, Mather had promptly received a very strong indication that he had made the right decision: "at the very same instant when he was thus driven to *this theme*, the *thunder* was directed by the God of Heaven to fall with very tearing, though no killing effects, upon [Mather's] own house." Not only that sermon, but the interruption by the messenger who brought Mather the news that his house had been struck by lightning, and also Mather's immediate decision to continue the sermon without a pause, after he had learned that his wife and daughter were safe — all these became part of the church history of New England.

The inclusion of such extemporaneous materials, and the reprinting of whole title pages from the biographies and some of the other sermons that had been published separately before 1702, intensify the sense of incoherence that must trouble any reader of the 800-page folio volume. Yet Mather achieved in the *Magnalia* a work that has stood for 276 years as a major expression of the New England literary imagination. Although often scorned or mocked by some of the very people who use its unique information and (save for the theology) its historical interpretation, *Magnalia Christi Americana* is also a major work of American historiography. It deserves a place beside the best histories of George Bancroft, William H. Prescott, Francis Parkman, and Henry Adams. Deliberately projected on the grandest of epic and typological scales, it deserves to stand near (if necessarily below) the shelf of expansive works that includes *Moby-Dick* and the novels of Yoknapatawpha County.

The outline that Mather printed on one of his title pages (Figure 13) will serve as an adequate outline of the history. After a General Introduction on the value of church history, and the problems and advantages of writing one in New England, he began with the founding of New England in Book I, which he ended with a sermon that he had preached in 1698, *The Bostonian Ebenezer*. Books II and III and much of Book IV constitute the heart of the narrative, the lives of the governors, then the lives of the ministers, and (after some documentary information on Harvard College) the lives of some noteworthy men connected with Harvard. Book V is a collection of documents, with some commentary, from the synods of Congregational churches, and the last two books are concerned, respectively,

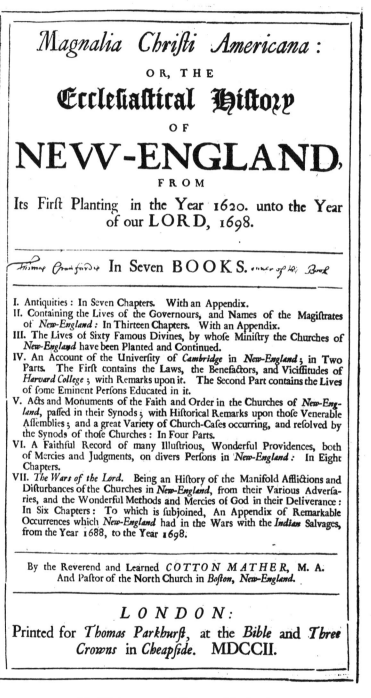

# *Magnalia Christi Americana :*

## OR, THE

# Ecclefiaſtical Hiſtory

### OF

# NEVV-ENGLAND,

#### FROM

Its Firſt Planting in the Year 1620. unto the Year
of our LORD, 1698.

*Thomas Cranford* In Seven BOOKS. *owner of this Book*

I. Antiquities : In Seven Chapters. With an Appendix.
II. Containing the Lives of the Governours, and Names of the Magiſtrates
of *New-England :* In Thirteen Chapters. With an Appendix.
III. The Lives of Sixty Famous Divines, by whoſe Miniſtry the Churches of
*New-England* have been Planted and Continued.
IV. An Account of the Univerſity of *Cambridge* in *New-England ;* in Two
Parts. The Firſt contains the Laws, the Benefactors, and Viciſſitudes of
*Harvard College ;* with Remarks upon it. The Second Part contains the Lives
of ſome Eminent Perſons Educated in it.
V. Acts and Monuments of the Faith and Order in the Churches of *New-Eng-
land,* paſſed in their Synods ; with Hiſtorical Remarks upon thoſe Venerable
Aſſemblies ; and a great Variety of Church-Caſes occurring, and reſolved by
the Synods of thoſe Churches : In Four Parts.
VI. A Faithful Record of many Illuſtrious, Wonderful Providences, both
of Mercies and Judgments, on divers Perſons in *New-England :* In Eight
Chapters.
VII. *The Wars of the Lord.* Being an Hiſtory of the Manifold Afflictions and
Diſturbances of the Churches in *New-England,* from their Various Adverſa-
ries, and the Wonderful Methods and Mercies of God in their Deliverance :
In Six Chapters : To which is ſubjoined, An Appendix of Remarkable
Occurrences which *New-England* had in the Wars with the *Indian* Salvages,
from the Year 1688, to the Year 1698.

By the Reverend and Learned *COTTON MATHER,* M. A.
And Paſtor of the North Church in *Boſton, New-England.*

## *LONDON :*

Printed for *Thomas Parkhurſt,* at the *Bible* and *Three
Crowns* in *Cheapſide.* MDCCII.

13. Title page of Cotton Mather's
*Magnalia Christi Americana.*

with remarkable providences and with "the wars of the Lord." The outcome of those wars is still unresolved at the end of the history, though New England's "grievous decade" seems to have ended.

The *Magnalia* confronts Mather's biographer with several peculiar problems. Like the life of any writer, this biography must represent the creation of Mather's major works. Since neither the manuscript of the history nor Mather's diaries for 1694 and 1695 have been found, one cannot retrace Mather's composition. Except for the works published before their chronological place in the narrative (the biography of Eliot, for example, and the sermon on thunderstorms), one must assume that Mather composed the history in the order of its final appearance in the London edition of 1702. His biography of William Phips is a singular exception, because the news of Phips's death did not come to Boston until a few days before Mather had the lives of five first-generation ministers ready for separate publication in May 1695. Since Phips was presumably still the incumbent governor of Massachusetts when Mather wrote Book II, the lives of New England's governors, his biography could hardly have formed a part of Mather's original design, but by the time Mather wrote Phips's life in 1695-96 he certainly knew that it would form a splendid addition to his lives of the other governors and that it provided an excellent opportunity to incorporate into his history of New England the revolution of 1689, the controversy over the new charter, and the witchcraft trials.

Thus the life of Phips, like the sermon about thunderstorms, constitutes at once a part of the history and an earlier, immediate statement about Mather's contemporaneous experience. When he wrote the biography in 1695 and 1696, Mather did use the "statue" that he erected therein as a threat which might "knock out the brains" of any partisans of Elisha Cooke who dared try to pull it down. Mather did call these partisans "base Tories" when he received the first copies of his life of Phips from London in December 1697, and he took some pleasure in the "anguish" that he thought its publication caused them. But Mather's interested motives and topical comments in this single biography or any other should not prevent us from seeing the value of the separate life in the larger historical work in which he reprinted it. When we treat the *Magnalia* as a single work, loosely connected though its baroque components certainly are, we come to see the very best literary expression of an attitude that

Mather had been developing at great personal cost — and with brief compensatory flights of exhilaration — throughout his life: the identification of his own life with the history and prospects of his native land.

By calling attention to the power of Mather's imagination in these years, I do not mean to emulate Sir William Phips by salvaging the treasure from Mather's baroque galleon and leaving the hulk itself under deep seas. If *Magnalia Christi Americana* is epic, prophecy, "auto-American-biography," jeremiad, hagiography, it is all these by virtue of being what Mather plainly intended it to be, a history. It is Mather's historical imagination and his fidelity to the historical record that justify the *Magnalia's* continuing survival. Readers of this history learn some things better from this historian of New England than they can learn from any of his modern successors, even though on many subjects he has obviously been superseded. When Mather said that New England, whether it should live anywhere else or no, must live in his history, he did not mean only that he wanted to project into the future his dream of the past, New England as it ought to have been or as it might have been, but New England as it actually had been and as it might yet be once again. Despite all its faults and its other aims, the *Magnalia* cannot be adequately understood either as a separate book or as a part of Cotton Mather's life unless it is also regarded as a history, an effort to achieve what Mather called an impartial record. He himself lives in that history not only as the representative celebrant of New England's best myths, but also as New England's faithful biographer and historian.

It is true that every page of Mather's huge folio volume seems to call attention to the historian's own personality. Even when he seems actually to have tried to conceal his identity, as in some of his anonymous writings, his strong personal mark can be easily identified; his Uncle Nathanael instantaneously recognized it in 1695 when a group of sermons that Cotton had sent off in 1692 to be published anonymously in London, turned up there unexpectedly after they had apparently been lost forever as part of a cargo taken by pirates in the Atlantic. Mather wrote the *Magnalia* as a defensive provincial, bringing light out of darkness to the great world of English readers and "entertaining" them — especially in his elaborate General Introduction and in the opening paragraphs of his innumerable biographies — with learned parallels and allusions. "Readers of history," he declares (quoting Polybius), "get more good by the objects of their emulation, than of their indignation." And he frankly wrote to celebrate virtue. "How," he asks, "can the lives of the commendable be written without commending them?" He warns us that he will suppress the names and some of the deeds of evil men, and many of the controversies between worthy men. And he writes the lives of the New England saints, his revered father's and grandfathers' generations, who by the dozen may seem to modern readers no more distinguishable from one another than all those portraits of Madonnas in Italian museums seemed to Mark Twain's innocents abroad.

Yet Mather was essentially a faithful historian, both in questions of fact and in interpretation. On the Pilgrims' departure from England to Holland, for example, or John Winthrop's now celebrated speech explaining the differences between civil and natural liberty, or the revolution of 1689 and the Salem witchcraft trials—on these and many other subjects one can now watch Mather following his sources. When I do so, I find him a consistently intelligent editor and reporter, whose paraphrases and summaries are remarkably free of distortion. One must be careful with documents that Mather himself wrote, because he sometimes remembers (or wishfully supplies) a different intention from the one our judgment would prefer, but I believe it is fair to say that we would lose very little if his report of the documents we can now check were the only surviving version of them. I believe he was genuinely concerned for accuracy when he invited every reader to point out errors of fact in his immense work, and that when he declared himself an impartial historian he did not mean to deny his passionate allegiance, but rather to declare a standard of justice.

Mather was also a more sophisticated thinker about historical objectivity than his reputation would lead us to expect. He understood and rejected the argument that in order to claim impartiality a historian had to restrict himself to "bare *matters of fact, without all* reflection." On that issue he cited Tacitus, who had declared the historian's privilege of narrating past actions *with praise or blame.* Although Mather did not completely anticipate modern debates about relativism, he certainly understood that it would be ridiculous for a Christian historian, who had sworn a covenant of faithful service after renouncing his own sins, to pretend that he saw no difference between virtue and vice. It is in this context that we should reread his rhetorical question: how can the lives of the commendable be written without commending them?

As an interpreter of New England church history, moreover—from church government and membership to the character of Governors John Winthrop, Sir Henry Vane, William Bradford, and Sir William Phips—Mather stands up surprisingly well even today. If we make minor allowances for the lapse of time, I believe that most specialists will set Mather's characterizations of John Winthrop beside those of Samuel Eliot Morison, Perry Miller, and Edmund Morgan—Mather was, after all, the first historian to see the importance of reprinting Winthrop's speech on civil liberty—and that they will find his interpretation of seventeenth-century changes in church membership rather close to the thesis of Edmund Morgan's fine study. Readers of this biography may also see the value of Mather's interpretations (excepting the diabolical and Providential) by following him (in the life of Phips) and later historians' accounts of the Salem witchcraft trials and the grievances and revolution against Sir Edmund Andros.

One of Mather's major achievements for Puritan readers of his own time, besides the collection of perishable information about seventeenth-century leaders, was the use of history to show the meaning of sainthood in New England. When sympathetically read, as in Sacvan Bercovitch's excellent book *The Puritan Origins of the American Self,* Mather's demonstration can still give the modern reader an unsurpassed view of the realms in which New England saints lived. Mather's John Winthrop ("as patient a lawgiver as Lycurgus") lived at once in the worlds of typology, classical antiquity, seventeenth-century piety and politics. He was the American Nehemiah, Mather said, builder of the walls of New England, and his exemplary function *as a New Englander* helped to define his role both in his actual life and in Mather's history. The seventeenth-century New England saint acted in this world for the glory of God, aware that his action was exemplary both as an imitation of biblical models and as an expression of New England's values.

Despite his anticipation of the Millennium, moreover, and his comparison of New England saints with great historical figures from

Augustine to Luther and Calvin, Mather knew that he had to acknowledge uncertainty, both his own and that of his subjects. Credulous though he sometimes was, he knew that there were sharp limits to his historical knowledge, and he knew that neither Christian historians nor eyewitnesses were always reliable authorities. He warns us, for example, that John Winthrop's *History of New England* is not an adequate source for the character of Winthrop's political rival, Sir Henry Vane.

Mather set his lives of the New England saints in a frame that allows him to celebrate the complexity of God's historical plan even as he sometimes uneasily concedes that the glorious experiment may fail and that the Golden City prophesied in Scripture may not after all be found in America. His first book, called "Antiquities," describes the founding of New England. Historical knowledge, Mather implies here, is progressive. Christian writers (he was to say some years later) had superseded the pagan chroniclers who had located in Joppa the bones of the sea monster from which Perseus had rescued Andromeda. Christians knew about the true story of Jonah and the whale, and the bones at Joppa were probably those of Jonah's whale. In the same way, Christian writers ignorant of America's existence are corrected in the *Magnalia* by a frankly provincial, explicitly American historian who boasts that he now writes from a region whose very existence could not have been proclaimed during the time of Pope Zachary without the risk of excommunication. Mather rejoices that he is not only beyond the range of the Pope's excommunication but also beyond any need to be protected by such an authority.

The idea of progressive historical knowledge is built into the history itself, and Mather knew that he too was subject to it, just as he knew that Luke and Paul had failed to include America when they wrote about "all the world." He argues that concealment of America's existence over the centuries was a more remarkable Providence than the actual discovery. But he reserves especial admiration for the timing of the Providential revelation to Columbus. The three key events that transformed the world near the beginning of the sixteenth century, he says, were the "Resurrection of Literature," the discovery of America, and the Reformation. The Pilgrims and Puritans who act in Mather's history are not merely defenders of a completed Reformation; they actively *pursue* the ideal of continuing reformation. Near the end of his brief chapter on the Plymouth colony, Mather quotes a very important sermon by John Robinson, pastor of the Pilgrim congregation during their long interlude in Leiden, exhorting his flock, as they embarked for England and America, to be alert for *further* truth that would surely break forth out of God's Holy Word. In that sermon Robinson criticizes the Lutherans and Calvinists for their refusal to go beyond what Luther of Calvin saw. He reminds the departing Pilgrims (as Mather by quoting him reminds readers of the *Magnalia*) that the covenant which binds them together binds them also to "be ready to receive whatever truth shall be made known unto you from the written Word of God." The rest of Mather's vast history reports what New Englanders had learned in the last eight decades of the century.

Mather's fundamental uncertainty influences the form of this first book and many of the later ones in the *Magnalia,* reinforcing the pattern of alternation that we have already noticed in Mather's personal view of New England's fortunes during the first thirty years of his own life. Faith in the progressive destiny of the Lord's people does predominate; even the jeremiad assumes that God will restore His favor if His people truly reown their covenant with Him. The wonders of the Christian religion in America include demographic triumphs: while the population of the world doubled during the last 360 years, Mather notes, in little more than 50 years 4,000 New England immigrants somehow managed to multiply into more than 100,000. They converted a "desert wilderness" into "a garden." And these desert colonies that had boasted an extraordinary number of Cambridge and Oxford graduates among their clergy in the first generation can now (only 60 years later) count 104 Harvard graduates preaching in their churches. The historian of these wonders can also point to physical abundance, which he typifies most grandly in the whale fishery's recent capture of a fifty-five-foot cow with a twenty-foot calf: "for unto such vast *calves,* the *sea monsters draw forth their breasts.* But so does the good God here give his people to suck the abundance of the seas!"

Against this celebration of abundance Mather sets the contrary theme of declension both spiritual and (at times) physical. He concedes that for more than twenty years now since the days of King Philip's War "the *blasting strokes* of Heaven" have fallen "upon the secular affairs" of New England. And from the early years of the

Plymouth colony he establishes an old Latin proverb as the counter-point that has been taken up, in the three centuries since he wrote, as the main theme of many studies of colonial New England: "The chief *hazard* and *symptom of degeneracy*" in the churches, he says, "is in the verification of that old observation, *Religio peperit divitas, et filia devoravit matrem;* Religion brought forth *prosperity,* and the *daughter* destroyed the *mother.*" One would expect gratitude to the God "who *gives them power to get wealth,*" but "the enchant-ments of this world make them to forget their *errand into the wild-erness.*" So we alternate. Sometimes we concentrate on the blasting strokes: a great fire destroys many homes; a thousand people die of smallpox and other causes in a town of four thousand, and a hun-dred buildings are burned down. Sometimes we stress the Providen-tial blessings: the town afflicted by smallpox has now grown to num-ber seven thousand, with more than a thousand houses. If no new towns have been founded since the devastating Indian wars of the 1670s, the old towns have doubled in population nonetheless.

Mather strives to find some rational coherence in the evidence. At first he insists that the *sole* motive for colonizing Massachusetts was religious zeal, and by way of contrast he candidly reports the rejoin-der of a group of Maine colonists who would not allow a visiting preacher to rebuke them for betraying the religious purpose of their colony: "Sir," one of them protests, "You are mistaken, you think you are preaching to the people at the [Massachusetts] Bay; our main end was to catch fish." For such worldly motives, Mather argues, the northern people suffered one disaster after another, while the early Puritans of Massachusetts have often "thriven to ad-miration." And in Massachusetts itself calamities have not been evenly distributed. Providence does not merely intervene to reward those towns that are blessed with "a good ministry"; in this matter, as in many others, the divine purpose is attached to mundane rea-soning. Mather contends—as Larzer Ziff has recently done—that the cold climate and barren land might not have allowed New Eng-land towns to flourish better than more fertile colonies if they had not enjoyed the extraordinary discipline of their churches and con-gregations. But then Mather also concedes that one subsidiary mo-tive for the founding of Massachusetts included both disgust with European corruption and a conviction that "the whole earth is the *Lord's garden,* . . . to be tilled and improved by" the sons of Adam:

why then, his English Puritans ask, "should we stand starving here for places of habitation, and in the meantime suffer whole countries so profitable for the use of man, to lie waste without any improvement?" Here, as in Max Weber's version of Puritanism, a worldly motive was acceptable and implicitly more effective if subordinated to a religious one.

The alternating pattern gives our doctrinaire historian freedom to incorporate all kinds of evidence without abandoning his essential faith. When he highlights the "blasting strokes" and the threat of disaster, he is like the preacher who calls for repentance. Indeed, he expresses not the slightest discomfort about incorporating into the text of his history several entire sermons of his own. In these he is the immediately present Pastor, exhorting his flock to improve. At other times, in the more disinterested stance of the historian, he can calmly report that like Jesus in the wilderness the people of New England have been "*continually* tempted by the Devil" in their wilderness — with "a new assault of extraordinary temptation" almost every five years. And when he sings his theme of the Christian wonders in America, he is holding up past models for emulation and celebrating the glory of the God who will yet deliver New England. Doubts about the future appear in the framing introductory book, "Antiquities," and more insistently in the last book, on the wars of the Lord. The lives of the saints, which fill Mather's second, third, and fourth books, are balanced later on by chilling circumstantial narratives of executions, confessing yet unrepentant murderers, Indian wars, witchcraft, and an astonishingly well depicted succession of confidence men who invade Boston at the very end of the century and utterly deceive some congregations. The complexity of the secular world, and many of the controversies that Mather frankly underplays in his biographies, appear in these later books along with a large number of original documents which emphasize Mather's conviction — iterated and refined in our own century by scholars from Perry Miller and Samuel Eliot Morison to Edmund S. Morgan and Michael Kammen — that New England church government was a *mixed* government, that embattled and perplexed seventeenth-century synods repeatedly sought and followed a *middle* way, as Mather insists in his account of the Half-Way Covenant.

Even in Mather's lives of the saints uncertainty plays a major role. Every reader must share a little of Peter Gay's resistance to the sameness in those lives, to the pattern not only of similar conversions but of happy endings, exemplary Christian deaths. But here, as in the study of Italian portraits of Madonnas, familiarity enables one to see important distinctions, and familiarity with Mather's own early life enables one to see their source in Mather's own experience. It is precisely his intention to show that so many of the lives of first-generation ministers were outwardly and inwardly similar. When one reads the entire history consecutively, the resemblances among these lives may become monotonous, but they are also impressive and even moving, and it is Mather's great theme of variation within essential uniformity that makes both his emotional and his historical case. To the allegorical Puritan mind and to the casual modern reader, all these men are saints. To the historian glorifying God in his narrative and instructing posterity by their example, these men are unique versions of an essential type. The challenge Mather faced was to make their uniqueness evident and memorable within the allegorical forms.

Before we consider the differences, I believe it is important to look more closely at the value of the repetition. As we see one after another in the first generation of ministers experience the crisis of conversion, of resistance to Anglican ceremonies, and of persecution by Archbishop Laud, we receive a convincing impression of a central historical reality: many accomplished men had to experience this religious and social crisis individually. For the secular reader of history, the impression of that fact is more memorable than the Providential deliverances that Mather sometimes underlines. And of course one of the main similarities among some of the most eminent lives is the recurrence of perplexing, often terrifying doubt. Richard Mather, John Cotton, Thomas Hooker, Thomas Shepard, Nathanael Rogers, Jonathan Mitchell—Mather gives strong evidence to show that every one of these founding fathers was seriously troubled by challenges to his faith or to his assurance of his own salvation years *after* he had already been preaching the Gospel. Thomas Hooker remarks as he takes his last look at England from his departing ship that in his lifetime religion may never again be defended with the same genuine ardor as in the days of the English oppression. And in the same brief speech he prophesies the declension of piety that has been noted by American historians ever since the seventeenth century. Some of the churches will decline when they have liberty in America, Hooker declares in Mather's narrative as he leaves England: "Adversity had slain its thousands, but prosperity would slay its ten thousands!" Ezekiel Rogers, an extraordinarily successful preacher in England, fears nonetheless that he is unregenerate, and his "lively spirit" has the misfortune to inhabit what Mather calls "a crazy body." Mather depicts him in a memorable image during his old age in Rowley, Massachusetts, as a tree of knowledge stooping to let the children "pick off the apples ready to drop into their mouths." William Thompson, suffering what Mather calls the prevalent New England disease of "splenetic maladies," is sometimes tempted like many others to suicide. While preaching at Braintree, he falls into "a black melancholy" which disables him for many years, and only as Thompson approaches death does the Devil flee and "God himself draw near." John Warham is so afflicted by a "deadly . . . melancholy" that he refuses to accept communion himself while serving it to the members of his church. "Some," Mather scrupulously reports, say that Warham was still "in a cloud" when he died, "though some have asserted, that the cloud was dispelled, before he expired." Nathanael Rogers laments his brief subscription in 1627 to articles of Anglican conformity in England. It had seemed only prudent, Rogers wrote at the time, "But it was my weakness as I now conceive it; which I beseech God to pardon unto me." Four years later, Rogers added a note which Mather prints in the history: "This I smarted for, 1631. If I had read this, it may be, I had not done what I did." "Reader," Mather comments, "in this one passage thou hast a large history, of the thoughts and fears, and cares, with which the *Puritans* of those times were exercised."

In no other historical work that I know can we find so pervasive and so well integrated a representation of doubt and uncertainty in the individual Puritan's life. Mather's strength as a historian grows out of the range and the number of his examples, and the persistence of his theme — the piety, the faith, the struggle, the perplexity, and the resignation in dozens of actual lives. However we may discount his partisanship, the unquestionable reality of their losses, their suffering, and their anxiety comes through as a major achievement of his narrative method, which of course owes something to John Foxe's Book of Martyrs. To know that dozens of successful, learned ministers left England is to be impressed by their danger and their commitment; to read dozens of their lives as in various cir-

cumstances they decide to leave is quite another, more powerful experience. The variety and the specific detail of Mather's individual-
izing anecdotes make their historicity generally unquestionable. Of
all the characters who die exemplary deaths in the *Magnalia,* only
Richard Mather struggles to get off his deathbed and into his study
on the day before his death, for fear of wasting time; only Richard
Mather asks his son in his dying request to honor the Half-Way
Covenant. Only Thomas Hooker says that a Pastor must be compassionate toward frightened sinners and severe with "crafty and
guileful souls," of whom "sharp rebukes make sound Christians."
"Indeed," Mather says, "of some he had compassion, making a difference; and others he saved with fear, pulling them out of the fire."
Only John Cotton gives up supper in his later years so that he can
study longer, "resolving rather to wear out with using, than with
rusting." Only Thomas Parker, the celibate, sweet-voiced singer, re-
tains his excellent voice until very old age because, Mather's source
reasons, "his teeth held sound and good until then; his custom being to wash his mouth, and rub his teeth every morning." Only
John Avery, shipwrecked on his way to preach at Marblehead, challenges the Lord not to save his life but to keep His promise " 'to deliver us from sin and condemnation, and to bring us safe to Heaven
. . .' Which he had no sooner spoken, but he was by a *wave* sweeping
off, immediately wafted away to Heaven indeed."

The lives of the governors, though perhaps the best of Mather's
historical achievements, need not take so much space here, but it is
important to notice that even the most assured of those men also
labor at times in perplexity. Even John Winthrop is tempted by "disconsolate thoughts of black and sore *desertions.*" Perhaps the best
example is Mather's own friend Sir William Phips, whose absolute
conviction that destiny will make him rich leads him to persevere in
his search for the wrecked Spanish treasure ship, and who, when he
finds it, cries out, "Thanks be to God; we're made!" This sweet-
tempered yet choleric hero, whom Mather compares ineptly to
Francisco Pizarro at one point during his adventures, becomes in
Mather's portrait not only the "Knight of Honesty" who makes the
heathen virtue of patriotism into a Christian virtue, but the first
self-made man in American literature. Yet even this favorite of
Providence comes to fear, as we have seen in our narrative of Mather's own life, that by granting him extraordinary prosperity without

assuring him of his conversion to a saving faith Providence may have decided to "put him off with a portion" here on earth, without saving his soul hereafter. He does repent of his sins, of course, in the declaration of faith that he presented to Cotton Mather just before leading the expedition to capture Port Royal from the French, and he does conquer Port Royal. Trusting Providence again, however, in the much more ambitious and presumably much more important campaign in the war against Antichrist, the invasion of Quebec, Phips suffers a humiliating disaster. Neither he nor his biographer can understand what signs might have told them that the siege of Quebec would fail, although neither one questions the conviction that an English conquest of Quebec would have served to advance Christian liberty. In the Salem witchcraft crisis, moreover, Mather's Phips comes to see belatedly that, whatever the individual innocence or guilt of the people who were condemned in 1692, the Devil's most effective strategy had been to set the Lord's people fighting among themselves like so many men in a blindman's buff, sinfully and hotly mauling one another in the dark.

In William Bradford, John Winthrop, and Phips, moreover, Mather re-creates the characters of three representative rulers whose unique qualities and experiences reinforce the central theme of variety among the typical saints. All three are to some degree willing to treat their enemies or opponents leniently, for example, but in each of the three lives Mather establishes that willingness with an anecdote whose historicity seems authentic and whose import deepens the peculiar lines of the individual portrait. The Bradford anecdote comes from Bradford's own history *Of Plymouth Plantation*. Mather condenses Bradford's account of the colonists who by pleading liberty of conscience won the Governor's permission to be excused from working on Christmas Day, a holiday which most Pilgrims as well as other Congregationalists deplored as popish superstition. When Bradford finds some of these people playing games on a supposedly religious holiday during which most of the colonists have to work, he orders the celebrants back to work because, he insists, his own conscience will not allow some colonists to play while others have to work.

Moderation is even more important to the characterization of Mather's Winthrop than of his Bradford, for Winthrop stands among the founders as the chief exemplar of the middle way. Mather emphasizes the combination of firmness and leniency in the famous example of Winthrop's speech to the General Court in 1645 after his acquittal on a charge of exceeding his legitimate authority. Here Winthrop exemplifies his moderation both by insisting on standing trial and by the substance of his remarks after his acquittal, remarks which themselves define the middle way of civil liberty—covenanted liberty for which a Christian who knows the opposite dangers of licentious anarchy and tyranny will venture his life when he must. In a simpler incident, too, Mather's Winthrop exemplifies moderation in his treatment of a man who has been stealing Winthrop's firewood, a commodity that had to be brought to the Boston peninsula from the mainland. When Winthrop's associates inform him of the theft, Winthrop tells them that he will cure the man of stealing if they will bring the man to him. When the poor man appears, Winthrop gives him a generous supply of firewood and tells the observers that he has thus cured the man of stealing.

Phips appears in Mather's history as a fat, irascible adventurer, but despite his "choleric" temperament he too knows when to forgive and relent, and when to dismiss the untrustworthy. The most memorable variations on the theme of leniency in Phips's life come during the risky months of his search for the treasure, when threats of mutiny endanger both his enterprise and his life. Mather shows him subduing one group of mutineers by turning the ship's guns on them after he has outwitted and isolated them; Phips does not kill these men but discharges them at the first opportunity. His political shrewdness and the loyalty he elicits from one key member of the crew reveal qualities of leadership that may be profitably compared with the traits of Bradford and Winthrop, but of course he expresses these in a context of physical danger before he himself has become a Christian. He is the knight of honesty rather than Moses or Nehemiah. Threatened by a different rumbling among the men who eventually find the great Spanish treasure with him, he regains their support by a combination of firmness and generosity, and he keeps his word to them after the treasure has been found.

❦

MATHER PREDICTED in his General Introduction that he would be criticized both for the "simple, submiss, humble *style*" of his history and for having embellished his prose "with too much of ornament, by the multiplied references to other and former concerns, closely couched for the observation of the attentive in almost every paragraph." Here again Mather calls our attention to a form of uncertainty, by his anxious self-defense and especially by his projection of the opposite standards that he says critics will use in censuring his prose. We need not try to make him seem modern; he himself appeals to a classical anecdote to reveal the subjectivity and unreliability of criticism. Critics of the sculptor Policletus begged him to create a sculpture according to their standards, Mather says, but then unanimously condemned the work with which he obliged them, and they praised the other work that he had secretly done according to no standards but his own. Attentive and inattentive readers have observed the ornament and the multiplied references in the prose of the *Magnalia*. No critic that I know has ever complained of the simple quality of Mather's style, however, and few have noticed it at all. The prose of the *Magnalia* is both baroque and plain.

Probably the two commentators who have made the most accurate observations about the intended value of Mather's ornaments and allusions are Nicholas Noyes, who wrote a prefatory poem for the first edition of the *Magnalia,* and Sacvan Bercovitch. Noyes praises Mather for holding the reader fast with his clever designs,

> Whilst *Wit* and *Learning* move themselves aright,
> Thro' every line, and *Colour* in our sight,
> So interweaving *Profit* with *Delight;*
> And curiously inlaying both together,
> That he must needs find Both, who looks for either.

Bercovitch, in the most perceptive and extensive recent commentary, shows that Mather's closely couched allusions often go further than the obvious purpose of entertaining sophisticated readers with witty puns and learned parallels from classical and biblical antiquity. They set the history of New England in the history of the world, and especially of the Reformation. They not only display the provincial historian's learning but project the qualities of the great men of Western history into the American "wilderness," where the model for the last Reformation has been established.

Despite Mather's claim of entertainment in nearly every paragraph, however, he concentrates the most allusive of these passages (after the General Introduction) in the opening and concluding paragraphs of his biographies. His narrative prose is characteristically graceful, economical, straightforward, and even his wit and punning often call upon plain diction. Throughout the history one finds passages like the following anecdote near the end of the life of Phips.

In the meantime, I cannot but relate a wonderful experience of Sir *William Phips,* by the relation whereof something of an *antidote* may be given against a *poison,* which the diabolical *figure-flingers* and *fortune tellers* that swarm all the world over may insinuate into the minds of men. Long before Mr. *Phips* came to be Sir *William,* while he sojourned in *London,* there came into his lodging an old *astrologer,* living in the neighborhood, who making some *observation* of him, though he had small or no *conversation* with him, did (howbeit by him wholly undesired) one day send him a paper, wherein he had, with pretenses of a rule in *astrology* for each article, distinctly noted the most material passages that were to befall this our *Phips* in the remaining part of his life; it was particularly asserted and inserted, that he should be engaged in a design, wherein by reason of enemies at *court,* he should meet with much delay; that nevertheless in the *thirty-seventh* year of his life, he should find a *mighty treasure;* that in the *forty-first* year of his life, his *king* should employ him in as great a *trust beyond sea,* as a subject could easily have: that soon after this he should undergo an hard *storm* from the endeavors of his adversaries to *reproach* him and *ruin* him; that his adversaries, though they should go very *near* gaining the point, should yet *miss* of doing so; that he should hit upon a vastly *richer matter* than any that he hitherto met withal; that he should continue *thirteen years* in his *public station,* full of action, and full of hurry; and the rest of his days he should spend in the satisfaction of a *peaceable retirement.*

Mr. *Phips* received this undesired paper with trouble and with contempt, and threw it by among certain loose papers in the bottom of a trunk, where his lady some years after accidentally lit upon it. His lady with admiration saw, step after step, very much of it accomplished; but when she heard from *England,* that Sir *William* was coming over with a commission to be governor of *New England,* in that very year of his life, which the paper specified; she was afraid of letting it lie any longer in the house, but cast it into the *fire.*

Now the thing which I must invite my reader to remark, is this, that albeit Almighty God may permit the *devils* to *predict,* and perhaps to *perform* very many particular things to men, that shall by such a *presumptuous and unwarrantable juggle* as *astrology* (so Dr. *Hall* well calls it!) or any other *divination,* consult them, yet the *devils* which *foretell* many *true* things, do commonly *foretell* some that are *false,* and it may be, propose by the things that are *true* to betray men into some fatal misbelief and miscarriage about those that are false.

Very singular therefore was the wisdom of Sir *William Phips,* that as he ever treated these *prophecies* about him with a most *pious ne-*

*glect,* so when he had seen all but the *two last* of them very punctually fulfilled yea, and seen the beginning of a fulfillment unto the *last but one,* also, yet when I pleasantly mentioned them unto him, on purpose to *try* whether there were any occasion for me humbly to give him the serious *advice,* necessary in such a case to anticipate the *devices of Satan,* he prevented my advice, by saying to me, *Sir, I do believe there might be a cursed snare of Satan in those prophecies: I believe Satan might have leave to foretell many things, all of which might come to pass in the beginning, to lay me asleep about such things as are to follow, especially about the main chance of all; I do not know but I am to die this year: For my part, by the help of the grace of God, I shall endeavor to live as if I were this year to die.* And let the reader now attend the event!

I have deliberately chosen here a passage that makes no claims to eloquence or wit. Some of the sentences are long, and their characteristic structure is complex, but the narrative moves directly and easily, the diction is consistently unpretentious, and the rhythm under firm control, with emphasis in the abundant parallel elements falling consistently on the words whose meaning requires the greatest emphasis. Here, as in the most serviceable prose of Benjamin Franklin, one could not easily delete anything except the parenthetical information about astrology and Dr. Joseph Hall, whose meditations Mather had admired for twenty years.

IN CELEBRATING the value of Cotton Mather's uncertainty, I do not mean to drag him into the twentieth century. I hope to illuminate qualities in his view of history and in his predicament that give twentieth-century observers an unusually good opportunity to understand him and his own time. Mather, like many of us, believed that historians in some generations have a better opportunity than their predecessors to understand certain historical problems. He and other Puritan historians knew that they could not be sure they understood their own motives or those of historical and contemporaneous characters. Mather could even describe himself in one uncharacteristic moment as a "seeker" in his effort to understand conflicting evidence about the character of Sir Henry Vane. Both in his own life and in his *Magnalia,* Mather had difficulty reading the intentions of Providence, the direction of history, although his faith told him that the Millennium was imminent. One of his most poignantly valuable passages in the *Magnalia* describes the ironic misery of saints who had emigrated to America for the religious benefit of their descendants but who eventually found that some of their own grandchildren could not even be baptized, because neither parent in the intermediate generation had joined the church. Sometimes Mather could show that Providence rebuked the strictest interpreters of Scripture: the most vehement leaders who insisted that the Devil could not appear in the shape of an innocent person are confuted in the *Magnalia* by sworn testimony that victims have been afflicted by specters in the shapes of those very leaders themselves! And ultimately the entire community can make gross errors in the name of the Lord—as when they resist the Devil's assault in the form of witches, only to discover too late that his real strategy has mixed lies with truth to foment universal suspicion, has discredited authority, and has caused at least some false convictions by seducing the courts into accepting the Devil's testimony.

In all these perplexities, however, Cotton Mather never doubted for long that history was moving toward a good ending decreed by the wisest of beings. Nor in all his reporting of villains, backsliders, and confidence men did he doubt that heroes and saints had really existed. "*Suffering* as well as *doing*," he said, "belongs to the complete character of a Christian." Both while writing the *Magnalia* and in the year of its belated publication, he himself experienced a full measure of suffering and doing. And in this fourth decade of his life he experienced the definitive separation of his own personal and spiritual life from the political life of Congregational New England.

# IX

## Suffering and Doing: The Mystery of Particular Faiths and Deaths

⁂

I set apart the Day following, for the Duties of a secret Fast, that I might humble myself before God under the rebukes of His Providence, who at the same time that wicked Men are from abroad assaulting me with a Storm of Malignity, to ruin all my Opportunities to glorify Him, does Himself also visit me with Deaths and Griefs at home in my own Family; and that I might obtain from Him, Assistances to carry it patiently and cheerfully under my Trials, and bring forth such Fruits of greater Serviceableness (especially among the *Children* of my Flock) as are to be expected of me.

Cotton Mather, *Diary*, February 7, 1701

THE PROCESS of separation had begun with the inauguration of the new charter in 1692, and it ended with the death of Abigail Mather ten years later. Passionately engaged in immediate issues both local and international, Cotton Mather could not see this process in the historical perspective that now makes it seem evident. He still felt sure that the Millennium was imminent. He still hoped for great changes abroad and for victories in Boston, Cambridge, and Canada. And throughout this grievous decade he continued to achieve Particular Faiths that overwhelmed all his doubts with the kind of ecstatic knowledge he had always craved and often enjoyed. When events confirmed the accuracy of his Particular Faiths, he rejoiced and sought hungrily for more of those exhilarating experiences. But when two of his most dearly treasured Particular Faiths miscarried despite his successful entreaties for divine confirmation of them, he found himself acting, at the age of forty, in a world almost completely transformed. His father, still vigorous and articulate at sixty-three, had been forced out of the Harvard presidency and was now certain never to reenact his glorious mission at the

Court of St. James. Abigail, the "good thing" Cotton Mather had been granted in answer to his prayers long ago, had been taken from him.

❧

EVEN WHILE writing the *Magnalia,* Mather could not always live in the high regions of Providential history. His vocation required him to act energetically in his neighborhood. Unaware of the changes we have noticed, he fulfilled his pastoral and civic duties. Within less than a year after he had persuaded the members of his church to accept the Half-Way Covenant, he found himself obliged as Pastor to pronounce the equivalent of excommunication on a young woman who was "by covenant under ecclesiastical inspection in this church." Mary Cooly, "having been convicted of living in *adultery,* with many aggravations of her crime," had not only failed to repent but "fled from the admonitions that should have brought her to repentance." The Pastor of her congregation had therefore to carry out a vote of the brethren and declare her "cut off from the ecclesiastical privileges and expectations" of those in the covenant. Just as in the excommunication of John Farnum thirty years earlier, the church held out the prospect of "seasonable repentance" to this absent sinner in the very declaration that she now belonged visibly to the kingdom of Satan. And two years later — although Mary Cooly did not return to the fold — a married woman in the church who was formally threatened with excommunication did give such convincing written and oral evidence of repentance that the members voted to restore her to full communion.

Mather's manuscript record of actions taken by the Second Church contains relatively few disciplinary judgments, but the number does increase in these years of the mid-1690s, and the offenses range from the trivial to the grave. Mather had to admonish two young women who had consulted a fortune teller in the spring of 1695, and to suspend from communion a man who (in a vain effort to protect himself from disciplinary action) had falsified the number of militiamen on regular guard duty. The church naturally took an interest in any member's failure to live up to his "oath for the faithful discharge of his trust," and it did restore this sinner's access to communion when he submitted "a penitent confession" three months later. By separate votes of the church Mather pronounced the censure of admonition on a man convicted of reveling and drunkenness, but scrupulously noted in the church record that the man had confessed only to the reveling. A woman "convicted of stealing in five or six horrid instances, and of lying many times on the occasion thereof," was excommunicated in the summer of 1697 and restored to communion eight years later. Abigail Day, who lived in the almshouse, was admonished by a vote of censure because she had defamed both the quality of the "laudable diet" there and the virtue of the keeper, who she said had "several times made attempts upon her chastity." She persisted in her charges against the keeper, but she did apologize for having said that "she would thank neither God nor man for such victuals." Mrs. Sarah Cock was excommunicated in 1697 for adultery, and for the same offense in 1698 Mather had to carry out the sentence of excommunication on Mercy Short, whose body and soul he had fought hard to rescue from the Devil in 1692-93.

Disciplinary matters, of course, were only a tiny fraction of the Pastor's concerns. Besides his catechizing and his regular pastoral visits, Mather occupied himself busily with a number of other duties and projects. He collected £80 to ransom three young Bostonians from Turkish slavery. He collected £60 "for the propagation of the Gospel unto the dark places in our borders," and wrote a circular letter urging the ministers of Massachusetts to support that work. He collected £55—more, he boasted, than any other church contributed—for relief of the poor during a famine that struck Massachusetts in the spring of 1696. During these months he fasted more often than he had usually done, sometimes more than once a week, and he explicitly tried to relate that intensification of his own fasts to the needs of the people. He said he wanted to emulate three biblical models, renowned for fasting, whom Jesus had made "miraculous *feeders* of other men." "I would fast," Mather wrote, "that my neighbors might be *fed*." Nor did he neglect political means of relief. He sent a letter to the governor of Connecticut, which had enjoyed a good harvest in 1696, requesting grain for the poor in Massachusetts. And he himself gave "several pieces of eight" to a poor Baptist preacher in Boston. In 1697 he wrote a little book called *Gospel for the Poor,* which he intended especially for the growing number of poor people suffering in England. When he heard that the ship carrying that manuscript to England had been captured, he published the book in Boston. When he heard reports in 1699 that a revolution had liberated New Spain from Spanish colonial rule, he taught himself enough Spanish to prepare a brief tract, *La religion pura,* twelve essential articles of Protestant faith, and *La fe del christiano,* for distribution in "the Spanish Indies." He baptized four black people in the Second Church, wrote an Indian primer, a pamphlet for Jews, a *Monitory and Hortatory Letter to those English who debauch the Indians,* and (although he himself was very well paid) *A Monitory Letter* warning the people not to starve their ministers. He contrived the catechism for Jews in a way that allowed him to cite Old Testament passages for the main articles of Christian belief, and although he wanted to convert at least one Jew to Christianity he announced in his preface that he would be content if Jews "would but return to the faith of the *Old Testament,* and believe with their own ancient and blessed patriarchs."

Mather acted energetically in local matters, too. His barber, on joining the church at last in 1700, testified that Mather's indefatigable offers of unsolicited advice, warnings, and lessons had been the chief means of converting him. On the same day Sara Winsley, a servant in the Mather household, joined the church with a similar profession of his influential tactics. Mather continued to attend and to advertise the "private meetings" of Christians that he had helped to organize throughout the North End, and he had thirteen or fourteen of them going strong by the end of 1701. He made periodic drives to attract more young people to the church, both by preaching sermons especially for them in his own church and at the regular Thursday Lecture, and by nurturing the Young Men's Associations that he had founded. His Reserved Memorials report an attendance of one hundred at a meeting of one of these societies in 1700. He founded a Society for Suppression of Disorders in 1702, and another for the Propagation of the Christian Religion, drawing up rules for them as he had done for other kinds of groups. He preached to the convicts in the prison on a Sunday afternoon after his regular service. He spent most of a week in "miserable Watertown" negotiating the settlement of an angry disagreement in the church there. He persuaded the Boston judges and selectmen to put the jail into more nearly decent condition, and he organized a committee to find work for the poor.

As his sermons, tracts, and biographies appeared in the bookshops at the rate of fifteen or twenty new titles every year, Mather became firmly established in the mid-1690s as one of the most successful preachers in New England. Neither the loss of his political influence nor the criticism provoked by Robert Calef's charges seems to have diminished Mather's audience or the range of his invitations. Within a year after the Salem witchcraft trials, he had initiated what developed into an annual visit to both Salem and Ipswich. The people of Salem received him "with much respect and honor," and turned out in great numbers to hear him. He preached in both Salem and Ipswich at least once every September for the rest of the decade — presumably with the endorsement of John Wise, the Ipswich minister who had signed a petition in favor of John Proctor in 1692 and would soon again oppose the Mathers on an issue of church government. Large crowds also attended Mather's sermons and lectures in Boston, Reading, and Watertown. He was invited to speak before the legislature, and some of his regular turns at the Thursday Lecture were extraordinarily well attended. It was about this time that Increase Mather calculated the average weekly attendance at the services in the North Church on the Lord's Day at fifteen hundred people, and no evidence indicates that the attendance decreased when Increase Mather was forced to move to Cambridge for two years in order to retain the presidency of Harvard College. In the last five years of the century Cotton Mather preached at least a hundred sermons a year; besides the ones that he himself arranged to have printed, a fair number were solicited for publication by people who had heard them.

Only a part of this unusual attention should be attributed to peculiar circumstances or to that celebrity which is hardly distinguishable from notoriety. Mather himself recognized that at least some of the extraordinary number of people who came to his Thursday Lecture just after the first copies of Robert Calef's book arrived in Boston from London were curious to see how he would react to the ridicule in Calef's book. And if Mather's sermon before the execution of Sarah Threeneedles attracted the largest audience of the century, as he said it did, the five thousand people surely came not only to hear Mather's two-hour sermon but also to see the young woman hanged for the murder of her "base-born child." Although the General Court ordered this Lecture moved from the uncertain meetinghouse of the First Church to the larger and newer South, thousands of auditors were unable to get into the building, and Mather himself was able to get into the pulpit only "by climbing over *pews* and *heads.*" But there is no reason to disbelieve Mather's report that his sermon in the prison moved some of the inmates to tears, or that the crown that came "from all the towns in the neighborhood" to hear him preach at Reading was unusually large. He preached with great intensity, and with a strong belief in the value of adapting his sermons to the immediate circumstances. Whatever else Ralph Waldo Emerson might have said in criticism of this Old Calvinist preacher, he could not have indicted him with the dull Unitarian preacher who failed to perceive that the snowstorm going on just outside his own church was as great a miracle as any scriptural miracle the man was laboring to defend. Mather did write out most of his sermons in advance, but he always prayed for divine guidance just before he began to preach, and he once set aside his prepared sermon in order to preach extemporaneously on a snowstorm — just as he did for the thunderstorm that damaged his own house. He may have been insensitive to the repulsive effect of his personality on some of his auditors, but he certainly paid close attention to what he thought of as the people's immediate needs.

The Reserved Memorials indicate clearly enough why Mather's preaching in these years might have expressed unusual intensity. He had not abandoned his chiliastic hopes. Excluded from direct political action, he tried to prepare for the great new Reformation (which he still hoped would occur in 1697) by resuming his frequent fasts, during which he sought new assurances and new ways of acting for God's glory. His Reserved Memorials in those years must not be mistaken for a record of his daily life. Abstracted from more hasty notes and written retrospectively from year to year, they emphasize once again his meditative Saturday fasts in preparation for the Lord's Day, especially for communion services. But they do show the particular spiritual gifts he prayed for, and the kind of response he thought he received. He repeatedly asked for more guidance from his own special angel and for a renewal of Particular Faiths, those exhilarating and thus far infallible promises of a specific blessing to be conferred on his family or the Lord's people. To pray on these Fast days or on other important occasions, he would often lie prostrate on the floor of his study, and he often felt gloriously rewarded by the approach of the divine spirit. "Doubtless," he wrote about one of those experiences, "the *Angel* of the Lord made me sensible of his approaches. I was wondrously irradiated." And then —the date here is September 19, 1697—came the assurance:

> My Lord Jesus Christ, shall yet be more known, in the vast regions of *America;* and by the means of poor, vile sinful *me,* He shall be so. Great *Britain* shall undergo a strange revolution and reformation; and sinful *I* shall be concerned in it. *France* will quickly feel mighty impressions from the almighty hand of my Lord Jesus Christ: and I shall on that occasion sing His glorious praises. Nor was this all, that was then told me from Heaven: but I forbear the rest.

Mather's journals and sermons in the hopeful passages that he wrote during these years vibrate with an irrepressible ebullience, a passionate excitement that must have enlivened his preaching as well. Sometimes his pious euphoria resembles the almost manic expansiveness that would later characterize Herman Melville's letters during the composition of *Moby-Dick.* On one of his visits to his colleague John Bailey, who was gravely ill, Mather spoke "with a certain serious and sacred *hilarity*" about the relative merits of praising Christ among myriads of angels in Heaven, and preaching Christ to hundreds of mortals on earth. "But sir," Mather asked, "have you prepared a *song?*" And when Bailey asked him what *he* would say upon arriving in Heaven, Mather answered: "I'll say, 'Behold, O ye Holy Spirits, the most wretched and loathsome sinner, that ever arrived among you: but it is our Glorious Christ, that hath brought me hither.' I'll say, 'Sirs, here is one come among you, that was the most abominable sinner that ever was in the world, and yet I have as good a righteousness as any of you.' I'll say, 'Oh! ye illustrious angels, if you don't wonderfully glorify the grace of the Lord Jesus Christ, in fetching so vile a sinner into these mansions, you'll never do it!' "

Until the end of 1697, these euphoric expressions and the secret assurances from Heaven strengthened Mather's chiliastic hopes. He repeatedly prayed for the overthrow of Louis XIV and the liberation of French Protestants, and he found his reward again and again in thrilling assurances that there would be a tremendous revolution in France. Since New England was virtually at war with New France throughout the period that Mather's history of the fighting would call "the grievous decade" in 1698, these prayers about France had a local as well as Millennial significance. And in November and December 1697 prominent signs in the external world reinforced his private assurances. Heavy rains saved the harvest "when a few days of drought more" would have caused a *"terrible famine."* A large French and Indian force was defeated by English and American troops during a "descent on our frontiers," and *"the Angel of the Lord"* smote a French naval force "with such a wasting sickness" that the squadron of fifteen men-of-war had to abandon its plan to attack Boston from the sea early in November. On the special day of thanksgiving to commemorate these blessings, Mather received further assurances of forthcoming reformation in England and of a "mighty *revolution*" soon in France. On the night of December 9, just after he had prayed to one of his private groups of Christians on the peace that would come to the world with the sudden destruction of Antichrist's kingdom at the Second Coming of Christ, he learned that peace had been declared in Europe and that "the *Turk*" had received "such an overthrow . . . as looks like the *second woe passing away.*"

Even after 1697 passed without the destruction of Turk or Pope or Sun King, Mather did not question the validity of his Particular Faiths. No date had been attached to those assurances of revolution; he had not relied on Particular Faiths in naming 1697 as the year of the Second Coming but had computed it himself by adding 180 years to the date of Luther's Reformation. Mather continued throughout the rest of the century to experience Particular Faiths about the eventual revolution in France, and his Particular Faiths on several other subjects were so dramatically verified, as we shall see, that his miscalculation of the Millennium did not lead him to question his special messages. He continued to feel close to the heavenly world through other experiences, which also added strength to his preaching. He was present, for example, when his "dear friend" John Bailey died on December 12, 1697, and he recorded Bailey's last words: "His glorious angels are come for me!" Bailey had been working on a sermon on the thirty-first Psalm, "Into Thy hands I commend my spirit," and on the day of his death he had asked Mather to preach a sermon on that text. Mather thought it a special providence that Bailey's funeral was scheduled on the day of Mather's regular turn to give the Lecture. Before "a vast assembly," then, he preached on Bailey's text the sermon that he quickly published as *A Good Man, Making a Good End,* which he later slipped into the flexible structure of his *Magnalia.* Mather believed that the remarkable circumstances under which he had received his text for the sermon gave additional "pungency" to the truths that he preached in it, and his skillful use of Bailey's diaries apparently did help to make the sermon "an acceptable entertainment."

While the intensity of Mather's chiliastic faith and of his reliance on divine guidance gave special force to his preaching during these years, he was not alone in these beliefs. Samuel Sewall, who belonged to the South Church and who took a neutral or critical position in the Mathers' most painful controversies during these years, not only published an apocalyptical book of his own in 1697. He also treated Cotton Mather as a connoisseur of such heavenly mysteries. Mather happened to be dining at Sewall's new house in 1695 on the day that a prodigious hailstorm broke 480 squares of new glass there. Mather was in the kitchen when the sudden volley of hail struck the house. He had just asked about the Providential meaning in allowing a disproportionate number of ministers' houses to be struck by lightning. A volley of hailstones broke through the glass, Sewall wrote, "and flew to the middle of the room, or farther: People afterward gazed upon the house to see its ruins. I got Mr. Mather to pray with us after this awful providence; he told God He had broken the brittle part of our house, and prayed that we might be ready for the time when our clay-tabernacles should be broken. . . . I mentioned to Mr. Mather that Monmouth made his descent into England about the time of the hail in '85, summer, that much cracked our southwest windows."

Sewall, moreover, did not approach the most celebrated moment of his own life with a concern mainly for correcting any injustices that he and the Court of Oyer and Terminer might have done in the witchcraft trials of 1692. He, like Cotton Mather, kept a watchful eye on divine judgments against his own family. His diary shows that for weeks before the day on which he stood to hear his bill of confession read to his church in 1697 he had great reason to be "conscious of the reiterated strokes" of God upon himself and his family. Nor did Sewall stand on an ordinary day; the special fast proclaimed for January 14, 1697, lamented a number of sins for which the whole province was called to repent, and the articles of confession had been written by Cotton Mather. Mather's list of sins to be repented went far beyond the usual cries of apostasy, drunkenness, profanity, and luxury. He included grave mistreatment of the Indians, and (following "*wicked sorceries*") "errors, on both hands . . ., which we have cause to bewail with much abasement of soul before the Lord." He included both "*unjustifiable hardships*" imposed on dissenters, and the "scandalous contentions and animosities" with which "we have been inflamed one against another." Nor did he forget fraudulent business deals or oppression of the poor. During these trying weeks there is little difference between the tone of Mather's and Sewall's diaries; both men strive to break the possible connection between their conduct in 1692 and the mortality and danger that now afflict their individual families.

Mather's reputation as a man who lived close to the invisible world depended as much on his personal experience as on his authorship of such proclamations. He found some of the heavenly communications in his study too precious or dangerous to record, but he showed no reluctance to share other extraordinary experiences with the widest audience available, and he became known as a man to whom strange things happened. During one Lord's Day service in 1696, while praying "for some of our *sea-faring* friends," he experienced a Particular Faith that some of them would be granted special mercy. Within a few minutes after his prayer, everyone in the congregation could hear the great guns fired by a ship in distress in the bay; "and Heaven sent that *help*," so that the ship got safely into harbor. A week later, when Mather abandoned his prepared sermon in order to preach extemporaneously on the "mighty *snow* upon the ground," he chose a line from the sixty-eighth Psalm: "She was white as the snow in Salmon." Toward the end of the sermon he was suddenly moved to predict that some members of his church would soon be brought up for censure for "horrible scandals." Within a few months he had to excommunicate several women for theft or adultery, and within the next two years two other women and one man were excommunicated for fornication or adultery. Mather did not fail to remind the church of his prediction.

During one of his journeys to preach at Reading, a round trip of twenty-six miles, his horse's front legs broke through the rails of a bridge, and the horse plunged breast-deep onto the rails. Mather kept his seat, and the horse, though losing a shoe, leaped clear, with a strength that astonished both Mather and his companions. By preventing his injury in similar accidents, "the good angels" showed him and his companions "sensible" evidence of their protection on three occasions while he was riding to Dedham to "preach the *unsearchable riches of Christ;* a subject whereof the angels are the glad students, and would be glad to be the preachers." Mindful of this special protection, Mather found himself filled with "an inexpressible satisfaction" as he began to deliver that sermon, a radiant assurance that "the Spirit of the Angel of my Lord Jesus Christ, would assist me wonderfully" as he preached. "And it was with me," he said afterward, "even beyond my assurance." Surely his auditors felt some awareness of that special exhilaration during the sermon itself, just as the members of the General Assembly, before whom he preached a week later, obeyed his exhortation to stand and reenact their faith in Jesus "as a *sin-offering*" when Mather told them that they "should not stir out of the place" until his exhortation had been obeyed. As if participating in a revival, the legislators rose at his command and joined at least figuratively in his cries to the Lord pleading Christ's sacrifice "for our deliverances."

More prodigious experiences occurred within his own family. The terrible judgment of mortal illness, so different from anything that his parents had suffered during his own childhood, continued to threaten Cotton Mather's children during the 1690s. Just as one of those deaths had been attributed to witchcraft in 1693, so another was attended by strange circumstances of a different kind. On January 28, 1695, his infant daughter Mehitabel died suddenly in her nurse's arms — "not known to be dying, till it was dead," he wrote a week later; "of some sudden stoppage by wind; *the wind passed over the flower, and it was presently gone!*" This fourth death among his children brought him more rebellious temptations from Satan than the others had provoked, but he soon found some hope that a countervailing spirit had led him to "a patient and cheerful submission." He inscribed on one of the headstones an expression of his faith, "Your Bones Shall Flourish like an Herb," and he wrote a hymn of resignation based on Job 1:21. But he found it hard to understand the strange coincidence on the morning of the child's death. He had been praying in his study and had followed his usual method of praying for each of his children by name, but this time he had neglected to mention Mehitabel. He remembered having rebuked himself for being "so sottish, as having *three* children to forget *one* of them." But when he finished his prayers a messenger came to tell

him that Mehitabel had died an hour ago. He did not blame his forgetfulness for her death—"Alas, the child was overlaid by the
nurse!" he wrote—but he considered his forgetfulness a Providential
sign that before the father had begun to pray the child had already
"gone beyond the reach or use, of our *prayers*."

Similar prodigies attended the cures and the deaths of his other
children. He had a Particular Faith that Hannah would recover
from her convulsions in May 1698, and she did. Little Nanny, while
playing in Mather's study with her two sisters, fell into the fire and
was severely burned, in January 1699; in praying for her recovery,
Mather attained not only assurance of her quick improvement but
also a promise of eternal mercy for all his children. Six weeks later,
Katy, his eldest daughter, was badly burned by a fire started in her
headdress by a candle she was carrying. Mather, extremely distressed by this new calamity, feared he had delayed too long in keeping the promise he had made while praying for Nanny's recovery—a
promise to preach more often and more effectively on the duties of
parents and children. Scheduled to preach on the night of Katy's injury, he discarded his prepared sermon and chose instead to use the
opportunity that Providence had so painfully called to his attention.
Later in the year he published two sermons on the promised subject,
one for parents and one for children, under the title *A Family Well
Ordered*. When another of Nanny's fevers induced convulsions the
following June, her father agonized again over the new calamity imposed on "this little bird, that had already undergone so much," but
fasting and meditating on Job brought him a Particular Faith in her
recovery. He "wrestled with the God of Jacob, for my threatened
family, as once *Jacob* did for his," and he pleaded for God's pity,
acceptance, help. On this occasion, and another in 1700, he stood
by his Particular Faith even after the physician had predicted the
child's death, and Mather's faith was vindicated each time by her recovery on the day after he had kept a private Fast day for her.

On the same day, moreover, Mather received the strongest inti-
mation he had yet been granted that Increase Mather would one
day be sent to England on an important mission for the glory of
Jesus Christ. Confident that this mission would concern a new charter for Harvard College, Cotton Mather shared the good news with
his father, along with another Particular Faith that had been
granted him at the same time: his own son, whose birth was immi-

nent, would glorify Jesus Christ on earth after both Cotton and Increase Mather had gone to Heaven. The same assurance was reinforced with a radiant splendor about three weeks later, when the son
was born, "a hearty, lusty and comely infant," on the morning of a
Lord's Day for which a communion service was scheduled. The delighted father preached that morning on the enjoyment of Jesus
Christ as the great blessing desired by good men both for themselves
and for their children, and in the afternoon he baptized this first
surviving son and named him Increase in honor of the grandfather.
Not until twenty-five years later, after his own father's death, did
Cotton Mather learn that this precious son, a torment in his lusty
youth, would not survive to glorify Christ on earth after Cotton
Mather's departure for Heaven. In his infancy, however, little
Cressy's strong constitution did support his father's Particular Faiths
on several occasions when convulsions seemed to threaten his life,
and especially in one illness that the physician called fatal.

Until the end of 1702, the same principle worked in reverse. After
the birth of Samuel in 1700, Mather made several futile attempts to
"get my heart raised, unto a *Particular Faith* for that child," that
the Lord would accept him "for the service of His churches in this
world," but this experience actually reinforced his belief in the validity of his other Particular Faiths. His inability to experience the
same sort of assurance for Samuel as for the other surviving children
reminded him of the central psychological truth of evangelical Protestantism: "a man cannot believe, *when* and *what* he will." Mather
resigned himself to living "in a continual apprehension" that Samuel, though "a lusty and hearty infant," would soon die, and the
anxious father could not resist sharing his supernatural reasons for
this anxiety with both his wife and his father. He would not have
thought it prudent to tell them only the good results of his special
pleas. The significance of the angels' silence became evident about
three weeks later, when Samuel, having suffered for forty-eight
hours in extreme convulsions, died. In the worst of his fits on the
night of his death, this tiny infant terrified the people sitting up with
him. At about midnight he suddenly broke into "a very great *laughter*" as he came out of one of his fits.

Mentioned in his own sermons and in gossip throughout the community, prodigies of these kinds were associated with Cotton Mather's reputation among people who revered him and those who de-

spised him. He himself perceived that many of the people who flocked to see and hear him whenever he went out were probably expressing a simple curiosity, and a modern observer can understand the natural desire to see what this controversial, voluble man, with so strange a history of communicating with good and bad spirits, would say next. Benjamin Colman, one of Mather's chief antagonists in a controversy between the churches at the turn of the century, observed that Mather's writing gave an inadequate sense of his literary skill: nobody who had never heard Mather speak, Colman said, and especially nobody who had not heard him in conversation, could form an adequate impression of his verbal skill or the force of his personality. The agility of Mather's mind, the aptness and quickness with which he responded to immediate stimuli in conversation and in the pulpit, must have drawn people to hear him even as the same qualities — along with his irrepressible impulse toward constant action in God's service — probably tempted him to speak and write too much. He was both offended and perplexed when someone warned him in 1700 that the people were now prejudiced against him because he had published too much.

His literary achievements, his divine assurances, the love and care of his own angel, and his frequent exposure to large audiences — all nurtured the very vanity that offended some of his critics. He struggled in obedient Christian exercises to subdue his vanity and pride. But both the fasts with which he commemorated his superlative filthiness, and the thanksgivings with which he acknowledged the blessing of his extraordinary achievements, expressed the vanity that they were supposed to check. When he was only thirty-four, he gave thanks for having been allowed to publish while still a young man more books than any other American had ever written, and for having been "read, and prized, and serviceable, not only all over these American colonies, but in *Europe* also." On the evening of the same day he went into his church and tried to give himself up to "my Lord Jesus Christ, that He may glorify Himself, in making yet a *greater use* of me than ever." He lay down on the floor of the pulpit and thanked the Lord for "the *use* which He had made of me" there.

It was on this day in August 1697, moreover, that he gave thanks for having been allowed to complete his *Magnalia Christi Americana*. Although he would continue to add sermons, documents, and even some extended narratives before he finally ventured three years later to send the history to London for publication, he now thought he had finished the book. To supplement his special thanksgiving, he copied into his Reserved Memorials the long paragraph from his General Introduction in which the Pastor-historian explains how many other demanding obligations he has been meeting while composing the history. That paragraph starts out as a modest apology pleading extenuation for inadequacies, but it grows and swells both in learned allusions and in the enumeration of Mather's immense and varied labors (including the publication of a score of other books) during the very brief time that he had taken to write so large and complex a history. Here too he is at first only the representative Protestant minister, whose many duties in the world give him much less leisure for study than he believes Catholic scholars enjoy. But the mention of his "Biblia Americana," on which he had been working briefly during almost every day of the same period, sets him off on an expansive advertisement for that cherished dream, in which he had hoped from the time he originally conceived it to bring together in one work all the "treasures of *illustration*" that had been scattered in hundreds of books by learned commentators and, "by a *labor,* that would resolve to conquer all things," to include "all the *improvements*, which the *later ages* have made in the sciences." He would feel "an inexpressible pleasure" in bringing that new enlightened learning into biblical exegesis, and he could not repress his great joy in announcing now that "in a few months" he had "got ready a huge number of *golden keys*, to open the pandects of Heaven." His novelties would be rare and entertaining, but they would not offend the judicious or the orthodox. If allowed to live only a few more years, he would hope to give the world in his "Biblia Americana" "a volume *enriched* with better things, than all the *plate* of the *Indies;* yet not I," he concluded, remembering belatedly to draw back, "but the grace of Christ with me."

In these heady moments, vanity becomes an inadequate word for what Mather expresses. Pride and vanity are swallowed up in a merging of self with divine intentions to use the author's learning, pride, and vanity in an extension of divine glory. The Particular Faiths, the extraordinary deliverances, the angelic visions, and the prodigious signs that Mather had received, all served to reinforce his ability to achieve that union. The family name, moreover, enabled him to achieve a similar union on a more earthly plane. He had been reminded since childhood of the special honor in the conjunction of his eminent grandfathers' names to designate his own identity, and of course he revered his father. Now that both Cotton and Increase Mather were actually identified in political controversy that brought the family names into public ridicule or condemnation, Cotton Mather found it easy to perceive those assaults mainly as attacks upon the family name, and as efforts to weaken the Mathers' ability to serve Christ's interests in the world. In 1697 the sanctity of the family names became an even more sensitive conception when Cotton Mather's favorite uncle, John Cotton—perhaps his best friend outside the immediate family, the man with whom he had exchanged the most openly affectionate correspondence ever since his early teens—fell into disgrace at Plymouth and had to leave his congregation there because he was charged with adultery and "undue carriage in choosing elders." The church council gathered from neighboring towns to hear the charges, made a remarkably lenient recommendation to the Plymouth church—too lenient, Samuel Sewall and Increase Mather apparently believed—and one persuasive witness charged long afterward that Mr. Cotton had been falsely accused of adultery. Without commenting on his uncle's guilt of adultery, Cotton Mather did say that he had been justly condemned to silence, but "extreme anguish" over the news of "my poor uncle" led him to pray once again about the danger to the family name: "I was afraid, lest the Lord should bring His dreadful judgments upon *me* also, for my sins against Him, and leave me to things that might horribly wound *His* name and work in *mine*, and be the horrible astonishment of all His *churches*." Prostrate on his study floor, Mather received assurances that his own sins had been pardoned and that God would glorify His infinite grace by "employing me to serve my Lord Jesus Christ exceedingly."

IT WAS NOT through disgraceful sins that Cotton Mather's own name came into some disrepute during these years of his celebrity as a preacher and writer. He suffered for defending his past conduct, traditional beliefs about the Devil's powers, the principles of Congregationalism, the integrity of the ministry of Boston, and the good name and good hopes of his father. Both he and his opponents associated the name of Cotton Mather with the causes he defended, and the passionate intensity of his engagement was also magnified by threats to the validity of one of his Particular Faiths.

Robert Calef persisted throughout the decade in adroitly baiting his hypersensitive antagonist. Calef had a fine instinct for Mather's vulnerability, both on scriptural issues and as the tender custodian of the family's and the religion's good name. In 1694, 1695, and 1696 Calef discharged barbed, witty letters at Mather, addressing them directly to him or else writing to Thomas Brattle or Samuel Willard in flagrant ridicule of Mather's arguments. He provoked Mather to send him some papers and arguments early in 1694, and when Mather insisted that they be returned promptly without having been copied, Calef replied that he could understand very well why Mather did not want such "crude matter and impertinent absurdities . . . to spread." Mather sent him Richard Baxter's *The World of Spirits*, as an "ungainsayable" defense of the powers accorded devils and witches; Calef replied that he knew no ungainsayable book but the Bible, and he later circulated a hilarious list of Baxter's untenable statements and contradictions, which he attributed to senility. Mather complained that Calef had attacked his sermons, and Calef replied that he had only questioned Mather's "interpretation of a *thunderstorm* (that broke into his house) which savored so much of enthusiasm." Calef demanded scriptural authority for the Devil's covenant with witches to do evil, and for the witch's power to invoke that covenant in commissioning the Devil to kill. Mather replied by offering Calef the freedom of his library and the testimony of his own unforgettable experience. Calef dismissed this response as "a bare assertion, together with [Mather's] own bigoted experiences," and he repeated his request for scriptural texts rather than Mather's allusion to "multitudes of histories to confirm" his belief. He even attacked the veracity of Mather's biography of Phips in 1697.

To crown the method of ridicule, Calef not only called on Mather to stop choking his own conscience, to stop pretending that he still believed in discredited fantasies that had caused unjust deaths. He quoted Baxter's very words to show that if Mather really believed what he claimed to believe, he stood "in the broad path to heathenism, devilism, popery or atheism." And in 1695 Calef wrote a letter to Samuel Willard, Pastor of the South Church, in which he copied "Certain Proposals made by the President and Fellows of Harvard College" for the collection of remarkable providences in New England. Calef suggested that the sudden death of Judge John Richards, the death of two of Judge Samuel Sewall's sons, the accidental death of a layman who had been prominent in the witch hunt, the explosion of a Salem gun that blew Deputy Sheriff George Herrick to pieces, and above all the eventual charges that magistrates and ministers were witches — Calef suggested that the President and Fellows should include all these as remarkable providences intended for their moral instruction. The way of God, Calef noted here, quoting Richard Baxter once again, "is to shame the sinner, how good soever in other respects, that the sin may have the greater shame, and religion may not be shamed, as if it allowed men to sin; nor God the Author of religion be dishonored; nor others be without the warning; but the way of the Devil is, to hide or justify the sin, as if it were for fear of disparaging the goodness of the persons that committed it; that so he may hereby dishonor religion and Godliness itself." This weaver knew how to fabricate arguments that wrapped his antagonists comically in the language and logic of their own condemnation. Unfair though it often was, his method was entertaining and infuriating.

Apparently with the help of Thomas Brattle and the acquiescence of Samuel Willard, Calef gathered his arguments and circulated his documents until 1697, when at last he had his manuscript ready to be submitted to a printer. Either a Boston printer refused to accept it, for fear of offending the Mathers, or Calef understood that he had virtually no chance of getting the book printed in Boston, because he knew that both Increase and Cotton Mather, galled by his insistent sarcasm, would try to block its publication there. When Calef sent the manuscript off to London in 1698, Cotton Mather noted the event in his diary as one more threat against his own usefulness in the Lord's service. While Mather's beloved church history, "strangely delayed," bounced heavily from one London printer to another between 1700 and 1702, Mather was consoled by Particular Faiths that it would indeed be published to the honor of the Lord and His people in New England, but he could not help reflecting that Providence had allowed Calef's libels to move easily through the press and to arrive impudently in Boston while the publication of his own precious work remained uncertain. Tradition has libeled President Increase Mather with the completely undocumented charge of having Calef's book burned in Harvard Yard. Certainly Cotton Mather burned with anger and shame when an unusually large crowd turned out to hear his Lecture just after the accursed book arrived in Boston, and he burned with righteous indignation when a group of his friends published *Some Few Remarks* in his defense. In his own copy of Calef's book he inscribed a paraphrase from the Book of Job (31:35, 36): "My desire is that mine adversary had written a book. Surely I would take it upon my shoulder, and bind it as a crown to me." His resolution to forgive Calef and to pray for him served a disciplinary purpose in Mather's continuing effort to develop Christian resignation, but it also put the large reservoir of his human anger under additional pressure.

That anger erupted both visibly and audibly when the welfare of Harvard College, the validity of a Particular Faith, the principles of Congregational ordination and church government, and the name of Increase Mather all came into jeopardy. Throughout the last two or three years of the century, Cotton Mather himself noticed that the alternating pattern of his spiritual and emotional life moved in wider arcs. The rapture and the gloom, the praise and the criticism, the success and the frustration, all grew more intense. He noticed that he often suffered "torturing pains" in his head for some days before "doing some special service for my Lord Jesus Christ," and he blamed these on the Devil, just as he thanked an angel or a Particular Faith for some of his recoveries. The deaths of his children and the accumulation of opposition to himself and his father were balanced by extraordinary rapture in prayer and by achievements like the *Magnalia* and the developing "Biblia Americana." On one of his days of secret thanksgiving in the autumn of 1698, Mather felt himself carried "into the suburbs of Heaven . . . and filled . . . with *joy unspeakable and full of glory.*" Afterward he not only felt faint and ill but also found himself "effectually *buffeted*" by unnamed temptations and vexations in his neighborhood.

Through all his accumulating difficulties in the outer world, moreover, he continued to enjoy public successes and marks of official respect. His annual salary was raised to £150, plus firewood, in the winter of 1699. When the new royal governor was finally appointed in 1699, Cotton Mather was chosen to write the letter greeting him for the elders of all the churches, and in a ceremony at the Town House Governor Bellomont graciously asked Mather to read that address aloud to him. Mather was chosen to give the right hand of fellowship to a new minister ordained in the church at Charlestown, and the election sermon before the Governor and General Court in 1700. Perhaps his most satisfying triumph in a public controversy during this difficult period came in 1699 and 1700, when he helped to expose an English brickmaker named Samuel Axel, who had taken the name of Samuel May and had won over a large following by misrepresenting himself to the Baptist congregation in Boston as an ordained minister. Cotton Mather went to hear one of May's sermons and reported it immediately to his father, who recognized it as a plagiarism and soon found in his own library the book from which it had been copied. Cotton Mather was astonished to find that public exposure of the plagiarism did not silence May's insistence that he himself had written the sermon, and Mather was outraged to see that for several more months many people continued to flock after this "incendiary" fraud. By some of these people Mather was blamed rather than thanked, months after he had demonstrated the plagiarism. At last several women swore before a magistrate that May had tried to seduce them, and after May was therefore obliged to leave town Mather was further vindicated by letters from England proving the imposture.

But although this "detected wolf" went "off with a stink," the language with which Mather rebuked his sheepish followers, both in a published Lecture called *A Warning to the Flocks* and in a characteristic letter admonishing the Baptists to repent of their misplaced confidence, provoked more hostility against himself. Mather had treated the Baptists more civilly than most of his colleagues had treated them, but he had been criticized for meddling in the Baptist church's affairs and for trying to silence a colleague whom many people considered harmless. Now he was offended by his critics' unwillingness to thank him or to apologize for their unjust complaints against him. In this brief period between 1699 and 1701, all his troubles in the world of affairs seemed to be coming together.

The Baptists were the least of the antagonists whose errors threatened the Mathers' version of traditional Congregationalism. Cotton Mather had complained earlier about the ordination of the young Pastor in Charlestown to whom he had given the right hand of fellowship in 1698. Mather had been pleased with the effect of his own fervent charge on that congregation; almost every person there, he was told, had "either wept or trembled" during his speech. But he was worried about the Pastor's reluctance to conform to Congregational principles, the very basis for the unusual passion in Mather's moving remarks about the significance of the ordination. A year later Mather infuriated Benjamin Wadsworth, the young Pastor of the First Church, by lobbying with "the principal gentlemen" of that church in an effort to impose a reliable old Teacher upon them. And just after the departure of the Baptist impostor, the Brattle Street Church controversy developed toward a crisis. Mather thought the Baptists and Anglicans were united against him.

Like the angry debates with Robert Calef, the struggle over the Brattle Street Church brought together antagonists who had opposed the Mathers in politics during the time of Governor Phips, and who continued to oppose them at Harvard College. Both Increase and Cotton Mather understandably perceived these separate issues as parts of a converging assault upon the best traditions of New England Congregationalism. The founders of the new church in Brattle Street were not only beginning a new congregation without adequately considering their binding covenants to the churches to which they already belonged; they deliberately chose a minister who had been ordained by the London Presbytery in England because it seemed unlikely that the Boston ministers would make his ordination possible by agreeing to participate in the traditional laying-on of hands in his own church. It was true that young Benjamin Colman (Harvard, 1692) had been "born and bred here" before going to England for his theological training, but the manner of his installation in the new church seemed to violate both Presbyterian and Congregational traditions, and the *Manifesto* that he and the brethren of his church published in New York and circulated in Boston seemed as outrageously threatening as the book by Robert Calef. Cotton Mather said flatly that the principles of the *Manifesto* would "utterly subvert our churches, and invite an ill party through all the country, to throw all into confusion on the first opportunities."

Scholars from Williston Walker in the nineteenth century to Perry Miller in the twentieth have agreed with the Mathers that the founders of the new church were as much interested in excluding the Mathers from control of Harvard as they were in establishing new rules for worship and church membership. William Brattle, now Pastor of the Cambridge church, and John Leverett had counteracted some of Increase Mather's ideas at Harvard College ever since Mather's long absence during his mission to England, when they were tutors at the college, and Brattle's brother Thomas, treasurer of Harvard, donated the land in Boston on which the new meetinghouse was built. Although both Increase and Cotton Mather were too sensitive to underestimate the personal significance of the new movement, they had good reason to see grave threats to New England's first religious principles in the seemingly minor innovations proclaimed in Colman's *Manifesto*. Besides abandoning the traditional "relation" of religious experience that many of the churches had required of prospective members before admitting them to communion, the new church denied the need of an explicit covenant, and was willing to give "all baptized male adults who contributed to the minister's support . . . a voice in his selection." If generally adopted, these innovations would soon overwhelm the traditional power of the visible saints, members in full communion, and the danger seemed all the more threatening because of William Brattle's power in the Cambridge church and Solomon Stoddard's long-standing practice, which he now vigorously urged in a new book, of admitting to full communion in Northampton any person who had "a good conversation and a competent knowledge"—in short, anybody whose behavior was not scandalous. As early as 1697 Increase Mather had warned the Cambridge church and the students at Harvard against failing to require new members to narrate their religious experience before joining the church, and he had published that admonition as a preface to Cotton Mather's biography of Jonathan Mitchel, late Pastor at Cambridge. A few months later, Increase and Cotton Mather had sent a letter of admonition complaining that the Charlestown church had betrayed traditional liberties by allowing all residents to vote on the call to a new minister.

Strenuous negotiation by Cotton Mather and the other ministers in Boston eventually brought a brief, nominal truce in the Brattle Street church affair, but the coincidental attacks from Robert Calef, Colman's *Manifesto*, Stoddard's work, and Increase Mather's opponents at Harvard increased the pressure under which Cotton Mather's temper finally exploded. The Brattles, John Leverett, and some others wanted to move Increase Mather out of the Harvard presidency. With help from Elisha Cooke, they eventually achieved a stroke that might force Mather to resign, for the same reason that had led him to refuse the presidency when it had been offered to him nearly twenty years before. The General Assembly voted in July 1700 to require the President of Harvard to reside in Cambridge, as a condition attached to their renewal of Increase Mather's appointment. In 1693 and 1695 the General Court had voted that the President must live in Cambridge, but Mather had ignored the decree. Now he could not ignore it. Once again Mather left the decision to his church, but this time he made his distaste for Cambridge unmistakably plain.

The Mathers, Samuel Sewall, John Higginson and other believers in the old New England Way knew that Increase Mather had no choice. Abandoning Harvard to the innovators meant losing control of the one place in which a small group of faithful descendants might preserve the founders' principles by training young ministers to uphold them in the churches. The Mathers already complained that their opportunities to glorify the Lord had been "much abridged and abated" by prejudices that were likely to prevail against them "in the *apostatizing generation*," and they felt sure that the agents of both Solomon Stoddard and the Brattles were virtually pandering to that apostatizing mood. Almost at the moment of the General Assembly's vote concerning Increase Mather's residence, the Mathers attended a meeting of ministers at which President Mather condemned Stoddard's new book as the most daring and explicit of all attacks upon "the *state* of our churches." With Stoddard present in the room, Mather accused him of furnishing "a profane generation of people in the country, with cavils against the churches, and the good things observed in them." Far from advancing the Reformation, Mather declared, Stoddard was pushing New England's churches from the admirably "primitive" condition they now enjoyed and plunging them into the miserable condition that "the *Romish apostasy*, after some centuries," had brought on them.

But seeing that he had to move to Cambridge did not make Increase Mather like the prospect. At sixty-one he hated to leave his home, his church, and the seat of the political influence and action that remained to him. He did not relish the provincial setting or the constant proximity of the young men whose future was so obviously at stake, and he must have found little consolation in the knowledge that he could attend William Brattle's church in Cambridge. Cotton Mather worried about the "strange melancholy, and disconsolate condition of mind" that his father was taking to Cambridge, "the place, which of all under Heaven, was most abominable to him. If he would be cheerful," Cottton Mather perceived, "all would be easy." But the gloomy attitude might bring still more dishonor on the Christian cause by weakening the President's effectiveness. After the Second Church had voted to permit Increase Mather's move to Cambridge for the good of the college and the country, Samuel Sewall had a difficult time consoling him by appealing to his sense of duty and even to his sense of shame. If their ancestors had willingly come out of England into the wilderness, Sewall implied, after reminding Mather that the Council's vote for him had been unanimous, a man ought to be ready to move from Boston to Cambridge without too much complaint.

The departure of his father at a low point in this miserable year of controversy left Cotton Mather alone once again in charge of the largest congregation in New England. Anxious about his own ability to keep his people from growing "foolish and froward" in these apostatizing times, Mather also worried about his ability to withstand his personal enemies in Boston and the convergence of all "enemies of the evangelical interests" against himself. He knew that he did not have the extraordinary prudence for successful diplomacy in verbal hostilities, especially when the enemy fired blasts against the family names and character. He knew that "the special vice" of Boston, as of other intellectual communities then and now, was "for men, even *good men*, to *speak evil* of one another," and although he resolved to suppress that vice in himself and (by preaching) in others, he knew that he was sometimes provoked into vicious language by attacks upon the family name or the Lord's cause.

Despite these anxieties, he did get through the year without any egregious displays of anger, for he confined himself to some angry language in his diaries and some strong rhetoric in the exchange of pamphlets with the Brattle Street group, the Stoddardeans, and Robert Calef. He even endured the slanderous charge of forgery when some of "that malignant company, who have lately built a new *church* in *Boston*," accused him of fabricating the signatures of two venerable preachers whose support he had claimed for the Mathers' side of the Congregationalist debate. When the opposition questioned the authenticity of John Higginson's and William Hubbard's *A Testimony to the Order of the Gospel*, they accused Mather of having misappropriated the endorsement of the two oldest ministers in the country. Since this charge was made in the legislature, Mather happily reported that "God put it into the heart of the reverend old Mr. *Higginson*" to write directly to the deputies there, "solemnly" acknowledging his signature and giving his reasons. Mather hailed the news of this "triumphant vindication" as "better than a feast unto us, at the end of our *fast*."

As THE CONFLICT against so many different antagonists continued, however, it was the threat against the Particular Faith, and a gratuitous affront to Increase Mather, that made Cotton Mather explode. For three years he had been assured by one Particular Faith after another that his father would go to England on an important mission before going to heaven, and on several occasions both father and son believed the government was about to send President Mather to London to arrange for a new charter for Harvard. As early as June 1698, when the Mathers were sure they had a commitment for that mission, the Reverend James Allen, Senior Fellow of the Harvard Corporation, had proposed it to the Governor's Council. But the Governor had turned it down, as King William had rejected a similar charter in 1692, because the proposed charter limited the Governor's power to be a Visitor. Again in June 1700, the Mathers felt sure they had Governor Bellomont's promise to endorse the mission, but "some of our Tories" dissuaded both Bellomont and Lieutenant Governor Stoughton from supporting Increase Mather's candidacy, and Cotton Mather accused Stoughton of using "all the little tricks" to "confound" the mission. Even so, Cotton Mather believed, the decision would have been affirmative if some favorably disposed members of the Council had not been "inconveniently" called away from the meeting at the time of the vote.

This most recent disappointment struck Cotton Mather with extraordinary force, not only because it embarrassed his reverend father and brought more smirking ridicule upon the family name, but also because it seemed to him an explicit Providential denial of his faith in Particular Faiths. Only a week after he had at last sent the manuscript of his church history to England, both he and his father had "unaccountably" been reassured by Particular Faiths that Increase Mather would be sent on a Christian mission to England. Because Cotton remembered that the plan had miscarried several times just before it had seemed about to be adopted, he had explicitly asked (while "prostrate on my study floor before the Lord") whether a Particular Faith, which he "had always taken . . . to be a work of Heaven on the minds of the faithful," could turn out to be "a deceit." If it should, he had pleaded, he would be "cast into a most wonderful confusion," and he had begged the Lord to renew the Particular Faith about his father's mission to England—if that faith "were not a delusion."

Immediately after he had made this plea, he had experienced the most exhilarating "afflatus" since the first radiant appearance of an angel in his study in the 1680s. During the prayer, which he himself described as an argument, his heart had felt "the coldness of a stone upon it, and the straitness that is to be expected from the bare exercise of reason." But now he had felt "an inexpressible force" on his mind, an afflatus that he could not describe: "none knows it, but he that has it," he wrote afterward. The communication was as plain as if an angel had actually spoken it: the Lord Jesus Christ loved both Increase and Cotton Mather, and delighted in their service; He had not allowed them to be deceived in their Particular Faith. Increase Mather would go to England to glorify Jesus Christ, and the Mathers' Particular Faith about this matter would itself bring Jesus Christ "illustrious revenues of praise." At first their Particular Faith would seem to be absolutely defeated, pronounced dead, "but the Lord Jesus Christ, who *raises the dead*, and is *the Resurrection and the Life*," would give it a new life. "*He will do it*," Mather exulted, "*He will do it!*"

Weeping with joy at this glorious message from the invisible world, Mather had risen from his prostrate position and gone to his Bible, where he had found on "the first place I opened" a text endorsing both his Particular Faith and his faith in it: "There stood by me the Angel of God, whose I am, and whom I serve: saying, Fear not, thou must be brought before Caesar: I believe God, that it shall be even as it was told me." This sign had brought on more tears, and the confirmation of the "death sentence" in the Governor's decision encouraged Mather to write "*Wait! Wait!*" in the expectation that his father's mission would soon enjoy the promised resurrection.

Mather waited, during a year of troubles that included the appearance of Calef's book and Colman's *Manifesto*, the death of little

Samuel, the accusations of forgery, the coolness of a ministers' meeting toward the Mathers' answers to Solomon Stoddard, and the failure of Increase Mather's valiant effort to live in Cambridge. Particular Faiths about the success of the church history and of his father's
eventual mission served with his own busy and effective labors to
counteract these miseries, but the waiting and the miseries also built
up pressure. Almost predictably, as in one of Mather's Particular
Faiths, the explosion was set off not by one of those "many enemies"
whom Mather had resolved to forgive, but by a peace-loving friend
and supporter whose vote in the Governor's Council seemed a be-
trayal of Increase Mather. The President had tried for some months
in 1700 to live in Cambridge without moving his family there, but at
last he had asked to be replaced unless he could be allowed to live in
Boston. The General Court had offered the appointment to Samuel
Willard, who had promptly declared his own unwillingness to live in
Cambridge, whereupon the General Court had given him virtual
control of the college by appointing him Vice President. Since no
law required the Vice President to live in Cambridge, and since Willard did not differ greatly from Mather on doctrinal questions, the
personal insult to Increase Mather seemed blatant. Willard, in effect, was allowed to preside over the college on terms that had been
explicitly refused to Mather.

Cotton Mather could not allow the insult to go unanswered. En-
countering Samuel Sewall in Wilkins' bookshop a day or two after
the Council's vote to appoint Willard Vice President, Mather be-
rated him for having treated Increase Mather worse than one would
treat a "Neger" (the spelling is Samuel Sewall's). Obviously enraged,
Mather could not let that allusion to Sewall's recent antislavery
pamphlet stand by itself. He was speaking so loud that people in the
street could hear him, and he made the meaning of his allusion explicit. He shouted that whereas "one pleaded much for Negroes,"
Sewall had used Increase Mather "worse than a Negro. That was my
father," he exclaimed.

Sewall, of course, was appalled. He remembered having sent Increase Mather a haunch of very good venison ten days earlier, and
he insisted that his speech in Council had not betrayed his old
friend. Both in a letter to Cotton Mather and in another meeting at
Wilkins' shop to which he invited Mather two days later, Sewall protested that he had only said residence in Cambridge was not the real

issue: the question, he had argued, was whether Mr. Mather would read and expound the Scriptures to the students—if not, Sewall had said, the example of the refusal would do more hurt than the good done by moving to Cambridge.

But Cotton Mather was not to be placated only two days after his original outburst. As Sewall and several sober gentlemen reminded him, the author of a recent book on the evils of speaking with a cruel tongue must have known how extraordinary it was in Boston for a minister to rage at a member of the Governor's Council in the street. When Sewall tried to elicit an apology by asking whether Mather had spoken according to Christ's rule the other day, Mather replied that, having spoken to Sewall then, he did not need to speak again. But he immediately did speak again. He charged the Council with lying, hypocrisy, and trickery. He objected to Sewall's speech to the Council. He said that Jonathan Corwin, a member of the Council, had complained to him of Sewall's speech, asking why one should dedicate books to such a man. Meanwhile, as Sewall asked Mather whether he would like to have a complaint about his own pastoral behavior shouted at him in the street, Mr. Wilkins tried unsuccessfully to persuade Mather to move the argument into an inside room, as curious people in the shop and on the street took in the show. Only after several more days of diplomatic missions from Joshua Moody, Richard Wilkins, and Joshua Gee could Sewall report in his diary that the two Mathers "seem to grow calm."

⚜

Because the Particular Faith concerning Increase Mather's mission had mentioned no specific date, its apparent failure in 1701 was not conclusive. The characteristic resiliency of Cotton Mather's lifelong movement between gloom and joy did not desert him after the encounter with Sewall. Only three days after the second meeting in Wilkins' shop, while the scandal and the negotiations were still expanding, Mather was encouraged by a new Particular Faith about the publication of his church history. Because it was not only the major work of his life but also, he believed, his major service to New England and the glory of God, he was naturally distressed to learn that its publication was still in doubt, and prayers on this subject replaced his father's aborted mission as his major public request in the secluded Fast days that he held during the next few months. He was rewarded with several more Particular Faiths on the subject during the next several weeks. "It will be so! I have prevailed! I have prevailed!" he wrote on one of these occasions, and his Particular Faiths about the book on other Fast days in January and February induced "floods of tears."

We must remember, too, that throughout these years he found the strength to continue his writing, his preaching, his pastoral duties, and his ingenious good works as his spirits fluctuated between "considerable elevation" and gloomy anxiety. Great crowds still came to hear him preach, and it was within these early months of 1702 that he worked successfully on proposals to found a Society for the Suppression of Disorders, to improve the condition of the jail, to find work for the poor, and (from the Congregationalist's perspective) to reform the jury lists.

Now, however, he entered the longest period of suffering that he had ever experienced, and it ended in the absolute contradiction of one of his most precious Particular Faiths. He would have grieved over his wife's death any time, for although he rarely mentions her in his Reserved Memorials she and his father were the two people whom he loved most, and on whom he was most dependent. In accounts of his fasts and meditations, as in his narrative of Mercy Short, Abigail Mather appears chiefly as a silent companion, a cooperative assistant, "my dear consort," when summoned to the study for prayer on a special occasion or when mentioned as a participant in the family's daily worship. But even in those pages the strength of Mather's affection for her invigorates the prose both in the months of his desperate prayer for her survival and in a few of his earlier allusions to her. He demonstrated this affection in their fertile sexual life, in his care for her spiritual welfare, and in his closeness to her family, as well as in his daily life with her and the children. During her mother's final illness it was Cotton Mather who assuaged the dying mother-in-law's fears of death, and when Abigail grieved over her father's prompt remarriage her husband tried unsuccessfully to console her once again, as he had done after the deaths of their own children. The seven-year difference in age did encourage her to treat him with a certain deference, for she had been only sixteen at the time of her wedding to the celebrated and precocious young minister. Even after they had been married sixteen years, half of her entire life, she still addressed him as Mr. Mather, at least when other people were present. Worn out by her coughing and by months of suffering in her bed while relays drawn from nearly a hundred watchers attended her, she once sighed to those at her bedside, "I shall make you weary!" Then immediately, perhaps before she saw the look on her husband's face, she reassured him: "I don't mean you, Mr. Mather!"

Other signs of Mather's "extravagant fondness for her" include his tender consideration for her feelings about her brothers. John, the eldest, was just Cotton Mather's age, but in this fortieth year of his life he fell into "idle, profane, drunken, and sottish" ways. Anderson and Harry, her two younger brothers, who had both been babies at the time of her wedding, now fell into grave physical trouble. She knew that Anderson—"her darling," Cotton Mather wrote, "I had almost said, her idol"—probably had consumption, and that he had gone to London in hopes that the sea air might cure him. Before she herself became ill, Abigail had lamented this favorite's departure by saying passionately that she hoped God would never let her live to hear of Anderson's death. When the news of his death arrived in September, her husband not only remembered that wish but arranged to conceal Anderson's death from her (along with the news of John's disgrace and of Harry's capture by a French privateer) even though the family dressed in mourning for a time thereafter. Mather, of course, considered Providential the arrival, three hours after Abigail's death, of a letter addressed to her from "the gentlewoman in whose house her brother died; giving her an account of him, and of the manner of his hopeful death."

In his care of the children, too, Mather showed his affectionate respect for his wife. His long days and nights in the study did not keep him from doing his fond duty as a parent charged with their spiritual instruction. Like his father and grandfather Mather, he abominated corporal punishment, against which he later published some of the strongest, most humane criticism written in his time. It was in 1699 that he advised parents to practice "a *sweet authority*," to avoid "such harshness and fierceness as may discourage your children. Our authority should be so tempered with kindness, and meekness, and loving tenderness, that our children may *fear* us with *delight*, and see that we love them with as much delight." Banishing the child from his presence was usually Mather's most severe punishment, and he understood that its effectiveness depended on the pleasantness of being in his presence. He relied on resourceful teaching, both by ingeniously promising to teach his children "some curious thing" as a reward and by using as a punishment the refusal to teach them something. Although he clearly favored the intellectual prospects of his sons, he did believe in the spiritual and practical education of girls, too, and he took a special interest in sharpening his children's wits — at mealtime, during witty homilies at the time of daily worship, and in rigorous catechizing. In March 1702 he attracted one of the largest of all his crowds to two lectures called *Cares about the Nurseries,* the nurture of the young. Abigail was his affectionate partner in the family instruction on which those lectures, and his *A Family Well Ordered,* were based. And of course he gave some of those sermons partly to fulfill his promise of thanksgiving for the deliverance of the ailing and injured children over whom he and Abigail had prayed together.

His extravagant fondness for her, then, would have led him to keep her with him here "upon any terms." What made the dreadful experience excruciating was the defeat of a long series of Particular Faiths assuring him, against both her own wishes and medical evidence that he could not deny, of her recovery. And before her last illness began, Mather escalated his pious observances in a way that made his Particular Faiths all the more powerful. In March 1702 he began to keep all-night vigils in emulation of the "primitive Christians" who had used that device "for the sake of a devout conversation with Heaven." Mather had given up his usual plans for a Fast day on Saturday the fourteenth, for fear of injuring his health after a strenuous day of preaching on Friday. Finding himself stronger than he had expected to be on Saturday evening, he resolved to try his first vigil. He sent Abigail off to bed by herself, and once again lay down on the floor of his study, where he was "rewarded with communications from heaven, that cannot be uttered." During that long night he received assurances about the time and manner of his own death, and promises of mercies intended for his family. "If these be *vigils,*" this connoisseur of mystical communion observed, "I must (as far as the *sixth* Commandment will allow) have some more of them!"

He was not greatly surprised the next day when his sermon at the communion service in the North Church was interrupted by a report that one of the chimneys of his house had caught fire — a crisis that sent his "great congregation" running out of the meetinghouse to help extinguish the fire. He had already observed that his periods of "sweet and intimate communion with heaven" were likely to be followed immediately by "some vexation on earth." When his wife suffered a miscarriage on May 25, soon after a series of new vigils had irradiated his mind "with celestial and angelical influences" about the fine prospects for his church history, he read the new misfortune in the same way. He had recently received praise from a fellow minister remarking that one of Mather's books had made him see how full of excellency Jesus must be to enable a writer to "fill a book with such excellent things!" That praise had sent Mather into "ecstasies," for he had always had an enormous need for approval, and he believed that setting other hearts to contemplate the glory of God was "the highest pitch of my felicity." After such delights, and a subsequent interview in which he ingeniously reassured another young minister who consulted him in dread of being unregenerate after all, he might almost have expected the miscarriage. The midwife informed him that Abigail had not only miscarried of a son but was also delivered of "a *false conception*" at the same time. Mather dutifully humbled himself before the Lord, asking himself especially whether he had ever troubled the Congregational churches with any false conception, but he could not find himself guilty of that offense, and even though he found himself unaccountably dull during a special day of prayer that he kept for Abigail's recovery, he was not surprised when "the blessed breezes of a *Particular Faith*" blew over him "from heaven" as he prayed "with my dying wife" at her bedside on June 6.

A second Particular Faith confirmed his hope as he prayed alone in his study that afternoon, and once again he persuaded himself, even as he noticed that he was often instructed in the same way, that the first biblical passage to which he opened, contained a special message for him. He found in his Psalmbook the hundred and eighteenth, with the Lord's answer to prayer and the Psalmist's exultant affirmation:

> I shall not dy, but live, and shall
>     the works of Jah declare;
> The Lord did sorely chasten me,
>     but me from Death did spare.

He went to Abigail's room and assured her that she would live.

As she grew worse despite these assurances, he read the experi-

ence as a severe trial of his faith. He persisted in his belief even when
the physician was called out of the meetinghouse on the Lord's Day
by attendants who felt sure Mrs. Mather was dying, and even after
Mather himself was called up to her bedside late that night for the
same reason. From there he went to his study for another vigil,
which was rewarded with yet another Particular Faith. He himself
came to suspect that she might be dying after another week of great
weakness, but his faith "held out comfortably under the trial." On
June 24, in a special day of private prayer, he felt his strongest assurance thus far that, although in dying circumstances, his wife would
recover and that Jesus Christ would thereupon have special glory
among His people because of His intercession as the Mathers' *"family sacrifice."*

The agony continued for another six months. Psalms and Particular Faiths reassured him, but his medical experience forced him to
see as early as the last week of June that she must die of this illness.
When he observed that the disappointment of his Particular Faith
would greatly aggravate the calamity of her death, his assurance of
her recovery was soon renewed by "the Lord, and His Angel."
Mather persisted, therefore, even after Abigail herself had given up
hope. A new smallpox epidemic afflicted Boston early in July, and
as Abigail grew weaker Mather, in the seventh fast that he had kept
especially for her, gave her *up* to the Lord even though he said he
"could not *give her over.*" Once again the assurances washed over
him, with promises that the Lord would be glorified exceedingly by
her recovery. In this vigil and others the retrospective account now
begins to introduce qualifications: "I thought" and "I think" pre-
cede accounts of the reassurance from heaven in July, but after he
was kept awake all night on August 1 to see her die — "and therewith
[to] see the terrible death of my prayer and faith" — the "strange
irradiation" was again unmistakable. Mather continued through
the summer to read this experience as a special exercise to keep his
faith and prayer employed.

He found that conviction reinforced on the night of August 23, at
the end of a full Lord's Day of preaching and private devotion.
While sitting in his study, he distinctly heard a voice commanding
him: "Go into your great chamber and I will speak to you!" He went
to the largest room upstairs, the one most secluded, and lay on the
floor. There he soon felt again that "inexpressible afflatus come

from heaven upon my mind," and he wept and found himself speaking aloud at the same time:

> "And now *my Father* is going to tell me, what He will do for me. *My Father* loves me, and will fill me with His *love,* and will bring me to everlasting *life. My Father* will never permit anything to befall me, but what shall be for *His interest. My Father,* will make me a *chosen vessel* to do good in the world. *My Father* will yet use me to glorify His Christ, and my opportunities, my precious opportunities to do so, shall be after a most astonishing manner continued and multiplied. Particularly, my treatise of, THE TRIUMPHS OF CHRISTIANITY, *my Father* will send His holy angels to look after it, and it shall not be lost. The condition of my dear *consort, my Father* will give me to see His wonderful favor in it. *My Father* will be a *Father* to my *children* too; He will provide for them, and they shall every one [of] them serve Him throughout eternal ages."

On the twenty-ninth of August he tried a new way of placating the Lord, the same kind of thanksgiving day with which the leaders of Massachusetts had helped to end King Philip's War in 1676. Although both he and Abigail had suffered, he gave thanks for the fourteen weeks through which the Lord had upheld her. A day of praise, he reasoned, might be "followed with salvations, beyond what any *days of prayer* had yet obtained." Keeping this day was especially difficult because Abigail's condition was terrifying the day before the scheduled thanksgiving, but her frantic husband's perseverance was again rewarded by a new Particular Faith that revived "at the strangest rate imaginable," and the poor woman also began "to have some strange revivals."

The prayer that Mather uttered while administering communion to his church the next day is one of the most exquisitely self-torturing declarations of ambiguous faith, argument, and desperate anxiety in all the devotional literature of New England. He wept as he offered it, under the force of what he felt was "an inexpressible irradiation from heaven" on his mind. *"Surely,"* he simultaneously declared and pleaded at the start of several sentences, "Thou art our Father . . . . *Surely* Thy Christ, is ours." Surely Christ has washed away our sins, "or else Thou wouldst never have made our sins to become so bitter, and loathsome unto us, and made us wish for nothing so much as deliverance from our sins. Surely, we stand before Thee in the righteousness of Christ; or else Thou wouldst never have made us to renounce and abhor all our own *righteousness*" and flee only to His. Surely the Holy Spirit had "taken a saving possession of us, or else" we would never have changed, become reconciled to the "self-denying points of Christianity," nor ever preferred affliction to sin, nor "have relished it, as the chief delight under Heaven, yea a very Heaven itself, to be *always doing of good. Surely,* these are the *seals* of God upon us. . . . God uses not such *seals* as these upon reprobates." Persuaded by "a mighty Light, broke in upon our minds, . . . We are sure this persuasion must either be from *Satan,* and from a deceived and a deluded *heart;* or else it must be from the *Holy Spirit* of God. But we are sure, the persuasion, is not from *Satan,* and from our own sinful *heart,* because we no sooner enter- tain it, but it fills us with love to God, and care to please Him and serve Him; . . . it causes us to abound in the work of the Lord; it in- spires us with a zeal for Thee; it constrains us to a watchful, useful, fruitful and humble walk before Thee. We are sure then, that the persuasion is from the *Holy Spirit* of God. And now, *behold, what manner of Love is this!*"

Few better statements were ever made of the basis on which a troubled Puritan might judge the assurance that a regenerate per- son would sometimes feel, but of course the personal meaning here applies to Mather's threatened family and his threatened faith as well. More skillfully than his father had done in the crisis that nearly incapacitated him in the years after Richard Mather's death, Cotton Mather articulated in this prayer an argument, a declaration of faith, and an exemplary demonstration of the process of receiving and certifying grace — and he directed all of these simultaneously to himself, to his congregation, and to the Almighty Being whose decrees the prayer was designed at once to celebrate and to influ- ence.

As Abigail grew steadily worse, however, Mather began to suspect that the assurances he won at several of his regular vigils were not tests of his faith but "admirable demonstrations" of the Lord's reluc- tance to deny his most fervent requests. Therefore, he reasoned, Providence might "one month after another delay the thing which I fear," only to prepare both the husband and the wife for her inevi- table death. Mather began to suspect that he had interpreted too certainly, too narrowly, the divine assurances that his prayers had been heard. Toward the end of October, having languished more than twenty weeks, Abigail began to show plainly "the symptoms of

an hopeless *consumption.*" Mather resigned her to the Lord in the
vigil that he kept that night, but again he was astonished by extraordinary signs of encouragement. Abigail dreamed of a remedy—a
mixture of spring water, dissolved mastics, and gum isinglass—and
the physician endorsed it when she told him about it the next day.
She revived for awhile thereafter, and so of course did her husband's
hopes.

Those new hopes had not yet been threatened by the twenty-ninth
of October, when another of Mather's Particular Faiths was joyously
fulfilled. On that day he saw for the first time a copy of *Magnalia
Christi Americana,* which had just arrived from London. He invited
his friend Edward Bromfield, who had helped to start the book on
its way to publication in England, to spend the day with him in his
study in special thanksgiving. But his blessings, as always, came
along with new trouble. His daughter Nibby came down with smallpox on the thirtieth, as the epidemic spread throughout the neighborhood.

This time the epidemic was compounded of both scarlet fever and
smallpox, but the Mather children were spared the scarlet fever.
The one disease sufficed. As his wife began to decline once again,
Mather visited many of the afflicted people in his neighborhood,
wrote a pamphlet of *Wholesome Words* for those he could not visit,
and saw his warm study, the best refuge from the nasty November
weather, "sanctified" as a hospital ward for his ailing children. Of
course he interpreted his own eviction as a humbling providence in
return for his failure to serve the Lord as well "as I should have done
in my study." Little Nanny had the worst case among the three children, but Increase was "also pretty full and blind, and sore," and
the "godly maid" who cared for them had a terrible case that permanently unsettled her mind. With both the maid and Abigail so
ill, the children kept calling their father to pray for them, sometimes a dozen times a day.

He gave most of his time to Abigail, who was now obviously dying.
He prayed with her and tried to prepare her with the liveliest commentaries on heaven that he could devise. He tried to dispose her
(and himself) as well as he could to what he called "a glorious resignation." For that attitude, Abigail needed no help. She had long
since decided that she would never recover, and her slow, painful
decline strengthened her wish to die. A short time before she died,

her husband asked her to tell him faithfully whether she had observed any fault in his behavior that she would advise him to rectify. She said that she knew of none. Providence, she told him, had made her husband's behavior a blessing that had brought her much nearer to Himself.

Two hours before the death of his "lovely consort," Mather knelt beside her bed, took her hand, "the dearest in the world," and solemnly gave her up to the Lord. To show the genuineness of his resignation, he "gently" put her hand down on the bed, resolving that he would never again touch it. This, he wrote later, "was the hardest and perhaps the bravest action, that ever I did," and Abigail told him that she signed and sealed his act of resignation. Although she had continually called for him before, she did not ask for him again. Her last intelligible words were addressed to her own father, who also wept at her bedside: "Heaven, Heaven will make amends for all."

Mather managed to pray with his father-in-law and the other mourners in the room, and three days later to preside, as he had done for his brother and his children and as he would one day do for another wife and his own mother and father, at Abigail Mather's funeral. He gave each of the nearly one hundred faithful watchers who had watched at her sickbed a copy of one of his books, either *Ornaments for the Daughters of Zion* or *Death Made Happy and Easy,* and he pasted into each book a conventional, hastily composed epigram, which expressed his affection, his resignation, and his endorsement of his wife's dying words:

Go then, my DOVE, but now no longer *mine;*
Leave *Earth,* and now in *heavenly Glory* shine.
*Bright* for thy Wisdome, Goodness, Beauty here;
Now *brighter* in a more *angelick Sphaere.*
JESUS, with whom thy Soul did long to be,
Into His *Ark,* and Arms, has taken thee.
Dear *Friends,* with whom thou didst so dearly live,
Feel thy *one Death* to *them a thousand* give.
Thy *Prayers* are done; thy *Alms* are spent; thy *Pains*
Are *ended* now, in *endless* Joyes and Gains.
   I faint, till thy last Words to Mind I call:
   Rich Words! HEAV'N, HEAV'N WILL MAKE AMENDS FOR ALL.

On the Lord's Day, December 6, he preached her funeral sermon, on Ezekiel 24:16, proscribing mourning for the prophet's wife even though the Lord should take away "the pleasure of thine eyes," and again on the tenth he preached a sermon on the province's day of general thanksgiving. In Boston alone, eighty people died of small-pox that month, and the thanksgiving was hardly joyful. But every Puritan knew where the blame for such calamities had to be as-signed. On the thirteenth, Mather preached a sermon on the fourth chapter of John, on coming to Jesus for healing mercies. One of his chief doctrines here condemned his own misreading of Particular Faiths: "Though faith be no folly, yet faith may be mixed with folly; and particularly with the folly of limiting the Wisdom of God, unto our own way of answering it."

The community's rituals of support and one or two special ges-tures helped him, as well as his faith and his multiple duties helped him, to endure the first months of grief. His children recovered from the smallpox and escaped the scarlet fever, but the maid's mind was so badly affected by her nearly fatal attack of smallpox that she could no longer care for the children. Mather, who had often wept at other times but only in what he called "joy for the Sal-vation of God," now found that he wept almost every day, and he feared that his eyes were thus being weakened. He took some com-fort from a magnanimous gesture of the congregation, which built "a costly tomb" for Abigail Mather and the five Mather children who had been buried with ordinary gravestones. He was also dis-tracted from his grief for a while by a strange ordeal that required unusual delicacy.

Scarcely a month after his wife's death, while the maid's disability and the multiplicity of his duties made him wonder how the chil-dren would be cared for, a handsome young woman in his congre-gation began a determined campaign to marry him. She was only about twenty years old, and her reputation had been "under some disadvantages," but she had a fine education, and Mather admired both her "rare wit" and "extremely winning . . . conversation." She wrote him letters, visited him at home, and proposed importu-nately. When he protested that there were many difficulties in his situation, including his pious way of living "in continual prayers, tears, fasts, and macerating devotions and reservations," she insisted that she "desired nothing so much as a share in my way of living." He was strongly tempted, but when his family and members of his congregation complained that it was unseemly to consider remarrying so soon and that the woman's reputation was unacceptable, the courtship gradually ended. Mather did have the consolation of inducing his unsuccessful suitor to undergo a tearful conversion.

Besides the loss of his wife, it was the miscarriage of his Particular Faith that confused and pained him. In the little time that he had to himself in the weeks after Abigail's death, he tried to reason out the significance of both her death and his erroneous faith. At first he rationalized in a blatant effort to find advantages in the catastrophe: perhaps her removal "unto a better world" had also been meant as a blessing for him, for she could hardly have survived without "continual weakness, and languor, and sorrow, that would have been uneasy to us all." Perhaps, he reasoned, his own health might have been destroyed if she had "recovered . . . so far that I should have run the venture of sleeping with her." His own "feeble constitution" might have "run into a consumption." The children, too, would have suffered in their education. And besides, Abigail herself would have suffered greatly from "the dreadful change on her father's family." Her father's prudent remarriage had "extremely broken her spirit," and her brothers' respective illness, death, and disgrace would have tormented her still more miserably.

But that sort of obvious searching into the wisdom of Providence did not answer Mather's perplexity about the Particular Faith. He might understand the Providential reasons for letting her die even though his own "extravagant fondness for her would upon any terms have detained her here." Yet he could not forget all those moments of irradiation that had absolutely assured him of her recovery. He could only conclude, after hours and days of perplexity, that his wife herself "had in the court of Heaven put in a bar" against the fulfillment of his faith. Her own secret requests, he decided, had "overruled the effect of all my prayer and hope concerning her."

That was as far as he could go to solve the particular question. On the more general "mystery" of his practical Christianity, he had more difficulty. He tried to answer it in his sermon on December 13 by hedging the definition of the Particular Faith itself. When we receive an answer saying that the Lord has heard or that the Lord will receive our prayer, he said, we must not be too ready to *"limit* the sense of the Holy Spirit, by our own strong affections to the *temporal blessings,* and conclude, *the thing must be done in just such or such a manner.* No," the Holy Spirit may only mean to do "something towards the temporal blessing" to show His willingness to gratify us before He carries "the matter unto another channel," wherein all our desires will be "more than answered." Although this seems to a secular intelligence only another way of saying that the Particular Faith, if specific, might not be valid, Mather concluded with a strong reaffirmation of the creature's duty to resign his own will to that of Omnipotence: "The bravest effort of a true and a strong *faith,* is, to leave all entirely unto the Lord, and be satisfied with the infinite wisdom of His conduct." He resolved to observe "a more exquisite caution" than he had ever exercised toward Particular Faiths, and for years thereafter he virtually abandoned the doctrine. Not until the disappearance of his son Increase at sea in 1724 did another of his Particular Faiths prove false.

AT THE AGE of forty, then, Cotton Mather settled into the busy routine of his middle age. He had begun ten years earlier the major works of his life. Now that the *Magnalia* was in print, he continued to labor steadily on his "Biblia Americana" and to press his unsuccessful campaign, inaugurated in the *Magnalia* itself, to find a publisher for that immense compendium. Except for good works in the community and complex negotiation and maneuver in the politics of the Congregational churches, he now virtually withdrew from politics. The successor to Governor Bellomont, who had died in England while on the assignment that Increase Mather had hoped to perform, was the Mathers' old enemy Joseph Dudley. During the second month of Abigail Mather's last illness, Cotton Mather had made the humiliating gesture of welcoming Dudley with a sermon on the character of *A Good Man,* delivered in the presence of the new Governor and the General Court, but that alliance could not last, and Mather's political influence was soon restricted to the delivery of a few election sermons. He concentrated more than ever on works of practical piety in the remaining decades of his life, and attended more closely to works of scientific description and meditation — including *The Angel of Bethesda,* the medical work that he had begun soon after the Salem witchcraft trials, and *The Christian Philosopher,* foreshadowed by his sermon *The Wonderful Works of God* and by his *Winter Meditations.* During these years he also be-

came an elder statesman of religious and scientific affairs, whose letters to the Royal Society eventually won him election as a Fellow and
whose growing correspondence extended into the pietist movement
in England and Germany.

In the last twenty-five years of his life Mather's spiritual and psychological condition continued to alternate between the exalted and
gloomy moods that his theology both decreed and helped him to endure. He never abandoned his passionate concern for the welfare of
the Lord's people in New England, but the arrival of his published
*Magnalia,* the death of Abigail Mather, and the miscarriage of his
Particular Faith virtually completed the separation of his personal
life from his country's political life, the separation that had become
evident ten years earlier. After 1702 his chiliastic hopes were largely
confined to a few general statements and one soaring election sermon on Boston's possible choice as the New Jerusalem, in a time
that was now unspecified and unconnected to any one political
group. Cotton Mather lived vigorously in his community for exactly
a quarter of a century after his fortieth birthday, but after 1702 the
Mather whose personal and spiritual life were united with the life of
New England lived nowhere else but in his *Magnalia.*

NOTES

INDEX

# *Notes*

*Preface*

Page

xiii "phenomenon to be analyzed." Nathaniel Hawthorne, *The Whole History of Grandfather's Chair,* in *True Stories from History and Biography* (Columbus, 1972), p. 105.

*I. A Covenanted Childhood*

1 "the founding of Massachusetts Bay." *The Autobiography of Increase Mather,* ed. M. G. Hall (Worcester, Mass., 1962), p. 286: "I . . . was married to the then only daughter of Mr. Cotton . . . in honor to whom I named my eldest son Cotton."

2 *"an happy father."* Cotton Mather, *Parentator* (Boston, 1724), pp. 22-23.

"the Half-Way Covenant." See Kenneth B. Murdock, *Increase Mather, the Foremost American Puritan* (Cambridge, Mass., 1925), pp. 80-85; and Robert Middlekauff, *The Mathers: Three Generations of Puritan Intellectuals, 1596-1728* (New York, 1971), pp. 113-139.

4 "nonconforming clergymen." See Gerald R. Cragg, *Puritanism in the Period of the Great Persecution, 1660-1688* (Cambridge, 1957).

"displayed on London Bridge." See John Gorham Palfrey, *The History of New England* (Boston, 1858-1890), II, 428, 429; III, 80. The governor was Sir Henry Vane; Hugh Peter's head was displayed on London Bridge.

5 "wishes to the Crown." A century later, Governor Thomas Hutchinson, who knew what it was to suffer between the orders of the Crown and the demands of his fellow colonists, described Boston's treatment of the agents Bellingham and Norton in a worthy epigram: "The [returning] agents met with the fate of most agents ever since. The favors they had obtained, were supposed to be no more than might well have been expected, and their merits were soon forgot; the evils which they had it not in their power to prevent, were attributed to their neglect or un-

Page

necessary concessions." *The History of the Colony of Massachusetts Bay,* ed. Lawrence S. Mayo (Cambridge, Mass., 1936), I, 190-191.

"in several parts of the world." Increase Mather, *Autobiography,* p. 288; Cotton Mather, *Parentator,* p. 29.

6    "original relation to the universe." Ralph Waldo Emerson, *Nature* (Boston, 1836), p. 5.

6-9   "the drama of John Farnum's salvation." The narrative of Farnum's excommunication, including all the quoted speeches, can be found written in Increase Mather's hand in the records of the Second Church, in the Massachusetts Historical Society. I have quoted them here with the permission of the Society and the Second Church.

10    " 'Ton would go see God," and "towards me and mine." I am indebted to Professor Michael G. Hall for these manuscript diary entries of Increase Mather's. The original copies are in the American Antiquarian Society.

"all but one of the sons." Timothy, the farmer (1628-1685).

10-11   "as soon as he could speak" to "work that he had missed." The facts and quotations in this paragraph are taken from "Paterna," an unpublished autobiographical manuscript addressed by Cotton Mather to his son, pp. 3-4 of a typescript that I have made and deposited in the Alderman Library, University of Virginia. Quoted with the permission of the Alderman Library, which owns the manuscript. All citations of this manuscript refer to this typescript.

11    "beyond the age of seventeen." The statistics may be found in Cotton Mather, *Corderius Americanus* (Boston, 1708), p. 18.

"when Cotton was twenty." The quotations from Maria Mather's diary are from Cotton Mather's funeral sermon for her, *Maternal Consolations* (Boston, 1714), pp. 43-44n.

"rule over the family." Cotton Mather adopted the same role for himself. See his extended comparison of himself as advocate, his father as judge, and his own son as guilty offender. *The Diary of Cotton Mather,* ed. Worthington C. Ford (Boston, 1912), I, 583.

12    "the beating of children." See Increase Mather, *The Life and Death of Richard Mather* (Cambridge, Mass., 1670), p. 44. Compare Cotton Mather, *Bonifacius,* ed. David Levin (Cambridge, Mass., 1966), p. 87.

"particular earthly afflictions." Increase Mather, *Autobiography,* p. 301.

"affectations of pre-eminency." The phrase is Cotton Mather's, from the *Diary,* I, 16. Katherine Anne Porter used the phrase as the title for her satirical chapter on Mather's childhood, "Affectation of Praehiminincies," *Accent,* II (Spring 1942), 131-132.

"faithful Christian service." See Proverbs 9:7, 27:5; Cotton Mather, "Paterna," p. 8; and David Levin, *In Defense of Historical Literature* (New York, 1967), p. 42.

13    "love and approval." Cotton Mather, *Maternal Consolations,* pp. 6, 42-44.

Page

13  "with as much delight." Cotton Mather, *A Family Well Ordered* (Boston, 1699), pp. 22-23.

"as if we came to *Play*." Cotton Mather, *Corderius Americanus*, p. 28.

14  " 'designed' him for the ministry," Increase Mather, *Autobiography*, p. 301.

15  "later described this experience." See the opening paragraphs of Jonathan Edwards' spiritual autobiography in Samuel Hopkins, *The Life and Character of . . . Jonathan Edwards* (Boston, 1765), pp. 24-25; and *The Journal and Essays of John Woolman*, ed. Amelia Mott Gummere (New York, 1922), chap. I. Compare Mather, "Paterna," pp. 3-5.

16  "in the years before 1672." Here again I am indebted to Michael Hall for entries from the manuscript diary of Increase Mather.

"betwixt these two strong arms." The description of Boston in this paragraph is taken from John Josselyn's *An Account of two Voyages to New England* (London, 1674), pp. 160-163. See also Walter M. Whitehill, *Boston: A Topographical History* (Cambridge, Mass., 1959), pp. 3-21.

18  "wickets in the streets." In "Paterna," pp. 23, 24, Cotton Mather remarks that he was already preaching when no older than other boys who were "playing at their *marbles* or *wickets* with one another in the streets." He preached his first sermon at the age of sixteen.

"on Cotton Hill." The other half of the large double house had been occupied by Governor Henry Vane until his return to England after the Antinomian Controversy of the 1630s. Maria Mather's brother Seaborn Cotton sold that half of the house to John Hull, the mintmaster, in 1664. When Leonard Hoar first came to Boston, and served briefly as assistant to Mr. Thacher in the South Church, he stayed with the John Hull family in this house. It may be that Increase Mather's friendship with Hoar began there. See Chapter II.

"the reaction of Increase Mather." The ensuing narrative of Increase Mather's troubles is based on his *Autobiography*, pp. 287-296.

20  "this typical predicament." We can find it echoed in the diary of Michael Wigglesworth, the preparatory meditations of Edward Taylor, and the diaries of Cotton Mather, Samuel Sewall, and Jonathan Edwards.

22  "as from the dead." Cotton Mather, *Diary*, I, 36.

"Cotton Mather's stammer." Cotton Mather later wrote ambiguously about the date of the onset of his affliction, but the first contemporaneous allusion is in Increase Mather's diary for October 7, 1674, during Cotton's first year at Harvard College. See Increase Mather, *Autobiography*, p. 301; and Cotton Mather, *Diary*, I, 70, 77, 111.

*II. Harvard College*

23-24  "When Cotton Mather enrolled" to "of his property." Cotton Mather, "Paterna," pp. 4-5; Increase Mather, "The Diary of Increase Mather,"

Page

*Proceedings of the Massachusetts Historical Society*, III (1855-1858), 316 (hereafter cited as *MHS Proceedings*); Samuel Eliot Morison, *Harvard College in the Seventeenth Century* (Cambridge, Mass., 1936), II, 423-428 (further citations of this important book will use the initials *HSC*).

24  "fifteen to twenty-one." The biographical information in the next few pages comes from John L. Sibley, *Biographical Sketches of Graduates of Harvard University* . . . (Cambridge, Mass., 1873-1975), vols. II and III. Grindall Rawson, born in 1659, was fifteen years old when he and Cotton Mather entered Harvard. John Pike and James Minot, both seniors, were born in 1653.

"father's pulpit." John Cotton resisted the call to succeed his father in the Hampton church after Seaborn Cotton died in 1686, but did accept the call when it was offered to him again ten years later. Sibley, *Graduates*, III, 2-5.

25  "heard them in church." Cotton Mather, *Magnalia Christi Americana* (London, 1702), IV, 202.

"learned men." See *The Diary and Autobiography of John Adams*, ed. Lyman Butterfield (Cambridge, Mass., 1961), III, 259.

"in verse and prose." Samuel Eliot Morison, *The Founding of Harvard College* (Cambridge, Mass., 1935), p. 333.

"had already begun to study it." Mather, "Paterna," p. 4.

26  "Benjamin Tompson" to "verses on Job." Mather, "Paterna," p. 4.

"to school at Paul's." Cotton Mather, *Corderius Americanus*, p. 28.

"preferring Duport to Homer." See Cotton Mather, *Bonifacius*, p. 85.

"Gassendi." Pierre Gassendi (1592-1655), a French materialist philosopher, tried in his scientific writings to reconcile a mechanistic atomic theory with orthodox theology. It was Gassendi's astronomical work that Cotton Mather cited most approvingly in his own later scientific writings. See Cotton Mather, *A Voice from Heaven: An Account of a Late Uncommon Appearance in the Heavens* (Boston, 1719), p. 4, which praises Gassendi's remarks on the aurora borealis. For seventeenth-century New England education, Gassendi's chief scientific value was his advocacy of an analytic method of research, working from smaller to large questions.

"the discovery of America." See Chapter VIII.

27  "failure of his presidency." See Morison, *HSC*, II, 639, where the letter is reprinted.

The account of Hoar's experience in England and his accession to the presidency of Harvard is based on Morison, *HSC*, II, 390-414.

28-29  "which you do yet enjoy" to "destroy themselves forever." The quotations are from Morison's text of Hoar's letter to Josiah Flint, *HSC*, II, 639. The interpretation is my own.

29  "investigators of the controversy." Morison, *HSC*, II, 404.

30  "to make him *odious*." *Magnalia*, IV, 129. Cited also by Morison, *HSC*, II, 402; and by Palfrey, *History*, III, 94, n.4.

Page
30  "a more modern work." Morison, *HSC*, I, 233.

"cruel young men." Morison, *HSC,* II, 402-407.

"would be punished." *Publications of the Colonial Society of Massachusetts,* XV (1925), 58. For an extended critical account of this issue, see David Levin, "The Hazing of Cotton Mather: The Creation of a Biographical Personality," *In Defense of Historical Literature,* pp. 45-56. Compare Morison, *HSC,* I, 82; II, 420-421.

31  "able to repent." Morison, *HSC*, I, 81-83, 121-132; II, 461-463.

"by the local jailer." *The Diary of Samuel Sewall,* ed. M. Halsey Thomas (New York, 1973), I, 5.

32  "prohibition of hazing." Morison, *HSC,* I, 82-83.

"of their misconduct." The quoted statement comes from Jeremy Belknap's transcription of a diary of Increase Mather's which Belknap dated July 16, 1674, and printed in *MHS Proceedings,* III (1855-1858), 317.

"home to Boston." *MHS Proceedings,* III, 317.

"begging the Lord to accept him." Increase Mather, *Autobiography,* p. 301.

33  "I had designed him." Increase Mather, *Autobiography,* p. 301.

"Trouble is near." Increase Mather, *The Day of Trouble is Near* (Cambridge, Mass., 1674).

"order to the college." See Morison, *HSC,* II, 406.

"with the sword." Increase Mather, *Autobiography,* p. 302.

"against the President." Sewall, *Diary,* I, 4.

"external as well as internal." Sewall, *Diary,* I, 8.

"deprived of his students." *MHS Proceedings,* III, 319.

"his original matriculation." *MHS Proceedings,* 2nd series, XIII (1899-1900), 347.

"reminded . . . of Hoar's severity." Morison, *HSC,* II, 407.

"treatment of Hoar in Cambridge." *MHS Proceedings,* III, 319.

34  "moving Harvard . . . to Boston." *MHS Proceedings,* 2nd ser., XIII, 347.

"friends in New England." The date was November 28, 1675. *MHS Proceedings,* III, 319.

"scholars at the college" and "from Harvard once again." *MHS Proceedings,* 2nd ser., XIII, 349.

35  "dangerously severe." In 1657, John Cotton and another student had received cash compensation for their injuries. Morison, *HSC,* I, 82-83.

" 'speaking part' of the occasion." Cotton Mather, *The Angel of Bethesda,* ed. Gordon W. Jones (Barre, Mass., 1972), p. 226.

35-38  "miserable affliction" to "as long as you live." Mather, *Bethesda,* pp. 227-231.

39  "more than one academic generation." Mather, "Paterna," p. 4.

"two birds with one stone." Mather, "Paterna," p. 5.

40  "imaginary maladies" and "done him more damage." Mather, "Paterna," pp. 6-7.

Page

40-41  from "consulted his father" to "his eminent father and grandfathers." Mather, "Paterna," pp. 5-6.

41  "improve his behavior." Mather, "Paterna," p. 8. See Joseph Hall, *Occasional Meditations*, 3rd ed. (London, 1633); and Henry Scudder, *The Christian's Daily Walk* (London, 1628).

42  "serve his Creator." Cotton Mather, "Paterna," pp. 53-57. Compare Mather's *Diary*, the earliest surviving copy of which begins several years later: I, 71-73, 81, 83.

"preparations for the Lord's Day." Morison points out, however, that even so sober and respected a minister as Joseph Green (A.B. 1695) repented in his diary for having sinned during his college days in ways that squandered time: "fowling, fishing, profanity, Sabbath breaking, card-playing, dancing, and roistering." *HSC,* II, 464.

43  "lust for long hair." See Morison, *HSC,* I, 88-89.

45  "reeked of tobacco fumes." Morison, *HSC,* I, 94.

46  "what was called seniority." Morison, *HSC,* I, 58ff.

"at £ 3 or more." Morison, *HSC,* I, 59.

46-47  "The curriculum" to "Gassendi." Morison, *HSC,* I, 139-284.

47  "the Arts course of Cambridge." Morison, *HSC,* I, 165.

"*Eupraxia*, or well-doing." Morison translates: "doing the right thing at the right time," *HSC,* I, 163-164.

"flowers in his head." Morison, *HSC,* I, 172.

48  "philosophers and orators." Quoted in Morison, *HSC,* I, 179, from a translation owned by Nicholas Udall.

"for the glory of God and our own good." Quoted in Morison, *HSC,* I, 239.

"paid off the mortgage." Morison, *HSC,* I, 106.

49  "vengeful attacks upon them." The factual basis of this paragraph is Alden T. Vaughan, *New England Frontier: Puritans and Indians, 1620-1675* (Boston, 1965), and Douglas Leach, *Flintlock and Tomahawk: New England in King Philip's War* (New York, 1958); for a much more adversely critical narrative of the New England Indian wars, see Francis Jennings, *The Invasion of America: Indians, Colonialism, and the Cant of Conquest* (Chapel Hill, 1975).

50  "higher than 20 percent." Leach, *Flintlock*, p. 131.

51  "a deplorable desolation." Cotton Mather, quoted by the editors of the 1858 edition of Sewall's diary, *Collections of the Massachusetts Historical Society*, 5th ser., V (1878), 28.

"volumes in his library." Increase Mather, *Autobiography*, pp. 302-303; Sewall, *Diary*, I, 28.

"just after the fire." Cotton Mather, *Diary*, I, 128, 133.

52  "I will not preach in a corner." Sewall, *Diary*, I, 30.

"bewildering misery." See Chapter IX.

"a particular benefit." See Cotton Mather, *Magnalia,* IV, 142.

53  "coming to dwell here." Sewall, *Diary*, I, 30.

"wife would surely recover." See Chapter IX.

Page

53    "son . . . would be rescued." Despite such an assurance, Mather's son In-
      crease was lost at sea in 1724. See Cotton Mather, *Diary*, II, 759-760.

      "had ever exprefenced." Sewall, *Diary*, I, 44.

53-54 "take no notice of them" to "the next twenty years." Morison, *HSC*, II,
      462-464.

54    "Oxford, or Edinburgh." Quoted in Morison, *HSC*, II, 471.

      "and one gallon to other students." Morison, *HSC*, II, 465.

      "no Body will see." Quoted from the almanac for 1682, in Morison,
      *HSC*, II, 466.

55    "catch up with them" to "languishing consumption." Morison, *HSC*, II,
      467-468.

      "the sense of sentences." Morison, *HSC*, I, 170.

      "Under rhetoric" to "by the first cause." Morison, *HSC*, I, 174, 166; II,
      608-609.

56    "parents . . . present." Morison, *HSC*, II, 469-470.


         *III.  The Call of the Gospel and the Loss of the Charter*

58    "without becoming clergymen." Thomas Brattle, who achieved some sci-
      entific distinction, and William Stoughton, deputy governor of Massa-
      chusetts and chief justice of the special court that tried the witchcraft
      cases in Salem, were two other Harvard Masters of Arts who did not
      follow a minister's vocation.

      "experience of conversion." Morison, *HSC*, I, 148-150; Mather, *Diary*, I,
      26.

      "horribly overwhelmed" to "condition of *midnight.*" Mather, "Paterna,"
      pp. 6-7.

59    "easy ways to hell" and "Suspect thyself much." Thomas Shepard, *The
      Sincere Convert* (London, 1640), pp. 148, 138.

      "constant joy" to "upon the Lord." Anne Bradstreet, "To My Dear Chil-
      dren," in *The Works of Anne Bradstreet*, ed. Jeannine Hensley (Cam-
      bridge, Mass., 1967), p. 243.

60    "my own *experience.*" Mather, "Paterna," p. 20.

      "raptures almost insupportable." Mather, "Paterna," p. 13.

      "new life of Soul." Mather, "Paterna," p. 52; Mather, *Diary*, I, 36-37.

      "heavenly way of living" through the end of this paragraph. Mather,
      *Diary*, I, 36-37. Compare Jonathan Edwards' spiritual autobiography:
      "a high, sweet, great, and gentle holiness, an awful majesty of sover-
      eign meekness." Hopkins, *Jonathan Edwards*, p. 28.

60-61 "in all this" to "a pardoned *soul.*" Mather, *Diary*, I, 39.

61    "have seen these conditions." Mather, "Paterna," p. 38.

      "came over me" to "assuring of it." Mather, "Paterna," p. 18.

62    "during the sermon?" Mather, *Diary*, I, 38.

      "I shall be" to "Hell unto me." Mather, *Diary*, I, 43.

      "Proud thoughts . . . best performances." Mather, *Diary*, I, 15.

63    "*buy off* guilt" to end of paragraph. Mather, *Diary*, I, 71-73.

Page
63   "which Mather destroyed." See, for example, I, 37, 42, 51, 52, 57, 63, 71-72.

"tutored during these years." Mather, *Diary*, I, 41. The allusion may also be to his own children, if he wrote this retrospective version after his marriage four or five years later, or simply as a young bachelor who presumed that he would one day become a father. One cannot date the manuscript precisely. Compare I, 11.

64   "adolescent 'pollutions.' " Mather, *Diary*, I, 79; see also pp. 92, 107, 439-458.

"a very valuable [letter]" to "hath *sealed*." Mather, *Diary*, I, 78.

"*unclean temptations*" to "or corruptions." Mather, *Diary*, I, 79-80.

"a minister stricken" to "the *evil Spirit*." Mather, *Diary*, I, 79-80.

65   "as vile . . . not prevent it." Mather, *Diary*, I, 30.

"*have no faith*." Mather, *Diary*, I, 79-80.

"for the success of the Gospel here" to "three-hour sermon." Mather, *Diary*, I, 80. Mather says he had little more than an hour to prepare the sermon on Acts 11:21: "And the hand of the Lord was with them so that a great number believed and turned to the Lord."

"extraordinary occasion" to "in my soul." Mather, *Diary*, I, 81. Fifty years later, young Benjamin Franklin, who acknowledged the influence of a later form of Mather's schemes for moral improvement, tried to achieve "moral perfection." "As I knew, or thought I knew," the difference between right and wrong, Franklin wrote in some amusement many years afterward, "I did not see why I might not always do the one and avoid the other." *The Autobiography of Benjamin Franklin*, ed. Benjamin Labaree et al. (New Haven, 1964), p. 148.

"What! . . . murders?" to "splenetic maladies." Mather, *Diary*, I, 81.

66   "ruin his health." Cotton Mather, *Early Piety, Exemplified in the Life and Death of Nathanael Mather* (London, 1689), pp. 4-5.

"killed himself with study." Mather, *Early Piety*, pp. 4, 8-55.

"Yea, tis well . . . if I avoid a consumption." Mather, *Diary*, I, 81; see Mather, *Early Piety*, pp. 17, 55-56.

67   "Englishmen and Europeans were." John Duffy, *Epidemics in Colonial America* (Baton Rouge, 1953), p. 22.

"less than a month." Increase Mather, *Diary, March 1675 - December, 1676. Together with extracts from another diary by him, 1674-1678* (Cambridge, Mass., 1900), pp. 20-21.

"become infected." Duffy, *Epidemics*, pp. 46-48.

"Samuel Sewall . . . survived." Sewall, *Diary*, I, 46.

"Shepard . . . died." Cotton Mather, *Magnalia*, IV, 18.

"four decades later." Mather was one of the first people in the English-speaking world to encourage inoculation against smallpox, and during the epidemic of 1721-22 he was roundly abused for urging Dr. Zabdiel Boylston to inoculate healthy people. The fairest account of this episode is in Otho Beall and Richard Shryock, *Cotton Mather, First Figure in American Medicine* (Baltimore, 1954). A brilliant but less fair

Page

account is in Perry Miller, *The New England Mind: From Colony to Province* (Cambridge, Mass., 1953), pp. 346-366.

68  "publication outside Mexico." Thomas Thacher, *A Brief Rule to guide the common-people of New-England how to order themselves and theirs in the small pocks, or measels* (Boston, 1678; facsimile reproduction, ed. Harry R. Viets, Baltimore, 1937). The broadside has no page numbers.

"one miserable position to another." William Bradford, *Of Plymouth Plantation*, ed. Samuel Eliot Morison (New York, 1952), pp. 270-271.

69  "that are behind." Letter of Cotton Mather to John Cotton [November? 1678], *Massachusetts Historical Society Collections,* 4th ser., VIII, 383-384. See also John Cotton to Increase Mather, August 26, 1678, ibid., p. 246.

70  "God's controversy with New England." The phrase is used in the synod's report, by Increase Mather, in Williston Walker, *The Creeds and Platforms of Congregationalism* (New York, 1893; rpt., 1960), p. 414. See Michael Wigglesworth's poem, *God's Controversy with New England*, written during the great drought of 1662.

" 'hath half ruined . . . the town' of Boston." William Hubbard, quoted in Walker, *Creeds*, p. 412, n. 2.

"What are the evils" to "may be reformed?" Increase Mather, in Walker, *Creeds*, p. 414.

70-71  "contending parties" to "May 31." Palfrey, *History*, III, chap. 7.

71  "all persons . . . country." Edward Randolph, *A short Narrative of my proceedings . . . [in] N. England*, in *The Andros Tracts*, ed. William H. Whitmore (Boston, 1868-1874), I, 2.

"to the people." Palfrey, *History*, III, 320.

72  "to be sent to Boston." Palfrey, *History*, III, 324.

*The Necessity of Reformation*, reprinted in Walker, *Creeds*, pp. 423-437.

72-73  "The grandeur of God's achievement" to end of paragraph. Walker, *Creeds*, p. 424.

73  "like to follow." Walker, *Creeds*, pp. 425-426.

"out of his sight." Walker, *Creeds*, p. 426.

"given to prove." Psalms 78:8, 37; 81:11. Jeremiah 2:5, 11, 13. The report also cited an example from the New Testament, Revelation 2:4, 5.

"for their own bickering." Walker, *Creeds*, p. 427.

"ornamental dress . . . (Isaiah 3:16)." Walker, *Creeds*, p. 428.

"Sabbath-breaking . . . Jeremiah 17:27." Walker, *Creeds*, p. 429.

73-74  "Inordinate affection . . . Isaiah 5:7." Walker, *Creeds*, p. 431.

74  "with our fathers." Walker, *Creeds*, p. 426.

"action, revival, community." For revivalism, see Miller, *From Colony to Province*, pp. 105-118.

"this projecting age." Jonathan Swift, *A Project for the Advancement of Religion and the Reformation of Manners* (London, 1709).

Page

74  "keep one another alive." Cotton Mather, *Religious Societies* (Boston, 1724), p. 2. This little book, including Cotton Mather's first sermon, was written in 1679, but he did not publish it until forty-five years later.

75  "to one another." Mather, *Religious Societies*, p. 3.
"many valuable interests." Mather, *Religious Societies*, p. 4.
"questions laid out by Mather." Mather, *Religious Societies*, pp. 5ff.
"points of *practical piety*." Mather, *Religious Societies*, p. 6.
"Society of the Free and Easy." See Franklin, *Autobiography*, pp. 161-163.

76  "when it may be said" to "our peace." Mather, *Religious Societies*, p. 3. The verse concludes, in the Geneva version, "But now are they hid from thine eyes."
"The peace of a believer . . . sanctification also." Mather, *Religious Societies*, p. 6. "Sanctification" here means improved obedience to God's will; justification, forgiveness through the unmerited gift of grace.
"there is a sweetness . . . their *wages*." Mather, *Religious Societies*, p. 6.
"mother of destruction." Mather, *Religious Societies*, p. 14.
"*excellency* in them" to "worth of them." Mather, *Religious Societies*, p. 15. Compare Jonathan Edwards, "Spiritual Autobiography," in Hopkins, *Jonathan Edwards*; and "The Excellency of Christ," in *The Works of Jonathan Edwards* (London, 1817), VI, 399-430.
"The other circumstances . . . with *opportunity*." Mather, *Religious Societies*, p. 15.
"Lose this *NOW*" to "eternity depended on." Mather, *Religious Societies*, p. 17.
"uncommon *advantages*" to "*joy of the LORD*." Mather, *Religious Societies*, pp. 18-19.

77  "a dreadful eternity." Mather, *Religious Societies*, p. 13.
"very potent sermon." Mather, *Parentator*, p. 85.
"lovest is sick." Mather, *Parentator*, pp. 87-88.

78  "oblige the better party." Quoted in Palfrey, *History*, III, 356.
"great estates in land." Quoted in Palfrey, *History*, III, 357.
"errors and blasphemies." Quoted in Palfrey, *History*, III, 337.

79  "towed the ship away." Quoted in Palfrey, *History*, III, 338.

79-80  "The Bostoneers" to "kingdom much more." Quoted in Palfrey, *History*, III, 339 n. 2.

80  "at the King's charge." Quoted in Palfrey, *History*, III, 343.
"habit of meeting." Sewall, *Diary*, I, 52. See also letter of Cotton Mather to John Cotton, January 19, 1682, New York Historical Society.
"stately cedars crack!" Letter of Cotton Mather to John Cotton, March 28, 1682, Harvard College Library.
"not altogether unapprehensive." Draft of letter from Cotton Mather to John Cotton, April 1682, Boston Public Library.
"summer of 1681." Mather, *Diary*, I, 22.

82  "Great rumors" to "arms to meeting." Sewall, *Diary*, I, 49.

Page

82   "at the door." Sewall, *Diary*, I, 49.

     "midnight or past." Sewall, *Diary*, I, 52.

     "increased the excitement." See letter of Cotton Mather to John Rich-
     ards, November 13, 1682, in *Selected Letters of Cotton Mather*, ed.
     Kenneth Silverman (Baton Rouge, 1971), p. 11.

82-83  "At the wedding" to end of paragraph. Sewall, *Diary*, I, 53.

83   "Two days later" to "north end of the town." Sewall, *Diary*, I, 53-54.

     "Increase Mather's house." Sewall, *Diary*, I, 54.

     "invented by man for convenience." Mather, *Diary*, I, 26, and Samuel
     Mather, *The Life of the Very Reverend and learned Cotton Mather*
     (Boston, 1729), pp. 5-6.

84   "Grief never made good poet." Cotton Mather, *A Poem Dedicated to the
     Memory of the Reverend and Excellent Mr. Urian Oakes* . . . (Boston,
     1682), in the facsimile edition published by the Club of Odd Volumes
     (Boston, 1896), p. 3.

     "Oh! the *Name* . . . Under the Cross!" Mather, *A Poem*, p. 15.

85   "A *great Soul* . . . *always low.*" Mather, *A Poem*, pp. 11-12.

     "The earth . . . on the ground." Mather, *A Poem*, p. 8.

86   "Lett not the Colledge . . . Hallelujah's ring." Mather, *A Poem*, p. 16.

     "congregation approved." Ms. diary of Increase Mather, September 8,
     1681. Quoted in Murdock, *Increase Mather*, p. 107.

88   "may be supplied." *Massachusetts Archives*, XI, 16-17; quoted in Mori-
     son, *HSC*, II, 441. See also the ms. Church Record, pp. 3-4 (reading
     upside down from the back of the book).

     "in 1690." When his father was in London, and perhaps going to stay
     there. See Chapter VI.

     "pulpit of . . . Church of *Boston.*" Mather, *Diary*, I, 37.

     "Thanksgiving proclamation . . . in October 1681." Mather, *Diary*, I,
     43. The resolution was adopted October 21, and the day of Thanks-
     giving celebrated on November 24.

89   "very backward" to " 'any other' candidate." Increase Mather, *Autobiog-
     raphy*, p. 310.

     "small and mean." Mather, "Paterna," p. 16.

     " £ 70 per year." Mather, *Diary*, I, 47.

     "render me unserviceable." Mather, *Diary*, I, 49, 51.

90   "my removal from them." Mather, *Diary*, I, 53.

     "make him their Pastor." Church Record, pp. 3-4, reading upside down
     from the back of the book.

     "prospective members away." Church Record, vol. III. See also Mur-
     dock, *Increase Mather*, p. 150.

     "dozens of new memberships." Mather, *Diary*, I, 68.

     "four times that number." In 1698, Increase Mather remarked that the
     average attendance at his church was fifteen hundred people. See
     Chapter IX.

     "advised him to accept." Mather, "Paterna," p. 16.

     "member of this church." Church Record, vol. III.

90-91 "My father was President" to "providence of God." Mather, *Diary*, I, 26.

91 "a day for ordination." Church Record, III, 43.

"the advancement of learning." Mather, *Magnalia*, IV, 132.

"any knowledge." Increase Mather, *An Essay for the Recording of Illustrious Providences* (Boston, 1684).

92 "catastrophic judgments" to "natural law." See Increase Mather, *Kometographia* (Boston, 1683); and Murdock, *Increase Mather*, pp. 145-146.

"proposed in 1679." Otho H. Beall did some splendid detective work to prove that some of Cotton Mather's *Curiosa Americana*, his unpublished letters to the Royal Society in 1712, were based on papers of the Philosophical Society of the 1680s. My account of the Philosophical Society is based on Professor Beall's fine article, "Cotton Mather's Early 'Curiosa Americana' and the Boston Philosophical Society of 1683," *William and Mary Quarterly*, 3rd ser., XVIII (1961), 360-372.

93 "always happened." Beall, "Mather's Early 'Curiosa,'" pp. 369-370.

93-94 "Cotton's Almanac" to "*Julian* ones." Cotton Mather, *The Boston Ephemeris. An Almanack for the (Dionysian) Year of the Christian Era* (Boston, 1683).

95 "from the dead." Mather, *Diary*, I, 36.

"days of thanksgiving." Mather, *Diary*, I, 18.

"richest of my enjoyments." Mather, *Diary*, I, 20.

"signalize me . . . Hallelujah." Mather, *Diary*, I, 34.

"one of the worst kinds of thievery in the world." Cotton Mather, *Theopolis Americana* (Boston, 1710), p. 15.

"a *Spanish Indian*" to "thus to *measure*." Mather, *Diary*, I, 64-65.

"the vocal reader." Mather, *Diary*, I, 23.

96 "ruled the household." Mather, *Diary*, I, 23-24.

"this nation" to "in New England." Mather, *Diary*, I, 22. The fast was proclaimed by the General Court in a resolution adopted May 30, 1681, and was observed on July 7.

"Within his own church . . . their liberation." Mather, *Diary*, I, 41-42. Here Mather cautioned himself against superstition in the regularity of the observance.

"the *South* church." Mather, *Diary*, I, 12.

97 "For Richard Middlecot . . . the North Church." Mather, *Diary*, I, 13-14.

"objects of their charity." Mather, *Diary*, I, 54.

"the smaller towns." Mather, *Diary*, I, 65.

98 "at their first meeting." Mather, *Diary*, I, 67-68.

"the glory of God." Mather, *Diary*, I, 76.

"serviceable to man." Mather, *Diary*, I, 62.

"my *love* thereunto." Mather, *Diary*, I, 60.

99 "unto his *incommunicable*." Mather, *Diary*, I, 61.

"Mather's desire . . . 'thy own praise.'" Mather, *Diary*, I, 66-67.

"into his 'excellencies.'" Mather, *Diary*, I, 67.

Page

100  "to general criticism." See Mather, *Diary*, I, 70, and the "Paterna" entry that seems to imply, years later, some early opposition to his election as Pastor of the Second Church, pp. 69-70.

"that have died" and "the room thereof." Mather, *Diary*, I, 65.

"in his autobiography." Increase Mather, *Autobiography*, p. 300.

"make me a blessing." Mather, *Diary*, I, 69.

"into the fire." Mather, *Diary*, I, 73.

100-101  "During a walk" to end of paragraph. Mather, *Diary*, I, 68-69.

101  "In the fall . . . vote of submission." See Palfrey, *History*, III, 383-385; and *Massachusetts Archives*, CVI, 305.

101-102  "Cotton Mather kept up . . . jail sentence." Letter of Cotton Mather to John Cotton, December 20, 1683, American Antiquarian Society.

102  "found in America." Letter of Samuel Sewall to Cotton Mather, December 25, 1684. Printed in Sewall, "Diary" (*Massachusetts Historical Society Collections*, 5th ser.) V, 58.

102-103  "In his written arguments" to end of paragraph. Palfrey, *History*, III, 381-383.

103  "We know that" to "great a sin." Increase Mather, *Autobiography*, p. 308. One of the three surviving accounts of the meeting says Mather did not speak until after the vote. David Lovejoy, *The Glorious Revolution in America* (New York, 1972), pp. 154-55.

"Not one . . . the Bostonian example." Increase Mather, *Autobiography*, p. 308.

103-104  "In the legal battle . . . cancelled the charter." Palfrey, *History*, III, 387-394.

105  "for several years." Increase Mather, *Autobiography*, pp. 309-310; Palfrey, *History*, III, 556-558; Murdock, *Increase Mather*, pp. 183-185.

"servant of Antichrist." Palfrey, *History*, II, 480-481.

### IV. From Vision to Bereavement

106-107  "When the angel . . . were imminent." Mather, *Diary*, I, 86-87.

107  "Behold he was . . . envied him." Ezekiel 31:3, 4, 5, 7, 9. Mather, *Diary*, I, 86.

108  "Therefore thus saith . . . caused them to mourn." Ezekiel 31:10-15.

109  "next day's worship." Mather, *Diary*, I, 88.

"when he could." Mather, *Diary*, I, 89.

"He expresses . . . 'unsavory salt.' " Mather, *Diary*, I, 91.

"strife and sin." Mather, *Diary*, I, 93.

109-110  "some foolish discouragements." Mather, *Diary*, I, 92.

"He calmed himself . . . 'theater enough.' " Mather, *Diary*, I, 93.

"by James's accession." Mather, *Diary*, I, 93.

"to deliver New England." Mather, *Diary*, I, 94.

111  "for many years." Sewall, *Diary*, I, 63, 147.

"He kept . . . predicament." Mather, *Diary*, I, 97.

"never forsake him." Mather, *Diary*, I, 98.

Page

112 "from on high." Mather, *Diary*, I, 98.

"of the world." Mather, *Diary*, I, 98.

"out of the world." Mather, *Diary*, I, 99; Sewall, *Diary*, I, 63.

113 "a lover of Jesus Christ." Mather, *Diary*, I, 99; *Sewall*, Diary, I, 63.

113-114 "He resolved . . . first conception." Mather, *Diary*, I, 102-103.

114 "profitable exercise." Mather, *Diary*, I, 103.

"his prayers." Mather, *Diary*, I, 100-101.

"Samuel Sewall . . . and wine." Sewall, *Diary*, I, 63.

115 "end of the world." Mather, *Diary*, I, 102; *Magnalia*, IV, 206.

"such a father." Mather, *Magnalia*, IV, 202.

"older people." Mather, *Magnalia*, IV, 206.

"affection for him." "This was the short life of my dear Shepard. I confess my affection unto him to have been such, that, as the poet says, 'I am half buried since he is dead,' or, 'He is but half dead since I am alive.' Nevertheless, this affection hath not bribed my veracity in any part of the character which I have given of him; for as on the one side, I count it base to throw dirt on the face, which dust hath been cast upon; so, on the other side, I think, that painting becomes dead people worse than living." Mather, *Magnalia*, IV, 207.

"on the hearse." Sewall, *Diary*, I, 66.

116 "fulfill the curse." Sewall, *Diary*, I, 67.

"the waterside." Sewall, *Diary*, I, 72.

117 "an attack." Sewall, *Diary*, I, 77.

"the harbor." Sewall, *Diary*, I, 79.

"governor had arrived." Sewall, *Diary*, I, 70.

"cryer of fish." Sewall, *Diary*, I, 75-76.

118 "autumn or winter." Sewall, *Diary*, I, 84.

"Mather's lecture." Sewall, *Diary*, I, 85.

"shall lose it." Sewall, *Diary*, I, 86.

"so empowered." Sewall, *Diary*, I, 71-72.

"a special order." Sewall, *Diary*, I, 73.

"offend England." Sewall, *Diary*, I, 83.

119 "bloody a peace." Sewall, *Diary*, I, 85.

"Old Testament." Sewall, *Diary*, I, 83.

"religious experience." Sewall, *Diary*, I, 76.

"its mother." Sewall, *Diary*, I, 83.

"such a holiday." Sewall, *Diary*, I, 90.

"in several years." Even here the uncertain status of the government became an issue, for William Stoughton and Joseph Dudley refused to participate in sentencing Morgan. The question seems to have been whether the government now had power to execute a felon. Sewall, *Diary*, I, 98.

119-120 "Increase Mather . . . following day." Sewall, *Diary*, I, 98; Mather, *Diary*, I, 122.

120 "concourse of people." Mather, *Diary*, I, 122.

"nearly three centuries." This memorably accurate phrase is Samuel

Page

Eliot Morison's, paraphrased in Miller, *From Colony to Province*, p. 204.

121 "of the earth." Isaiah 45:22.

122 "by your *hearing*." Increase and Cotton Mather, *The Call of the Gospel applied unto all men in general, and unto a Condemned Malefactor in particular,* 2nd ed. (Boston, 1686), p. 43.

"of your *own*." Mather, *Call of the Gospel,* p. 68.

"be *saved*." Mather, *Call of the Gospel,* p. 50.

"*Believe and be saved*." Mather, *Call of the Gospel,* p. 47.

"partake hereof." Mather, *Call of the Gospel,* pp. 52-53.

"these INVITATIONS." Mather, *Call of the Gospel,* p. 54.

"burn in Hell." Mather, *Call of the Gospel,* pp. 72-73.

"He warned" to "free grace." Mather, *Call of the Gospel,* pp. 81-82.

123 "Soon after" to end of paragraph. Sewall, *Diary,* I, 99.

"in either." Mather, *Call of the Gospel,* p. 31. Remember that Increase Mather's lecture was printed in Cotton Mather's book, along with the Exhortation by Joshua Moody.

"He cited . . . 'bodies too.' " Mather, *Call of the Gospel,* pp. 24-25.

"soul is filled . . . without *end*." Mather, *Call of the Gospel,* pp. 10-11.

125 "so often avoided." Mather, *Call of the Gospel,* p. 29.

"other sins" to "never-dying soul." Mather, *Call of the Gospel,* p. 32.

"Consider 3" to "*innocent blood*." Mather, *Call of the Gospel,* p. 33.

"compassion on you." Mather, *Call of the Gospel,* p. 35.

"When the service . . . of Jesus." Mather, *Call of the Gospel,* p. 115.

125-126 "Morgan asked" to end of paragraph. Mather, *Call of the Gospel,* pp. 120-121.

126 "Morgan stumbled" to end of paragraph. Mather, *Call of the Gospel,* pp. 122-123.

"Christ wants" to "help and comfort." Mather, *Call of the Gospel,* p. 123.

"unto Life!" Mather, *Call of the Gospel,* p. 123.

127 "I pray God" to "I come." Mather, *Call of the Gospel,* pp. 135-136.

"later works." See Thomas J. Holmes, *Cotton Mather: A Bibliography* (Cambridge, Mass., 1940), I, 111-113. I have used the second edition of *Call of the Gospel* for this account, because it contains Mather's dialogue with Morgan.

127-128 "On April 7" to "shame for sin?" Mather, *Diary,* I, 125. For the Cheever trial, see Sewall, *Diary,* I, 103-106.

128 "unto His glory." Mather, *Diary,* I, 106.

"Mather disclaimed" to "good thing." Mather, *Diary,* I, 106-107.

129 "Mather kept" to end of paragraph. Mather, *Diary,* I, 109-110; "Paterna," pp. 90-91.

130 "a lovely and worthy" to end of paragraph. Mather, "Paterna," pp. 90-91.

"splendid affair." Mather, *Diary,* I, 126-127; Sewall, *Diary,* I, 110.

"against him." Mather, *Diary,* I, 125-126.

Page
130  "joyous celebration" to "Charlestown." Mather, *Diary*, I, 126-127.

"On the ninth" to "divine delights." Mather, *Diary*, I, 107.

"in these pages." See Sewall, *Diary*, I, 110.

131  "as a magistrate." Sewall, *Diary*, I, 111.

"Englishmen's liberties." Sewall, *Diary*, I, 110-122; Palfrey, *History*, III, 485-487.

"spake . . . changing." Sewall, *Diary*, I, 113.

131-132  "new offices" and "gesture of concern." Sewall, *Diary*, I, 114.

132  "under protest." Palfrey, *History*, III, 486.

"Gentlemen . . . our relief." Reprinted in Palfrey, *History*, III, 486.

133  "Wednesday of October." Sewall, *Diary*, I, 115.

"toward Heaven." Sewall, *Diary*, I, 116-117.

134  "was refused." Sewall, *Diary*, I, 119-120.

"A raucous group . . . 'good people.' " Sewall, *Diary*, I, 121.

"the Sabbath." Sewall, *Diary*, I, 122.

"to meet." Sewall, *Diary*, I, 123-124.

"their meetinghouses." Sewall, *Diary*, I, 128.

135  "God's people." Sewall, *Diary*, I, 128.

"from abroad." See, for example, Sewall, *Diary*, I, 139.

"own boundaries." Mather, *Diary*, I, 132.

136  "where I am." Mather, *Diary*, I, 129.

"joys and griefs." Mather, *Diary*, I, 131.

"surrounded with" to "of divinity." Mather, "Paterna," p. 94.

"exceeded one hundred." Mather, *Diary*, I, 131-132.

136-137  "a course" to "these exercises." Mather, "Paterna," pp. 87-88.

137  "forever blest." Mather, "Paterna," p. 97.

"God's glory." Mather, *Diary*, I, 133; "Paterna," p. 93.

137-138  "His first child" to "any harm!" Mather, "Paterna," p. 94.

138  "of a Christian." Cotton Mather, *Right Thoughts in Sad Hours* (London, 1689), p. 1.

"*unto good.*" Mather, *Right Thoughts*, pp. 5-6.

"a *fool.*" Mather, *Right Thoughts*, p. 7.

"the stars." Mather, *Right Thoughts*, p. 8.

140  "*Hand* of the Lord." Mather, *Right Thoughts*, p. 10.

"very *obscure.*" Mather, *Right Thoughts*, p. 11.

"*God* to men." Mather, *Right Thoughts*, p. 14.

"to be comforted." Mather, *Right Thoughts*, p. 14.

"for good." Mather, *Right Thoughts*, p. 15.

"know hereafter." Mather, *Right Thoughts*, pp. 16-17.

"I am this day" to "afflicted people." Mather, *Right Thoughts*, pp. 18-19.

"before the Lord." Mather, *Right Thoughts*, p. 20.

141  "unto them." Mather, *Right Thoughts*, pp. 27-29.

"*A wound*" to "our *God.*" Mather, *Right Thoughts*, p. 34.

"very glorious." Mather, *Right Thoughts*, p. 35.

"given back." Mather, *Right Thoughts*, pp. 47, 48.

Page

141  "dear lambs again." Mather, *Right Thoughts*, p. 50.

"bosom of Jesus." Mather, *Right Thoughts*, p. 53.

"crying aloud" to "*of Heaven.*" Mather, *Right Thoughts*, p. 54.

## V. Witchcraft and Revolution

143  "his initials." See Chapter III.

144  "sedition and treason." Murdock, *Increase Mather*, p. 183.

"a great knave." Murdock, *Increase Mather*, p. 185.

"Soon after . . . getting aboard." Murdock does not mention the pursuit, but Cotton Mather says that a strong easterly wind forced the pursuers into Nantasket, whereas *The President* had already gone beyond the point and into the open sea. The wind, he said, was "fresh testimony of God's presence" with Increase Mather. In March Increase had preached a farewell lecture on Exodus 33:15: "If Thy presence go not with us, carry us not hence." Letter of Cotton Mather to John Cotton, April 11, 1688, University of Virginia Library. Mather, *Parentator*, p. 108; Sewall, *Diary*, I, 162, 163, 164; Murdock, *Increase Mather*, pp. 183-189.

"our religion." Church Record, vol. III.

146  "and other guests." Sewall, *Diary*, I, 178.

"Governor's Council." Sewall, *Diary*, I, 164.

"Spanish galleon." Sewall, *Diary*, I, 169.

"forty years." Sewall, *Diary*, I, 173.

"Mather deplored . . . '5 English persons.' " Sewall, *Diary*, I, 175, 176.

"unjust wars." Cotton Mather, *Soldiers Counselled and Comforted* (Boston, 1689), Epistle Dedicatory. See *Military Duties* (Boston, 1687), p. 25.

147  "publish the book." Cotton Mather, *Memorable Providences, Relating to Witchcrafts and Possessions* (Boston, 1689), pp. x, 33. All further references to this work use the abbreviation *MP*.

" 'cataleptic' seizures." *MP*, p. 3.

"Martha . . . at once." *MP*, pp. 2-3.

"sometimes they . . . move at all." *MP*, pp. 4-5.

148  "such extreme fits." *MP*, p. 2.

"to hoodwink them." *MP*, p. 2. See also Cotton Mather, *Pietas in Patriam: The Life of . . . Sir William Phips*, in *Magnalia*, II, 61.

"t'other too." *MP*, pp. 3-4.

"The children . . . at night." *MP*, p. 6.

"inquired into it." *MP*, p. 6.

"deny her guilt." *MP*, p. 6.

149  "When asked . . . repeated unto her." *MP*, pp. 6-7.

"The Devil . . . superstitious remedies." Increase Mather, *Illustrious Providences*, pp. 184, 118, 188-189.

149-150  "At the trial . . . 'the whole assembly.' " *MP*, pp. 7-8.

Page

150    "looking very pertly" to "confessed all." *MP*, p. 8.

"confirm her guilt." *MP*, p. 9.

150-151    "A six-year-old . . . he recovered." *MP*, p. 10.

151    "Mather insisted . . . Glover accused." *MP*, p. 12.

"any offense." *MP*, p. 13.

151-152    "They barked . . . 'the floor.' " *MP*, pp. 14-15.

152    "God Himself." Mather, Preface to *MP*; "Discourse on Witchcraft," *MP*, passim.

"the poor victims." *MP*, p. 17.

"debauched age." *MP*, p. 18.

"over her again." *MP*, p. 19.

153    "hear a word!" *MP*, p. 19.

154    "thrown herself." *MP*, p. 20.

"hurt her back." *MP*, p. 21.

"He demonstrated" to "read a word." *MP*, p. 22.

154-155    "Now he brought" to "honest historian." *MP*, pp. 24-25.

155    "upon the *floor*." *MP*, p. 27.

155-156    "One of" to "any devotion." *MP*, p. 28.

156    "When Martha" to "told a word." *MP*, p. 31.

"by that history." *MP*, p. 33.

156-157    "He spoke Latin" to "fit went over." *MP*, p. 39.

157    "of *witches*." *MP*, p. 41.

"the children." *MP*, p. 44.

158    "books devoured him." Mather, *Magnalia*, IV, 211.

"in North Boston." Mather, *Magnalia*, IV, 219.

"Never did" to "can know it?" Mather, *Magnalia*, IV, 221.

159    "with the Lord." Mather, *Magnalia*, IV, 221.

"of the year." Sewall, *Diary*, I, 180-181.

"I have now" to "close his eyes." Mather, *Magnalia*, IV, 221; Sewall, *Diary*, I, 181.

"sore terrors" to "in his mind." Mather, *Magnalia*, IV, 219.

160    "Study killed him." Mather, *Magnalia*, IV, 211.

"emphatically mixed." Mather, *Magnalia*, IV, 215.

"should allow." Mather, *Early Piety*, p. 39; *Magnalia*, IV, 218.

161    "characteristically explicit." Mather, *Magnalia*, IV, 218.

"*time* to *pray*." Cotton Mather, *Small Offers for the Tabernacle* (Boston, 1689), p. 37. See also Levin, "Introduction," *Bonifacius*, p. xiii.

"to be serviceable." Mather, *Small Offers*, pp. 19ff.

"his middle age." See chapter IX.

"given away." Mather, *Diary*, I, 291.

"just historian." Mather, Introduction to *Early Piety*.

162    "his own church." Letter of John Cotton to Increase Mather, September 10, 1688, *Massachusetts Historical Society Collections*, 4th ser., VIII (1868), 257.

162-163    "If an antagonist" to "English liberties." Lovejoy, *Glorious Revolution*, pp. 340-350. See Miller, *From Colony to Province*, pp. 153-155.

Page

Though disagreeing on this question with both of these scholars, I have of course learned a great deal about the subject from them, and my very brief account of the Glorious Revolution in this chapter is especially indebted to David Lovejoy's twelfth chapter. On earlier appeals to English liberties, see above, Chapter III. See also Murdock, *Increase Mather*, pp. 190-245.

163    "his agency there." Increase Mather, *New England Vindicated from the Unjust Aspersions* . . . (London, 1688); *A Narrative of the Miseries of New England* (London, 1689).

    "administrative means." Lovejoy, *Glorious Revolution*, p. 231.

164    "for his fall." *Narratives of the Insurrections*, ed. Charles M. Andrews (New York, 1915), p. 173.

165    "within the Council." See William Stoughton et al., *A Narrative of the Proceedings of Sir Edmund Androsse and his Complices, Who Acted by an Illegal and Arbitrary Commission from the Late K. James* (Boston, 1691); and a pamphlet probably written by Joseph Dudley, *New England's Faction Discovered* . . . (London, 1690), which gives the Andros side of the argument. Both of these, along with several other valuable documents, are reprinted in *Narratives*, ed. Charles Andrews. Although I have used the original versions of some of these documents, I shall refer to those that Andrews reprinted by citing *Narratives* and the page numbers.

    "among the people." Quoted in G. B. Warden, *Boston, 1689-1776* (Boston, 1970), p. 7.

167    "of his crew." Andrews, *Narratives*, p. 216n.

    "restraint and coordination." Among the best nineteenth-century accounts are those in Justin Winsor, ed., *Memorial History of Boston* (Boston, 1880-81), and John G. Palfrey, *History of New England*. Some of the best recent accounts, besides Lovejoy, are in Richard S. Dunn, *Puritans and Yankees: The Winthrop Dynasty in New England, 1630-1717* (Princeton, 1962), and G. B. Warden, *Boston*.

    "had been spilt." Andrews, *Narratives*, p. 207.

    "former employments." Andrews, *Narratives*, p. 167.

168    "destroy Protestantism." Cotton Mather, *Declaration of the Gentlemen, Merchants, and Inhabitants of Boston, and the County Adjacent* (Boston, 1689). Reprinted in Andrews, *Narratives*, pp. 175-178.

169    "fairly published." The last clause is written in the margin of the original; see Andrews, *Narratives*, p. 178n.

171    " '*Christian*' virtue." Mather, *Magnalia*, II, 42.

    "[is] treason." Mather, *Magnalia*, II, 44.

    "could no more . . . *English* Crown." Mather, *Magnalia*, II, 44.

172    "taking of arms." Andrews, *Narratives*, p. 182.

    "principal gentlemen" to "ungoverned *mobile*." Mather, *Magnalia*, II, 45.

    "in the world." Mather, *Magnalia*, II, 45.

    "from England." Mather, *Magnalia*, II, 45-46.

Page

*VI. Struggling toward the Millennium*

174    "Andros' dominion." Andrews, *Narratives*, p. 190.
176    "speaking with tongues." Cotton Mather, *The Wonderful Works of God Commemorated* (Boston, 1690), pp. 52-53.
       "to confess." Mather, Postscript to *Wonderful Works*, p. 60.
       "the shepherdess" to "God on earth." Mather, *Wonderful Works*, pp. 40-41.
       "coming true." See Chapter IV.
177    "any breath." Mather, *Wonderful Works*, p. 55.
       "The worst" to "our own *passions*." Mather, *Wonderful Works,* pp. 29-30.
       "half our prayers." Mather, *Wonderful Works,* p. 34.
       "exemplar, Increase Mather." Mather, *Wonderful Works*, p. [iv].
178    "to their homes." See Palfrey, *History*, III, 589-590.
       "until 1693." Church Record, vol. III; Robert G. Pope, *The Half-Way Covenant* (Princeton, 1969), pp. 194-197.
180    "*fall with them*." Mather, *Magnalia*, II, 47.
       "and Sara Mather." Mather, *Magnalia*, II, 47; Church Record, vol. III.
181    "destructive enemies." Sewall, *Diary*, I, 251.
       "joined the church." Sewall, *Diary*, I, 255.
182    "against modifications." Murdock, *Increase Mather*, p. 229.
       "Increase Mather's request." Letter of Cotton Mather to Thomas Hinckley, April or May 26, 1690, Boston Public Library.
       "stay in England." Sewall, *Diary*, I, 238.
       "public servants." Quoted in W. C. Ford's note, Mather, *Diary*, I, 140.
183    "Your Son, C.M." Mather, *Diary,* I, 137-140.
184    "the native Americans." Cotton Mather, *The Triumphs of the Reformed Religion in America* (Boston, 1691), pp. 1-78.
185    "mortification, brother." Mather, *Triumphs,* p. 31.
       "The cheering confirmation" to "Daniel Quincy." Sewall, *Diary*, I, 259, 260, 261-262.
       "to flow in." Sewall, *Diary*, I, 266.
186    "the very ruins" to "the challenge." See Mather, *Triumphs*, pp. 78, 83, 124.
186-187  "citizens of the WORLD" to "Henry Adams." Mather, *Wonderful Works*, pp. 25-27.
187    "the solar system." Sewall, *Diary*, II, 779. Sewall complains of a sermon by Mather on December 23, 1714.
188    "lies and slander." See Cotton Mather, *The Principles of the Protestant Religion Maintained* (Boston, 1690); and *Little Flocks Guarded against Grievous Wolves* (Boston, 1691).
188-189  "Mather's reaction" to "next day." Sewall, *Diary*, I, 268.
189    "*some*, that" to "*serviceable*." Letter of Cotton Mather to John Cotton, October 17, 1690, University of Virginia Library. Mather marked the date in Latin as the second anniversary of his brother Nathanael's memorable and lamented death.

Page
189-190 "Phips's fleet" to "misadventure." Sewall, *Diary*, I, 269-271.

190 "defend it himself." Sewall, *Diary*, I, 271.

"criticize Sir William." Quoted in Alice Lounsberry, *Sir William Phips* (New York, 1941), p. 230.

"out of joint." Sewall, *Diary*, I, 272.

"chest and clothes." Sewall, *Diary*, I, 272-273; see also Lounsberry, *Phips*, pp. 211-214.

191 "by himself." Mather, *Diary*, I, 140-141; and letter to John Cotton, September 14, 1691.

"after his return." See *Andros Tracts*, II, 279ff.

"Mather learned" to "General Court." Letter of Cotton Mather to John Cotton, September 14, 1691, in *Diary*, I, 141-142.

192 "Mather felt obliged" to "will be well." Letter of Cotton Mather to John Cotton, December 8, 1691, Southern Historical Collection, University of North Carolina.

"at a gnat." Sewall, *Diary*, I, 276. The sermon was preached on March 19, 1691.

193 "returning to God." Cotton Mather, *A Midnight Cry* (Boston, 1692), p. 64.

"our awakening." Mather, *Midnight Cry*. The quoted clause is part of Mather's extended subtitle for the sermon.

"NEW REFORMATION" to *"blessed Reformation."* Mather, *Midnight Cry*, p. 62.

194 "In the winter" to *"hastens greatly."* Quoted in Holmes, *Bibliography*, II, 836-839.

194-195 "Mather resolved" to "blessed Reformation." Mather, *Diary*, I, 161-163; letter to John Richards, February 13, 1692, Massachusetts Historical Society. See also Pope, *Half-Way Covenant*, pp. 194-197.

195 "Mather's instigation" to "Richards and others." Letter of Cotton Mather to John Richards, December 14, 1692, Massachusetts Historical Society.

*"somewhat awake."* Letter to Richards, December 14, 1692.

196 "had been lost." Mather, *Diary*, I, 151-152.

197 "out of excrement." See Samuel Parris, Church Record, March 27, 1692; Charles W. Upham, *Salem Witchcraft* (Boston, 1867), II, 95.

"tormentors were." John Hale and Samuel Parris, the Salem Village minister, both deplored the witch-cake as an invitation to Satan. In the abundant literature on the Salem witchcraft trials, two recent books represent valuable approaches that differ without being mutually exclusive. *Salem Possessed,* by Paul Boyer and Stephen Nissenbaum, is subtitled *The Social Origins of Witchcraft* (Cambridge, Mass., 1974). It builds ingenious new interpretations on the foundation laid by Charles W. Upham (*Salem Witchcraft*, 1867), by making a much more professionally thorough investigation into the local history of Salem and Salem Village. Chadwick Hansen's *Witchcraft at Salem* (New York, 1969) gives perhaps the best account of the afflicted girls' medical condition, and perhaps the best argument (though by no

Page

    means a conclusive one) for the guilt of some of the defendants. I am indebted to *Salem Possessed* for my summary of local events, and I have also profited from subsequent conversations with Stephen Nissenbaum.

197   "therapy of Martha Goodwin." See Chapter V.

    "Even Sarah Good" to "a topknot." *What Happened in Salem*, ed. David Levin, 2nd ed. (New York, 1960), pp. 6-8.

198-199   "most powerful confession" to "Burroughs." Levin, *Salem*, pp. 66-69.

199   "the same time." Levin, *Salem*, p. 10.

    "fraud and delusion." Mather, *Magnalia*, II, 61.

200   "convict the innocent." As the summer brought on more executions, others did write privately to the court. See, for example, the letter of Robert Pike to Judge Jonathan Corwin, August 9, 1692 (in Hansen, *Witchcraft at Salem*, pp. 139-141); and a sermon by the Reverend Deodat Lawson, preached at Salem Village in March, then published a few weeks later: *Christ's Fidelity the Only Shield against Satan's Malignity* (Boston, 1692).

    "existence of witches." Mather, *Memorable Providences*, p. 41; see above, Chapter V; and *The Wonders of the Invisible World* (London, 1862), p. 42: the sermon preached August 4, 1692, Proposition I.

201   "Mather conceded" to "kill themselves." Reprinted in Mather, *Magnalia*, VI, 76-77.

    "to injure him." See Chapter III.

    "Mather associated" to "Shubael Dummer." Cotton Mather, *Fair Weather* (Boston, 1692), pp. 19-20, 86, 91.

    "imminent arrival." Mather, *Midnight Cry*, p. 8.

202   "*I leave thee.*" Mather, *Midnight Cry*, p. 17.

    "Synod of 1679." See Mather, *Diary*, I, 161.

    "seize this moment" to "of *gold*." Mather, *Midnight Cry*, p. 27.

    "preparation thereunto." Mather, *Diary*, I, 147.

    "the ultimate Reformation." Mather, *Midnight Cry*, pp. 44-46, 62.

202-203   "high treason" to "our land." Cotton Mather, *The Wonders of the Invisible World*, p. 87.

203   "in the spring." Mather, *Diary*, I, 148.

204   "suspicion of witchcraft." Letter of Sir William Phips to the Earl of Nottingham, in *Narratives of the Witchcraft Cases*, ed. G. L. Burr (New York, 1914), pp. 198-199.

    "*over the water.*" Mather, *Diary*, I, 148.

    "determine cases." Letter of Phips to Nottingham, in Burr, *Narratives*, pp. 198-199.

    "counted so themselves." *MP*, p. 28.

205   "persons thus abused." Levin, *Salem*, p. 107.

    "may unhappily" to "wished for." Levin, *Salem*, p. 107.

206   "really tormented." Levin, *Salem*, p. 108.

    "Mather recommended" to "free speech." Levin *Salem*, pp. 108-109.

    "spiritual nourishment." Levin, *Salem*, p. 109.

Page

206    "witches themselves." Levin, *Salem*, p. 110.

207    "religious societies." Cotton Mather, *Good Things Propounded* (Boston, 1692), p. 44.

       "*institutions* of our Lord." Mather, *Good Things Propounded*, p. 44.

208    "evil cause." Mather, *Good Things Propounded*, p. 44. Kenneth Murdock long ago pointed out Mather's distinction between civil and spiritual jurisdictions in this sermon. See Holmes, *Bibliography*, II, 769-770. For the comparable language in Jefferson, see *A Bill for establishing Religious Freedom* (1779; rpt., Charlottesville, 1975).

       "*the aliens.*" Mather, *Good Things Propounded*, p. 44.

       "in a *bedlam.*" Mather, *Diary*, I, 149.

       "for witchcraft." Mather, *The Wonders of the Invisible World*, p. 100; and *Magnalia*, II, 62-63.

       "informal group." Mather, *Diary*, I, 143.

208-210 "Its arguments" to "detection of witchcrafts." Reprinted in Levin, *Salem*, pp. 110-111.

210    "biography of Phips." He did not omit it from *Wonders of the Invisible World*, in October 1692.

211    "On August 5" to "ring leader." Letter of Cotton Mather to John Cotton, August 5, 1692, in Mather, *Diary*, I, 142-143.

       "recording them." Mather, *Diary*, I, 142-143.

211-212 "Mather repeated" to "spectral ones." Letter of Cotton Mather to John Foster, in Silverman, *Selected Letters*, pp. 41-42.

212    "a suspected" to "this danger." Silverman, *Selected Letters*, pp. 41-42.

       "the innovation." Letter to John Foster, quoted in Silverman, *Selected Letters*, pp. 42-43.

213    "Thirty-two of his neighbors" to "make him confess." Levin, *Salem*, pp. 62-63.

       "his execution." Sewall, *Diary*, I, 294.

       "righteous sentence." Sewall, *Diary*, I, 294.

215    "verdict of guilty." Levin, *Salem*, p. 126.

216    "in the world." Letter of Cotton Mather to William Stoughton, September 2, 1692, in Silverman, *Selected Letters*, p. 43. I have been unable to find the holograph of this letter. Silverman's text is a typewritten transcript in the American Antiquarian Society.

       "not exposed." Letter of Cotton Mather to John Cotton, October 20, 1692, Boston Public Library.

       "as he said later." Letter of Cotton Mather to Stephen Sewall, September 20, 1692, New England Historical and Genealogical Society.

       "in the *dark.*" Mather, *Wonders of the Invisible World*, p. 84.

217    "being accused." Letter to Stoughton, September 2, 1692, in Silverman, p. 43.

       "where, at last." Letter of Cotton Mather to Stephen Sewall, September 20, 1692.

       "from jail." Hutchinson, cited in Lounsberry, *Phips*, p. 273.

218    "of the trials." Sewall, *Diary*, I, 297.

Page
218    "so be deceived." Levin, *Salem*, p. 122.
       "to be condemned." Levin, *Salem*, pp. 125-126.
219    "never intended" to "condemned unjustly." Levin, *Salem*, p. 118.
       "to 'vindicate' " to "risked." Letter of Cotton Mather to John Cotton,
          October 20, 1692.
219-220 "raging asperity" to " 'Return' in June." Levin, *Salem*, p. 126; and letter
          of Cotton Mather to John Cotton, October 20, 1692.
220    "crafty, busy" to "upon us." Mather, *Diary*, I, 151.
       "the witchcraft." Mather, *Diary*, I, 151.
       "work of Darkness." Mather, *Wonders of the Invisible World,* p. 4.
221    "various occasions." Levin, *Salem*, pp. 112, 114-115. Much of this testi-
          mony about Burroughs' strength was hearsay, and the one witness who
          had actually seen him lift a gun by putting his right forefinger in the
          muzzle of the seven-foot-long barrel had been persuaded not to testify
          during the trial itself, Mather conceded; but the witness had come for-
          ward and given a sworn deposition after the trial had ended.
       "specific indictments." Levin, *Salem*, pp. 130-131.
222    "*Invisible World.*" Mather, *Diary*, I, 153-154.
       "*written right.*" Mather, *Diary*, I, 154.
       "unblemished reputation." Mather, *Diary*, I, 154.
       "the *New-Covenant*" to "he can." Mather, *Diary*, I, 157-159.


                    *VII.  Two Brands, Two Deaths, and a Sadducee*


224    "County of Essex." Cotton Mather, "A Brand Plucked out of the Burn-
          ing," in Burr, *Narratives*, p. 260.
       "returned upon her." Burr, *Narratives*, p. 260.
       "help was requested." Sewall, *Diary*, I, 302.
       "the cursed specters" to "the text." Burr, *Narratives*, p. 260.
225    "with the Devil." Burr, *Narratives*, pp. 260-261.
       "the new court." Sewall, *Diary*, I, 302. William Stoughton was again
          chief justice, and Richards, Sewall, and Wait Winthrop were justices.
       "form of knowledge." See above, p. 76.
226    "rats-bane." Burr, *Narratives*, p. 265.
       "afflicted her." Burr, *Narratives*, p. 264.
       "fifteen minutes." Burr, *Narratives*, p. 266.
       "and comprehension." Burr, *Narratives*, pp. 269-271, 272-273, 275.
       "witch-wounds." Burr, *Narratives*, p. 264. It is also a "property" of
          "wounds" caused by hysteria and hypnotic suggestions. See Hansen,
          *Witchcraft at Salem*, pp. 10-11, 83, 181, 201.
       "her throat." Burr, *Narratives*, p. 264.
       "returned unto her." Burr, *Narratives*, p. 264.
       "invisible forms." Burr, *Narratives*, pp. 278-279.
227    "she shouted" to "tell them?" Burr, *Narratives*, pp. 272-273. All the
          quoted lines are Mather's version of the dialogue.
       "scoffing" to "believing." Burr, *Narratives*, p. 277.

Page

227    "uncomfortable uproars." Burr, *Narratives*, p. 276.

228    "First Mercy" to "jumped over him." Burr, *Narratives*, p. 281.

       "what had happened." Burr, *Narratives*, p. 281.

       "much of" to " 'apply' it." Burr, *Narratives*, p. 281.

229    "have learned." Burr, *Narratives*, p. 282.

       "unaccountably folded" to "bookshelf." Burr, *Narratives*, pp. 282-283.

       "that superstition." Burr, *Narratives*, p. 283.

       "the *mother*." Mather, *Diary*, I, 164.

230    "haunted chamber" to "that night." Burr, *Narratives*, p. 284.

231    "on the floor." Burr, *Narratives*, p. 286.

       "his lips." The text for Mather's other sermon was Hebrews 11:17: "By
       faith Abraham offered up Isaac, when he was tried, and he that had
       received the promises, offered his only begotten son."

       "closed up." Mather, *Diary*, I, 164; Sewall, *Diary*, I, 308.

       "his posterity." Mather, *Diary*, I, 164.

232    "better dissipated." Burr, *Narratives*, p. 286.

       "appointed governor." See Warden, *Boston*, pp. 39-42.

233    "were reelected." Warden, *Boston*, p. 44.

233-234 "our animosities!" Sewall, *Diary*, I, 300.

234    "Increase Mather." Sewall, *Diary*, I, 309-310.

       "He put" to "that afternoon." Mather, *Diary*, I, 168-169; Sewall, *Diary*,
       I, 311. In November 1694, when both Mathers stayed away from a tes-
       timonial dinner that Phips refused to attend even though it was given
       in his honor, Cotton Mather said that he himself would have attended
       if he had not been "sick of a grievous pain in his face." Sewall, *Diary*,
       I, 323. See Chapter IX.

       "rising generation." Mather, *Diary*, I, 164-165.

       "extraordinarily large." Sewall, *Diary*, I, 310.

       "similar occasion." The earlier sermon was "A Blessed Medicine for Sin-
       ful Madness." See Mather, *Warnings from the Dead* (Boston, 1693).

       "bought up." Mather, *Diary*, I, 165.

235    "Mather accepted" to "the fleet." Mather, *Diary*, I, 167; Sewall, *Diary*,
       I, 311.

       "the almshouse." Mather, *Diary*, I, 177-178.

235-236 "A company" to "go elsewhere." Mather, *Diary*, I, 176-177.

236    "to receive." Mather, *Diary*, I, 162.

       "serviceable." Mather, *Diary*, I, 163.

236-237 "publish them" to "his death." Mather, *Diary*, I, 163.

237    "the Revolution." Gordon Jones, Introduction, *Angel of Bethesda*, p.
       xxvi.

       "*Reformation*." Mather, *Diary*, I, 166.

       "until September." Mather, *Diary*, I, 166.

       "eternal *advantage*." Mather, *Diary*, I, 169.

237-239 "in August 1693" to "its publication." Mather, *Diary*, I, 169-171.

239    "the Devil." Mather, *Diary*, I, 171.

239-240 "got nothing!" to "any questions." Mather, *Diary*, I, 172.

Page
240   "before 1688." Burr, *Narratives*, p. 291.
      "her healers." Robert Calef, *More Wonders of the Invisible World* [Lon-don, 1700], reprinted as volume II in *The Witchcraft Delusion in New England*, ed. Samuel G. Drake (Boston, 1866; rpt., 1970), p. 49. All references below are to this edition, hereafter cited as Drake, II.
      "any answer." Drake, II, 49.
240-241 "Mather lays" to "none withdrew." Drake, II, 49-51.
241   "tonight." Drake, II, 51-52.
      "was outraged." Mather, *Diary*, I, 172.
      "the Mathers." Mather, *Diary*, I, 172-173.
242   "lied about them." Hansen, *Witchcraft at Salem*, pp. 190-193.
      "further quibbling." Drake, II, 62-74.
243   "other places." Drake, II, 14.
      "this country." Drake, II, 13. Calef did concede that not all the con-victed people deserved "so high a character." Drake, II, 14.
      "be guilty." Drake, II, 9.
      "by the Devil." Mather, *Diary*, I, 172, e.g., wherein Mather receives an answer to his prayer that God will protect him "as well from *unreason-able men* acted by the devils, as from the devils themselves."
      "where it ought" to "scandalous libel." Drake, II, 55.
244   "his own spirit." Mather, *Diary*, I, 172-173.
244-245 "hindered from" to "under affliction." Mather, *Diary*, I, 173-174.
245   "Phips's Council." Mather, *Diary*, I, 175.
      "forgive his critics." Mather, *Diary*, I, 173.
      "meet withal." Mather, *Diary*, I, 175.
      "glorious Lord." Mather, *Diary*, I, 175.
246   "be delivered." Mather, *Diary*, I, 175.
      "October tenth." Drake, II, 38.
      "a very proper" to "permanently cured." Drake, II, 40-41.
246-247 "Having observed" to "been dissembled." Drake, II, 30-32, 36-37.
247   "own congregation." Drake, II, 42-43.
      "for the libel." Drake, II, 46-48.
247-248 "During the winter" to "quickly recovered." Mather, *Diary*, I, 178-179.
248   "in tears" to "us all." Mather, *Diary*, I, 179.
      "everlasting benefits." Drake, II, 47.
      "rebuked a servant." Sewall, *Diary*, I, 318.
249   "February 18, 1695." Sewall, *Diary*, I, 323-324; Lounsberry, *Phips*, p. 304.
      "the Sabbath" and "in the face." Sewall, *Diary*, I, 323.


*VIII.  The Lord's Remembrancer*

250   "rhapsody." Mather said it was "made up (like the paper whereon 'tis written!) with many little rags, torn from an employment, multifarious enough to overwhelm" him. General Introduction, *Magnalia*, p. [xxvii].
250-251 "A strange" to "own house." Cotton Mather, *Brontologia Sacra: The*

Page
*Voice of the Glorious God in the Thunder* (London, 1695), pp. i-ii.
251  "of New England." Mather, *Brontologia*, pp. 4-5; *Magnalia*, VI, 16.
253  "May 1695." See Holmes, *Bibliography*, II, 512, 806-809.
     "pull it down." Mather, *Magnalia*, II, 73. See also *MHS Proceedings*,
     2nd ser., XV (1901-1902), 319; and Holmes, *Bibliography*, II, 809.
     "caused them." Mather, *Diary*, I, 245.
254  "a history." Beginning with Barrett Wendell nearly a century ago, a
     number of scholars have expressed similarly high evaluations of the
     *Magnalia*, and especially in recent years the work of George H. Wil-
     liams, Austin Warren, and Sacvan Bercovitch has treated Mather's
     imaginative powers with respect. For more than two centuries, more-
     over, the book has had another kind of life in our literature, the noto-
     rious life of the target for satire and burlesque. Ever since John Banis-
     ter in 1710 called Mather "the mad enthusiast, thirsting after fame,"
     who "by endless volumes thought to raise a name," other American
     readers have shared his severe judgment:

> My belly's full of your Magnalia Christi.
> Your crude Divinity, and History
> Will not with a censorious age agree.

     From Washington Irving and Nathaniel Hawthorne to Vernon L.
     Parrington, Perry Miller, Peter Gay, and John Seelye, American writ-
     ers who might otherwise disagree about the Puritans have wryly de-
     plored the pedantry, the repetitiousness, and the self-regard of
     Mather's *Magnalia*. Even Kenneth Murdock, in the first scholarly edi-
     tion of the *Magnalia*, takes a deeply apologetic tone in defending the
     book and its author. See *Magnalia Christi Americana*, ed. Kenneth B.
     Murdock, with the assistance of Elizabeth W. Miller (Cambridge,
     Mass., 1977), pp. 37, 46; Sacvan Bercovitch, *The Puritan Origins of
     the American Self* (New Haven, 1975); Austin Warren, "Grandfather
     Mather and His Wonder Book," *Sewanee Review*, LXXII (1964),
     96-116; Miller, *From Colony to Province*, p. 33 and passim; John See-
     lye, *Prophetic Waters: The River in Early American Life and Litera-
     ture* (New York, 1977); George Williams, "The Idea of the Wilderness
     of the New World in the *Magnalia*," in the Murdock edition of the
     *Magnalia*, pp. 49-58.
     "in his history." Mather, *Magnalia*, p. [xxi].
     "impartial record." Mather, *Magnalia*, p. [xxii].
     "in the Atlantic." See Cotton Mather, *Batteries upon the Kingdom of the
     Devil* (London, 1695); and Holmes, *Bibliography*, I, 71-73.
255  "commending them?" Mather, *Magnalia*, p. [xxvi].
     "standard of justice" and "*praise or blame.*" Mather, *Magnalia*, p.
     [xxii]. See also Gustaaf Van Cromphout, "Cotton Mather: The Puri-
     tan Historian as Renaissance Humanist," *American Literature*, LIX
     (1977), 327-337.
256  "Morgan's fine study." Compare Mather, *Magnalia*, II, 8-15; Samuel

Page

Eliot Morison, *Builders of the Bay Colony* (Boston and New York, 1930), pp. 51-104; and Edmund Morgan, *The Puritan Dilemma: The Story of John Winthrop* (Boston, 1958), and *Visible Saints: The History of a Puritan Idea* (New York, 1963). Compare also Mather and Francis Parkman on Sir William Phips, Count Frontenac, and the siege of Quebec: *Magnalia*, II, 47-49; and Parkman, *Count Frontenac and New France under Louis XIV* (Boston, 1892), pp. 235-285.

256     "Edmund Andros." See Chapters V and VI.

"as Lycurgus." Mather, *Magnalia*, II, 8.

"New England's values." Bercovitch, *American Self*, passim, and especially pp. 55-56, 71.

257     "Sir Henry Vane." Mather, *Magnalia*, II, 18.

"Jonah's whale." Cotton Mather to James Jurin, June 5, 1723. The letter is in the Royal Society in London. Mather attributes this hypothesis to William Jameson, late professor in the University of Glasgow. Although Mather wrote this letter more than twenty years after the *Magnalia* was published, he expressed similar historical and "scientific" skepticism throughout his adult life. I am grateful to the Royal Society for permission to examine Mather's letters.

"such an authority" and "all the world." Mather, *Magnalia*, I, 2.

"the Reformation." Mather, *Magnalia*, I, 2.

258     "Word of God." Mather, *Magnalia*, I, 14.

"his own life." See above, Chapters IV, V, and VI.

"100,000." Mather, *Magnalia*, I, 23.

"a garden." Mather, *Magnalia*, I, 17, 18, 23.

"their churches." Mather, *Magnalia*, I, 27-28.

"of the seas!" Mather, *Magnalia*, I, 13.

"of New England." Mather, *Magnalia*, I, 27.

259     "*the wilderness.*" Mather, *Magnalia*, I, 14.

"a thousand houses." Mather, *Magnalia*, I, 31.

"population nonetheless." Mather, *Magnalia*, I, 29.

"to admiration." Mather, *Magnalia*, I, 15.

"recently done." Larzer Ziff, *Puritanism in America: New Culture in a New World* (New York, 1973), p. 113.

260     "any improvement?" Mather, *Magnalia*, I, 18.

"*continually*" to "five years." Mather, *Magnalia*, VII, 4. See George H. Williams, "Idea of Wilderness," in the Murdock edition of *Magnalia*, pp. 49-58.

"wars of the Lord." See the reproduction of Mather's title page in Figure 13.

"Michael Kammen." See Michael Kammen, *People of Paradox: An Inquiry concerning the Origins of American Civilization* (New York, 1972), pp. 171-172.

"Half-Way Covenant." Mather, *Magnalia*, V, chap. 10 and 17.

261     "Christian deaths." Peter Gay, *A Loss of Mastery: Puritan Historians in Colonial America* (Berkeley and Los Angeles, 1966), pp. 64-65.

Page

261 "preaching the Gospel." See, for example, Mather, *Magnalia*, III, 126.

262 "ten thousands!" Mather, *Magnalia*, III, 63.

"into their mouths." Mather, *Magnalia*, III, 103.

"draw near." Mather, *Magnalia*, III, 118-119.

"before he expired." Mather, *Magnalia*, III, 121.

"were exercised." Mather, *Magnalia*, III, 106.

"Book of Martyrs." *Acts and Monuments of these Latter and Perilous Dayes* (1563). Mather borrowed the first three words for the title of Book V.

263 "Half-Way Covenant." Mather, *Magnalia*, III, 129.

"of the fire." Mather, *Magnalia*, III, 65.

"rusting." Mather, *Magnalia*, III, 26. Mather does use the same proverb, in a different context, for Jonathan Burr, III, 79.

"every morning." Mather, *Magnalia*, III, 147. Mather's account of these peculiarities comes to the reader through the words of his source for them, Nicholas Noyes.

"Heaven indeed." Mather, *Magnalia*, III, 77.

"sore *desertions*." Mather, *Magnalia*, II, 14-15.

"we're made!" Mather, *Magnalia*, II, 41.

264 "soul hereafter." Mather, *Magnalia*, II, 46.

"in the dark." See Chapter VI.

"have to work." Mather, *Magnalia*, II, 4.

265 "when he must." Mather, *Magnalia*, II, 12-13.

"of stealing." Mather, *Magnalia*, II, 10.

"Mather shows" to "been found." Mather, *Magnalia*, II, 39-42.

266 "every paragraph" and "but his own." Mather, *Magnalia*, p. [xxiii].

"for either." Mather, *Magnalia*, p. [x]. See also Van Cromphout, "Mather as Renaissance Humanist."

"Bercovitch" to "established." *American Self*, passim.

267 "plain diction." Of Archbishop Laud's effort to "Romanize" the Anglican Church, for example, Mather says: "This was not the first instance of a shipwreck befalling a vessel bound for Rome; nor will it be the last: a vessel bound [on] such a voyage must be shipwrecked, though St. Paul himself were aboard." Mather, *Magnalia*, III, 4-5.

267-268 "In the meantime" to "the event!" Mather, *Magnalia*, II, 69.

268 "Sir Henry Vane." Mather, *Magnalia*, II, 18.

269 "joined the church." Mather, *Magnalia*, V, 63.

"leaders themselves!" Mather, *Magnalia*, II, 63.

"Devil's testimony." Mather, *Magnalia*, II, 62, 64.

"Suffering . . . Christian." Mather, *Magnalia*, II, 23.


*IX. Suffering and Doing*


271 "in the covenant." Church Record, vol. II, March 19, 1664.

"full communion." This was Hannah Bishop, who on March 23, 1696, was censured for having promised to marry one Daniel Hodgson although her own husband had been at sea for less than a year and although nobody had reported his death. Mrs. Bishop had apparently gone to live with Hodgson in Rhode Island but had not formally married him. She submitted her repentance in a letter to the church in June, and then appeared before the church to "acknowledge what she had written. Hereupon, the church voted, satisfaction, and she was restored unto the communion." Church Record, vol. II, March 23 and June 14, 1696.

271-272  "Mather had" to "for adultery." Church Record, vol. II, April 8, 1695; May 31, 1696; August 2, 1696; April 4, 1697; July 26, 1697; May 22, 1698.

272  "in 1692-93." See Chapter VII; and Mather, Diary, I, 261.

"Turkish slavery." Church Record, vol. II, August 11, 1695.

"that work." Mather, Diary, I, 217-218.

"other men." Mather, Diary, I, 192.

"might be fed." Mather, Diary, I, 193.

"in Massachusetts." Mather, Diary, I, 223.

"preacher in Boston." Mather, Diary, I, 209.

273  "book in Boston." Mather learned that Sir Henry Ashurst had somehow obtained the original manuscript after all, and that he had spoken to a printer about publishing it in London, but no copy of either the English or American edition has survived. Holmes, Bibliography, I, 439.

"Spanish Indies." Mather, Diary, I, 284-285.

"starve their ministers." Two of those baptized were the infant children of Samuel, a servant of Robert Howard; the fourth person baptized was Katherine, the wife of a chair maker named Thomas. See Church Record, Vol. II; and Mather, Diary, I, 278. The tract for Jews was called The Faith of the Fathers. Mather, Diary, I, 298-299. The Indian Primer, based on the Savoy Confession of Faith, was published in May 1700. Mather also published An Epistle unto the Christian Indians in 1700. Both monitory letters were written and printed in 1701. See Mather, Diary, I, 342, 347, 351.

"blessed patriarchs." Mather, Diary, I, 298.

"converting him." Mather, Diary, I, 346.

"influential tactics." Mather, Diary, I, 346.

"in 1700." Mather, Diary, I, 399.

"regular service." Mather, Diary, I, 272; September 1698. Again in 1700 he preached to a group of captured pirates and other prisoners in the jail. Mather, Diary, I, 331.

"the church there." Mather, Diary, I, 235.

"for the poor." Mather, Diary, I, 422.

274  "to hear him." Mather, Diary, I, 232.

"fifteen hundred people." Letter of Increase Mather to William Stoughton, December 16, 1698, in Sewall, "Diary" (Massachusetts Historical Society Collections, fifth ser.), V, 493.

"had heard them." Mather, of course, was usually eager to publish his

Page

sermons and his other work, but apparently he was sometimes impor-
tuned by printers and booksellers for copies of lectures and sermons
that promised a good sale. Consider the sermon at the execution of
James Morgan, above, Chapter IV. Probably the sermons on children
were similarly attractive in 1699. See Sewall, *Diary*, I, 296.

274   "Calef's book." Mather, *Diary*, I, 374.

"base-born child" to "*pews* and *heads.*" Mather, *Diary*, I, 277, 279. Sewall gives no number of auditors, but says that the crowd was "very vast
. . . , and the street full of such as could not get in." Mather, *Diary,* I,
400.

"unusually large." Mather, *Diary*, I, 274.

"to defend." Ralph Waldo Emerson, *An Address Delivered before the
Senior Class in Divinity College, Cambridge* (Boston, 1838), pp. 19-
20.

"his own house." Mather, *Diary,* I, 213.

275-276   "Doubtless" to "forbear the rest." Mather, *Diary*, I, 234.

276   "with a certain" to "do it!" Mather, *Diary*, I, 234; the date is September
24, 1697. Compare letter of Herman Melville to Nathaniel Hawthorne, June 1(?), 1851, in *The Letters of Herman Melville*, ed. Mer-
rell R. Davis and William H. Gilman (New Haven, 1960), p. 128.

277   "Heavy rains" to "in November." Mather, *Diary*, I, 241.

"soon in France." Mather, *Diary*, I, 242.

"*passing away.*" Mather, *Diary*, I, 243.

"revolution in France." Mather, *Diary*, I, 241-242, 243, 301.

277-278   "He was present" to "entertainment." Mather, *Diary*, I, 244.

278   "Samuel Sewall" to "in 1697." *Phaenomena quaedam Apocalyptica Ad
Aspectum Novi Orbis configurata. Or, some few Lines towards a de-
scription of the New Heaven as it makes to those who stand upon the
New Earth* (Boston, 1697).

"southwest windows." Sewall, *Diary*, I, 330-331.

"and his family." Sewall, *Diary*, I, 361-367.

279   "He included" to "the poor." Mather, *Diary*, I, 215-216.

"individual families." Sewall, *Diary*, I, 361-367; Mather, *Diary*, I, 214-
217.

"into harbor." Mather, *Diary*, I, 212.

"or adultery." Mather, *Diary*, I, 213, 226, 244, 258, 268, 309.

"and his companions." Mather, *Diary*, I, 274.

279-280   "the good angels" to "deliverances." Mather, *Diary*, I, 237-238.

280-281   "not known" to "our prayers." Mather, *Diary*, I, 185-186.

"and she did." Mather, *Diary*, I, 258-259.

"his children." Mather, *Diary*, I, 282-283.

"his attention." Mather, *Diary*, I, 293-294.

"this little bird" to "for her." Mather, *Diary*, I, 303-305, 376-377.

282   "gone to Heaven." Mather, *Diary*, I, 305-306.

"a hearty" to "called fatal." Mather, *Diary*, I, 307-308, 336, 337, 340,
348.

Page

282 "get my heart" to "his fits." Mather, *Diary*, I, 380, 382.

283 "simple curiosity." Mather, *Diary*, I, 272-273.

"his personality." Benjamin Colman, *The Holy Walk and Glorious Translation of Blessed Enoch* (Boston, 1728), pp. 23-24.

"published too much." Mather, *Diary*, I, 340.

"own angel." Mather, *Diary*, I, 229.

"superlative filthiness." Mather, *Diary*, I, 311.

"*Europe* also." Mather, *Diary*, I, 228.

" 'of me' there." Mather, *Diary*, I, 229.

284 "treasures" to "pandects of Heaven." Mather, *Diary*, I, 229-231.

"Christ with me." Mather, *Diary*, I, 231.

"choosing elders." Sewall, *Diary*, I, 378.

"apparently believed." Sewall, *Diary*, I, 378, 379.

285 "of adultery." In 1735 an aging man who had worked near Plymouth at the time of the scandal thirty-eight years earlier wrote a letter to a Boston minister claiming that many people in Plymouth had known the charges to be false. See *Colonial Society of Massachusetts*, XXVI (1927), 80-81; and *MHS Proceedings,* LVI (1922-23), 30-31. M. Halsey Thomas argues that we should mistrust the aging man's memory, because John Cotton had been excommunicated from the First Church of Boston in 1664 (and reinstated six weeks later after penitent confession) "for lascivious unclean practices with three women and his horrid lying to hide his sin." But Thomas gives no reason for the extraordinary mildness of the council's verdict. Had the council been thoroughly convinced of a minister's notorious adultery, it would not merely have "judged it best that the Pastor should cease his work amongst them and the church dismiss him with such expressions of their love and charity as the rule called for." The council would have recommended an adulterer's outright excommunication. And the Plymouth Church itself vowed only to release or dismiss him, not to excommunicate him. Apparently the members did not wish to prevent him from preaching elsewhere. Sewall, *Diary*, I, 378-379.

"Mather did say" to "exceedingly." Mather, *Diary*, I, 236.

286 "to spread." Drake, II, 86.

"to senility." Drake, II, 86, 113-119.

"enthusiasm." Drake, II, 86.

"his belief." Drake, II, 91.

"biography of Phips." Drake, III, 149-159.

"or atheism." Drake, II, 123.

"in New England." Increase Mather was President, and Cotton Mather a Fellow, along with some other Fellows sympathetic to Calef.

287 "Godliness itself." Drake, II, 111-112; the Baxter quotation is from *The Cure of Church Divisions* (London, 1670).

"publication there." In 1701 a printer did refuse to print a book by Benjamin Colman that attacked the Mathers. See Walker, *Creeds*, p. 479.

"Lord's service." Mather, *Diary*, I, 264.

Page

287    "strangely delayed." Mather, *Diary*, I, 371.

"remained uncertain." Mather, *Diary*, I, 265.

288    "his defense." Mather, *Diary*, I, 374.

"additional pressure." Mather, *Diary*, I, 265, 339.

"Christ." Mather, *Diary*, I, 344.

"his recoveries." Mather, *Diary*, I, 345.

"his neighborhood." Mather, *Diary*, I, 278.

"aloud to him." Mather, *Diary*, I, 302.

289    "helped to expose" to "imposture." Mather, *Diary*, I, 315-316, 324-325, 351; Holmes, *Bibliography*, III, 1196.

"a stink." Mather, *Diary*, I, 324.

"misplaced confidence." Mather, *Diary*, I, 325, 329; see *A Warning to the Flocks against Wolves in Sheeps' Clothing* (Boston, 1700), pp. 24-79.

289-290    "during his speech" and "the ordination." Mather, *Diary*, I, 275.

290    "Teacher upon them." Mather, *Diary*, I, 317.

"against him." Mather, *Diary*, I, 318.

"Congregational traditions." Mather, *Diary*, I, 377, 386.

"first opportunities." Mather, *Diary*, I, 326.

"church membership." Walker, *Creeds*, p. 473; Miller, *From Colony to Province*, p. 244.

291    "his selection." Walker, *Creeds*, p. 473.

"not scandalous." Solomon Stoddard, *The Doctrine of Instituted Churches* (Boston, 1700), p. 21.

"new minister." Walker, *Creeds*, p. 475.

"Brattle Street church affair." Mather, *Diary*, I, 332.

292    "Mather's appointment." Mather, *Diary*, I, 358-359.

"ignore it." Murdock, *Increase Mather*, pp. 345-346.

"apostatizing generation." Mather, *Diary*, I, 340.

"apostatizing mood." Mather, *Diary*, I, 338, 384-386.

"observed in them." Mather, *Diary*, I, 385.

"brought on them." Mather, *Diary*, I, 386.

292-293    "strange melancholy" to "effectiveness." Mather, *Diary*, I, 360.

"too much complaint." Sewall, *Diary*, I, 433.

"names and character." Mather, *Diary*, I, 360.

"the special vice" to "in others." Mather, *Diary*, I, 333, 348. He published this Lecture as *The Good Linguist; or, Directions to avoid the Sins of the Tongue* (Boston, 1701). No copy of it had been found by the time Holmes published his bibliography.

"the Lord's cause." Mather, *Diary*, I, 330-331, 338-339.

293-294    "that malignant company" to "our *fast*." Mather, *Diary*, I, 395.

294    "charter in 1692." Murdock, *Increase Mather*, p. 346.

"a Visitor." Sewall, *Diary*, I, 394-395.

"Mathers felt sure" to "the vote." Mather, *Diary*, I, 356.

295    "explicitly asked" to "resurrection." Mather, *Diary*, I, 355-356; the biblical text is Acts 27:23-25.

Page
296 "refused to Mather." Murdock, *Increase Mather*, pp. 354-358; Morison, *HSC*, II, 498-534; Miller, *From Colony to Province*, pp. 237-240.

"stand by itself." Samuel Sewall, *The Selling of Joseph* (Boston, 1700), was the first antislavery tract published in New England.

296-297 "He shouted" to "grow calm." Sewall, *Diary*, I, 454-456.

297 "church history." Mather, *Diary*, I, 407.

298 "floods of tears" and "gloomy anxiety." Mather, *Diary*, I, 410, 411.

"jury lists." Mather, *Diary*, I, 422-423.

"allusions to her." Mather, *Diary*, I, 405, 430-455.

"prompt remarriage." Mather, *Diary*, I, 452.

299 "Mr. Mather!" Mather, *Diary*, I, 452.

"extravagant fondness" to "hopeful death." Mather, *Diary*, I, 452-453.

"in his time." Mather, *Bonifacius*, p. 87.

"much delight." Cotton Mather, *A Family Well Ordered*, pp. 22-23.

300 "teach them something." Mather, *Bonifacius*, pp. 44, 46, 47.

"upon any terms." Mather, *Diary*, I, 452.

"primitive Christians" to "more of them!" Mather, *Diary*, I, 421-422.

301 "on earth." Mather, *Diary*, I, 422.

"my felicity." Mather, *Diary*, I, 426.

"after all." Mather, *Diary*, I, 427-428.

"on June 6." Mather, *Diary*, I, 430-431.

"she would live." Mather, *Diary*, I, 432.

302 "*family sacrifice.*" Mather, *Diary*, I, 432-433.

"given up hope." Mather, *Diary*, I, 434-435.

"her recovery." Mather, *Diary*, I, 434-435.

"again unmistakable" and "prayer employed." Mather, *Diary*, I, 437.

302-303 "Go into" to "eternal ages." Mather, *Diary*, I, 438.

303 "in 1676." See Chapter II.

"strange revivals." Mather, *Diary*, I, 439.

303-304 "He wept" to "*is this!*" Mather, *Diary*, I, 440-441.

304 "Mather began" to "been heard." Mather, *Diary*, I, 441-442.

305 "hopeless *consumption.*" Mather, *Diary*, I, 443.

"husband's hopes." Mather, *Diary*, I, 444-445.

"This time" to "times a day." Mather, *Diary*, I, 446-447.

305-306 "He gave" to "AMENDS FOR ALL." Mather, *Diary*, I, 447-450.

307 "healing mercies." Mather, *Diary*, I, 463.

"answering it." Mather, *Diary*, I, 453.

"being weakened." Mather, *Diary*, I, 457.

"ordinary gravestones." Mather, *Diary*, I, 450.

"determined campaign" to "tearful conversion." Mather, *Diary*, I, 457-458, 466-470.

308 "more miserably." Mather, *Diary*, I, 451-453.

308-309 "put in a bar" to "exquisite caution." Mather, *Diary*, I, 453-454.

"General Court." Mather, *Diary*, I, 434.

310 "sermon on . . . the New Jerusalem." *Theopolis Americana* (1710).

# Index